The Political Life of Mary Kaldor

THE Political Life OF Mary Kaldor

Ideas and Action in International Relations

Melinda Rankin

LYNNE RIENNER PUBLISHERS
BOULDER
LONDON

Published in the United States of America in 2017 by
Lynne Rienner Publishers, Inc.
1800 30th Street, Boulder, Colorado 80301
www.rienner.com

and in the United Kingdom by
Lynne Rienner Publishers, Inc.
3 Henrietta Street, Covent Garden, London WC2E 8LU

Library of Congress Cataloging-in-Publication Data
Names: Rankin, Melinda, author.
Title: The political life of Mary Kaldor : ideas and action in international relations / by Melinda Rankin.
Description: Boulder, Colorado : Lynne Rienner Publishers, Inc., 2017.
Includes bibliographical references and index.
Identifiers: LCCN 2016041281 | ISBN 9781626375932 (hardcover : alk. paper)
Subjects: LCSH: Kaldor, Mary. | Political scientists—Great Britain—Biography. | World politics—1945–1989. | World politics—1989–. | Human security. | Civil society. | Globalization—Political aspects. | Intervention (International law).
Classification: LCC JC257.K35 R36 2017 | DDC 327.092 [B]—dc23
LC record available at https://lccn.loc.gov/2016041281

British Cataloguing in Publication Data
A Cataloguing in Publication record for this book is available from the British Library.

Printed and bound in the United States of America

The paper used in this publication meets the requirements of the American National Standard for Permanence of Paper for Printed Library Materials Z39.48-1992.

5 4 3 2 1

For Lila, Jim, and Ali

Contents

Acknowledgments

THIS BOOK IS THE RESULT OF ENORMOUS GOODWILL AND GENEROSITY. Over the course of the project, I have incurred a great number of debts.

First and foremost, I wish to thank Nick Bisley and Judy Brett at La Trobe University. It was both a privilege and an honor to work with them.

My work on the project was supported by the La Trobe University Postgraduate Research Scholarship and the La Trobe Postgraduate Research Travel Grant.

I wish to thank my colleagues in the politics and international relations program, the majority of whom went out of their way to provide counsel and support and contributed immensely to the intellectual life of the school. Similarly, I wish to thank my colleagues in banking and financial services who supported this project in various ways, particularly Greg Adamson, William (Bill) Lowres, Gaj Premnath, and Matt Wakely.

A special thanks to Dieter Esche for his unique and extensive historical insights into the social movements and politics of Central and Eastern Europe, the European Nuclear Disarmament (END) movement, and the Helsinki Citizens' Assembly.

Many thanks also to Thomas Weber, who provided many documents from his personal archives, invaluable criticism of various drafts of the book, and constant personal interest and support for the project.

A big thank you to Bryan Mabee for his wonderful support throughout the life of this project and for providing necessary criticism on a draft of the book.

I am incredibly thankful to all those who granted interviews, all of whom were incredibly busy and with more pressing immediate concerns, particularly those in Hungary, the Balkans, and South Caucasus who shared their wonderful hospitality.

I would like to thank the staff at the following archives, many of whom went to great lengths to track down elusive files: Darren Treadwell at People's History Museum of Labour History, Manchester, United Kingdom; Ora Lehel Tari at the Open Society Archives, Budapest; Pauline Adams and Anne Manuel at Somerville College Archives, Oxford University; Tracy Wilkinson at the archives of Nicholas Kaldor, Kings College, Cambridge University; Clare Elsey at Her Majesty's Stationary Office Parliamentary Papers in London; Silvia Gallotti and Catherine McIntyre at the European Nuclear Disarmament Archives, London School of Economics.

Many thanks also to those who allowed access to or provided materials from their personal archives, most particularly Mary Kaldor, Padraic Kenney, Patrick Burke, Andy Roberts, and Tamás Csapody.

I am indebted to many peers and colleagues who provided support, advice, and constructive criticism throughout the life of the project, particularly Luca Anceschi, Nicholas Barry, Peter Beilharz, Magda Karagiannakis, John King, Raymond Madden, John Taylor, Les Holmes, Derek McDougall, Charles Barclay Roger, George Lawson, Iavor Rangelov, Sabine Selchow, Dominika Spyratou, Marika Theros, Peter Wilson, Ari Kerkkanen, Tarak Barkawi, James Crawford, Adam Fagen, Alejandro Colas, Tony Simpson, Michael Pugh, Tony Thirlwall, Florent Schaeffer, and Gillian Wylie.

Many thanks also to James Der Derian for his excellent advice and support during the final stages of the project, as well as to the Centre of International Security Studies.

I wish to thank Taylor & Francis for permission to include in this book portions of my article "New and Old Wars: Organized Violence in a Global Era," *Global Change, Peace and Security* 26, no. 2 (2014): 223–225, www.tandfonline.com.

My most sincere gratitude goes to my parents, for their intellectual support and for their constant encouragement, and to my friends, both in Australia and abroad, for their irreverence and humor.

Finally, a great debt is owed to Robert Horvath, who was the impetus for returning to study. Robert took this project seriously, and he encouraged me to pursue it when it was just a seed of an idea.

Of course, all mistakes are my own.

—M. R.

1

The Politics of Mary Kaldor

IN THIS BOOK, AN INTELLECTUAL BIOGRAPHY OF MARY KALDOR, I explore her political life from her privileged beginnings as the daughter of Lord Nicholas Kaldor, a Keynesian economist, to her development as a public intellectual who has combined activism, scholarship, and policy work to influence some of the most significant contemporary debates in international relations. Throughout her career, Kaldor has explored a broad range of questions surrounding the responsibilities of the state and society; the legitimacy of organized violence; ways to engage citizens in a democratic polity; the political responsibilities of the cosmopolitan citizen; the role of the military industrial complex in maintaining a market of insecurity; political and social dimensions of warfare as central to capitalism; the delinking of civil society from the state and the rise of global civil society; the importance of reconceptualizing contemporary wars as "new wars"; and the need for military intervention to protect civilians in a state of violence.

A leftist peace activist and academic in the 1970s and 1980s, Kaldor was opposed to military intervention during the Gulf War in 1991. Yet, as I argue in this book, through her direct experience of war in the Balkans and Caucasus, she became a supporter of humanitarian intervention and the use of force to defend civilians.

Although I explore some of Kaldor's academic work, I focus more on her political life, highlighting the events and people that shaped Kaldor's political and intellectual formation. I particularly focus on two social movements in which Kaldor was heavily involved: European Nuclear Disarmament (END) and the Helsinki Citizens' Assembly (HCA). Kaldor was cofounder of both of these, and they provided the organizational base for much of her activism.

In the pages that follow, I look at the experiences that underpin the central questions that have preoccupied Kaldor throughout her intellectual and political life, charting how both the questions and the answers have changed over time. Exploring how her familial, political, historical, social, and geographical environments informed these questions and answers, I also consider the development of Kaldor's character and how her character shaped her particular style of public intellectual debate.

Early Political Life

The origins of many of Kaldor's later intellectual questions on the responsbilities of the state and society and the legitimacy of organized violence lie in her parents' political engagement and experiences. Kaldor's Hungarian-born father, Nicholas Kaldor, was a Keynesian economist, a liberal who was engaged in European reconstruction after World War II and the development of the British welfare state. Her British mother, Clarissa Kaldor, née Goldschmidt, was a descendent of the prominent Jewish D'Avigdor-Goldsmid family and was committed to democratic socialism. Clarissa campaigned with Bertrand Russell in the Campaign for Nuclear Disarmament (CND) and was elected Labour Party local councilor. Both Kaldor's parents shared a commitment to Fabian principles and a Victorian sense of public duty, which set an example of political activism for their four daughters.

The experiences of her father's Hungarian family gave her a broader European context from which to pull her ideas: her grandmother's memories of the Holocaust and her relatives' experiences of the Hungarian Uprising of 1956 and of the Cold War. In her early family life, Kaldor adopted democratic socialism from her mother, who, although committed to socialism because she believed that state and society played a role in ensuring social and economic equality, always emphasized the *democratic* in response to the totalitarianism of Eastern Europe. Yet her mother's idea of democratic socialism was challenged within the family context in response to the Hungarian Uprising. Arguably, Kaldor's most formative experience as a child was listening to the arguments between her mother and her Hungarian uncle immediately following the Hungarian Uprising. Kaldor's uncle asked her mother why the West had not intervened during the uprising to defend Hungary against the Soviets, and her mother had replied that an intervention would have triggered a nuclear war, killing both families on either side of the Iron Curtain. Much later, this personal exchange would form the basis for Kaldor's academic questions about the effectiveness of violence and revolution as forms of protest, the use of nuclear weapons, and the threat of organized violence to suppress political dissent and human rights.

In this way, Kaldor's distinct intellectual, political, and family milieu provided the rich context for her earliest political discussions and debates. Kaldor and her siblings were encouraged to be intellectually confident, to be involved in the nuclear disarmament protests of the 1950s and 1960s, and to challenge the state on issues of militarism and the Cold War. They also participated in debates with their father on economic policy, supported their mother in her political campaigns, and, through their parents' political networks, met the most influential figures of the British left. As a teenager, Kaldor was already involved in various forms of political campaigning and public protest concerning the responsibilities of state and society and the legitimacy of nuclear weapons.

Somerville College, Stockholm International Peace Research Institute, Sussex, the Labour Party, and Protest

Kaldor's acceptance into Somerville College, Oxford University, to study economic policy was in many ways a continuation of her heritage. Yet what distinguished Kaldor from her parents and siblings were the generational changes taking shape in British society more broadly, such as the emerging counterculture and the shifting dynamics in gender equality. As the youngest sibling, Kaldor started her university studies as women were being admitted to many of the previously male-dominated colleges for the first time. As the first female editor of the Oxford university newspaper, *Isis,* in 1965, Kaldor was participating in and defining political debates and was not averse to voicing controversial views, at one point criticizing the Labour Party government, for which her father was an adviser.

Upon completing her honors in philosophy, politics, and economics, Kaldor began her career through her family connections at the newly founded Stockholm International Peace Research Institute (SIPRI). While at SIPRI, Kaldor gained access to distinguished scholars and political elites, such as Alva Myrdal, SIPRI's founder and first chair. Myrdal profoundly influenced Kaldor. Not only did Myrdal question state militarism and was later awarded the Nobel Peace Prize for her campaign against nuclear weapons, she had also revolutionized gender equality in Swedish public policy. For Myrdal, SIPRI was about involving ordinary people in the decisions that states make in relation to nuclear weapons and the trade in armaments, and she questioned the legitimacy of the international arms trade based on a narrative of defense and security. Myrdal argued that people should be informed and involved in the security policies that are developed in their name. Moreover, Myrdal's constructivist ideas of the defense narrative, not just regarding nuclear weapons but conceptions of the Cold War in general, informed Kaldor's later ideas. Another important influence on Kaldor at SIPRI was Julian Perry Robinson, a chemist and lawyer, whom she eventually married. Robinson's strong work ethic left a lasting impression on Kaldor, encouraging a prolific approach to her own work.

During the late 1960s and throughout the 1970s, Kaldor was building on her political and intellectual inheritance from her family, particularly in relation to activism, policy views, and scholarship. At Oxford and SIPRI, Kaldor had focused on policy. She and continued to do so upon her appointment at Sussex University as a research fellow in 1969. Again Kaldor experimented academically with questions of foreign policy, the economics of arms trade and weapons production, and their relationship with the state. She also worked to shift the products of the weapons industry into socially useful technology to break what she considered to be the military industrial complex's economic dependency on war or the threat of war.

Yet, although Kaldor's early environment played a key role in shaping her ideas on violence, the state, and society, something must also be said of her character. What distinguishes Kaldor from her siblings, aside from being the youngest in the context of the 1960s emerging counterculture, was her total self-confidence. Whereas all her sisters were raised to be intellectually confident, Kaldor shared the self-assurance and extroverted nature of her father, which enabled her to approach establishment elites and debate political policy in a wider national arena. For example, Kaldor's involvement in the British Labour Party's National Executive Committee (NEC) in 1975, in the Study Group on Defence Expenditure, the Arms Trade and Alternative Employment, saw her play a more direct role in debating public policy. Up until 1975, Kaldor did not intellectually separate her activism, scholarship, and policy, yet her involvement with the NEC saw her increasingly move between the roles of scholar, activist, and policy adviser, and she assumed the social confidence to fuse the three approaches together in order to solve her intellectual questions.

European Nuclear Disarmament

As a response to the deployment of nuclear weapons across Europe by the North Atlantic Treaty Organization (NATO), Kaldor cofounded END in 1980 with E. P. Thompson, Dan Smith, and Ken Coates, among others. END was determined to unite Eastern and Western Europe against nuclear deployment. However, more than just a movement for a nuclear-free Europe, END opposed the Cold War altogether and questioned the legitimacy of preparations by both the Soviet Union and the United States for a nuclear war.

In the early stages of END, Kaldor formed an intellectual partnership with Thompson, which informed much of Kaldor's initial approach to campaigning and devising strategy in these years and saw her expand her activism to include Europe and the United States. Thompson often deferred to Kaldor for conceptual and strategic advice and considered her the central figure of END.

During this time, Kaldor continued to address the practical problem of militarism and the economics of the arms trade through her academic scholarship. She also explored political and social dimensions of warfare as central to capitalism and the system of states through important texts such as the essay "Warfare and Capitalism" and the book *The Baroque Arsenal*. Kaldor concluded that communism was essentially a war economy, whereas capitalism was dynamic and improved the political and economic position of the working class. Yet capitalism was also implicitly founded on socially organized physical violence as a means of coercion and solving conflict. More particularly, capitalism eradicated forms of individual physical violence but in doing so revealed the brutality of socially organized physical violence as a coercive force and means of persuasion. Although still involved in the NEC, Kaldor was also working with Labour Party members of parliament (MPs), such as Robin Cook, to influence policymakers and politicians alike who were responsible for Europe's defense policy.

Nonetheless, although Kaldor and Thompson were intellectual leaders within END, their ideas regarding who should be involved in END and how to end the Cold War differed greatly. Kaldor believed that END should be more inclusive and emphasized participatory democracy over party politics. Although loyalty was important to her, Kaldor also had an independent mind and encouraged others to assert their own independence, particularly by not confining END debates to a "party line." Kaldor attempted to influence and persuade other END members to decentralize control and to reflect a plurality of views and debates within the wider peace movement, including those in Eastern Europe.

Kaldor's ideas regarding how to resolve the Cold War were also developing in ways that conflicted with many in END. During the 1980s, three key intellectual tools shaped her thinking. First, Kaldor placed importance on the notion of linking peace and human rights. Not only was she against nuclear weapons because of their direct consequences, as demonstrated in Hiroshima and Nagasaki, but also because nuclear weapons suppressed democracy and legitimized oppression in Eastern Europe. Her Hungarian family's personal experiences of the Cold War had seen her uncle imprisoned for advocating a democratic and independent Hungary and her aunt and cousin detained in labor camps. Although Marxism inspired her, Kaldor also drew on notions of democratic socialism and liberalism from her familial milieu, and she interpreted communism to be fundamentally undemocratic. Kaldor's activism with a new generation of Eastern European dissidents and independents, who largely viewed communism as autocratic, reinforced this view. As Kaldor became increasingly active with Eastern European dissidents and was sympathetic to their view of democratic freedoms, she and Thompson came to disagree about what human rights meant and, therefore, how peace and human rights were linked.

Second, the emerging concept of politics "from below," which emphasized participatory forms of politics, influenced Kaldor's views. Although she was well connected to the political elite in Britain, particularly to those in the Labour Party, and across Europe, she increasingly prioritized connections with grassroots and independent groups, reflecting her sympathy with a participatory rather than representative form of democracy. Although Kaldor was initially inspired by Thompson's notion of "history from below," as advanced in his seminal book *The Making of the English Working Class*, the practice of activism in the early 1980s revealed that Kaldor's own brand of politics from below was heavily influenced by both her associations with Eastern European activists and also Mient Jan Faber's more egalitarian notions of "détente from below." Unlike Thompson, who was suspicious of democratic and grassroots approaches being adopted within END, Kaldor emphasized greater direct participation. Moreover, Kaldor believed that the ending of the Cold War and the development of democracy in Eastern Europe could only evolve from below, in other words, from the social and political changes advanced by grassroots movements and with the involvement of ordinary people.

For Kaldor, this emerging philosophy also meant supporting the direct participation of dissidents and independent movements in Eastern Europe across the wider END movement. Although Thompson was one of the first to engage with contacts in Eastern Europe, he found that the new generation of independents were increasingly aligned with liberal democratic principles rather than with communist, or "renewed" socialist, movements. Although Thompson was a major proponent of history from below, in reality he found practicing politics from below difficult, which limited his ability to establish partners in Eastern Europe. Kaldor's emphasis on participatory democracy, rather than renewed socialism, enabled her dialogue with dissident and grassroots independents but also brought her into direct conflict with END's cofounders, such as Thompson and Coates, and others in the broader END movement.

These conflicts revealed Kaldor's ideas on liberal debate. For Kaldor, genuine debate was not about accepting differences nor discussing themes that united activists between the blocs. Rather, liberal democracy was about being able to debate differences; it was about being able to disagree and to take responsibility as an active citizen for a state's decisions, whether that citizen agreed with them or not. Moreover, Kaldor began to argue that the debate about the legitimacy of the bloc system and the acknowledgment of the political and economic arrangements that underpinned the nuclear arms race were critical to the peace movement. Although so-called nuclear deterrence was supposed to prevent a war in Europe, Kaldor argued that the threat of war served to continue the conflict, which gave the raison d'être for the bloc arrangement. For Kaldor, ordinary people in Europe ought to be involved in and responsible for starting this debate.

Third, Kaldor's engagement and activism with her Eastern European counterparts informed her intellectual and scholarly understanding of the concept of civil society. Many Eastern European activist groups, with whom Kaldor would increasingly form intellectual alliances, such as Solidarity (Solidarność in Polish), Charter 77, and the Peace Group for Dialogue, were convinced that independent civil society was the most effective social and political mechanism for democratization in their countries and for ending the Cold War. This perspective contrasted with the usual top-down approaches, such as a violent revolution that toppled a government or a power shift, which replaced one totalitarian regime with another. Kaldor argued that Eastern European scholars, such as Adam Michnik, reinvented previous notions of civil society by delinking civil society from the state. During the mid-1980s, Kaldor started to explore the term *civil society* in her academic work. For example, in an article co-authored with Ferenc Miszlivetz, for example, Kaldor and Miszlivetz argued that any shift in power in Eastern Europe must be about redefining the relationship between state and civil society. In this respect, they drew on Václav Havel's the "Power of the Powerlessness" and Michnik's ideas on civil society, which emphasized a change in the level of political analysis. High politics was no longer the source of political legitimacy. Rather, low politics or politics of the everyday was at the heart of civil society and necessary for any effective democratic transition. However, not all members of British END, nor the wider END network, agreed about the merits of civil society. Thompson, for example, was skeptical. Although Kaldor and Thompson remained friends, their disagreements served to further separate them intellectually.

Much later, Kaldor explored the notion of civil society in terms of global civil society. For Kaldor, the social contract was an important feature that was tied to the Kantian idea of universal civil society. Although the social contract between the state and the individual remained a key feature, within an increasingly international context, Kaldor argued, individual contracts were also being expanded beyond the nation-state. In the same way that individuals pay taxes to a government in exchange for an end to anarchy and war within their own state, individual social contracts have expanded beyond the state to include economic, social, and political contracts between individuals from different nation-states, and these contracts mitigate anarchy and war between those states. Kaldor viewed civil society as the principal means through which many social contracts between individuals are negotiated and reproduced, both within the state and across the interstate system.

Kaldor remained a scholar at Sussex University during the 1980s, while continuing her involvement as an activist and policy adviser, a task that was not without its challenges. Kaldor's attempt to blend activism with her scholarship made securing academic tenure and attracting funding for her research difficult. Nonetheless, these difficulties ultimately served to reinforce her determination to remain an independent scholar. Kaldor became more creative in the ways that she sourced her funding, and in doing so she developed an "entrepreneurial" approach to her scholarship.[1]

As academia, activism, and policymaking continued to intertwine, Kaldor's ideas on how to solve the Cold War were drawn from debates with intellectuals, dissidents, and policy think tanks from both sides of the Iron Curtain. For example, the concept of dealignment was shaped by her interaction with international scholar Richard Falk. For Kaldor and Falk, a policy of dealignment was about developing foreign policy that was beyond the blocs and outside the US-Soviet axis, with the focus being on more democratic political structures, both between and within states. Although Kaldor and Falk conceded that an international consensus was required, they argued that dealignment should be built on a pluralist debate that involved a participatory democratic approach.

At the same time, Kaldor was also becoming an influential figure within the British END, particularly with respect to her engagement with Eastern European dissidents behind the Iron Curtain. Not only did she continue to debate with Eastern European dissidents, but she also began to ensure that Eastern European independents were included at the END conventions by personally inviting them during her field trips.

Helsinki Citizens' Assembly

In the time leading up to the fall of the Berlin Wall, Kaldor's involvement in the debates on civil society, politics from below, and the link between peace and human rights saw her shift her energies away from END to become a cofounder of the HCA. Born out of the ideas of END, the HCA was a grassroots activist group that encouraged citizens from Eastern and Western Europe, as equal partners, to be directly involved in the future of the region, and this alliance had a significant impact on the Velvet Revolution and other nonviolent or "negotiated" revolutions across Eastern Europe.

With the fall of the Berlin Wall, the possibility of a new world order gave hope for a cosmopolitan and democratic Europe in which, Kaldor argued, the HCA would be a version of the Organization for Security and Co-operation in Europe (OSCE), but from below. Nonetheless, Kaldor's initial euphoria was soon reconsidered with the advent of the Gulf War. Against the military intervention in Iraq, Kaldor questioned the socially organized and sanctioned violence against that country, which, she argued, was presented as a state of exception. Kaldor also questioned the absence of a liberal debate, both in Parliament and more broadly in British society, in making the decision to commit to the war.

At the same time Kaldor took over as cochair of HCA in 1991, the prospect of a new world order was further diminished with the rise of violent nationalism in Europe. Kaldor responded to the wars in the Balkans and Caucasus with a series of public campaigns in an attempt to prevent war by political means. As war engulfed these areas, Kaldor initially viewed the conflicts as the absence of politics and, embracing a left liberal position, believed that politics from below and the strength of civil society could curtail the violence.

Characteristically Kaldor was comfortable in the role of leader and media front for the HCA's campaigns, which included briefing and taking questions from the media, writing scholarly and newspaper articles, organizing conferences, and involving scholars and political elites, as well as grassroots groups, in public debates. Yet Kaldor's interaction with activists in war zones also revealed less traditional leadership qualities, in which her loyalty and commitment to fellow campaigners extended to friendship and personal acts of solidarity. As in the 1970s and 1980s, the personal and the political merged, and this blending served to influence her work.

As it grew increasingly clear that the wars in the Balkans and Caucasus could not be resolved with a political solution from below or be curbed by high-level diplomatic engagement, Kaldor began the process of solving what she considered to be a series of ontological problems in the way that war, violence, and intervention were framed. Increasingly, two problems dominated Kaldor's thinking. First, Kaldor could not reconcile her experience of war with her conceptual understanding of conventional or Clausewitzian warfare. Unlike conventional wars between two discrete armies supported by states and viewed as a nation-building exercise, the wars in the Balkans and Caucasus saw the unravelling of the state. Although war still stemmed from an organizing principle anchored in a narrative of nationalist identity, it was declared in the defense and purity of the "state" by political and quasi-political elites against their own citizens, as opposed to conventional war in which the threat remains external. Kaldor observed that violent actors were also accorded some legitimacy by the fact that international diplomats and intermediaries attempted to negotiate a settlement with them, even while they committed war crimes, in order to arrange a cease-fire and to determine new borders based on ethnicity.

Increasingly, Kaldor shifted her position on warfare to view violence framed as a form of politics, although not a legitimate one. Therefore, Kaldor argued that foreign diplomats could no longer negotiate with political and military elites to stop violence where there was evidence they had suspended the rule of law and, therefore, jettisoned political legitimacy. Second, although Kaldor had championed civil society and politics from below as preventing war, she increasingly realized that civil society could not survive in a situation of abject violence and that military intervention was required. However, military intervention did not require armies to pursue an "enemy" but to defend civilians from organized violence and to uphold the rule of law. More specifically, she came to argue that war must be stopped by military intervention before a political solution could be agreed upon, because such a solution relied upon citizens' arriving at a political settlement through the process of a liberal debate, a debate that could not occur in the context of violence.

New Wars and Cosmopolitan Law Enforcement

Whereas at the beginning of the wars in the Balkans and Caucasus, Kaldor believed that political problems could and should be solved from below, during the course of the wars Kaldor increasingly assumed a cosmopolitan liberal position. As she accepted the limits to politics from below in curtailing the violence, she proposed that a political process could only start once civilians were protected from violence. This step required a top-down multilateral force to initially curtail the violence until citizens felt safe enough to participate in a debate to solve political disagreements and discuss the future of their country.

After the war in Bosnia and Herzegovina (BaH), Kaldor arrived at the conclusion that the wars in the Balkans and Caucasus were what she termed *new wars*, as distinguished from conventional war, and that to end them required cosmopolitan law enforcement, which included, but was not limited to, military intervention. Kaldor's ideas on new wars and cosmopolitan law enforcement developed simultaneously as an argument to explain why state violence is never an internal affair, and why, as members of a global civil society, we are all responsible for stopping organized violence and affording other citizens the protection enjoyed in Western countries in the form of civic policing. In 1999, Kaldor published *New and Old Wars: Organised Violence in a Global Era* in an effort to continue to stimulate public debate regarding contemporary notions of war and international law enforcement and to further expand on her existing conceptual framework. Aiming her ideas at policymakers, activists, scholars, and a wider public, Kaldor attempted in her exposition of the concept of new wars to change the way in which policy elites and the United Nations responded to war but also endeavored to involve the wider public in a discourse about the responsibilities of the state and society and the legitimacy of using violence to solve political problems.

Kaldor's activist experiences of war in Kosovo further refined her understanding of how military intervention should be conducted. Through a series of scholarly articles and public debates, Kaldor continued to challenge conventional understandings of war, the manner in which armies should conduct themselves in the theater of war, and the legitimacy of organized violence executed by the state. Kaldor concluded that, with the exception of the civilian role of policing and upholding the rule of law domestically and internationally, the state had lost its legitimacy to engage in organized violence.

The Evolution of Kaldor's Political Life

In contrast with the elite-focused politics of her family, Kaldor's career must be understood in the context of the social movements of the 1970s, 1980s, and 1990s, from which she learned particular forms of political organization and activism, such as the debate, the forum, and the assembly, and the power of grassroots networks to create a politics from below. Although since the beginning of her career, Kaldor has occupied the space between policymaking, academia, and activism, one could argue that she has never firmly belonged to any of them. Even though she identifies first and foremost as an academic, she views policymaking and activism as inseparable from her scholarship, a perspective that influences the nature of her work and thinking in response to her experiences.

Up until the wars in the Balkans and South Caucasus, Mary Kaldor's intellectual and activist preoccupations were focused on moving away from a war-based system driven by the military industrial complex and instead establishing a society that was not based on war and militarism in either the Western or the Eastern bloc states. Her work at SIPRI, her book *The Baroque Arsenal,* and her work on conversion of the military industry were all products of these preoccupations. For Kaldor, the 1980s shift in security was not just about changing the relationship between state and society but conditional on participatory forms of politics from below, the link between peace and human rights, and a thriving civil society.

However, the publication of *New and Old Wars* saw a turning point in her career. In the 1990s, Kaldor set the agenda on a wider public debate, which reexamined the nature and character of contemporary war and questioned the legitimacy of war as an extension of state policy. Moreover, Kaldor argued that war was not a legitimate form of politics nor did it solve contemporary political conflict. Nevertheless, a tension remained in her work in that she believed that force was always necessary to protect civilians from organized violence.

Since the late 1990s, Kaldor's ideas regarding new wars and cosmopolitan law enforcement have influenced debates in the Pentagon, the European Union, and NATO. But, for Kaldor, the most important debates regarding the legitimacy of organized violence by the state are the public discussions that take place from below. The most important question that still remains, therefore, is not *if* we are involved but *how* all of us, each and every one of us, are involved in the social organization of violence in an increasingly global civil society.

For Kaldor, this involvement meant being able to challenge the state and society on matters of violence and to question the legitimacy of decisions made regarding organized violence in the name of a state, all to a broader audience. At the heart of Kaldor's self-confidence and self-assuredness was a political philosophy that fundamentally recognized political legitimacy as beginning at the grassroots level. Questions such as those about the legitimacy of state violence, citizen engagement in a democratic polity, and the political responsibilities of the cosmopolitan citizen were triggered initially within the context of her early family life but have been reconstituted and refined through the course of her involvement in social movements, her role in policymaking, and her continued connection to academia. In this sense, both context and character are key to understanding her political life and her ideas on society, the state, and the legitimacy of state violence.

Political Biography as a Different Kind of Analytical Lens

In this intellectual biography of Mary Kaldor, I trace the historical underpinnings between the subject's life and work and the broader context to which Kaldor responded. The organization of this book is both thematic and historical-chronological in approach in order to explore how Kaldor's character and context shaped her thinking over time. As Robert Skidelsky, academic and biographer, argues, biography "is above all about character and context, not about proposition."[2]

Even though I explore Kaldor's character and context, I also reflect on Kaldor's political life. According to Judith Brett, academic and biographer, the objective of political biography is to convey the story of a "political life in such a way as to make that life intelligible" and to understand what makes some "unable to leave politics alone."[3] In this way, I seek to reflect some sense of what Kaldor felt and thought about the key conflicts and experiences in her life, to draw out the distinctive strategies that contributed to her accomplishments and failures, and, lastly, to explore how Kaldor may have changed and personally responded to life's events and endeavors.[4] I hope to illuminate the way Kaldor's ideas concerning organized violence were informed and the questions that drove her.

A biography of Mary Kaldor, a political biography in particular, provides for a different kind of analytical lens in four ways. First, unlike other forms of analysis of Kaldor's work, which start and end with her scholarly texts, an intellectual biography incorporates outside research. Historical context provides insights into Kaldor's life and the events that influenced her academic texts. Even though these insights and events are implicit in her writing, they are not provided by Kaldor herself. Kaldor also endeavored to make her work accessible and, in doing so, simplified complex concepts to solicit broader public debate. For those who adhere to traditional theoretical and philosophical disciplines, such as traditional international relations theory, Kaldor's academic writings and speeches could appear rather idealistic or simplistic. Yet an historical examination of the relationship between Kaldor's life and work may not change realist views of her work, but it attempts to illuminate the richness and subtle nuances of Kaldor's debates. These nuances were often forfeited in her academic writings so as to engage a wider public discourse. Moreover, Kaldor often ignored the disciplinary divides of political science, which meant that her work was perhaps not taken as seriously as it should have been. In short, a political biography of Kaldor's life contributes to understanding her writings and, thus, suggests how and why Kaldor arrived at her conclusions, rightly or wrongly, concerning political violence and military intervention.

Second, a political biography of Kaldor's life also serves as an analytic lens to reconsider the debates surrounding the legitimate use of force in the post–Cold War era. Kaldor's personal transition on the subject of intervention highlights the complexity of deriving an ethical and moral standpoint for contemporary notions of defense and security. Initially Kaldor held an anti-interventionist position to the First Gulf War in relation to Operation Desert Shield, which aimed to stop the Iraqi invasion of Kuwait, and she challenged the well-accepted principle that war and force were legitimate extensions of state politics. Yet her direct experience of the wars in the Balkans and Caucasus saw Kaldor shift toward humanitarian intervention in the form of cosmopolitan law enforcement to defend civilians from state and quasi-state violence. Understanding the evolution of these debates reveals how society frames contemporary war and security and how people understand the events that formed the contemporary basis for what might be termed the *responsibility to protect*.

Third, Kaldor's personal experiences also provide a window into the role of the individual in the development and formation of ideas. On the one hand, Kaldor's political life is one of privilege, well connected to the establishment and political elite, which enabled her to influence and effect change in matters of security. On the other hand, her activism, scholarship, and policy work also reflected a life that encouraged participatory democracy and politics from below. In this respect, a biography of Kaldor shows her preoccupation with where she believed legitimate forms of politics are situated within the state. Kaldor increasingly began to believe that questions concerning security should not start with established political or military elites. Rather, the most important decisions regarding war and security should be born out of a liberal discussion by ordinary citizens who then define public policy.

Kaldor's experiences in both the END and HCA provided her with the opportunity to test many of her ideas on political legitimacy, and through a review of her successes and failures, one gains a richer understanding of the process by which, and the reasons why, Kaldor formed her ideas on the legitimacy of violence, citizen involvement in a democratic polity, and the political obligations of the cosmopolitan citizen.

Lastly, and following on from above, a political biography of Kaldor's life provides a window into the relationship between policy, agency, and ideas. Kaldor is a complex and yet illuminating subject of intellectual biography, particularly within the realm of international relations scholarship, because, throughout her career, she has been an activist, policy adviser, and scholar, and she has viewed these three roles as inseparable. On the surface, this intertwining of roles makes Kaldor more difficult to pin down or pigeonhole: Is she an activist, policy adviser, or scholar? Or is she all of these things? Or is she none?

Traditionally, the study of international relations has rarely questioned the importance of exploring individual subjects and the context of their political thought. Yet the history of thought has played a central role in how we frame human action and consequently how we understand the unfolding of history.[5] Similarly, the discipline of international relations traditionally presents an ahistorical approach to how scholarship and theory evolve. As Duncan Bell, an academic, argues, "history, in its various manifestations, plays an essential, constitutive, role in shaping the present: in mainstream [international relations] this has often been disregarded."[6] I wish to explore the historical context of Kaldor's political thought and show how her scholarship and thought evolved over time to shape important events and ideas.

In this book, I draw extensively on several private and public archives, largely consisting of unpublished materials such as speeches, reports, memos, minutes, and letters. Given that some personal insights were difficult to gauge from primary documentation alone, I also conducted several interviews, face-to-face, by correspondence, or via telephone. Interviewees were selected on the basis of their personal and professional associations with Mary Kaldor and to reflect a diversity of views and experiences at each stage of her life. Interviewees ranged from her sisters and family friends to her contemporaries at Oxford, activist colleagues, and academic peers, to politicians, political advisers, and military practitioners. Not all desired interviewees were available (or living). Where an intended interviewee was not available, an attempt was made to identify an alternative contact (or series of contacts) with a similar perspective. Most face-to-face interviews were conducted in the Balkans, the South Caucasus, and Eastern and Western Europe.

I prioritize in-depth analysis over a complete list of all Kaldor's political activities. The biography is by no means an exhaustive or definitive intellectual study of Mary Kaldor. Rather, as the emphasis of the study is on what informed Kaldor's conceptual evolution on the subjects of violence, the state, and society, I directed my attention to key moments and people that influenced Kaldor's intellectual formation related to these themes and sought to examine critical shifts in her thinking.[7]

Given that Kaldor's work is still evolving and she continues to contribute to debate, one could not possibly make a complete assessment of her life's work or her legacy at this point. For this reason, I focus on the development of Kaldor's thinking on organized violence up until the publication of *A European Way of Security: The Madrid Report of the Human Security Study Group*,[8] and I omit much of her activism in other countries, such as Iraq, Afghanistan, and Syria, and many of her projects such as the Security in Transition project. Although Kaldor's notions of intervention were also challenged throughout these wars, these later debates, though important, were still evolving when this book was started. For example, Kaldor was still developing her ideas on human security with the Human Security Capability Group (HSCG). As coconvenor of the group, she published the report entitled *From Hybrid Peace to Human Security: Rethinking EU Strategy Towards Conflict*, which was presented to Federica Mogherini, the high representative of the European Union for foreign affairs and security policy, in 2016.[9] In other words, a complete survey of all the debates surrounding her thoughts on human security is difficult to conduct. Moreover, given the sheer volume of all Kaldor's work, which includes books, speeches, journal articles, policy papers, activist materials, and various experiences of activism, I thought focusing on the evolution of her ideas on organized violence, rather than the complete survey of her life's work, more effective.

As the first biography of Mary Kaldor, this study should be a starting point, with the expectation that further analysis and examination of Kaldor's work, including her activism in Tuzla and the debates surrounding the wars in Iraq, Afghanistan, and Syria, in which she was involved, will follow.

Notes

1. Martin Albrow, interview with author, 8 June 2011.
2. Robert Skidelsky, "Essay: Confessions of a Long-Distance Biographer," *Independent on Sunday*, 29 November 2003, http://www.skidelskyr.com/.
3. Brett, "The Tasks of Political Biography," pp. 74–75.
4. Ibid., pp. 74–75.
5. Bell, "International Relations."

6. Ibid., p. 116.

7. Although I explore Kaldor's political life and her early family life, the nature of her immediate domestic life with her husband and children is not a central feature of this study. The biography is limited to references to how Kaldor pursued her public political life in the context of her family commitments. That is not to say, however, that her immediate family did not influence her political life. The study of how her husband and children directly informed her political life remains outside the scope of this study and may require further study in the future. Similarly, other personal or familial influences could also be explored.

8. Albrecht et al., *A European Way of Security.* For example, it does not explore her activism or collaboration with civil society peers in other HCA countries (outside the Balkans and Caucasus), nor does it explore all of her experiences in the Balkans and Caucasus (such as her work in Tuzla).

9. Human Security Capability Group, *From Hybrid Peace to Human Security: Rethinking EU Strategy Towards Conflict: The Berlin Report of the Human Security Study Group*, London School of Economics, 24 February 2016, http://library.fes.de/.

2

Militarism and the State

What [Mary] Kaldor brought to bear to these ideas was her long history of political activism and that kind of sense that there isn't a disconnection between your political practice . . . and your intellectual world, the world of ideas that are moving in academia. For her, it was always part and parcel of the same thing. . . . It was there from the very start of her career. . . . If you actually think about her political activism in the peace movement, it was actually connected to her academic work on disarmament. The two, for her, are always connected.[1]

ON 16 MARCH 1946, MARY HENRIETTA KALDOR WAS BORN IN CAMbridgeshire, England, just before the death of her father's mentor, John Maynard Keynes. Her arrival came in the immediate aftermath of World War II and a week after the famous "Iron Curtain" speech was made by Winston Churchill. Denouncing the Soviet Union for carving up the European continent, Churchill declared that a new "era of anxiety" had begun.[2] What the world needed was something between magic and an intellectual revolution, and according to her father, Keynes's work held the answers. In a letter addressed to Keynes's bereaved wife, Lydia, Nicholas Kaldor articulated the importance of Keynes's work in his own life and those of his peers. Moreover, Nicholas believed that Keynes's ideas had the potential to change the world:

> There is no one to whom I owe so much in the formation of my thoughts and ideas; and this must be just as true of most economists of my generation. In the truest sense of the world he was our master who for many years exerted a magic influence on us all. He created an intellectual revolution in economics the likes of which only occurs once a century, if at all; and if the world after the war will prove a happier and more prosperous place for the ordinary man and woman, it will be very largely due to the fact that his ideas had caught fire.[3]

Kaldor was born just as her father increasingly assumed, "consciously or unconsciously, the mantle shed by Keynes."[4]

Nicholas Kaldor was born into a middle-class Jewish family in Budapest. As a young man, he traveled to London with a keen interest in the essays of the British Fabian Society and John Maynard Keynes, to study economics at the London School of Economics. Reflecting his characteristic confidence and enthusiasm, Nicholas had arranged to take tea on his first Sunday in England with Beatrice Webb, the renowned economist and sociologist, who was also a prominent member of the Fabian Society and cofounder of the school.[5]

The *Fabian Essays in Socialism* had also shaped the perspectives of Clarissa Elisabeth Goldschmidt, the British woman who would become Mary Kaldor's mother.[6] Clarissa was a democratic socialist who read history at Somerville College, Oxford, and was a fourth-generation descendent of Sir Isaac Lyon Goldsmid, the first Jewish baronet, who campaigned to secure civil and political rights for British Jews.[7] Both Nicholas and Clarissa shared a commitment to Fabian principles, a Victorian sense of public duty, and the love of their four daughters.

The youngest of the four, Kaldor also drew on her experiences as a second-generation descendent of the Hungarian diaspora, particularly in the context of World War II and the Cold War. Although Nicholas had emigrated from Budapest to Britain in 1927, Nicholas's mother, Joan Kaldor, his sister, Edith, and Edith's husband, Dr. Aurel Varannai, remained in Budapest in hiding during World War II.[8] At one point, Joan was discovered and detained by Nazi sympathizers but by various means managed to escape.[9] In 1946 Joan emigrated to England, horrified by her experiences during the Nazi occupation.[10] During the course of World War II, both Kaldor's parents supported Churchill's war on Nazi Germany, as they saw many of their Jewish relatives and friends attempt to escape the ensuing genocide.

Yet, despite the terrors of World War II, Nicholas's sister, Edith, and her husband, Aurel, along with their young daughter, Annamaria, had all remained in Budapest with varying consequences. As communism enveloped Eastern and Central Europe, Edith's husband, Aurel, who had become the Hungarian correspondent for Reuter's agency, remained committed to a democratic and independent Hungary. In 1948, Aurel was imprisoned for several years, two of which were in solitary confinement. Aurel had several convictions laid against him, one of which was for sending "secretly malicious and false reports to Reuter's about conditions in Hungary."[11] Moreover, Edith and Annamaria were detained in Stalinist labor camps.[12]

During the 1940s and 1950s, Nicholas Kaldor's attempts to get the Varannai family, and other relatives, out of Hungary were unrelenting. Over several years, Nicholas tried various diplomatic channels.[13] Yet not until after the Hungarian Uprising of 1965, when Mary Kaldor was eleven years old, did

Nicholas finally succeed in bringing his sister's family to the United Kingdom for the first time. According to Mary Kaldor, their visit was one of significant importance to her. Upon their arrival, her uncle asked her mother, "Why didn't the West save us? . . . Why didn't you stop the Russian tanks?" Her mother replied that the intervention would have led to nuclear war and the whole family would have been killed on both sides of the Iron Curtain.[14] Mary Kaldor later remarked that the "exchange was profoundly important in shaping my political thinking."[15] Mary Kaldor went on to say, "Of course we were very conscious of the horrors of fascism and communism with Rele [Aurel Varannai] in prison and Edo [Edith] in a labor camp, and I adored my cousin Csopi (Annamaria), who told me all about what she had gone through. The 1956 Hungarian [Uprising] made a big impact on me."[16] Nonetheless, despite the difficulties of Hungarian communist life and the opportunities promised to them in the West, Nicholas could not persuade his sister's family to stay in the United Kingdom. In 1956 they returned to Hungary.[17]

In response to the escalation of the Cold War, Mary Kaldor's mother and her sisters became increasingly involved as peace activists. For many Britons, their government's testing of the H-bomb in 1957 represented a dangerous obstacle to peace across Europe.[18] In April 1958, young Kaldor, at the age of twelve, began to attend protests, such as an Aldermaston March, with her older sister, Frances.[19] Clarissa was enormously supportive of her daughters and their political engagement, and encouraged by them, she became active in various peace campaigns, including attending the founding meeting of the CND, chaired by Canon Collins and Bertrand Russell.[20] In the 1960s, when Kaldor was sixteen years old, Clarissa's political activism led to an interest in a political career, and she campaigned for the seat of Arbury and was elected as the local councilor for labor.

As a young woman, Kaldor acquired a sensitivity to the potential and consequences of ideas. She and her sisters were constantly immersed in their parents' political discussions and those of their colleagues. Indeed, debate was a constant feature of their upbringing. As Frances Stewart, Kaldor's elder sister remarked, their "father was an obsessive intellectual" who always had "ideas—more often about politics and economic policies than economics—which he would discuss endlessly."[21] Every Sunday Kaldor would be in the midst of cabinet members from the Labour Party and other intellectuals who joined her family for lunch.[22] A close family friend, Robert Skidelsky, maintained:

> It's a very political family. They were intellectuals in the Labour Party, and Nicky Kaldor was closely connected to the more intellectual Labour leaders, like Tony Crossland in the 1950s and 1960s, and was in the Harold Wilson governments as an adviser. He was ennobled by and made a peer by Wilson, so he was then able to continue that in the House of Lords. And Mary's mother was very political as well. Very, very strong Labour Party supporters, as is Mary. . . . So that's her political base—she is left wing.[23]

Oxford

By the time Kaldor graduated with her A levels, she was already an activist. After spending the summer in then-Yugoslavia working on roads and as an exchange student in what is now Slovenia, Kaldor commenced her studies at Somerville College, Oxford, in September 1963. Kaldor thrived in Oxford's competitive intellectual environment, becoming actively engaged in the life of the university, just as Britain was reeling from the effects of an emerging counterculture and social revolution.[24] Although initially studying mathematics, Kaldor was drawn back to politics and economics, and she elected to pursue a degree in politics, philosophy, and economics, studying under several luminaries, including Robert Skidelsky, Margaret Hall, Elizabeth Anscombe, Anthony Kenny, and Philippa Foot. While at Oxford, Kaldor was also elected joint editor of the Oxford university newspaper, *Isis,* in 1965, making her one of its first female editors.[25] As a writer and editor of *Isis*, Kaldor was not averse to printing controversial views, including criticizing the government that her father advised. Indeed, Kaldor had argued that the Labour government under Prime Minister Harold Wilson was "morally and politically bankrupt" and, moreover, that "the political ineptness of raising MPs salaries immediately, while delaying old-age pensions for six months because of 'administrative difficulties,' is the most obvious example of a series of short-term tactical blunders."[26]

Kaldor's appetite and tenacity for public debate was a propensity that she shared with many of her contemporaries. For example, while coeditor of *Isis*, Kaldor first worked with Fred Halliday, a student in the same field as Kaldor at Queens College and the political editor of *Isis*. Halliday and Kaldor would become lifelong friends who shared an intellectual rigor and keenness for debate consistently throughout their respective academic careers. According to Kaldor, working with Halliday over the years made a huge impression on her:

> Later . . . we had a big conceptual disagreement about the nature of the Cold War. Fred saw it as the "Great Contest," to use Isaac Deutscher's phrase. And I argued that it was a mutual enterprise through which the United States and the Soviet Union maintained their dominance. We organized a project around our disagreement at the Transnational Institute [in Amsterdam], which turned out to be hugely stimulating and fun too. . . . I didn't change my mind and nor did he, but the discussions we had helped to sharpen my ideas and had a profound long-term influence.[27]

Although Kaldor was born into a privileged political family, she was also keen to remain independent and to differentiate herself from her family. The extent to which Kaldor attempted to defined herself as her own person was noted by Dame Janet Vaughan, then principal of Somerville College and a distinguished radiation pathologist and hematologist. Vaughan contended at the time:

> I admire [Mary] because she never allowed herself to be dominated by an extremely powerful family and this, at times, as I know has needed courage on her part. She has, at the same time, been extraordinarily good to some of her contemporaries who have needed every sort of help. She is, in fact, quite one of the nicest people and the most interesting people we have ever had in College. . . . When she leaves Oxford I shall watch her career with interest because I think she is one of the people who has much to contribute to the present generation's problems.[28]

Stockholm

Having achieved high grades and received a first at Oxford University, Kaldor once again was drawn to politics and economics.[29] A research position was offered at the newly inaugurated SIPRI. In 1967, at the age of twenty-one, Kaldor was eager to make her mark: "At that time I still saw myself as primarily an economist but I didn't want to be an economist like my sister and my father. I wanted to branch out . . . so this seemed like a *great* job."[30]

Kaldor's appointment at SIPRI and her move to Sweden revealed the extent to which she benefited from her parents' associations. Kaldor's position at SIPRI was through a close friend of her father, Robert Neild, a renowned economist. Neild had worked with Nicholas Kaldor several times throughout his career: first at the UN Economic Commission for Europe in Geneva in 1947, then at Cambridge from 1956 to 1958, and lastly in Her Majesty's Treasury from 1964 until Neild's appointment at SIPRI. As the first appointed director of SIPRI, Neild followed a similar recruitment model to Lord Victor Rothschild, another close friend of Nicholas Kaldor's, who had developed a new think tank in Whitehall at the time. Their approach was to "recruit the clever children of clever friends."[31] As Neild explained: "I think I recruited Mary straight from Oxford when she graduated with a good degree."[32]

One of the greatest influences on Kaldor during this period was Alva Myrdal, an activist, sociologist, and Swedish politician. Kaldor worked along side Alva and her husband, Gunnar, both later Nobel Prize laureates for peace and economics, respectively. Alva Myrdal had persuaded Prime Minister Tage Erlander that the Swedish government should initiate and finance SIPRI, and as such she was the first to take the helm as SIPRI's chair. Myrdal wanted outputs that were practical and useful to those struggling with arms control negotiations and disarmament and that were available to the general public.[33] Myrdal's analysis of the Cold War would inform Kaldor's career over the next ten years,[34] particularly her constructivist views of the Cold War as a mutual enterprise whereby both governments from East and West held a vested interest in continuing the threat of a nuclear war. Myrdal also held the view that ordinary people should have independent facts on arms control, traditionally the privilege of powerful governments.[35] As Kaldor explained: "Alva was amazing. Alva, I would say, in a way was the first person who [propounded] the idea of the Cold War as a mutual enterprise. Alva very much thought along those lines. You know, 'a plague on both your houses,' and that they [the United States and the Soviet Union] were reinforcing each other."[36]

During her tenure at SIPRI, Kaldor helped to gather the first statistics on the global arms trade, developing approaches to analyzing data still largely used today. She was one of three coauthors to write the chapters on the arms trade in the first two SIPRI yearbooks, for 1968–1969 and 1969–1970.[37] While developing the yearbooks, Kaldor worked directly alongside Frank Blackaby, an economist and former deputy director of the National Institute for Economic and Social Research (NIESR), and Frank Barnaby, a nuclear physicist who formerly worked at the Atomic Weapons Research Establishment in Aldermaston. Kaldor was also the principal author of the first edition of *The Arms Trade with the Third World*, developing the methodology for tracking the arms trade and valuing the data.[38]

While at SIPRI, Kaldor's personal, professional, and intellectual relationships began to form almost inseparably. In many respects, often no delineation could be found between Kaldor's personal and professional relationships, and many of the experts she worked alongside or collaborated with, such as Alva Myrdal, Robert Neild, Frank Barnaby, Frank Blackaby, and Joseph Rotblatt, or those who would soon become experts in their own right, such as Ulrich Albrecht, Karin Lissakers, Milton Leitenberg, Eva Göransson, Anders Boserup, and Randell Forsberg, became her close friends and future collaborators. Moreover, while at SIPRI, Kaldor also met her life partner, Julian Perry Robinson, who was a chemist, lawyer, and expert in chemical and biological weapons.

At the time that Kaldor was working on gathering the first arms trade statistics for SIPRI, much of Europe was experiencing the convulsions of the "revolutions" of 1968. Unlike many of her contemporaries who participated,[39] Kaldor was not involved in the 1968 demonstrations or communist party gatherings. Although sympathetic, she considered many of the people who were active in the protests to be "very macho."[40] Yet reluctance to become physically involved also reflected her sympathy for Fabian social and political reform, her belief in the enlightened role of government to facilitate change, and a deeply held skepticism of the merits of violent revolution.[41]

Sussex

After several years at SIPRI, Kaldor was keen to return home and to pursue independent research. In 1969, she relocated back to the United Kingdom to begin her role as a research fellow at the Institute for the Study of International Organisations (ISIO) at Sussex University. Although now based in Brighton, Kaldor continued to work with SIPRI as a consultant until 1970. Kaldor also applied to be admitted as a doctorate of philosophy (PhD) candidate at Sussex University, under the supervision of Keith Pavitt, and while Coral Bell was chair of the international relations program. In a letter of support for her candidature, Margaret Hall, an economist from Somerville College, maintained that Kaldor "is a person of exceptional academic ability. . . . I consider that the field of international relations is a most suitable field of research for her,"[42] and in 1972, Kaldor was accepted into the PhD program within the department of international relations. Building on her research at SIPRI, Kaldor had begun to write a book (later entitled *The Baroque Arsenal*) and decided to use the ideas toward her dissertation. The subject of her book was the relationship between technological innovation and the arms race. According to Zdenek Kavan, then a scholar within the international relations program at Sussex University, after already developing some of the initial methods for tracking arms and developing SIPRIs first yearbooks, Kaldor "wasn't your ordinary PhD student."[43]

Kaldor struggled with the Cold War orthodoxy of international relations, and after several years, she abandoned her doctorial studies. As Kavan explained, "[Kaldor] eventually ended up, for reasons that entirely escape me, with Coral Bell. I think that that was probably not particularly successful . . . and don't forget at the time it wasn't all that crucial to have a PhD to do an academic job. But as I said, she just chucked [it] in—chucked the [doctorate of philosophy]!"[44]

Her inability or unwillingness to conform the central thesis of her dissertation to the position of her international relations supervisor demonstrates Kaldor's very early difficulties with abiding by mainstream scholarship. This was Kaldor's first real challenge in adapting to an intellectual orthodoxy that did not fit with her own values and assumptions. Kaldor had closely adopted Myrdal's approach to the Cold War, as a mutual enterprise, a position that was at the time well outside the conventional discourse of mainstream international relations.

Yet Kaldor's intellectual sphere extended radically past her efforts to attain a PhD. While living in Brighton, Kaldor had involved herself in a rich political and intellectual milieu and had continued to pursue her scholarly interests, becoming an increasingly prolific writer. As an extrovert, Kaldor developed friendships readily at Sussex, all while retaining her connections with her peers at SIPRI and also with her contemporaries from her days at Oxford. For example, a fellow student from Oxford, Stuart Holland, was also now based in Brighton. After working as an adviser to the Labour Party (alongside Thomas Balogh and Nicholas Kaldor), Holland had moved to Brighton to also take up a position at Sussex University. In a few years, Holland and Kaldor would go on to cofound END together. Kaldor's partner, Robinson, was also offered a position at Sussex University in 1971. Kaldor and Robinson moved into their flat in Sussex Square, Brighton, directly across the hall from Holland, and would be based there for the rest of their lives.[45] Robinson's strong work ethic further stimulated Kaldor's diligence and industrious attitude toward her own endeavors.

Irrespective of the difficulties of pursing doctorial studies, Kaldor became a prolific academic writer. She continued to develop the ideas she had formed during her time as a PhD candidate,[46] and she further pursued a number of other research projects at both SIPRI and Sussex University,[47] which included producing monographs, coauthoring papers, and collaborating on research projects concerning the economic policy and the military industry. For example, Kaldor coauthored three SIPRI publications and an occasional paper, the latter with her ISIO colleague Javed Ansari, a Pakistan economist, concerning the Bangladesh "Liberation War."[48] She was also the sole author of a monograph on European defense industries.[49]

Moreover, Kaldor's ties with many of her SIPRI colleagues, her academic peers, and defense advisers continued to flourish. In 1970, Kaldor lectured at the International School on Disarmament and Research in Conflict at the University of Rome. In 1973, Kaldor, along with her other SIPRI colleagues, was a member of the International Peace Research Association's Panel on Militarisation and the Third World, a position she held until 1978. In 1978, she coauthored *A Short Research Guide on Arms and Armed Forces* and, in 1979, *The World Military Order*.[50] In 1974, Albrecht invited Kaldor to be visiting fellow at the Berghof Foundation, based in Berlin. That same year she also became an associate fellow at the Institute of Development Studies at Sussex University.

Visiting fellowships were important in forming Kaldor's early style, particularly in terms of engaging in public debate. For example, in 1972, Kaldor was invited as visiting fellow for half a year at the Center for International Studies at Massachusetts Institute of Technology (MIT),[51] one of the foremost institutions on the subject of security.[52] Kaldor's visit was proceeded by an altercation with an MIT professor in the same faculty, William W. Kauffmann, a renowned US nuclear strategist who divided his time between his academic work at MIT and acting as a consultant to the US Department of Defense. When the US Department of Defense delivered their annual expenditure report to Congress, written by James Schlesinger, secretary of defense under Richard Nixon and Gerald Ford, two years later, the report stated that despite a new era of détente and what was the "first peacetime defense budget in a decade," military spending should be increased by 8 percent to an allocation of $85.8 billion.[53] Aside from 1942, when the budget was set at $99.5 billion, this budget was the highest ever requested by the department. Questioning the seriousness of US détente and also the nature of the military industrial complex in light of such further expenditure, Mary Kaldor and coauthor Alexander Cockburn, a former Oxford graduate and political journalist, wrote an article in the *New York Review of Books* in response to Schlesinger's report and the budget request.[54] In their article, one of their footnotes detailed Kauffmann's role as the Pentagon's adviser in the report's recommendations. In reply to their article,

Kauffmann voiced his irritation for the authors' inaccuracies, one of which was their miscalculation of the extent of his influence on the report's strategy. Kauffmann concluded, "One assumes that Mary Kaldor is the author of this confusing footnote. If so I forgive her for creating an identity crisis. After all, one must recall: 'If to share some . . . errors fall/ Look on her face and you'll forget 'em all.'"[55] This dustup started what was to be a fascinating, sometimes bizarre, relationship with US defense advisers.

Marxism and Activism

At the same time that Kaldor pursued her intellectual projects at Sussex University and at various institutions abroad, she was also teaching in the School of International Relations at Sussex University. Although she taught a number of different subjects, perhaps the one that most influenced her work during the 1970s was a class concerning Marxist economics. Kaldor had been working on arms trade economics at SIPRI during the so-called revolutions of 1968, and, although she was skeptical of violent revolution, she was not impervious to contemporary debates surrounding Marxist discourse, then prevalent within academic scholarship in Britain and across Europe. Her parents had not been particularly fond of the ideas of Karl Marx. Her mother was adverse to any form of totalitarian politics and emphasized democracy in her approach to democratic socialism. Kaldor's father was a Keynesian economist and a liberal and had been quite critical of Marx, particularly his theories of exploitation and value.[56] Although Kaldor did not believe in the far-left revolutionary vision nor wholly in the economic systems prescribed by Marx, she nonetheless became fascinated by the Marxists' view of the dialectic, society, and agency. In teaching Marxist economics together with colleague Robin Murray, industrial economist at the Institute of Development Studies, Kaldor was drawn to Marxist theoretical perspectives. As Kaldor recalled:

> I definitely absorbed that way of thinking and was terribly excited and impressed by it, but I think I never was completely convinced. And I wasn't convinced, partly because . . . I didn't think you could solve the transformation problem, which is, how do you translate labor theory of value into prices? . . . And I didn't accept the falling rate of profit. . . . But I loved the stuff and . . . I mean that's the great thing about Marxism. It offers a big theory of society and . . . the whole idea of the dialectic and movement and change and struggle and the subjective and the objective.[57]

Contrary to her claim, one could argue that Marxism profoundly influenced Kaldor, particularly the notion that ideas and agency are interconnected. Marx's influential study, entitled "Theses on Feuerbach," criticized materialism and abstract idealism alike. For Marx, ideas should be applied actively to change the material world, a point best reflected in his famous assertion, "The philosophers have only interpreted the world, in various ways. The point, however, is to change it."[58] Like Marx, Kaldor directed her scholarship toward agency, but Marx was not the only influence that spured her preoccupation with agency and social change. Kaldor emerged from a family tradition of Fabian reformists and activists, who had been instrumental in social change, either through policymaking or activism or, at times, both. Nevertheless, Kaldor synthesized many of Marx's ideas. In this way, rather than marking a radical shift in Kaldor's approach, Marxism acted as an important frame of reference and set of conceptual tools. And to demonstrate Marxism in action, Kaldor taught many of her classes with a mixture of theory and action:

> I had the idea that we should make it practical, so we used to do it all day on a Wednesday, and in the afternoon, we would do something practical to illustrate [the concepts], so we did "exploitation." We went off to local factories. And then the trades union of one of the local factories that we visited asked us if we would help them negotiate with their company, and so we all got into this great project. It was a company that produced tele-printers for the post office in Brighton, and they were taken over by ITMT, and they shifted from mechanical production of tele-printing to electronic. . . . Shifting to a new technology had allowed the company to undermine all [union rights].[59]

At this same time, Kaldor became involved in the transitioning of military industry toward producing socially beneficial technology, starting with Vickers shop stewards and Lucas Aerospace. Kaldor was asked to act as a consultant for the Vickers Shop Stewards Combine Committee, from 1975 to 1979, which was tasked with considering options for steering the company from military technology to nonmilitaristic, civilian products. These projects extended to include alternative plans for Vickers at Newcastle and Barrow, which manufactured defense assets.[60] Kaldor also published a series of articles based on her research and activism on conversion studies.[61] During these projects, while traveling on an overnight train from Newcastle-upon-Tyne with a group of researchers working on similar options for transferring military technology to "socially useful production," Kaldor first met Hilary Wainwright, a British socialist and later editor of *Red Pepper*.[62] In addition to Wainwright, some of the other researchers on the project were also working with the Institute for Workers' Control (IWC), founded by Ken Coates, a Trotskyite and former member of the British Communist Party before becoming a member of the Labour Party, the latter from which he was expelled. On occasion, Kaldor attended IWC conferences and much later would work with Ken Coates to cofound END.[63]

By 1974, amid her activism and scholarship, Kaldor, at the age of twenty-eight, was pregnant with her first child. Joshua Kaldor-Robinson was born on 7 February 1975 at the Royal Sussex County Hospital in Brighton.

Labour Party Defense

Several months after the birth of her first child, Kaldor became involved with politics more directly. During the British Labour government under Harold Wilson and then James Callaghan, Kaldor cowrote the Fabians' *Defence Review: Anti-White Paper* in 1975, with Robin Cook (the future foreign secretary), David Holloway, and Dan Smith.[64] David Holloway, then lecturer at the University of Edinburgh and later professor at Stanford University, initiated the idea and invited Kaldor to be a cowriter. In doing so, he introduced her to Dan Smith, then general secretary for CND, and Robin Cook, who was at the time a central MP. Upon his first meeting with Kaldor, Smith remarked that, in comparison to his own activist career, Kaldor was very much the scholar: "Mary . . . was much, much more of an academic, much more influential. She had been at SIPRI for several years working on these arms trade registers." He went on to explain that at the ISIO, "she was writing articles which had equations in them and a whole theory of capacity expansion driving military industry."[65]

Not long after the *Defence Review: Anti-White Paper*, both Kaldor and Smith, among others, were invited to act as advisers for the Labour Party's NEC for a three-year study to consider the means and implications for reducing defense expenditure.[66] The chair of the NEC subcommittee, the Study Group on Defence Expenditure, the Arms Trade and Alternative Employment, was Ian Mikardo, a socialist and MP for the Labour and Co-operative Party.[67] The mandate for the study group was articulated in the Labour Party's 1974 manifesto, written by the NEC and the Parliamentary Committee. The mandate pushed for, among other things, a significant reduction in defense spending as a key component of the party's election policy.[68] As Chair Mikardo indicated, "the study group was not a policy-making body: its task was to consider the methods by which the Party's policy could be implemented."[69] The breadth of the study incorporated the possibilities for all aspects of British defense, including nuclear weapons and the arms trade, as well as sea, air, and land forces, and the subject was also to be considered in view of European defense more broadly, including NATO.[70]

Kaldor was a collaborator on the main report of the group. She also contributed to a series of subpapers, such as *Defence, Industrial Capacity and Economy*; she supplied documentary evidence to show that longer production runs for export purposes did not necessarily reduce unit cost; and she redrafted sections of the report detailing the strategic and political implications of defense cuts regarding a reduction in precision guided munitions (PGMs) among other weapons.[71]

Overall, the collaborative approach by the group entailed an arduous and iterative process of researching, redrafting, and debate of the drafts within the meetings. On one occasion, members were in such vehement disagreement that two members resigned in protest.[72] As chair, Mikardo begged dissenters to remain, encouraging them to "slog it out for a bit longer" and to continue to pursue their questions and concerns about the draft within the context of the group in order to correct and polish the draft.[73]

Much of Kaldor's earlier activist and scholarly work on the role of conversion for Vickers and Lucas Aerospace also fed into the NEC's study.[74] Expanding on her earlier studies, Kaldor conducted further research and interviews with workers in the shipbuilding industry, investigating alternative forms of technology that Vickers could produce, which included wave power, deep-sea mining, and an ocean barge system.[75] She also began to collaborate with Albert Booth, then labor secretary of state for employment, and they prepared a paper together on conversion at the Vickers Burrows shipyard.[76] The issue of military conversion was a particularly sensitive subject for Booth and his constituency. Not only was he an avid nuclear disarmament campaigner and the secretary of state for employment, but he also held the seat of Burrows, whose principal employer was Vickers, a company responsible for building the Polaris nuclear submarine.[77] Convincing his constituents that they did not need to rely on the economic demands of the military industry for their current and future employment was an altogether difficult task.

The first component of the report *Sense About Defence* was published in 1977 and essentially criticized the current Labour defense policy that required continued expenditure and ultimately weakened the British economy.[78] Not only had Britain developed nuclear weapons, escalating Cold War tensions and the risk of mutually assured destruction, but Britain, the authors of the report declared, could also no longer support the escalating demands of nuclear and defense policy. They argued that companies such as Vickers should be converted to produce socially beneficial technology. To support the main findings, two case studies were included: the first was written by Smith, who had researched the Tornado as a multirole combat aircraft, and the second case study, written by Kaldor, was focused on the antisubmarine warfare cruiser.[79]

To further make their case, members of the NEC wrote an additional report in 1979, entitled *Democratic Socialism and the Cost of Defence,*[80] which was edited by Mary Kaldor, Dan Smith, and Steve Vines, the new secretary of the NEC study group.[81] The findings highlighted the continuing "paradox" of an era of détente "accompanied by general rising military expenditure by the main military powers, and by a continuing and ever intensifying super power 'arms race.'"[82]

To show that the report also applied to a wider European context, the report's foreword was written by Olof Palme, the former Swedish prime minister, who was about to lead the Independent Commission on Disarmament and Security Issues.[83] Palme applauded the efforts of the study group to challenge the dominant narratives of what state security must look like in the context of the Cold War era: "It takes a good deal of hard work to examine all the relevant aspects of the conversion problems . . . [and] courage to question . . . national security . . . [which is] often regarded as being almost sacrosanct. The Labour Party Study Group therefore deserves our respect and admiration for this pioneering effort."[84]

Nonetheless, the study group's findings would receive very little applause from the Labour Party, despite the terms of the manifesto. Indeed, the report provoked intense controversy that went right to the heart of the party's security policy. In response to *Sense About Defence,* John Gilbert, then secretary of state for defense, was outraged over the findings. He called a press conference, at which he denounced the authors' call for further cuts of around £1.8 billion on planned defense spending for the 1980s, remarking that the cuts would be "highly irresponsible."[85] Taking advantage of the apparent confusion and bickering displayed by the Labour Party, the Conservative Party opposition pledged not only to repeal the most recent cuts but also to increase further defense expenditures, emphasizing that the Labour Party could not, and did not, have a coherent defense policy that would ensure the long-term safety of the British people.

Adding to the divisions in the Labour Party, David Owen became British foreign secretary in 1977. In support of disarmament and the study's findings, he appointed a disarmament panel, which included Kaldor as adviser. Kaldor later explained: "We talked about the cost of defense, and my whole idea was the problem of defense, that the defense industry itself permanently puts pressure [on government] for increases in military spending. So what you need to do is to start converting the defense industry to alternative uses so they're no longer dependent, and so we produced all these alternatives plans."[86]

On one level, the rising disagreement over military spending demonstrated that the Labour Party was not an unshakable, coherent, policymaking force but undeniably splintering into a series of factions. Yet, on another level, the disagreement also reflected the gravity and sheer complexity of the debates. That the Labour Party study group's mandate was to reduce spending but was subsequently rejected by Gilbert reflected growing disunity within the party on the nature of security and the legitimacy of nuclear defense. After Callaghan and the Labour Party lost control of government, giving way to the Conservative Party and Margaret Thatcher in 1979, the issue of reducing military expenditure deepened divisions within the Labour Party further. As Smith argued, although other issues were contributing to the Labour Party's splintering, the defense-spending issue itself revealed how underdeveloped the questions of defense were within both the Labour Party and the British community more broadly. As Smith put it,

> In [1978–1979], it was clear Labour was heading for a crash out of office. . . . On defense issues there was the Labour Party sort of establishment happening . . . [and then there was the] right wing . . . and basically there was "us." There wasn't any other sources of expertise closely connected to the Labour

> Party. I mean the Department of Peace Studies at Bradford University had only recently started. It was a school of peace studies, [but] it was part of another department, [and] there [were] no "conflict" and "development" courses [at that time].[87]

In opposition, the Labour Party continued their heady debates concerning nuclear defense policy. Michael Foot, the newly elected opposition leader of the British Labour Party, also concurred with the study group's findings and had campaigned for leadership of the Labour Party on the basis of reduced defense expenditure and unilateral nuclear disarmament. Indeed, Foot was committed to bringing "the question of stopping the arms race back to the centre of our politics, where it ought to be," promising to abandon the Trident nuclear missile program and to return cruise and Pershing II missiles back to the United States when Labour was reelected.[88] Kaldor remained involved in Labour Party defense policy during this time, but she was also interested in extending these debates to the broader community. For example, she organized a public debate with Michael Foot and Olof Palme, then head of the Common Security Commission (later referred to as the Palme Commission). For the moment, however, the prospect for a unified defense policy in the Labour Party remained untenable and ultimately resulted, among other reasons, in a party split.[89]

Political Economy of Militarism

Prior to her involvement in Labour Party policy, Kaldor was appointed a fellow at the Science Policy Research Unit (SPRU), during which time she continued to be a prolific writer.[90] SPRU offered her a platform that accommodated the mixing of academia, policymaking, and activism. Although intellectually confident, Kaldor found a mentor and colleague in Christopher Freeman, a British economist, who had been the founder and first director of SPRU, holding that position since 1966. Her preoccupation with assessing critically the evolution and development of military industry was supported and consistent with SPRU's mandate. Defense represented a significant public investment in research and innovation for military purposes, and Kaldor continued to focus her work on the military component of innovation within SPRU.[91] In addition to the intellectual support received from Freeman, possibly the most important long-term influence on Kaldor was Freeman's emphasis on "interdisciplinary collaborative methods of research."[92] This influence became important later when Kaldor directed large-scale projects in the 1990s and 2000s, such as projects funded by the United Nations University, whereby interdisciplinary collaboration became a major characteristic of her approach.

Working on military technology and disarmament at SPRU, Kaldor continued to combine politics and economics in her work. Moreover, although not completely subscribing to Marxism per se, Kaldor used many tools of Marxist social theory to underpin her scholarship. Marxism did not replace her economic and political ideas; rather, she synthesized her own ideas with Marxism. In two articles, for example, "The Significance of Military Technology" and "Military Technology and Social Structure," Kaldor explored how military technology affects society and how "it is the product of the level of society, itself the consequence of the particular mode of production."[93] In the article "General and Complete Disarmament," Kaldor and her coauthors explored various conceptual approaches to the social role of armament models, including, but not limited to, "demand/institution" (i.e., action-reaction) and "supply/institution" (i.e., bureaucratic politics). They also considered a Marxist framework, such as "demand/class" (i.e., arms retaining or opposing hegemony of capital) and "supply/class" (i.e., arms and the economy). In the Marxist model, the main actors are distinctly social groups, as opposed to states, governments, or corporations.[94]

Moreover, Kaldor began to explore the impact of different narratives of war on defense markets and policy. For example, she explored future prospects of military technology from a conservative, reformist, and radical (Marxist) worldview, in an article entitled "War," which she coauthored with Robinson. They investigated how military research and development (R&D) contribute to the changing character of war.[95] In "Technical Change and the British Defence Industry," Kaldor surveyed changes to the defense sector as an industry and market and the impact those changes had on the civilian market. In this analysis, she employed data from Jane's defense annuals, which reports on weapons technology and defense news, the British House of Commons, and the Rand Corporation, among other sources, as well as the observations of Friedrich Engels.[96]

Yet in a key argument she developed at this time, Kaldor asserted that, as one of the effects of constantly creating and advancing military technology, the technology's sophistication often surpassed its suitability and practical purpose in the theater of war, leading to what she referred to as "baroque techniques of force."[97] In "Arms and Dependence," Kaldor explored how military power is not simply about quantities of weapons or sophisticated weapons development but about the ability to "achieve specific political or strategic objectives through military means."[98] Sophisticated technology, she argued, may not necessarily reflect the way that contemporary war is fought nor serve as an advantage in real-life battle situations. Advances in the ferocity and accuracy of conventional munitions, for example, which may have served well in a conventional war, such as World War II, are not nearly as vital to a more contemporary war, such as the Vietnam War, which relied on force dispersal and guerrilla tactics.

Moreover, the way that technology was developed, Kaldor argued, was excessively expensive and inefficient and diverted resources from civilian technological innovation. In "The Armaments Sector," Kaldor argued that

British military investment ensured that less efficient and less profitable armaments industries survived and that, although military spending postponed an economic crisis, it precluded much needed change.[99] Moreover, she suggested that the military sector was mixed, with the state as a market and private companies as suppliers, ensuring a fragment of central planning within the capitalist system.

Kaldor argued that the shift to a US-led capitalist world reflected the character of the contemporary arms industry, which increasingly relied on a capitalist model of production, identifying and creating new arms markets, and a constant emphasis on military technological innovation, all to ensure lines of production were kept open, however misguided. In "The Role of Arms in Capitalist Economies," Kaldor maintained that the nature of US capitalism meant that US armament decisionmaking was decentralized, which resulted in a rapid, uneven expansion, combined with an uncoordinated technical development, inherent to the armament approach. Irrespective of the US capitalist model, an increasing mutual reliance remained between the US government and the armament industry. Thus over a period of time, efficient production and functional design of military technology was sacrificed as vested interests dictated armament design and procurement by default, in the absence of a clear, centralized policy. For Kaldor, because of the rigidity of the demand side (who were imagining a war on the model of the last war), the suppliers invented more and more elaborate developments within this evolutionary framework, leading to what Kaldor later called "baroque technology," which was a drag on the economy, not because of the size of military spending but because skills and design were being dragged along a distorted economic path. Drawing parallels with Britain before 1914, Kaldor argued that the armaments approach in the United States "must be understood in terms of a decline in the American economy and that the relatively high level of military spending (both in historical terms and in relation to other Western advanced industrial nations) reflects and reinforces this decline."[100] Although, she added, it did not necessarily follow that economic decline should be permanent. Influenced by Marxist scholar Christopher Cox, Kaldor drew on Marxism to buttress her socialist economic perspective and to make the point that importing a Western form of force produced distorting effects on the economies of underdeveloped countries:

> The form of force is thus the product of a particular society, but it can also influence society. Historically, this occurs through war between different types of armed forces. For example, the victory of [Oliver] Cromwell's New Model Army in the English Revolution represented a victory for a new form of social organisation, reflecting the rise of a new class. Today, it also occurs through the import of arms and appropriate force structure, through the adoption of a foreign form of force that is alien to local society [within underdeveloped countries].[101]

Kaldor went on to say, "It implies a major change in the relation to force, a change from a batch production type organisation to something which is more like an assembly line, involving considerable changes to hierarchy and skill differentials within the armed forces, themselves the historical reflection of complex class structures."[102]

But Marx was not always a component of Kaldor's intellectual studies. In "Economic Aspects of Arms Supply Policies to the Middle East," Kaldor explored the complexity of the arms trade from the West to the Middle East.[103] Kaldor argued that short-term economic interests increasingly dominated Western arms supply to the Middle East, namely that, in order to keep the West's own military production lines open, the industry increasingly targeted the Middle East. Yet, Kaldor argued, as military production was governed by conflictual and "uncontrollable competing interests," arms sales had complex economic and political consequences for both supplying and receiving markets.[104] For example, Kaldor argued, prior to 1970 on the basis of military aid, Iran received fewer arms than it demanded from the United States, because the US administration thought that excessive arms supply would create a burden on the Iranian economy. Nonetheless, by 1972 when the United States shifted its policy emphasis to one of increased arms sales, President Nixon promised the shah all the conventional weapons he wanted. In doing so, Kaldor argued, the political constraint necessary for the production of arms and arms innovation was influenced by economic and production interests. These interests ultimately had an impact on the way arms are developed and supplied, particularly in relation to the interests of the US military lobby groups and their quest to find new markets. Moreover, the receiving country and the region can also experience indirect negative effects, in this case the increase in Israeli defense spending in response to Iran's increased weapons supply.[105]

While at SPRU, at thirty-two years of age, Kaldor also published her first book as sole author, entitled *The Disintegrating West*.[106] Kaldor wrote the book in response to a series of international crises—namely the US withdrawal from the Bretton Woods Agreement, the Yom Kippur War, and the oil crisis of 1973—that precipitated a stock market crash and crises in the broader monetary system. But in the book, she also identified a series of problems in the preoccupation with US liberal capitalism, allowing it to become a dominant model of growth. Perhaps most strikingly, this book reveals Kaldor's conceptual approach for what today could be described a constructivist.[107] According to Kaldor, "I realized . . . that it was a matter of interpretation that affects how you act."[108] Yet, in the book, Kaldor also demonstrated an appetite for debate: "In the end . . . there was quite a row about it. . . . But it turned out to be very important in terms of my later thinking for [the book] *The Imaginary War*. It was about the way the Cold War framework contained conflicts between Europe and America."[109]

As when she was at SIPRI, Kaldor forged many important personal and intellectual relationships while at SPRU. She developed one particular lifelong friendship with Geneviève Schméder, a French economist then at the Organisation for Economic Co-operation and Development (OECD) with Kaldor's childhood friend, Emma Rothschild, in Paris. In 1978, Schméder came to conduct research at SPRU for eighteen months on a NATO grant. Initially, Kaldor wanted to collaborate with Schméder on issues of disarmament, military innovation, and peace, but Schméder adamantly refused. French academic discourse, Schméder argued, was generally monolithic about the Cold War, and regarding peace and security, mainstream French academia remained conservative, at best. After several "passionate discussions," Schméder remained steadfast: collaboration with Kaldor remained quite out of the question. However, a bond grew. Although, Schméder believed that Kaldor's views were hopelessly utopian, she also believed that Kaldor held original views on the nature of the Cold War and the arms race. She also found the disagreements and debates with Kaldor stimulating.[110]

> I think that Mary and I have completely different qualities, which made us rather complementary, because Mary is an extraordinarily imaginative person. She has a lot of ideas—she always has ideas and visions—and I'm a very rational and logical person, so you know the image for me is like when you launch a pigeon and you shoot them. She launches ideas and I shoot them, and the ones that are not shot are pretty good. And that is the way we always debate [ideas] together. So it makes us very complementary, and I [have to be] really convinced. I don't buy blindly what she says.[111]

At the age of thirty-three years, Kaldor was well connected, a renowned public intellectual, and the mother of two small boys. Oliver, Kaldor and Robinson's second son, was born on 16 July 1979 at East Sussex County Hospital.

Along with the work ethic encouraged by Robinson's own drive, Kaldor assumed the intellectual and social confidence to fuse scholarship, activism, and policymaking together. From the very beginning of her career, she considered the three as conceptually inseparable, but not until her work with the NEC did Kaldor have the opportunity to assume all three roles, and in doing so, her roles as an academic, activist, and policy adviser were now intertwined and seamless, each influencing the other. Kaldor's elder sister, Frances Stewart, maintained that obvious similarities could be identified between her father's and Kaldor's styles: "I think he [Nicholas Kaldor] and I think he and Mary *are* similar. [They] are much more bold than what I am about."[112] Yet, although Kaldor is a daughter of a famous intellectual family, by the mid-1970s, she had neither rebelled against nor remained dominated by them. Rather, she took elements of her family's tradition and then cultivated her own sense of public engagement. As Holland later recalled:

> [Mary had a] quite exceptional background, very privileged. . . . Mary was and was not her father's daughter. . . . She was much more radical than her father. . . . She shared her father's total self-confidence. . . . Mary had something, which I never chided her, but she would say (and you could take the intonation): "Well I think, et cetera, et cetera, et cetera." Big emphasis on the I . . . with the same kind of confidence as Nicky. "Well, I think," Nicky would say. Nicky would never say that Keynes is wrong, but Nicky would say that anything went, anything went. And she gained all this from him. . . . There is one interesting example: she wanted to call one of her books "The Coming War Between Europe and America," and Nicky said, "Are you sure that's going to happen?" I mean it may happen in our lifetime. It hasn't happened yet. "No, no. I think that's the right title" [Kaldor replied]. Nicky persuaded her that it was not the right title. So she was open to influence but not dominated by her father.[113]

Kaldor had the means and the connections to maintain her independence as a scholar. At the same time, she experimented with different forms of social activism and had the opportunity to influence the highest realm of state defense policy. The left political establishment was the environment that she was the most familiar with and one she considered her own. Kaldor saw no distinction between her family's connections and hers. Though she had inherited her famous parents' associations, Kaldor also had the luxury of not being dependent on them. Rather, they were very much her equals. Adapting and crafting her own style of public intellectual, Kaldor had the confidence to develop mature close relationships with her family's peers and contemporaries, while not being afraid of controversy and debate. As Smith recalled:

> It was a mixture, I think. And I don't think she would have ridden on the back of Nicky's connections. I don't think that would be her style. . . . I mean, though I remember her one time when she and Robin [Cook] and I were having a meeting in the House of Commons at some point in the late seventies, that she turned to Robin and she said, "Dan knows everybody." That was because I was working with the parliamentarians. But actually I think she had better and deeper and longer connections.[114]

Notes

1. Zdenek Kavan, interview with author, 1 July 2011. Kavan is a lecturer at Sussex University.
2. Winston S. Churchill, "Speech Upon Receiving an Honorary Degree," presented at Westminster College, Fulton, MO, 5 March 1946.
3. Skidelsky, *John Maynard Keynes*, p. 477.
4. Thirlwall, "Biography," p. 148.
5. King, *Nicholas Kaldor*, p. 89.
6. Mary Kaldor, interview with author, 24 June 2011; also see Shaw, *Socialism: The Fabian Essays.*
7. Sir Isaac Lyon Goldsmid was also designated baron da Palmeira by the Por-

tuguese government, became an officer of the Rose of Brazil, and was invested with the Order of the Tower and Sword. At his homes in both London and Kent, Sir Isaac Lyon Goldsmid entertained educationalists, musicians, politicians, artists, and other notables of the day, among them Klemens von Metternich, Louis Napoleon, and Queen Victoria. See Rozin, *The Rich and the Poor,* p. 77.

8. Edith Kaldor met and married her husband, Dr. Aurel Varannai, before Nicholas and Clarissa had met; Mary Kaldor, correspondence with author, 20 September 2012.

9. Frances Stewart, interview with author, 10 June 2011; also see "Joan's Diary Recalling the Nazi Occupation of Budapest," in Joan Kaldor, *In as Much . . .*, n.d., PA-MK-Brighton.

10. Ibid.

11. See "The Papers of Nicholas Kaldor" at Kings College, Cambridge (NK, GBR /0272/PP/NK No. 14); Kaldor quoted in Metta Spencer, "Two Talks in Pugwash, Hungary," p. 12.

12. "The Papers of Nicholas Kaldor" (NK, GBR/0272/PP/NK No. 14).

13. Ibid.

14. Kaldor quoted in Metta Spencer, "Two Talks in Pugwash, Hungary," p. 12.

15. Ibid.

16. Mary Kaldor, correspondence with author, 20 September 2012.

17. Ibid.

18. For example, see Nehring, "National Internationalists"; Minnion and Bolsover, *The CND Story*; Taylor and Pritchard, *The Protest Makers*.

19. Kaldor, correspondence with author, 20 September 2012; Kaldor, interview with author, 10 April 2011. The particular Aldermaston Marches were organized by CND and held on Easter on 4–7 April 1958.

20. Katharine Hoskyns, interview with author, 10 July 2012; Alan Johnson, "New Wars and Human Security: An Interview with Mary Kaldor," *Democratiya* 3 July 2007, online.

21. Frances Stewart, correspondence with author, 30 May 2012.

22. Jonathan Steele, interview with author, 13 July 2011.

23. Robert Skidelsky, interview with author, 23 June 2011.

24. See Donnelly, *Sixties Britain*.

25. Kaldor was the first female editor of *Isis*, and she was followed by the first solo female editor, Marina Warner, British writer and later professor of literature at Essex University. See Nicholas Wroe, "The Guardian Profile: Marina Warner," *Guardian* [London], 22 January 2000, online; Niels Sampath, correspondence with author, 24 February 2012.

26. Associated Press, "Wilson Flop as PM, Says Aide's Kin," *Ottawa Citizen*, 1 May 1965, p. 14.

27. Mary Kaldor, "Obituary of Fred Halliday," *OpenDemocracy*, 27 April 2010, online.

28. Janet Vaughan, Letter of Reference for Mary Kaldor, 11 November 1966, Somerville College Archives, Oxford.

29. Mary Kaldor, interview with author, 24 June 2011.

30. Ibid.

31. Robert Neild, correspondence with author, 16 April 2010.

32. Ibid.

33. Kaldor, *SIPRI at Forty*, p. 24.

34. Ibid.

35. See Myrdal, *The Game of Disarmament*.

36. Mary Kaldor, interview with author, 24 June 2011.

37. See SIPRI, *SIPRI Yearbook of World Armaments and Disarmament 1970;* SIPRI, *SIPRI Yearbook of World Armaments and Disarmament 1968/69.*
38. SIPRI, *The Arms Trade with the Third World 1971.*
39. See Allen and Styan, "A Right to Interfere?"
40. Mary Kaldor, correspondence with author, September 20, 2012.
41. Ibid.
42. Margaret Hall, "Confidential Reference on Applicant for Higher Degree Course in Arts and Social Sciences: Mary Kaldor," 10 April 1972, Somerville College Archives, Oxford.
43. Zdenek Kavan, interview with author, 1 July 2011.
44. Ibid.
45. Stuart Holland, interview with author, 23 May 2011.
46. As Kaldor later maintained, "I had planned to write the book and then thought why not make it a PhD book—it didn't seem very important to have a PhD at the time!" Mary Kaldor, correspondence with author, 20 September 2012.
47. See SIPRI, *Yearbook of World Armament and Disarmament 1968–69*; SIPRI, *Yearbook of World Armament and Disarmament 1970*; SIPRI, *The Arms Trade with the Third World*; Kaldor and Ansari, *The Political Economy of the Bangladesh Crisis*; Kaldor and Ansari, "Military Technology and Conflict Dynamics"; and Kaldor, *European Defence Industry.*
48. See Kaldor and Ansari, *The Political Economy of the Bangladesh Crisis*. This paper was developed further as a chapter in an edited book; see Kaldor and Ansari, "Military Technology and Conflict Dynamics."
49. Kaldor, *European Defence Industry.*
50. Albrecht et al., *A Short Research Guide on Arms and Armed Forces*; Kaldor and Eide, eds., *The World Military Order.*
51. Joan Smith, "Mary, Quite Contrary," *Sunday Times* [London], 24 January 1982.
52. Kaldor was also a visiting fellow at MIT again in 1983.
53. Schlesinger, *Report to Congress*, pp. 21–22.
54. Kaldor and Cockburn, "The Defence Confidence Game," 1974. The article was then developed further as an edited chapter; see Kaldor and Cockburn, "The Defence Confidence Game," 1975.
55. Kauffmann, "In Response to: 'The Defence Confidence Game,'" p. 33. Kauffmann's quip comes from from Alexander Pope, *The Rape of the Lock II*. Both Kaldor and Cockburn further replied: "It is evidently quite beyond the competence of any one person to have drafted the entire budget. However, our understanding was, and is, that Professor Kauffmann had an important part to play in the development of the strategic arguments as well as in the general policy statements in the defense budget. Professor Kauffmann's becoming modesty in referring merely to his 'work on defense budget' can be qualified by the fact of his presence, in a prominent position just behind Secretary Schlesinger, on the first day of the hearings on the defense budget before the Defense Subcommittee of the House Appropriations Committee, on February 26 of this year. There is no reason, incidentally, to conjoin confusion to the female countenance. The article, footnotes and all, was jointly written." Kauffmann also objected, in reply, to the misspelling of his name and the inaccuracy of the years cited for Robert S. McNamara's service as John F. Kennedy's and Lyndon B. Johnson's defense secretary.
56. Pasinetti, "Nicholas Kaldor: A Few Personal Notes."
57. Mary Kaldor, interview with author, 20 June 2011.
58. Marx, "Theses on Feuerbach," p. 101.
59. Mary Kaldor, interview with author, 20 June 2011.
60. Ibid.

61. Kaldor, "Workers' Initiatives for Conversion"; Kaldor, "Military Technology and Social Structure"; Mary Kaldor, *Economic Audit on Vickers Scotswood: Save Scotswood Committee*, February 1979.

62. Beynon and Wainwright, *The Worker's Report on Vickers*. Traditionally, Vickers was an engineering and armaments firm with a monopoly on government defense contracts. Hilary Wainwright stated, in relation to Kaldor: "Our first conversation had been in the mid-Seventies on an overnight train from Newcastle-upon-Tyne. We were among a group of researchers working with shop stewards at Vickers engineering on their alternative plans for 'socially useful production.'" Wainwright and Kaldor, "Tuesday Women (Between Friends)."

63. Stuart Holland, interview with author, 23 May 2011.

64. Cook et al., *Defence Review: An Anti-White Paper*.

65. Dan Smith, interview with author, 4 May 2011.

66. Keith Hill and Chris Ralph, minutes of meeting held on 27 February 1975, Study Group on Defence Expenditure, the Arms Trade and Alternative Employment: Sub-Committee of the National Executive Committee, International Department, London, 1975, the Labour Party, files of Ian Mikardo, Labour Party Archives, People's History Museum, Manchester; Dan Smith, correspondence with author, 14 April 2010. Kaldor was an adviser for the Labour Party NEC on defense and East-West relations from 1975–1987.

67. Ibid. The meetings were mostly conducted at the House of Commons and a few at Transport House, Smith Square.

68. February 1974 Labour Party Manifesto, Labour Party National Executive Committee and Parliamentary Committee, 11 January 1974.

69. Keith Hill and Chris Ralph, report of meeting held on 22 July 1975, p. 1, in Study Group on Defence Expenditure, the Arms Trade and Alternative Employment: Sub-Committee of the National Executive Committee, International Department, London, 1975, the Labour Party, files of Ian Mikardo, Labour Party Archives, People's History Museum, Manchester. In the minutes of the newly formed group, the chairman, Ian Mikardo, went on to say: "The NEC wanted to know what was the extent of the reduction in defence expenditure implied by the Party's commitment, and what were the employment implications of this reduction. The Group's job was to quantify the reduction, list the options for cutbacks in expenditure, examine the effects of these cutbacks on employment, and consider the ways in which possible resulting unemployment might be mitigated. The time-scale of five years over which the reductions were to be considered remained, but it was not a rigid guideline."

70. For example, see Paul Cockle, "Impact of Recent Changes in Italian Defence Expenditure on the Study Group's Assumptions of the Average European Defence Burden," Study Group on Defence, the Arms Trade and Alternative Employment: Sub-Committee of the National Executive Committee, International Department, London, n.d.

71. Mary Kaldor, *Defence, Industrial Capacity and Economy,* International Department, London, n.d., pp. 1–7, in the Labour Party, files of Ian Mikardo, Labour Party Archives, People's History Museum, Manchester; S. Vines, report of meeting held on 22 March 1977 at the House of Commons, Study Group on Defence Expenditure, the Arms Trade and Alternative Employment: Sub-Committee of the National Executive Committee, International Department, London, 1977, p. 3, in the Labour Party, files of Ian Mikardo, Labour Party Archives, People's History Museum, Manchester. The redrafting of a section of a chapter by Kaldor was in relation to Chapter 3. See S. Vines, report of meeting held on 17 May 1977 at the House of Commons, Study Group on Defence Expenditure, the Arms Trade and Alternative Employment: Sub-Committee of

the National Executive Committee, International Department, London, 1977, p. 2, in the Labour Party, files of Ian Mikardo, Labour Party Archives, People's History Museum, Manchester.

72. For examples of iterations and debates of the report by members of the group, see Keith Hill and Chris Ralph, report of meeting held on 19 April 1977 at the House of Commons, Study Group on Defence Expenditure, the Arms Trade and Alternative Employment: Sub-Committee of the National Executive Committee, International Department, London, 1977, in Labour Party Archives, Manchester. For example of members' resigning in disagreement, see Alan Lee Williams MP, letter to Ian Mickardo MP, 18 March 1976, Labour Party Archives, People's History Museum, Manchester; also see Keith Hill and Chris Ralph, report of meeting held on 29 April 1976, Study Group on Defence Expenditure, the Arms Trade and Alternative Employment: Sub-Committee of the National Executive Committee, International Department, London, 1976, p. 1, in the Labour Party, files of Ian Mikardo, Labour Party Archives, People's History Museum, Manchester.

73. Ian Mikardo, letter to Alan Lee Williams MP and Roderick MacFarquhar MP, 25 March 1976, in Labour Party Archives, Manchester.

74. Vickers at Newcastle, which made tanks, and Vickers at Barrow-in-Furness, which was a famous shipyard, were considered very early on as prospective case studies for the report, and representatives from Lucas Aerospace were later involved in the study group meetings. For information on the study group and the Burrows shipyards and Vickers, see Keith Hill and Chris Ralph, report of meeting held on 22 July 1975, Study Group on Defence Expenditure, the Arms Trade and Alternative Employment: Sub-Committee of the National Executive Committee, International Department, London, 1975, in Labour Party Archives, Manchester. For information on the study group and the involvement of Lucas Aerospace, see, for example, Keith Hill and Chris Ralph, report of meeting held on 11 December 1975, Study Group on Defence Expenditure, the Arms Trade and Alternative Employment: Sub-Committee of the National Executive Committee, International Department, London, 1975, in Labour Party Archives, Manchester. Also see Keith Hill and Chris Ralph, report of meeting held on 18 February 1976, Study Group on Defence Expenditure, the Arms Trade and Alternative Employment: Sub-Committee of the National Executive Committee, International Department, London, 1976, in Labour Party Archives, Manchester.

75. See Keith Hill and Chris Ralph, report of meeting held on 25 March 1976 of Study Group on Defence Expenditure, the Arms Trade and Alternative Employment: Sub-Committee of the National Executive Committee, International Department, London, 1976, in Labour Party Archives, Manchester.

76. Keith Hill and Chris Ralph, report of meeting held on 25 March 1976, Study Group on Defence Expenditure, the Arms Trade and Alternative Employment: Sub-Committee of the National Executive Committee, International Department, London, 1976, in Labour Party Archives, Manchester; Keith Hill and Chris Ralph, agenda, 4 June 1976, Study Group on Defence Expenditure, the Arms Trade and Alternative Employment: Sub-Committee of the National Executive Committee, International Department, London, 1976, in Labour Party Archives, Manchester; Kaldor and Booth, "Alternative Employment for Naval Shipbuilding Workers."

77. Julia Langdon, "Albert Booth Obituary," *Guardian* [London], 11 February 2010, online.

78. NEC Defence Study Group, *Sense About Defence: The Report of the Labour Party Defence Study Group* (London, Melbourne, New York: Quartet Books, 1977).

79. Dan Smith, "One: Tornado, the Muli-role Combat Aircraft (MRCA)," in NEC Defence Study Group, *Sense About Defence*, pp. 113–138; Mary Kaldor, "Two: The

Anti-submarine Warfare (ASW) Cruiser," in NEC Defence Study Group, *Sense About Defence*, pp. 139–144.

80. Kaldor, Smith, and Vines, *Democratic Socialism and the Cost of Defence*.

81. Keith Hill and Chris Ralph, report of the meeting held on 25 March 1976, Study Group on Defence Expenditure, the Arms Trade and Alternative Employment: Sub-Committee of the National Executive Committee, International Department, London, 1976, in Labour Party Archives, Manchester; Keith Hill and Chris Ralph, agenda, 4 June 1976, Study Group on Defence Expenditure, the Arms Trade and Alternative Employment: Sub-Committee of the National Executive Committee, International Department, London, 1976, in Labour Party Archives, Manchester; Kaldor and Booth, "Alternative Employment for Naval Shipbuilding Workers."

82. Mary Kaldor, Dan Smith, and Steve Vines, "Introduction," p. 4, in Kaldor, Smith, and Vines, *Democratic Socialism and the Cost of Defence*.

83. Independent Commission on Disarmament and Security Issues, *Common Security*.

84. Olof Palme, "Foreword," p. 1, in Kaldor, Smith, and Vines, *Democratic Socialism and the Cost of Defence*.

85. Gilbert, Tomlinson, and Wellbeloved, "The Ministerial Response," p. 532.

86. Mary Kaldor, interview with author, 20 June 2011.

87. Dan Smith, interview with author, 4 May 2011.

88. See Wittner, *Toward Nuclear Abolition III*, p. 135.

89. The "Gang of Four" (Shirley Williams, Bill Rodgers, David Owen, and Roy Jenkins) formed the Social Democratic Party. See Crewe and King, *SDP*.

90. Kaldor became a visiting fellow at SPRU in 1974, moved up to research fellow from 1976–1982, and later became a senior fellow from 1982–1993. From 1975 to 1980, Kaldor published the following: Kaldor and Cockburn, "The Defence Confidence Game"; Kaldor, "The Role of Arms in Capitalist Economies"; Kaldor, "European Military-Industrial Complexes"; Kaldor, "Arms and Dependence"; Kaldor and Robinson, "War"; Kaldor, "Economic Aspects of Arms Supply Policies to the Middle East"; Kaldor, *The Disintegrating West*; Kaldor, "The Military and Development"; Albrecht et al., "Forschungsführer Militär und Rustungsindustrie"; Curnow et al., "General and Complete Disarmament"; Kaldor, "The Armaments Sector"; Kaldor, "Military Technology and Social Structure"; and Kaldor, "The Significance of Military Technology."

91. Daniele Archibugi, interview with author, 22 June 2011.

92. Ibid.

93. Kaldor, "The Significance of Military Technology"; Kaldor, "Military Technology and Social Structure"; quote comes from Kaldor, "Military Technology and Social Structure," p. 50.

94. See Curnow et al., "General and Complete Disarmament," pp. 386–389.

95. See Kaldor and Robinson, "War."

96. Kaldor, "Technical Change and the British Defence Industry."

97. Kaldor, "The Role of Arms in Capitalist Economies," p. 331.

98. Kaldor, "Arms and Dependence," p. 46.

99. Kaldor, "The Armaments Sector."

100. Kaldor, "The Role of Arms in Capitalist Economies," p. 324.

101. Ibid., p. 323.

102. Ibid., p. 331.

103. Kaldor, "Economic Aspects of Arms Supply Policies to the Middle East."

104. Ibid., p. 221.

105. Ibid.

106. Kaldor, *The Disintegrating West*.

107. According to Robert Howard Jackson and Georg Sørensen, Nicholas Onuf first coined the term *constructivism* in relation to international relations in 1989; see Jackson and Sørensen, *Introduction to International Relations*, p. 166. Constructivism emphasizes the role of historically and socially constructed narratives in shaping world politics, and therefore, narratives can be reconstructed. For further information on constructivism, see Ruggie, "What Makes the World Hang Together?" p. 855, and Wendt, "Anarchy Is What States Make of It," pp. 396–399.

108. Kaldor, correspondence with author, 20 September 2012.

109. Ibid.

110. Geneviève Schméder, interview with author, 1 June 2011.

111. Ibid.

112. Frances Stewart, interview with author, 10 June 2011.

113. Stuart Holland, interview with author, 23 May 2011.

114. Dan Smith, interview with author, 4 May 2011.

3

European Nuclear Disarmament

You [Mary Kaldor] are, more than anyone else, the centre and anchor of END.[1]

THE DEFEAT OF THE BRITISH LABOUR PARTY IN THE 1979 ELECTION AND the rise of the government of Margaret Thatcher began a new era for European defense policy. Named the "Iron Lady" by the Soviet Defense Ministry,[2] she was aligned with the administrations of US presidents Jimmy Carter and Ronald Reagan.[3] Prime Minister Thatcher rallied political support for NATO's deployment of cruise and Pershing II missiles across Europe—including in Britain, Germany, the Netherlands, Belgium, and Italy—in response to the deployment of Soviet SS-20 missiles. The defeat of the government of James Callaghan also saw many of the NEC's recommendations regarding defense policy and military conversion relegated to the Labour Party archives as Labour returned to opposition under the leadership of Michael Foot.[4] Kaldor continued to act as an adviser for the Labour Party's NEC subcommittee on defense and East-West relations until 1987; however, her aspirations for détente dissipated along with those of many others across Europe. For Kaldor, NATO's deployment of a new generation of nuclear weapons four years after the signing of the Helsinki Final Act "seemed completely unacceptable to a generation who had seen the thawing of the Cold War."[5]

NATO's decision to deploy missiles across the continent in December 1979 triggered a wider European movement against nuclear weapons. Key to the movement was Ken Coates, now a leading figure in the movement and cofounder of the Bertrand Russell Peace Foundation (hereafter just the Russell Foundation).[6] According to Coates, the model itself derived from his discussions with Ralph Miliband and E. P. Thompson, British historian, writer, and socialist.[7] All three—Thompson, Coates, and Miliband—were previously members of the Communist Party of Great Britain, abandoning the party following the Soviet invasion of Hungary in 1956.[8] Coates recalled,

> The decision to deploy cruise and Pershing missiles across a wide arc of Western Europe greatly concerned Edward [E. P. Thompson]. . . . It was clear to me that Edward's concerns were justified, but that we needed a different proposal about what action should be taken. I consulted quite widely on this, and it was in conversation with Ralph Miliband that we discovered the formula upon which we ultimately settled, that there had to be a European-wide response to what was a European problem. I immediately put this to Edward on the telephone, and he became very excited, and wrote his first article in the *Guardian*.[9]

Although Thompson brought the broader issue of a greater nuclear presence across Europe to the attention of Coates, a conversation between Coates and Miliband provided the impetus to begin work on such a project.[10]

In further developing the idea of a wider European movement, Coates assembled a founding team under the name of European Nuclear Disarmament, or END. In addition to Thompson, Coates approached colleague and longtime friend Stuart Holland, also a longtime friend of Kaldor's. Holland was now a politician in the Labour Party and had been actively engaged with the political left across Europe.[11] Enormously encouraged by the END project, Holland suggested that Dan Smith and Mary Kaldor also become involved. Coates, who instantly agreed, knew them both from their work with Labour Party NEC and sent them invitations.[12] According to Coates, aside from their activism and her publications on arms control and conversion, the value in having both Smith and Kaldor on board was that they "were institutionally connected with all the people who could be most helpful in the Labour Party in taking up the issues of European nuclear disarmament."[13] Coates also chose Kaldor because of "her work in the Institute for Workers' Control and on defense conversion. . . . But also Stuart Holland spoke warmly of her."[14] By 8 March 1980, Coates had chaired the first END meeting, which also included E. P. Thompson, Stuart Holland, Dan Smith, Mary Kaldor, and Bruce Kent, then chair of CND.[15] As Smith recalled, "Ken was the one who kind of brought it all together. . . . He was the one who put us all around the table."[16]

END was important to Kaldor because it included the prospect of a pan-European antinuclear movement. END, an intellectual project born out of British left-wing politics, advanced the idea of a united Europe from East to West. The project was also personally meaningful, not only for Kaldor but for her family, because it included Hungary: "I remember . . . my father was really keen on it, and he'd never really been keen on CND, but he loved this and he loved the link with Eastern Europe."[17]

Kaldor's involvement with END also represented a turning point in her career and, in many respects, altered the course of her scholarship. Although Kaldor had not secured tenure at the University of Sussex during the 1970s, she had attracted numerous grants for various projects and had proved a serious, albeit controversial, scholar. Yet END heralded a more radical activist phase. As Kaldor later recounted, "END was a complete change of everything for me, I think. And I mean I still remember Ken Coates rang me up and said, 'Do you think that a nuclear-free zone is a good idea?' And . . . I sort of jumped on it. It felt absolutely right. And I just threw myself in to it. . . . What really made it [important] for me was the link between Eastern Europe and the fact that we were an anti–Cold War movement."[18]

Launch of a European Movement

In preparation for a wider END campaign, the END cofounders set about drafting an appeal for European disarmament. Thereafter referred to as the END Appeal, the document represented the group's ambitions for a Europe united against NATO's proposed nuclear ambitions.[19] The primary authors of the END Appeal were E. P. Thompson, Dan Smith, Ken Coates, Mary Kaldor, and Robin Cook.[20] Although some contention surrounds who wrote the first draft—Coates or Thompson—that ultimately the "drafting of the Appeal was a collective [endeavor]" is not in question.[21] On 28 April 1980, the END Appeal was launched at a press conference in the House of Commons.[22] Members of the British Labour Party attended in support of END and the END Appeal. For Coates, Kaldor and Smith had proven their ability to influence Labour Party politicians to become involved. END was closely connected with the Labour Party through such individuals as Robin Cook and Tony Benn, who attended the launch. Deeply proud of the moment, Benn noted in his memoirs: "At 11 [a.m.] I went into the House [of Commons] to launch the international campaign for a European nuclear-free zone; it is being simultaneously launched in Lisbon, Oslo, Paris, and Berlin."[23] Benn goes on to list several people of note who showed up. One could argue that Kaldor, Smith, and Holland had their mates show up to lend a little support to get END off the ground and provide the media attention END members wanted. As the daughter of a famous Labour Party family, Kaldor was particularly well connected and could probably pull a few favors. However, some level of support existed because many in the Labour Party were adamant that, regarding the subject of nuclear arms, Britain had left its defense policy in the hands of the military industry. As Benn maintained during the launch of END, "the real danger of nuclear weapons is that in the guise of defending people against a foreign threat, they place control of political action in the hands of domestic military establishments."[24]

The END Appeal went against the logic of existing peace movements by blaming the new generation of nuclear weapons squarely on both East and West, with the movement's slogan being "No cruise, no Pershing, no SS-20s!" The authors of the END Appeal asserted, "We must begin to act as if a united, neutral and peaceful Europe already exists," and "we must learn to be loyal, not to 'East' and 'West,' but to each other." They suggested that all people across Europe "from Portugal to Poland" should actively seek the removal of weapons and bases and determine policy for their own nations.[25] The notion of acting as if Europe were united would increasingly become an important conceptual tool among Eastern European dissidents during the 1980s.

By the time of its release, the END Appeal had garnered support both in the United Kingdom and across the world. Upon its release, 68 British MPs and nearly 200 other major public figures had signed it, and later thousands of prominent individuals in the West, alongside a much smaller but brave group behind the Iron Curtain, would add their signatures.[26] The influence of the END Appeal on campaigners continued throughout the decade. As one former member of END explained, the appeal provided the political framework for campaigning against nuclear weapons, and it did so "because END campaigners explicitly recognised it as such a framework."[27] Later, when British END became a membership organization in 1985, its members were required to sign a statement declaring, "I would like to join END. I endorse the END Appeal."[28]

END's ability to fund the organization's activities proved key to its success, and Kaldor, Thompson, Smith, and the Russell Foundation were instrumental in fund-raising. One of the initial sources of funding was Wilbur H. "Ping" Ferry, a US businessman, government adviser, and philanthropist. A close friend of Thompson, Kaldor, and Smith, Ferry's own ethical compass orientated along the "Kantian principle of the categorical imperative."[29] The goals of END appealed to Ferry. Although neither a communist nor anticommunist, Ferry intellectually and morally opposed the Cold War. Through funding activist groups and research, he aimed to open alternative spaces for debate on the subject of nuclear proliferation and the Cold War.[30] Ferry was also instrumental in opening doors to additional funding for Kaldor, Thompson, and Smith. For example, one of Kaldor's earlier trips in 1981 to the United States on behalf of END to raise awareness and funding was sponsored by Ferry. For this particular trip, he arranged a dinner for Kaldor at a country club, where he introduced her to twenty-five representatives of philanthropic foundations, such as the Rockefeller and Stern foundations, as well as to other individual donors.[31] By November 1981, $62,000 had been raised for END from the United States alone.[32] Just as importantly, Ferry also supported them with friendship, intellectual support, and advice on the US political terrain, along with arranging research fellowships behind the scenes.[33]

Thompson and the Public Life

Becoming the de facto leaders of END, Kaldor and Thompson developed a rich intellectual engagement and friendship. Thompson was, by now, an intellectual giant on the political socialist left, with the publication of *The Making of the English Working Class*, and willingly lent his celebrity-like status to raising the profile of the END campaign. A prolific letter writer, Thompson would constantly share his ideas, insights, and contacts with Kaldor and confided in her both professionally and personally. For instance, in one letter addressed to Kaldor, Thompson wrote:

> Mary, the pressures really are intense, as you know as well as anyone. . . . The media have decided I am a Personality—and one can't do anything about it except try to use it for END. . . . This is the most serious political work I have ever done or ever will do in my life, and I think this is true for you also . . . [and] for a brief while—maybe for eight or ten aching months—the pressure will be unrelenting, and we have to match it as we can.[34]

In many respects, Thompson saw the bulk of the work in setting up the office and structure of the organization as a joint effort between himself and Kaldor, with both acting as de facto chairs at various times until the role was formalized.[35] Thompson would often show his intellectual and personal support for Kaldor, encouraging her to take a leadership role within END, yet also showed concern for her personal well-being. In a letter addressed to Kaldor, Thompson wrote: "I do think we should implement the recommendation to have a formal chairperson. . . . Everyone would like you to do it. "[36] With Kaldor, Thompson also engaged in a series of correspondence concerning everything from how END should be managed to how to develop policy and strategy between Western and Eastern Europe:

> I think you and I for our speeches at Bonn and London ought to give out an advance press release (in your case in German also) with certain key points written clearly . . . [and] the END [press release] bit ought in my view just now be directed at the Russians: to show the peace movement is non-aligned and is not in their pocket: to stress the remaking of Europe is our objective, with ideological/security concessions from the East: and (depending on the then circumstance) perhaps saying explicitly that both blocs and both superpowers must stop meddling with Poland. . . . I think we need to stress once more negotiations by *actions* on both sides.[37]

Thompson was not simply a mentor to Kaldor. Thompson both encouraged and deferred to Kaldor, identifying her as the heart of END.[38]

With Thompson, Kaldor became the public face of END in both the United Kingdom and the United States, with the emphasis always on wider engagement and public debates. Her advocacy included numerous interviews in newspapers, letters to editors of various newspapers, public lectures, and seminars, as well as public appearances on television, which were supported by members of END, including those from the Labour Party. As Benn stated, "I watched Robin Cook and Mary Kaldor, the Labour Party's adviser on defence, talking about nuclear weapons on a marvellous party political broadcast. It was principled, serious, straight, with no rhetoric; I felt it was tremendously effective."[39] One of Kaldor's more famous seminars, which she organized and chaired, was a jointly held END–Labour Party public event, featuring co-speakers Michael Foot and Olof Palme, then head of the Common Security Commission.[40] Palme was deeply sympathetic to END, having already considered creating "a nuclear-free zone in Europe" prior to heading the commission.[41] At the END–Labour Party public seminar, Palme argued that ordinary people should be involved in the decisions made regarding nuclear weapons. Moreover, he asserted, "it is particularly important that people *not* adapt, that they don't say OK, [governments] know better, but that they say: we know better, because it is our lives and our future at stake."[42] In his letter thanking Kaldor for organizing the meeting, Palme added: "It was an experience for me, to meet such a large and engaged audience."[43]

Kaldor began to consider a career in Parliament. In 1981, with the support of Cook and Foot, Kaldor campaigned for the parliamentary seat of Dulwich in South London but failed to be selected as the Labour candidate.[44] Both Foot and Cook then pressed Kaldor to run again, this time for the seat of Hackney Central. Nonetheless, Kaldor pulled out of the campaign when she fell ill with hepatitis, from which she took several months to recover. Having to put many of her projects on hold gave Kaldor the opportunity to realize how overcommitted and complex her life had become. With her work in END, a rolling contract at Sussex, and a research project on the arms race, Kaldor could not reconcile all her activities with a parliamentary career. Moreover, Kaldor was also the mother of two small children, Joshua and Oliver, six and two years old, respectively. Although sharing parenting duties with Robinson, Kaldor was struggling to divide her time between her family and her intellectual life. As Kaldor later recalled, along with enjoying the freedom of academic life, "I just decided I didn't want to be a member of parliament. I just realized that I didn't want *that* life. . . . I realized what I [wanted]: and the children were young" and being a parent was "my favorite thing."[45]

The Politics of Protest

Although END's cofounders initially proceeded amicably in developing and launching the END Appeal, not long after, a heated debate ensued regarding the organization's processes and objectives, a debate that threatened to divide the END Coordinating Committee and, more specifically, the organization's cofounders. The development of the *END Bulletin*, the organization's magazine, and the organizing of the END convention process were illuminating examples. Originally, the primary purpose of the *END Bulletin* was to provide updates and information regarding END-supported events, meetings, and conferences, most particularly the END yearly convention, and the initial objective of the convention was to unite like-minded peace groups from across Europe. Organized by the Russell Foundation and the newly formed END Liaison Committee, the first convention was held in Brussels in 1982 and attended by myriad peace groups from across Western Europe. On a practical level, disputes concerned the organization's structure, allocation of resources, and management. On a more conceptual level, however, debates revealed differences over questions of representation and the nature of democratic participation.

More often than not, Kaldor found herself at the center of these debates, frequently as the instigator. In July 1980, the *END Bulletin* was launched out of the offices of the Russell Foundation in Nottingham, with the foundation acting as the principal organizing body for END.[46] The editors, Stuart Holland, Mary Kaldor, and Tony Simpson, struggled to develop a working rapport, and the relationships rapidly declined over a series of several months, due to two main issues. First, they clashed over the editorial style and content of the magazine. For example, cofounders with ties to the foundation—Ken Coates, Bruce Kent, and Stuart Holland—prioritized political parties within the wider European campaign for the convention process. These three cofounders also felt that the convention itself should be the priority in the *END Bulletin* and in the wider peace movement, suggesting that other members of END "systematically under-played" its importance.[47] Conversely, the "London-based" cofounders, such as E. P. Thompson, Mary Kaldor, and Dan Smith, were "interested above all in developing relations among movements" and wished to include more content in the magazine that fulfilled that goal.[48]

These differences came to a head in September 1982 when Holland and Simpson thought Mary Kaldor's plan for the eleventh issue of the *END Bulletin* did not include enough on the END convention.[49] Simpson "found the proposed schedule for *Bulletin* 11 . . . a complete downer. . . . We need a special END Convention issue of the *Bulletin*. Stuart and I have already started work."[50] In her reply, Kaldor charged that deciding "unilaterally and without consultation" the contents of the *END Bulletin*, excluding her from the editing process, was unreasonable.[51] Moreover, Kaldor argued that her own plan had been "misread" by Simpson and that she had "in fact put 6 pages in the outline of *Bulletin* No. 11 on the Convention."[52] In a letter to Coates regarding her exclusion from the editorial process, Kaldor maintained, "I was informed by Tony that he and Stuart were unilaterally going ahead with a Convention special issue," concluding that "there were in fact many occasions when I was overruled by Tony."[53]

The second issue involved differences of opinion over the management of the *END Bulletin* and of END more broadly. The cofounders aligned with the Russell Foundation favored a loose confederate style of management but one controlled from within the foundation offices. Conversely, the London-based END cofounders favored clearer roles and responsibility, a constitution, and greater transparency surrounding finance and decisionmaking processes. Ultimately they wanted END to be independent of the foundation and, at the same time, more decentralized.[54] According to Kaldor and those who aligned with her, a cycle was developing in which funds raised for the *END Bulletin*—a significant percentage by END founders and members in London themselves—were forwarded to the foundation office, which then controlled production of the *END Bulletin* but without clear accountability for how the funds were managed and allocated. After eighteen months, Kaldor and Smith were frustrated by an organization they viewed as "utterly opaque" and "utterly impossible."[55] Moreover, the lack of transparency in the foundation office began to affect their ability to continue to source funding. For example, Ping Ferry wrote to both Kaldor and Smith at the time, "My respect for your work and energy is undiminished . . . but I must confess that I find a five-month delay in getting some kind of financial accounting most annoying."[56]

Both Kaldor and Smith were adamant that the relationship between the Russell Foundation and END could not continue in its current form. Smith, who supported Kaldor's involvement as editor of the *END Bulletin*, was baffled by the actions of the foundation: both "the sudden request for financial support" by the foundation after END had raised funds and forwarded them on to the Russell Foundation and at the same time the editorial "repossession" of the magazine confirmed for Smith "the difficulties for END if it does not own its journal."[57] Although attempts were made to force greater accountability within the foundation, they were to no avail. Moreover, Kaldor began using her position as trustee on some of the funds, raised exclusively for END, to block finances to the foundation for the convention, forcing them to "plug the gap" with their own funds.[58] Thompson temporarily withdrew from the END Coordinating Committee in protest, a decision the Russell Foundation took as an attack on its political priorities.[59] Yet Smith believed that the disputes were ultimately about control of END:

> If you asked me, "What was it about?" I think I would go back to saying that Ken [Coates] liked to be the power behind the throne, but if the people who are clustered in front of the throne are not really sitting on it . . . if we have our own mind, and our own interests, and our own thoughts, you might find it quite difficult to control [them]. . . . [But] if you wanted to be a power behind the throne and you were trying, therefore, to move Edward Thompson and Mary Kaldor around the place [you would be wasting your time]. . . . It sounds very uncharitable towards Ken, but I think in the end it was because they wouldn't dance to his tune.[60]

For Kaldor, the falling out over *END Bulletin* No. 11 was more than just editorial bickering and not being included in the decision of how many pages the END convention should or should not have.[61] Rather, the falling out reflected a greater debate surrounding what END should stand for and how it should operate. The Coordinating Committee, she believed, was the committee of END, not of the Russell Foundation. Although she admired the foundation for its work, END and the *END Bulletin* as the main mouthpiece of the organization both needed to be independent. The editorial decisions needed to be decentralized, and the content of the *END Bulletin* needed to be more collaborative and inclusive, to represent a plurality of views, as opposed to following a "party line."[62] Kaldor was adamant that "if END is to survive, it has to expand and involve more people. We've got together a terrific, creative group of people and they have to feel it's their magazine if we are going to sustain their involvement."[63]

In addition, Kaldor argued that the magazine should not only report the events at the END convention in Brussels but itself be a site of contestation. In a letter to Coates, Kaldor maintained that "although I think the Convention is *very* important, I think there are lots of other important things happening too."[64] Kaldor also opposed the idea that the END Liaison Committee act as a supranational "executive committee" for disarmament movements across Europe.[65] When *END Bulletin* No. 11 was eventually published without her consultation, Kaldor was disappointed that the editorial had implied that END *was* the "European peace movement," representing all peace groups across Europe. In response, Kaldor wrote in her letter to Simpson and Holland:

> The editorial gives the impression that we regard END as a European organization which came into being at the Brussels Convention. This is not true and will upset many of our friends in Europe as well as supporters in this country. In persuading other peace movements to participate in the second convention, . . . I bent over backwards to make it clear that END is a British organization more than two years old and does not and can not claim to speak for Europe. The Liaison Committee is nothing more than a committee to prepare for END Convention. Furthermore we regard the Convention as one of the many activities of the new European movement; the others include demonstrations, conferences, contacts between local groups, etc. organised by the peace movements.[66]

Furthermore, Kaldor believed that both the *END Bulletin* and the END convention process reflected Coates and the Russell Foundation's top-down approach to politics, in which political groups and politicians were prioritized. Rather, Kaldor argued, the convention should also include activists and independent groups working from below. Showing her frustrations, Kaldor wrote: "I really was worried about the involvement of grass root peace movements in the Conventions project and I can't honestly say that you listened to my worries about this particular subject."[67] In this concern, Kaldor was not alone.

The majority of the members of the END Coordinating Committee also agreed that the organization needed to be independent of the Russell Foundation and more inclusive, emphasizing grassroots involvement. A letter addressed to Coates, on behalf of the Coordinating Committee, maintained that the "convention should be first and foremost, a meeting of such people from Eastern and Western Europe, rather than an occasion for speeches by well-known 'leaders.'"[68] The letter continued with a quote from Jürgen Fuchs, writer and East German dissident: "People . . . are struggling for peace and honest dialogue 'from below' and without protection and do not have offices with lots of telephones and imposing letterheads in the capital cities of their countries, who are most urgently dependent on an international dialogue at all levels and in which they will be included."[69]

A number of compromises and concessions were proposed between END and the Russell Foundation. Kaldor proposed that she herself take over the editorship of the *END Bulletin* and that the Russell Foundation hand over the editorial management of *END Bulletin* to the END Coordinating Committee. Coates was prepared to consider loosening his editorial control. However, he insisted that the magazine was to stay within the Russell Foundation offices: "We have never agreed to surrender our role as publisher. I don't really see why we should."[70]

By this stage, although respect between Coates and Kaldor remained, relations between them were severely bruised. In fact, Coates no longer trusted Kaldor, and Kaldor no longer trusted the Russell Foundation. Coates maintained that he could "no longer have confidence that [Kaldor] would make a good sole editor of the Bulletin."[71] Characteristically confident, Kaldor argued:

> Since, arrogantly perhaps, I have more faith in my own editorial judgment than Tony's, I proposed that I be sole editor. I certainly didn't want to claim exclusive powers; this is why I proposed that we should hold regular monthly meetings and that the magazine should be ultimately responsible to the Coordinating Committee. As long [as] production goes relatively smoothly, as it has done on this last issue, there is no pressing reason to have a primus inter pares editor.[72]

Despite her overly confident nature, or perhaps because of it, the END Coordinating Committee also thought Kaldor would make a more egalitarian editor. In August 1982, the END Coordinating Committee unanimously elected Kaldor as editor, to work in association with an "editorial collective" under the committee's administration. The committee also elected to formally separate END from the Russell Foundation.[73] The Russell Foundation declined to hand over the *END Bulletin*,[74] and a new *END Journal* was proposed by the Coordinating Committee. Thereafter the *END Journal* was under Kaldor's editorship, from December 1982 to May 1989, with thirty-seven issues published during that period.[75] Even without the obstacles that lay ahead for the wider peace movement, within the British END Coordinating Committee itself, politics was difficult to avoid.

Editor of the Journal

Unlike the *END Bulletin*, the *END Journal* empowered Kaldor, by providing her with a medium to represent what she believed was a greater plurality of ideas and debates and to report the myriad events across Europe. In her first editorial for the *END Journal*, Kaldor wrote that the strength of the END movement would be realized through the "exchange of ideas."[76] For Kaldor, this exchange of ideas would increasingly take place between East and West, particularly from below, meaning between activists and nonofficials from the two blocs. At the journal's inception, the intellectual and political dialogue between Eastern European samizdats and the *END Journal* was very much a lackluster, fruitless affair. Yet the *END Journal* became increasingly important because it was the most visible representation of the various END campaigns, both in Britain and abroad. Just as significantly, it was pivotal to the organization's objective to be an "ideas-disseminating" group.[77]

Although the *END Journal* was largely answerable to the British-based Coordinating Committee, Kaldor was keen also to create an "international advisory board," which would include activists from both Eastern and Western Europe.[78] Although the Coordinating Committee initially blocked this suggestion, Kaldor saw the value of such a board as a way to improve international coverage and the promotion of the *END Journal*, as well as to further expand the network and, therefore, the debates. As editor, Kaldor attempted to source her material broadly and encouraged Eastern European dissidents and Western peace activists alike to contribute.[79] She also included articles that where critical of her own views.[80]

The purpose of the *END Journal* was threefold. First, the *END Journal* was a vehicle to engage with others in the Western peace movements. Second, the *END Journal* was a vehicle for dialogue between END and the Eastern European dissidents. The *END Journal* and the conventions became a voice for dissident and opposition movements in Eastern Europe,[81] such as the Peace Group for Dialogue (PGD) in Hungary, Freedom and Peace (Wolność i Pokój) in Poland and Charter 77 in Czechoslovakia.[82] Lastly, the journal was also aimed at influencing and engaging with political groups and officials from the West but also from Eastern Europe. END's efforts often paid off more than Kaldor could have imagined. In 1984, Kaldor met with Miklós Barabás, general secretary of the official Hungarian Peace Council, in Budapest,[83] and when she explained the often archaic and underfunded nature of Western peace groups, Barabás replied: "What nonsense! The *END Journal* is a much better piece of propaganda than anything the Peace Movements in the Socialist countries can produce. And I know what a gigantic organisation must be required to produce something as good as the *END Journal*."[84]

Military Industry and *The Baroque Arsenal*

Even though Kaldor remained primarily an academic researcher whose publications included elements of advocacy and policymaking, she now aimed much of her academic writing at a wider audience. During the earlier 1980s, both Kaldor and Smith were regarded as the research arm of END. Kaldor drew on her experiences and connections as a researcher at SPRU and her associations with other institutions, such as the Transnational Institute in Amsterdam, where she had worked with Fred Halliday, and MIT, along with the relationships she developed through other temporary positions she had held across Europe and the United States. Smith was a researcher in London and later taught at Hampshire College, Amherst. Furthermore, both were also members of the Labour Party's NEC until 1987. Thompson contended: "When END originally got going there was a division of responsibility in which Mary and Dan [were] the peace researchers; the Russell Foundation looked forward to a Convention . . . ; the MPs were into inter-parliamentary work; and Bruce [Kent], Peggy [Duff] and I were supposed to do activist peace movement relations. . . . And of course all these areas have overlapped."[85]

While Kaldor and Smith produced research for END, they also collaborated with other researchers. For example, Kaldor and Smith would convene conferences on the Cold War and European nuclear disarmament across Europe and the United States with other researchers, both academic and nonacademic. One of these was the END Research Conference in Amsterdam in May 1981, supported by CND and the Transnational Institute. The purpose of the conference was to debate European nuclear disarmament as a concept and strategy. Kaldor and Smith felt that the conference needed to include more than just academics and that debate needed to be more than purely academic discourse. As Kaldor and Smith said, "in different ways, the participants were all active in disarmament movements in their own countries, and thus brought to the conference a scholarly concern to clarify the issues, together with a political concern to develop a strategy for disarmament."[86] Smith and Kaldor also continued to forge networks and initiate collaborative research.[87]

Aside from writing pamphlets, speeches, conference papers, and activist articles, Kaldor published a series of academic journal articles and coedited books, many of which were further developments of her work at SIPRI and NEC on the themes set out in earlier texts on military conversion and the political economy of the defense industry, but she now broadened her attention to wider European nuclear disarmament.[88] For example, in "Disarmament: The Armament Process in Reverse," Kaldor argued that the concept of the weapons system originated in the initial period of an extensive peacetime military buildup triggered by the Anglo-German naval arms race prior to World War I.[89] Furthermore, she asserted, although nearly all Western industrialized countries had reduced their armed forces since the war, their military economies remained "functionally organised around the weapons system."[90] War, for Kaldor, was viewed through the lens of complex economic policies, and "remov[ing] the causes of war was about undermining the political and economic basis for the armaments industry in industrialised countries."[91] Doing so would serve "to over-come the structural problems, weaknesses and divisions of different economic systems."[92] She went on to explain:

> The degeneracy of the weapons system is not without its effects on Western economy and society as a whole. As an object of use, the weapons system is the basis of military organisation both within individual nations and within the alliance as a whole. It is, at once, a symbol of legitimacy and Western Unity. The dominance of American weapons systems reflects the dominance of American strategic thinking and the American defence industry. . . . The Soviet Union could be described as the inverse of the Western armament sector. . . . Most disarmament efforts are aimed at the role of armaments as objects of use. . . . We also need to change the military-industrial culture which created them. Industrial conversion is one way of achieving this. . . . The conversion from war to peace needs to be seen not as the technical process of converting swords to ploughshares, but as a social process of finding a new mechanism for the allocation of resources.[93]

Kaldor also continued to address both defense policy and the economics of defense policy both domestically and abroad. Kaldor wrote the section of a memorandum to the House of Commons Defence Committee entitled "Industrial and Employment Implications of Polaris Replacement."[94] Any Polaris replacement, Kaldor argued in her submission, either as submarine-based cruise missile system or a submarine-based Trident system, would compete with the other defense programs within the scope of the existing research and development budget. Given the nature of the technology, Kaldor argued, the technological spin-off would be very small and face difficulties competing commercially in world markets. Also by 1978, Kaldor had begun working as a consultant on disarmament and development in the Swedish Foreign Office, where she wrote a report on behalf of the Swedish reference group to the UN Government Expert Study on Military R&D, published in 1984.[95] At the same point, Kaldor was also a consultant to the UN Group of Governmental Experts on Disarmament and Development. In December 1977, the UN General Assembly had adopted a resolution calling for a UN-sponsored study of disarmament and development. Proposed by the Nordic countries—Norway, Finland, Denmark, and Sweden—the terms of reference for the study were established by the tenth special session of the UN General Assembly in 1978.[96] As a part of the first study conducted during the period 1978–1981, Kaldor was selected to submit a report entitled *The Role of Military Technology in Industrial Development*.[97] In December 1984, the General Assembly announced the International Conference on the Relationship Between Disarmament and Development. The conference produced a final document containing a program of action that has served as the primary basis of subsequent General Assembly resolutions.[98]

Yet, due to her experiences working across Europe and with Eastern European dissidents, Kaldor's intellectual research interests began to broaden from the economic policy of weapons and security, disarmament, and peace[99] to include questions of democracy, the role of the state and society in organized violence, and the legitimacy of a political bloc system that was founded upon the threat of war.[100] For example, in "Nuclear Weapons and the Atlantic Alliance," Kaldor questioned the legitimacy of decisions about nuclear weapons within democracies, where these decisions are made by the very few and in secret.[101] Although she recognized that "societies must, of course, be defended against external military threats," this issue was "entirely separate from the question of nuclear weapons,"[102] not only because nuclear weapons could never be used in a limited defensive action but also because, as she elaborated in her article "Peace," the threat of nuclear war reinforced the bloc system of the Cold War. Although the coexistence of the two blocs, Kaldor argued in "Peace," relied upon the idea of a balance of force between two social and political systems, in reality the system provided a way of continuing the postwar military industrial complex and of preserving the order of international political arrangement.[103] Kaldor argued, "In both East and West, deterrence—fear of war, fear of the enemy (whether imperialism or communism)—apparently served to legitimise the political order, and the continued presence of American and Soviet troops in Europe."[104] Here, Kaldor developed what would later be described as a constructivist argument about nuclear strategy being "imagined" strategy. The initial détente process during the 1970s that lessened confrontation, she wrote in "Europe After Cruise and Pershing II," had in fact "reduced the legitimacy of the militarisation of East European society."[105] For this reason, a disarmament strategy was not just about changing the military industrial complex and military production. Rather, it was also about "dealignment," which meant ending the military division within Europe and between the East and West internationally, with the involvement of citizens from the East and West outside Cold War institutions. Though dealignment was an attempt to undermine the notion of deterrence, it was not, Kaldor argued, to be confused with neutrality.[106] Rather, as she argued in "Beyond the Blocs: Defending Europe the Political Way," greater citizen involvement, or "détente from below," was a form of participatory democracy that challenged the bloc arrangement.[107] This form of protest, Kaldor argued, was already evident in independent groups in Eastern Europe, such as Solidarity and Charter 77, as well as in the "new" Western European peace movements.[108]

In addition to the military industrial complex, Kaldor also began to explore the economics of war more directly. In "Warfare and Capitalism," for example, which is regarded as reflecting her Marxist tendencies, Kaldor argued that "the mode of warfare is just as important as the mode of production in shaping society."[109] Kaldor queried her reader that, if a nuclear bomb is too destructive to be used, how does the "contradiction between the bomb as object of consumption and the bomb as object of production ever get resolved? . . . The possibility of allocating more and more resources for increasingly otiose ends can become a reality, leading to the manufacturing of warfare to surpass the society which it's supposed to serve."[110]

Moreover, Kaldor's central idea was the notion that communist countries were basically war economies, an idea that was very important in her later analyses. The difference in social structures was not capitalism versus socialism but capitalism versus warfare. Kaldor argued that the battle was to war what the market is to capitalism, and so the war sector changes dramatically in war but hardly at all in peacetime, whereas capitalism is very dynamic. For Kaldor, the intersection between these systems explained the arms race. Although Kaldor continued to employ elements of Marxism in her writing, "Warfare and Capitalism" is in fact rather "un-Marxist":

> The Second World War changed the nature of capitalism and greatly improved the economic and political position of the working class with it. It may be that because capitalism is fundamentally based on coercion and conflict, it is impossible to imagine a capitalist society which did not rely on socially organized physical violence as a form of coercion and conflict "resolution." Warfare has been so central to the history of capitalism and the nation-state system. Capitalism might be said to represent "progress" in relation to previous societies because it eliminated forms of individual physical coercion and, by separating out and specializing different forms of coercion, exposed the brutality of socially organized physical coercion.[111]

Although Kaldor did not complete her PhD, she nonetheless continued the research project, which was eventually published in 1981 as *The Baroque Arsenal*.[112] The book was a culmination of her academic research, activism, and policy work. In *The Baroque Arsenal*, Kaldor argued that the social structure underlying weapons acquisition in both the United States and the Soviet Union led to ever more elaborate and sophisticated technology, as a result of which the weapons became increasingly unusable, and transferring the technology to alternative industrial uses became more difficult. Kaldor's activism at Vickers and Lucas Aerospace combined with her knowledge of the defense policy studies undertaken by the Labour Party ultimately informed her ideas in *The Baroque Arsenal*, and a reading of her written material over time reveals Kaldor's transition from less of an economist toward more of a political scientist.[113]

According to Alexei Pankin, Kaldor's ideas on the baroque arsenal even made their way into Mikhail Gorbachev's speeches. Pankin was a speechwriter working for Georgy Arbatov, the influential policy adviser to Gorbachev. Pankin said, "Kaldor's *Baroque Arsenal* was the book that made the greatest impression on me."[114] According to Pankin, working under difficult deadlines, he would translate Kaldor's words, along with those of E. P. Thompson, while Arbatov would submit them up the chain of command as speeches for Mikhail Gorbachev's "New Thinking" foreign-policy campaign during 1986–1987.[115] Pankin explained:

> Both [Kaldor and Thompson] were great stylists, so often it was easier for me to translate from their writings rather than formulate the same ideas myself. No attribution, of course. . . . I was the person who was capable to imitate Gorbachev's style so probably my submissions were most user friendly. On several occasions I recognized some of "my" passages in his speeches. What is important is that with all constraints on the person as high as [Gorbachev] was, he was not immune to that line of thinking.[116]

Notes

1. E. P. Thompson, letter to Mary Kaldor, n.d., PA-MK-END-E.Europe. Although the letter is not dated, from context, one can tell Thompson clearly wrote it in 1981 before 10 October.

2. Thatcher, *The Downing Street Years*, p. 65; Margaret Thatcher, speech presented at "Britain Awake," Kensington Town Hall, Chelsea, UK, 19 January 1976.

3. See Evans, *Thatcher and Thatcherism*; Fry, *The Politics of the Thatcher Revolution*; Thatcher, *The Downing Street Years*; Reagan, *An American Life*; Hargrove, *Jimmy Carter as President*; and Freedman, *The Politics of British Defence*.

4. Mary Kaldor, interview with author, 24 June 2011.

5. Mary Kaldor, speech presented at thirtieth anniversary of the Helsinki Final Act, Finlandia Hall, Helsinki, 1 August 2005, http://www.osce.org/cio/16243.

6. According to Stuart Holland, END "was entirely Ken's initiative." Stuart Holland, interview with author, 23 May 2011.

7. Ken Coates, correspondence with author, 20 April 2010.

8. See Beckett, *The Enemy Within*; and Klugmann et al., *History of the Communist Party of Great Britain*.

9. Coates, correspondence with author, 20 April 2010.

10. In a memo, the Russell Foundation maintained, "The original proposal that the appropriate form of the Nuclear Disarmament Campaign could be towards the creation of a nuclear weapons–free zone in all Europe came from the Scandinavian socialists, notably Olof Palme, but in its English form the suggestion that we should organize around this commitment was first made to the Russell Foundation by Ralph Miliband." Bertrand Russell Peace Foundation, "Memo on Relations Between END and the Russell Foundation, with Comments on Dan Smith's Text (Already Circulated)," 23 February 1982, PA-MK-END-GEN-1. A precedent for the proposal had been set by the Treaty of Tlatelolco, establishing the first nuclear-weapons-free zone. It was signed by twenty-one countries in Latin America and the Caribbean in 1968. See "Agency for the Prohibition of Nuclear Weapons in Latin America and the Caribbean (OPANAL)," http://www.opanal.org/index-i.html.

11. Stuart Holland, interview with author, 23 May 2011.

12. Coates, correspondence with author, 20 April 2011; Stuart Holland, interview with author, 23 May 2011; Ken Coates, letter to Mary Kaldor, 12 February 1980, PA-MK-END-GEN-3. Kaldor later maintained, "I had lots of contact with Ken. . . . I'd

been doing a lot of stuff on defence conversion and I'd been working with the Vicker's shop stewards and with Lucas Aerospace . . . [and] they were all connected." Quoted in Patrick Burke, *European Nuclear Disarmament*, p. 45. Also see Ken Coates, letter of invitation to Mary Kaldor, 12 February 1980, PA-MK-END-GEN-3.

13. Coates, correspondence with author, 20 April 2010.

14. Ibid.

15. Ken Coates, letter of invitation to Mary Kaldor, 12 February 1980, PA-MK-GEN-3; Ken Coates, correspondence with author, 20 April 2010.

16. Dan Smith, interview with author, 4 May 2011.

17. Mary Kaldor, interview with author, 24 June 2011.

18. Ibid.

19. END, "Appeal for European Disarmament."

20. According to the Russell Foundation, "Edward did the first draft of the END Appeal, which was modified in accordance with suggestions made by Dan Smith and others, before it was submitted to a consultative meeting, convened by the Foundation in London. At this meeting it was agreed that Mary Kaldor and Ken Coates would finalize the text with Robin Cook, and this was done." See Bertrand Russell Peace Foundation, "Memo on Relations Between END and the Russell Foundation, with Comments on Dan Smith's Text (Already Circulated)"; Wittner, *Confronting the Bomb*, pp. 83–84. April Carter also included Zhores Medvedev and Roy Medvedev, both of which were Russian dissidents. See Carter, *Peace Movements,* p. 117.

21. Stuart Holland claimed, "the first draft of the Appeal was by Ken. Ken was always drafting Appeals." See Stuart Holland, interview with author, 23 May 2011. However, according to Patrick Burke, E. P. Thompson wrote the first draft. See Burke, *European Nuclear Disarmament*, p. 45. Also, according to the Russell Foundation, E. P. Thompson was the first to draft the appeal. See Bertrand Russell Peace Foundation, "Memo on Relations Between END and the Russell Foundation, with Comments on Dan Smith's Text (Already Circulated)."

22. Chris McLaughlin, "Campaign Goes into Europe," *Labour Weekly*, 2 May 1980, p. 5.

23. Benn, *Conflicts of Interest Diaries 1977–1980*, p. 590. For a further history of END, see Burke, *European Nuclear Disarmament*, pp. 35–89.

24. Benn, quoted in McLaughlin, "Campaign Goes into Europe," p. 5.

25. END, "Appeal for European Nuclear Disarmament."

26. Wittner, *Confronting the Bomb,* p. 85.

27. Burke, *European Nuclear Disarmament*, p. 49.

28. Ibid.

29. James Ward, a biographer of Ferry's life, maintained that for Ferry, this imperative translated to "act as if the maxim from which you act were to become a universal law." Ward, *Ferrytale*, p. xx.

30. Ibid., p. xx.

31. Mary Kaldor, report for US trip, 13–29 November 1981, PA-MK-END-GEN-2.

32. Wilbur H. "Ping" Ferry, letter to E. P. Thompson, 24 November 1981, PA-MK-END-GEN-3.

33. Ward, *Ferrytale*, p. xx.

34. E. P. Thompson, letter to Mary Kaldor, n.d., PA-MK-END-E.Europe. While not dated, the letter was clearly written in 1981, before 10 October.

35. E. P. Thompson, letter to Meg Beresford, 14 September [1981], PA-MK-END-GEN-3. The letter is not dated, but it is clearly from 1981.

36. E. P. Thompson, letter to Mary Kaldor, n.d., PA-MK-END-E.Europe, p. 1. The letter is clearly written in 1981, sometime before 10 October.

37. Emphasis in original; ibid.

38. Ibid.

39. Benn, *The End of an Era Diaries*, p. 2.

40. See Independent Commission on Disarmament and Security Issues, *Common Security*.

41. Olof Palme had spoken of the idea of a nuclear-free zone in Europe at the Socialist International Disarmament Conference in Helsinki two years prior; see Olof Palme, letter to Ken Coates, 24 April 1980, PA-MK-GEN-3; also see Bertrand Russell Peace Foundation, "Memo on Relations Between END and the Russell Foundation, with Comments on Dan Smith's Text (Already Circulated)."

42. Olof Palme, speech presented at END and Labour Party public meeting at Caxton Hall, London, on 2 September 1981, PA-MK-END-GEN-2.

43. Olof Palme, letter addressed to Mary Kaldor, 8 October 1981, PA-MK-END-GEN-2; also see Stellan Andersson, "'You Can Never Say No to Noel-Baker': Olof Palme on Disarmament and the Peace Movement," paper presented at Peace Movements in the Cold War and Beyond International Conference, London School of Economics, London, 1–2 February 2008.

44. See Joan Smith, 'Mary, Quite Contrary,' *Sunday Times* [London], 24 January 1982.

45. Quote from Mary Kaldor, interview with author, 24 June 2011; Stephen Cook, "People Diary," *Guardian* [London], 7 June 1986; Stephen Cook, "People Diary," *Guardian* [London], 19 June 1986.

46. See Burke, *European Nuclear Disarmament*, pp. 76, 81.

47. Ken Coates, letter to Mary Kaldor, 29 July 1982, PA-MK-END-GEN-1; also see Burke, *European Nuclear Disarmament*, p. 82.

48. Burke, *European Nuclear Disarmament*, p. 82.

49. Tony Simpson, letter to Mary Kaldor, 6 July 1982, PA-MK-END-GEN-1.

50. Ibid. Also see Burke, *European Nuclear Disarmament*, p. 82.

51. Mary Kaldor, letter to Tony Simpson, 19 July 1982, PA-MK-END-GEN-1.

52. Mary Kaldor, letter to Ken Coates, 3 September 1982, PA-MK-END-GEN-1.

53. Ibid.

54. See Burke, *European Nuclear Disarmament*, pp. 82–85.

55. Mary Kaldor and Dan Smith, quoted in ibid., p. 85.

56. Wilbur H. "Ping" Ferry, letter to Mary Kaldor and Dan Smith, 25 May 1982, PA-MK-GEN-1.

57. Dan Smith quoted in Burke, *European Nuclear Disarmament*, pp. 82–85; also see Dan Smith, letter to Ken Coates, 4 October 1982, PA-MK-END-GEN-1.

58. See, for example, Ken Coates, letter to Mary Kaldor, 15 April 1982, PA-MK-GEN-1. The particular fund was the Conflict Education Library Trust, of which Kaldor was one of eight trustees. The funds in this trust were raised by Ping Ferry from US contributors for END activities. In a letter from Ferry to E. P. Thompson sent on to Kaldor, Ferry indicated that the funds were for "running END, ordinary travel, etc. It does not necessarily cover extra-ordinary costs—e.g., if a Theatre of Peace [multinational meeting] is decided on with END in a major contributing role." W. H. "Ping" Ferry, letter to E. P. Thompson, 24 November 1981, PA-MK-END-GEN-3.

59. Burke, *European Nuclear Disarmament*, p. 84; E. P. Thompson, letter to Meg Beresford, 14 September 1981, PA-MK-END-GEN-3.

60. Dan Smith, interview with author, 4 May 2011.

61. Mary Kaldor, letter to Ken Coates, 3 September 1982, PA-MK-END-GEN-1.

62. Mary Kaldor, letter to Ken Coates, 26 July 1982, PA-MK-END-GEN-1; Mary Kaldor, letter to Ken Coates, 23 April 1982, PA-MK-END-GEN-1; Mary Kaldor, interview with author, 24 June 2011.

63. Mary Kaldor, letter to Ken Coates, 31 March 1982, PA-MK-END-GEN-1.

64. Mary Kaldor, letter to Ken Coates, 3 September 1982, PA-MK-END-GEN-1 (emphasis in original).

65. Mary Kaldor and Dan Smith, "Shaping the Future: END Supporters Conference," *END Newsletter*, Autumn/Winter 1982, PA-MK-END-GEN-1.

66. Mary Kaldor, letter to Tony Simpson and Stuart Holland, 16 September 1982, PA-MK-END-GEN-1.

67. Mary Kaldor, letter to Ken Coates, 23 April 1982, PA-MK-END-GEN-1.

68. Roger Fieldhouse (on behalf of END Coordinating Committee), letter to Ken Coates, 12 January 1983, PA-MK-END-GEN-2.

69. Quoted in ibid.; Jürgen Fuchs, letter sent to END and Interkerkelijk Vredesberaad (IVK; Interchurch Peace Council), 28 December 1982, PA-MK-END-LC/CP. Fuchs was eventually expelled from East Germany and deported to West Germany, where he joined the peace movements based in Berlin.

70. Ken Coates, letter to Mary Kaldor, 15 April 1982, PA-MK-END-GEN-1.

71. Ibid.

72. Mary Kaldor, letter to Ken Coates, 23 April 1982, PA-MK-END-GEN-1.

73. The Coordinating Committee had agreed that (1) END's magazine should be under political and editorial control of the committee; (2) END's magazine should be produced by the editorial collective with Mary Kaldor as editor; and (3) END should have financial control of its own magazine. The Russell Foundation did not participate in the meeting. See Meg Beresford, letter to E. P. Thompson, 3 August 1982, PA-MK-END-GEN-1. Nonetheless, Smith maintained that Ken Fleet, a member of the Russell Foundation, attended on behalf of Russell Foundation but had not been advised on any action, and, soon after the meeting, Smith was advised by the Russell Foundation that it had no intention of handing over the *END Bulletin*. Hence, production of the publication would proceed as before. See Dan Smith, letter to Mary Kaldor and members of the Coordinating Committee, 8 November 1982, PA-MK-END-GEN-1. See END, "END Supporters' Survey: Summer 1982," PK-MK-END-GEN-1.

74. For example, in his letter to Kaldor, Coates maintained: "Your proposal that we hand over sole responsibility for the Bulletin to the Co-ordinating Committee has been carefully considered, and we don't think it is a reasonable thing to ask us to do. We founded both the Committee and the Bulletin, . . . [and] we think it's a good thing that we should continue to function in alliance." See Ken Coates, letter to Mary Kaldor, 29 July 1982, PA-MK-END-GEN-1.

75. Burke, *European Nuclear Disarmament*, p. 76.

76. Mary Kaldor, "Editorial," *END Journal* 1 (December–January 1982–1983), p. 1.

77. Burke, *European Nuclear Disarmament*, p. 76.

78. Mary Kaldor, letter to Peter Crampton, 14 January 1983, PA-MK-END-GEN-2. See also Mary Kaldor, "Proposals for the END Bulletin [Journal]," 27 October 1982, PA-MK-END-GEN-1.

79. Mary Kaldor, letter to END Coordinating Committee, 2 November 1982, London School of Economics Archives.

80. See, for example, Monks, "Détente or Cold War from Below?" p. 8.

81. Soper, "E. P. Thompson."

82. Wernicke, "The Race to Tip the Scales."

83. Though the Hungarian Peace Council was the first peace group in Hungary, it had little credibility. See Weber, "The Hungarian Peace Movement Today."

84. Mary Kaldor, "Memo to END Hungary Group and END Coordinating Committee: Notes on Hungary Trip—October 17 to 26, 1984," London School of Economics Archive END/12/6, London.

85. E. P. Thompson, letter to Meg Beresford, 1982, PA-MK-END-GEN-3.

86. Kaldor and Smith, "Introduction," p. ix.

87. Robert C. Johansen, letter to Mary Kaldor, 11 February 1982, PA-MK-END-GEN-2.

88. See, for example, Kaldor, "Technical Change and the British Defence Industry"; Kaldor, "Disarmament: The Armament Process in Reverse"; Kaldor, "Is There a Soviet Threat?"; Kaldor, "Military R&D: Cause or Consequence of the Arms Race?"

89. Kaldor, "Disarmament: The Armament Process in Reverse."

90. Ibid., p. 205.

91. Ibid., p. 219.

92. Ibid.

93. Ibid., pp. 212–215.

94. See Kaldor, "Industrial and Employment Implications of Polaris Replacement."

95. See Kaldor, *Military R&D*, 1984.

96. See Kaldor, "Arms and Dependence."

97. United Nations, Press Release DC/2897, "Governmental Experts to Review Relationship Between Disarmament and Development," 17–21 November 2004, online; Kaldor, *The Role of Military Technology in Industrial Development*.

98. Hovstadius and Wängborg, "Review Essay," p. 209.

99. For example, see Kaldor, *The Disintegrating West*.

100. See, for example, Kaldor, "Nuclear Weapons and the Atlantic Alliance"; Kaldor, "Peace"; Kaldor, "Beyond the Blocs"; Kaldor, "Europe After Cruise and Pershing II."

101. See Kaldor, "Nuclear Weapons and the Atlantic Alliance."

102. Ibid., pp. 10–11.

103. Kaldor, "Peace," pp. 255, 258.

104. Ibid., p. 257.

105. Kaldor, "Europe After Cruise and Pershing II," p. 78.

106. Kaldor, "Peace," p. 266.

107. Kaldor, "Beyond the Blocs."

108. Ibid., p. 19.

109. Kaldor, "Warfare and Capitalism," p. 262.

110. Kaldor, "Beyond the Blocs," p. 19.

111. Kaldor, "Warfare and Capitalism," p. 262.

112. Kaldor, *The Baroque Arsenal*. The term *baroque* to describe advance defense capability was coined by Herbert York; see York, *Race to Oblivion*, p. 44.

113. Kaldor, correspondence with author, 20 September 2012.

114. Alexei Pankin, correspondence with author, 5 October 2010.

115. Alexei Pankin, "A True Perestroika Scholar," *Moscow Times*, 12 October 2010, online.

116. Pankin, correspondence with author, 5 October 2010.

4

Linking Peace and Human Rights

> *E. P. Thompson, Mary Kaldor and a few others listened hard to the opposition groups in Eastern Europe and managed to convince the British peace movements that disarmament on its own was not enough—that a peace which left Eastern Europe without a nuclear threat but also without democracy was no peace at all.*[1]

KALDOR BECAME INVOLVED IN THE FOUNDING OF END NOT ONLY BECAUSE the organization promised to work against the Cold War but also because it promised to explicitly link peace and human rights together, the latter an issue of deeply personal importance to Kaldor as well as being of familial significance. As discussed earlier, Kaldor's uncle, her father's brother-in-law, was a dissident who had been incarcerated for several years in a Hungarian prison for speaking out against the regime, whereas her mother was a peace activist with a commitment to democratic politics in response to the violence and oppression occurring in Eastern Europe. As Kaldor recalled,

> I had to find a way of reconciling these two sides of my family. So I think that from a very early age I was against nuclear weapons and had an active interest in the peace tradition. At the same time, I had this very uneasy feeling that people who are involved in peace activism weren't really concerned about issues like human rights and the problem of communism in Eastern Europe. So somehow I wanted to bring those two [concerns] together.[2]

For Kaldor, the separation of peace and human rights was reflected in the opposing principles between US and Soviet foreign policy. Kaldor argued that this difference meant that the rhetoric of peace and human rights were purposely separated.

On the one hand, the foreign policy rhetoric in the United States was focused on the supremacy of human rights and democratic values and viewed in the context of "containment."[3] The US stance on Soviet human rights, some argued, generally coincided with US foreign policy interests. For example, President Jimmy Carter's criticism of the Soviet invasion of Afghanistan was not about the rights of the Afghan people but, as Carter argued, was "an assault on the vital interests of the United States . . . and such an assault will be repelled by any means necessary."[4] During the administration of President Ronald Reagan, US foreign policy continued to oscillate between aspirations for democracy, such as through Reagan's Project Democracy,[5] and blunt realism, with Reagan declaring that of "the great nations only those with the strength to protect their interests survive."[6]

On the other hand, the Soviet Union's foreign policy emphasized the importance of "peace." In 1981, Foreign Minister Andrei Gromyko asserted that "the fundamental underlying principles" of Soviet foreign policy were "proletarian internationalism and peaceful co-existence of states and differing social systems."[7] Contrary to the "West," which prioritized the rights of the individual, Soviet ideology emphasized the rights of society in its entirety. Therefore, Soviet internal and foreign policy highlighted economic and social rights over freedom of speech and freedom of association,[8] dismissing international human rights as "bourgeois."[9] Although certain brief historical moments could be identified when peace and human rights were formally linked together, such as during the signing of the Helsinki Accords in 1975,[10] for Kaldor, the logic of the Cold War was underpinned by the notion that peace and human rights were broadly separated or prioritized as competing interests.[11] But unlike scholars, such as Noam Chomsky, who saw the idea of "human rights" as a pretext for legitimizing US ideology and hegemony,[12] Kaldor believed that the US Congress was serious about human rights. Nevertheless, competing interests between various actors in the US State Department and the US Defense Department combined with the role of the military industrial complex made for an inconsistent human rights agenda.

Initially, Kaldor argued, peace and human rights were linked together in the END Appeal for tactical reasons.[13] The authors of the END Appeal attempted to "establish the integrity of the peace-movement" and to dissociate END from either US or Soviet rhetoric.[14] For example, through the END Appeal, all signers were asked to support "disarmament and peace," no matter where they came from and irrespective of any division between "Eastern" or "Western" blocs, and to denounce limits "placed upon the free exchange of ideas between persons, and [on the] civil rights of independent-minded individuals . . . in the West as well as the East."[15] Initially, Kaldor maintained, linking peace with human rights was a "formality," whereby END members officially supported the link as a way to protest against both the Soviet and US blocs more broadly and only thereafter felt increasingly bound to act on the idea: "It became a little bit more then a tactical argument in which people realized, if you had democracy in Eastern Europe, it would be easier to get rid of nuclear weapons."[16]

Protest in the West

The proposal in the END Appeal that peace and human rights were indivisible was a minority position within mainstream Western peace movements.[17] Throughout Europe, antinuclear peace rallies continued to increase in size and number from 1979 to 1981, particularly in autumn 1981 when a string of antinuclear peace marches took place across those countries set to receive NATO deployment: for example, 150,000 protestors attended marches in Rome and London, with 300,000 attending in Bonn, 120,000 in Brussels, and 400,000 in Amsterdam.[18] In Britain, the CND, then the largest grassroots lobby group in the United Kingdom, continued to harness its power as a single-issue peace group. At its peak in the 1980s, CND attracted around 400,000 protestors to the streets in October 1983, in what was considered the largest demonstration in British history, and, in 1985, membership of CND topped 100,000.[19] Peace and disarmament remained the primary and overriding objective of mainstream European movements, with their objectives ranging from a total eradication of nuclear weapons to, at least, curtailing the first launch missile of a nuclear weapon and the certain threat of mutually assured destruction on both sides of the Iron Curtain.[20] As a former UK defense secretary opined, "the disaster of the last conventional war" would be "child's play compared with what a new conventional war would be."[21]

Nonetheless, some argued that because mainstream demonstrations across Europe firmly described themselves as "peace" movements, they were more sympathetic toward the Soviet Union.[22] Most mainstream peace groups across Europe were known to have small, but vocal, openly pro-Soviet caucuses.[23] Moreover, a group such as CND was, as James Hinton argued, "adept at exploiting mass anti-American sentiment in its campaign against cruise missiles."[24] Others argued that the Soviet Union was explicitly involved in coordinating and funding elements of the Western peace movement.[25]

Conversely, those in the mainstream peace movement, such as CND, were adamant that promoting themselves as a single-issue "peace" movement was strictly a tactical approach to attract mainstream support. Some in the Western peace movement considered accusations of Soviet collusion as libel. For example, Dan Smith, who was later vice chair of CND, commenced civil action against the British Federation of Conservative Students for defamation, after it alleged that CND received Soviet funding. The federation later retracted the allegations, apologized, and paid the litigation costs.[26] Indeed, Bruce Kent, former general secretary of CND and cofounder of END, quipped that had the Soviet Union provided any funding to the Western peace movement, "it was certainly not getting to our grotty little office in Finsbury Park."[27]

That peace movements limited debate to a single-issue objective did not necessarily mean they were uninterested in human rights in Eastern Europe.[28] As Smith argued, Kaldor's position as both an activist and an academic meant that she approached the question of peace and human rights differently.[29] Kaldor was not a key member of CND because it did not address her concerns about the lack of human rights in Eastern Europe. Disarming nuclear weapons was not enough. The peace movements also needed to engage with the question of how to promote human rights behind the Iron Curtain. Nevertheless, groups such as CND rose to become the most powerful protest groups in British history simply because they were single-issue groups:

> The nuance here is quite important. Someone like Joan Ruddock, who was chair of CND at the time and is now a member of parliament, was not—is not—pro-Soviet, but she saw getting rid of nuclear weapons, [as a] single clear objective, [and we could] campaign for that. . . . The reason why you have a movement that focuses on an issue is because you can mobilize a bigger coalition and a bigger alliance. . . . You could reasonably disagree with the idea of nuclear disarmament and civil liberties in Eastern Europe being put into one campaign for reasons other than you "love" the Soviet Union.[30]

Across Western Europe, the debates surrounding the link between peace and human rights were magnified in West Germany. As one of the most militarized sites in the world, the border between East and West Germany, particularly in the city of Berlin, was an intensely fragile political landscape and considered the front line during any potential nuclear war between the United States and the Soviet Union.[31] Nonetheless, in the early 1980s, the prospect of further militarization prompted a new era of dissent within West Germany, the most well-known peace movement being the Breakfast Club (Frühstücksrunde).[32] An alliance of different peace groups and minor political parties, many of whom formed as a response to NATO weapons deployment,[33] developed and converged to organize the first major German peace demonstration in Bonn in October 1981.

Debate within mainstream West German politics and society surrounding the Bonn demonstration ensued. For example, some West German parliamentary members feared the protests would come across as a threat to their Soviet neighbors and could set off a chain reaction, leading both sides into a state of high alert; therefore, they recommended curbing the right to protest.[34] Nevertheless, the protests went ahead, and, attended by 300,000 protestors in Bonn, they represented the largest peace demonstration in West Germany's short history.[35]

Renown as a charismatic orator, Kaldor was invited to speak at the Bonn protest. In her address, Kaldor emphasized the need for grassroots democracy and dialogue between states. Kaldor also drew the link between peace and human rights:

> It is tremendously exciting to be here, at what is going to be an enormous rally, and to feel that we are part of . . . a movement that stretches across Europe. . . . We shall stop the cruise and Pershing missiles. . . . Together with

> the people of East Europe we shall remove the SS-20s . . . and end the senseless division of our continent. . . . [With] a movement for democracy and human rights . . . never again can the threat of war be used as an excuse to suppress freedom or independence. . . . We must . . . create our own alternative international system based on communications between peoples and not governments.[36]

Behind the Iron Curtain

Behind the Iron Curtain, East European dissidents were skeptical about the motivations of Western peace movements and accused them of being favorably disposed to the Soviet Union. In an essay addressed to the END convention in Amsterdam in 1985, entitled "Anatomy of a Reticence," Václav Havel argued that the word *peace* had been stripped of all its meaning. For Havel, those in the West who described themselves as peace activists and opposed nuclear weapons appeared, mostly unwittingly, as apologists for the Soviet system.[37] Similarly, George Konrád, a Hungarian independent activist and writer, maintained that although the United States had in the past characterized itself as on the "ideological leading edge" of human rights as an antithesis to the Soviet Union, leaders often downplayed human rights when they competed with their US foreign policy agenda. Realpolitik, he said, had triumphed over idealism. On the one hand, the United States showed moral outrage at the violation of human rights in Poland, but, on the other, the Soviets would demonstrate anger for violation of human rights in El Salvador, in which the US leaders were complicit. Konrád therefore concluded that this contradiction in words and deeds "suggests that we cannot expect our freedom from either of them. . . . We can only expect freedom from ourselves."[38]

For independent groups in Eastern Europe, the terms *human rights* and *peace* were highly contested, and linking them was a precondition for Eastern European dissidents to commence a dialogue with Western peace movements.[39] The most famous example was Charter 77's "The Indivisibility of Peace" in 1983, which, as the title suggests, argued for the indivisibility of peace from democratization and human rights. Charter 77 maintained: "To guarantee peace it is necessary to eliminate violence and injustice within states and guarantee respect by the state authorities in all countries of human and civil rights."[40]

Initially, within END, Thompson promoted ideas concerning linking peace and human rights and for pursuing engagement between Western and Eastern European dissidents. As the coordinator of END's Eastern Europe Committee, Thompson relentlessly sought contact and encouraged dialogue with Eastern European dissidents, constantly pushing END to further its links.[41] However, Thompson grew increasingly frustrated with END's pace.

For example, in early 1981, he began to criticize END's Coordinating Committee for doing "too little" and conducted workshops and meetings about how to better engage "Soviet and East European opinion."[42]

Yet how END's Coordinating Committee should engage Eastern Europeans on the subject of peace and human rights was not fully reconciled. At one such meeting, Kaldor's interpretation of the expected outcomes was focused on what dissidents, such as Victor Wysinski of Solidarity in Poland, thought about peace and civil rights.[43] In July 1982, Mary Kaldor and Mient Jan Faber, then secretary-general of Interkerkelijk Vredesberaad (IKV; Interchurch Peace Council), signed a joint statement advocating the link between peace and human rights, with representatives of the Solidarity Coordinating Office Abroad, based in Brussels. Gillian Wylie, a fellow member of END, argued that the ratification of the statement was rare within the peace movement because it equated peace with the Helsinki Process of "détente from above" and the prioritization of human rights together. "In doing so," Wylie argued, "Kaldor was signed up to a disputed view in the Western Peace movement."[44]

Within the Western peace movement, some regarded attempts to link peace and human rights with a mixture of contempt and alarm. Peace activists, such as Robert Borosage, argued that democracy in the East would only flourish when the Cold War thawed and the arms race halted. Therefore, Borosage suggested, the task of the Western peace movement was to change the direction of the leadership, from above, in both the West and East. Moreover, he argued, the Western peace movement had such moral and political force that Soviet leaders would be compelled to respond.[45] As Borosage explained, "one thing should be clear: the movement to end the arms race in the West cannot wait upon the growth of democracy in the East."[46] Similarly, within END itself, one could find vehement disagreement. Pieta Monks, an END activist and journalist, argued that the "preoccupation of some activists within END with the issue of human rights is potentially more dangerous and divisive to the British peace movement than anything [the British defense secretary] Michael Heseltine or President Reagan could dream up."[47]

Kaldor also found herself at odds with Ken Coates and E. P. Thompson, who were both furious that Kaldor had signed the statement with Solidarity. On one level, the issue was one of representation: Coates believed that Kaldor had not consulted all of the Coordinating Committee on whether to engage with Solidarity, and quite simply she had not followed the "party line." On another level, the difference reflected Coates's and Thompson's positions on the prospect for liberal democracy in Eastern Europe. Some believed that underlying Coates's and Thompson's outrage was their suspicion of Solidarity because the group was considered prodemocratic and anticommunist, neither of which resonated with Coates or Thompson.[48] According to Patrick Burke, an activist with END, Coates only associated and encouraged East Europeans who were "reform Marxists," and during the course of the 1980s, Coates "had no time for the liberals . . . even if they were peace activists, like Freedom and Peace in Poland."[49] Similarly, Thompson had reservations about liberal, pro-democratic groups in Eastern Europe, most particularly among the Poles. As Burke maintained, for Thompson, it was "not a question of getting *rid* of" communism; it was "a question of *renewing* it and making it better."[50] Likewise, Dieter Esche, a West German activist with the German Green involved in the END convention process, argued that, although Coates and Thompson had left the British Communist Party in response to the Hungarian Uprising of 1956, they had remained sympathetic to many of the ideas associated with "communist orthodoxy."[51] In essence, Esche argued, "for them the Soviet Union was not an error, but, let's say, a misled child."[52]

Violence, Totalitarianism, and Democracy

Thompson's reservations about liberal democracy created reservations among prominent dissidents. For example, when Charter 77 met with Thompson in his first trip to Prague in 1980, he was apparently greeted with awkward silence. Upon Thompson's return to the United Kingdom, in response to Thompson's article entitled "Notes on Exterminism" in the *New Left Review*,[53] a Czech dissident, writing under the pseudonym Václav Racek, explained the "silence" Thompson was "met with in Prague."[54] Although he believed that Thompson genuinely desired cooperation with Eastern European dissidents, Racek contended that Thompson had failed to understand the dynamics of ideology and totalitarianism in Eastern Europe.[55] In his open letter to Thompson, which both Thompson and Kaldor arranged to have published in the *New Statesman*, Racek argued:

> You don't concern yourself with any complex analysis of possible connections between ideology and bureaucracy on the one hand and aggression with invasion on the other. . . . But a true analysis of such interconnections in totalitarian regimes shows that the relation between ideology and bureaucracy and aggression and invasion is a necessary one. . . . I need not demonstrate this analysis to you, since it is very easily accessible. I refer to Hannah Arendt's *The Origins of Totalitarianism*.[56]

Here lay the impasse for Thompson and Kaldor. For Thompson, communism and respect for human rights were not mutually exclusive, whereas Racek, like Kaldor, believed that democracy and human rights were fundamentally absent from communism. Indeed, communism, in practice, could only ever be totalitarian, in the way that Arendt described.

Moreover, the importance Kaldor attributed to both peace and human rights appealed to many dissidents within independent Eastern European groups, such as Solidarity, Charter 77, and PGD and later the Alliance of

Young Democrats (Magyar Polgári Szövetség; FIDESZ) in Hungary. By December 1983, Jan Minkiewicz, a representative of the Solidarity office, had addressed members at the launch of the *END Journal*.[57] He also contributed an article on Solidarity to *END Journal*'s first issue.[58] In 1983 a working group was established to foster British END's Polish work. Members of this group, like those of other working groups, visited Poland and, on their return, publicized what they had seen and heard in various ways, such as in internal reports and articles in the *END Journal* and newsletters.

Kaldor's preoccupation with linking peace and human rights remained personal and political: "I think, for me, it was genuinely two goals. . . . I remember one person saying to me, 'You care more about democracy in Eastern Europe than you do about nuclear disarmament,' and me saying that 'I actually genuinely care about them both, equally.'"[59]

Notes

1. Neal Asherson, "EP Thompson: Defender of the Faithful Few," *Independent* [London], 5 September 1993, p. 21.
2. Kaldor, quoted in Schouten, "Theory Talk #30."
3. Packenham, *Liberal America and the Third World*; Blanton, "Foreign Policy in Transition?"; Kegley and Wittkoff, "The American Strategy of Containment," p. 45.
4. Jimmy Carter, quoted in Kegley and Wittkoff, "The American Strategy of Containment: Evolutionary Phases," p. xx; see also Forsythe, *Human Rights and U.S. Foreign Policy*, p. 2, and Forsythe, *Human Rights and World Politics*, pp. 110–114.
5. See Zakaria, "The Reagan Strategy of Containment." This Project Democracy is not to be confused with the secret operations dubbed by Oliver North as "Project Democracy," a program led by the Central Intelligence Agency (CIA) that bypassed Congress to fund covert operations in Latin America and Iran. See, for example, Richard Secord's testimony before the Joint Select Committee on 5 May 1987.
6. Ronald Reagan, quoted in Kegley and Wittkoff, *American Foreign Policy*, p. 77; see also Forsythe, *Human Rights and U.S. Foreign Policy*, p. 2.
7. Andrei Gromyko, quoted in Garthoff, "The Soviet Conception of Détente," pp. 108–109.
8. See Lambelet, "The Contradiction Between Soviet and American Human Rights Doctrine"; and Shiman, *Economic and Social Justice*.
9. Thomas, "The Helsinki Accords and the Political Change in Eastern Europe," p. 208.
10. See "Conference on Security and Cooperation in Europe."
11. See, for example, Cortright, *Peace*, pp. 280–292.
12. See, for example, Chomsky, *"Human Rights" and American Foreign Policy.*
13. Kaldor maintained that for "Western peace activists, supporting the struggle for democracy in Eastern Europe came to be seen not just as a tactical manoeuvre—a way to convince people in the West that peace activists were not pro-Soviet—but as an end in itself, and the most realistic strategy for overcoming the Cold War and bringing about disarmament." See Kaldor, "VII. 4 The Revolutions of 1989."
14. Kaldor, "A Movement for Peace and Democracy," p. 101.
15. END, "Appeal for European Disarmament."

16. Mary Kaldor, interview with author, 24 June 2011.

17. See Cortright, *Peace*, pp. 279–283; see also Galtung, "Violence, Peace, and Peace Research," pp. 167–191; also see Lawler, *A Question of Values*.

18. Other tactics of the peace movement included persuading hundreds of cities and nations to declare themselves nuclear-free zones, pressuring community and religious groups to take an ethical stance on nuclear weapons, and setting up permanent "peace camps" outside nuclear facilities (the most well known of which was the women's camp at Greenham Green). See Bess, *Realism, Utopia, and the Mushroom Cloud*, p. 136; for more information on peace movements across Europe during the early 1980s, see Kaltefleiter and Pfaltzgraff, *The Peace Movements in Europe and the United States*.

19. Wittner, *Confronting the Bomb*, p. 144.

20. Ibid.

21. Denis Healey, "Interview with War and Peace in the Nuclear Age: 'The Education of Robert McNamara Programme,'" London, part 2–3, 29 October 1986, http://openvault.wgbh.org/catalog/wpna-c55b60-interview-with-denis-healey-1986-part-1-of-3.

22. Kaltefleiter, "Introduction," p. 2; also see Carter, *Peace Movements*.

23. Nicholas Jones, "I Regret Nothing, Says Stasi Spy," BBC News, 20 September 2009, online.

24. Hinton, *Protests and Visions*, p. 200. James Hinton was an active member of the CND as chair of its Projects Committee and also an active member of END as chair of END Leamington.

25. See Glantz, *Soviet Military Intelligence in War*.

26. Dan Smith, quoted in EurActiv, "Ashton Faces Accusations Ahead of Parliament Hearing," *Efficacité et transparence des acteurs européens*, 26 November 2009, online.

27. Bruce Kent, quoted in Kate Hudson, "Soviet Funding? Rubbish," CND, 26 November 2009, online.

28. Dan Smith, interview with author, 4 May 2011.

29. Ibid.

30. Ibid.

31. Following Egon Bahr and German chancellor Willy Brandt's Neue Ostpolitik, translated as "New Eastern Policy," West Germany pursued a "normalization" foreign policy, which was based on "change through rapprochement" and establishing diplomatic engagement with East Germany. In what was considered a fragile political and military landscape, West German politics was preoccupied with ardently avoiding any direct confrontation with their East German neighbors that could trigger any further escalation on an already highly militarized border. See Egon Bahr, "Change Through Rapprochement," speech delivered at the Evangelical Academy, Tutzing, Germany, 15 July 1963; see also Fink and Schaefer, *Ostpolitik, 1969–1974*.

32. By the late 1970s, the prospect of additional militarization of the border between East and West Germany was a point of contention for many in German society. An article in *Der Stern* magazine mapping the sites of the thousands of existing nuclear weapons stationed across the Federal Republic, combined with the announcement by the administration of Ronald Reagan that the number of nuclear weapons stationed in West Germany would be further increased, ushered in a new era of protest in West Germany. Wittner, *Confronting the Bomb*, p. 145.

33. For example, the birth of the German Greens was partly in response to NATO weapons deployment in 1979. Led by Petra Kelly, the German Greens changed the political landscape in relation to both the antinuclear movement in West Germany and German parliamentary politics. See Wittner, *Confronting the Bomb*, pp. 70–71.

34. These MPs were mainly Christian Democrats; see Breyman, *Why Movements Matter*, p. 66.

35. Cooper, *Paradoxes of Peace*, p. 203.

36. Mary Kaldor, speech presented at peace demonstrations, Bonn, 10 October 1981, PK-MK-END-E.EUROPE.

37. Havel, "Anatomy of a Reticence." The piece was "to be delivered at a peace conference in Amsterdam, in my absence; and for an international collection of essays on European identity being prepared by the Suhrkamp publishing house." It first appeared in Czech in *Obsah*, a samizdat publication, in April 1985. Its first publication in English was as a Charter 77 pamphlet, *Voices from Czechoslovakia I* (Stockholm: Charter 77, 1985).

38. Konrád, *Anti-Politics*, pp. 23–24.

39. Burke, *European Nuclear Disarmament*, p. 170.

40. Charter 77, "The Indivisibility of Peace," p. 24.

41. Thompson's efforts to establish contact and nurture a dialogue with Eastern European dissidents preceded the founding of END. For example, see Thompson, *The Poverty of Theory and Other Essays*.

42. E. P. Thompson, letter regarding END—"Soviet & East European Advice," n.d., PA-MK-END-E.EUROPE. Although the letter is not dated, the letter clearly was written just prior to 15 March 1981. See also Stephen Lukes (chair of END), notes for the meeting on END East European links, 15 March 1981, PA-MK-END-E.EUROPE.

43. Mary Kaldor, letter to April Carter, 23 March 1981, PA-MK-END-E.EUROPE.

44. See Wylie, "Social Movements and the International Change."

45. Borosage, quoted in Gordon, "From the Other Shore," p. 408.

46. Borosage, quoted in ibid. See also Jan Kavan, speech presented at "The Influence of the Ideas of 1989 on Foreign Policy," public lecture series at the London School of Economics as part of the "Ideas of 1989," Centre for Global Governance, London School of Economics, online.

47. Monks, "Détente or Cold War from Below?" p. 8.

48. Padraic Kenney maintained, "To write about opposition to communism in the 1980s, one must begin with Poland. The Poles were the only ones ever to stage repeated challenges to communist rule, with major uprisings in 1956, 1968, 1970, 1976 and 1980. Solidarity, the last of these, was a more credible alternative to communism than anything else produced in Central Europe. Its influence throughout the region was incalculable." See Kenney, *A Carnival of Revolution*, p. 15.

49. Patrick Burke, interview with author, 10 May 2011.

50. Ibid.

51. Dieter Esche, interview with author, 31 March 2011.

52. Ibid.

53. Thompson, "Notes on Exterminism."

54. Václav Racek, letter to Edward Thompson, 12 December 1980, PA-MK-END-E.EUROPE.

55. Ibid.

56. Ibid. Also see Arendt, *Origins of Totalitarianism*.

57. Burke, *European Nuclear Disarmament*, p. 174.

58. Minkiewicz, "Solidarity."

59. Mary Kaldor, interview with author, 24 June 2011.

5

Politics from Below

By travelling around, by being at conferences, by being known, she did slowly build up [a network of Eastern European independents], and I give her all the credit for years when people were not interested, didn't believe that these dissident movements would ever amount to a single damn thing, which was probably more or less true. But nonetheless amongst those groups were people who then, when the possibilities arose, became influential and active. Mary was well ahead of the curve in understanding the importance of the role that they could—and would—play.[1]

A CORE OBJECTIVE OF THE END APPEAL WAS TO UNITE EUROPE "FROM Portugal to Poland" in protest against nuclear weapons.[2] Concurrently, authors of the END Appeal argued, "we must defend and extend the right of all citizens, East or West, to take part in this common movement and to engage in every kind of exchange."[3] Moreover, "we must commence to act as if a united, neutral and pacific Europe already exists. We must learn to be loyal, not to 'East' or 'West,' but to each other, and we must disregard the prohibitions and limitations imposed by any national state."[4]

Achieving these aims required developing an extensive network across Europe, and Stuart Holland and Mary Kaldor were central to assembling this network. In an END report written in 1980, Dorothy and E. P. Thompson declared, "We have, thanks to the work of the Russell Foundation, ICDP [International Confederation for Disarmament and Peace], and of Stuart Holland and Mary Kaldor, made important links in Western Europe. We are in good shape for commencing a new campaigning year in the autumn."[5] Similarly, the leaders of the Russell Foundation maintained that, without Holland and Kaldor, the initial END convention network could not have been established. In a memo, they concluded,

> [The] Russell Foundation could not have dreamed of launching the idea of a European conference or convention without being sure of the physical and

> moral help of the other members of the END [international] collective. In particular, the international contacts of Stuart Holland and Mary Kaldor were of decisive importance in bringing together, with the Russell Foundation's own extensive European contacts, a new type of convergence.[6]

Within END, however, no one could agree who exactly should be included in this international network.[7]

For those at the Russell Foundation and Stuart Holland, when deciding whom to include, the emphasis was on politicians, religious and political groups, and the unions. As a British parliamentarian, Holland had established connections across Europe, particularly with politicians and civil servants, including Willy Brandt (chancellor of West Germany), Andreas Papandreou (prominent Greek economist), Bruno Kreisky (chancellor of Austria), and António Ramahlio Eanes (president of Portugal).[8] The Russell Foundation, in particular, Ken Coates, also possessed a wide network of socialist party and union members, including Fernando Claudín, a leading Spanish ex-communist.[9]

The Russell Foundation emphasized top-down and representative approaches to initial END activities, such as conventions and consultations. For example, in November 1981, the foundation, in association with Italian Gruppo Parlamentare Misto—Sinistra Indipendente (Joint Parliamentary Group—Independent Left), conducted an initial conference or consultation in Rome to discuss the potential for a yearly European END convention.[10] The aim of the Rome consultation was to establish a permanent forum at the European level, a "European convention," that would effectively coordinate a series of initiatives for nuclear disarmament in Europe.[11] The Rome consultation was open to "the participation of political representatives," but the yearly convention process itself would aim to include "political, religious and social forces" against nuclear proliferation.[12]

At the Rome consultation, those present agreed that a provisional END Liaison Committee would be established to arrange the END conventions based on a representative approach. Although largely funded by the Russell Foundation, the END Liaison Committee was independent of the British END and met periodically in Brussels. Initially, the END Liaison Committee comprised three representatives of the peace movement: Ken Coates; Luciana Castellina, who was then an Italian member of the European Parliament; and John Lambert, founder of the leftist think-tank *Agenor,* whose aim was to increase left-wing political representation at the European level.[13] By July 1982, the END Liaison Committee, with the organization of the Russell Foundation, launched its first convention in Brussels. Conducted at a venue made available to END by the European Parliament, the convention assembled around 800 activists from twenty-four countries, including every country in Western Europe.[14] Official peace committees from Eastern Europe were, on this occasion, not invited.[15]

At the Grassroots

Kaldor was not against the convention process. In fact, she had been instrumental in establishing the network that brought the convention into being. Nevertheless she prioritized grassroots and independent groups across Europe over a movement that favored formal political representation. In support of the convention, Kaldor presented a paper with Michael Cooley of Lucas Aerospace on conversion, which received "enthusiastic reception."[16] Yet Kaldor saw the "main value of the Convention as a talk and meeting shop," not unlike the IWC, but on a "bigger and more ambitious" scale,[17] and she grew alarmed when Coates allowed what she described as "somewhat Vanguardist claims [to] creep into the descriptions of the Convention."[18] In response to an editorial by the Russell Foundation in the contested issue of the *END Bulletin* (No. 11), which implied that END *was* the European disarmament movement, Kaldor had written that British END "does not and can not claim to speak for Europe."[19] Kaldor was adamant that the top-down approach was politically limiting. Grassroots activists and independents from Eastern Europe, she believed, also needed to be included in the convention process. For this reason, Kaldor considered the convention as "one of the many activities of the new European movement," which also included demonstrations, dialogues, conferences, and contact among local groups, which were organized by a wider peace and human rights movement across both Eastern and Western Europe.[20]

Despite Kaldor's connections among the elite in Britain and across Europe, she sought to include grassroots activists in Western Europe as well as independents from Eastern Europe. For the convention process, Kaldor encouraged independent intellectuals such as Ulrich Albrecht,[21] but also she convinced larger grassroots groups to become involved, such as the Interchurch Peace Council (IKV), and No Nuclear Weapons in Norway and Denmark. At the same time, Kaldor was also involved in grassroots protests and debates across Europe outside the END convention process and would continue to expand such contacts through each meeting or protest. For example, at the Bonn demonstration, Kaldor made contact with several groups, information that she passed on to the END office for continued engagement. These contacts included the German trade union IG Metall, the German Peace Tax Campaign, a list of women who wanted to start a European women's committee for disarmament, and an activist interested in partnering his town with another nuclear-free town in Europe.[22]

In fact, Kaldor believed that the END convention should promote itself as a grassroots movement, with the convention providing an opportunity to "march through the institutions."[23] In other words, her goal was for the grassroots organizations to gain the backing of every conceivable organization in support of European nuclear disarmament. Although this approach still acknowledged the role of institutions and the political elite, Kaldor argued that change had to emerge from grassroots movements.[24]

These tensions were reflected more broadly across Europe. For example, Rudolf Bahro, then a member of the German Greens, argued that the peace movement should be completely autonomous from all institutions and political parties. During the Brussels Convention, Bahro and British Labour MP Tony Benn conducted a debate on the issue: Benn insisted that nuclear disarmament in Europe could be brought about through the election of a Labour government committed to the END convention's policies, whereas Bahro was adamant that an antiparty notion of "new politics" was the answer.[25] Bahro and Kaldor agreed that grassroots networks must be included, which meant also including Eastern European independents.

From Below

Increasingly, Kaldor began to locate her earlier democratic notions of grassroots participation, inclusiveness, and equity within the conceptual frame of politics from below. In the early years of END, Kaldor was inspired by Thompson's notion of "history from below," particularly as found in *The Making of the English Working Class*.[26] Unlike traditional history, which focuses on elites and the experiences of "great men," history from below casts ordinary people as its subject.[27] In terms of practical politics, however, Thompson had less faith in movements from below than did Kaldor, which contributed to significant tension in their intellectual partnership at END.

Compared with Thompson, Kaldor thought of politics from below in more participatory and liberal democratic terms. For example, at an END supporters conference in May 1982, aside from demanding greater contact with the East, the "general view seemed to be one of real concern" with the "lack of democracy within END."[28] Some supporters were concerned by what they saw as the undemocratic arrangement of END in which the Coordinating Committee was viewed as a "supreme policy making body," rather then the conference in its entirety, and the supporters were "vaguely constituted," often finding it difficult to participate in the decisionmaking mechanisms.[29] Members argued that the END membership be composed of "clearly identifiable supporters of END" and, in this way, "give END a more democratic image and reality."[30]

Both Kaldor and Dan Smith advocated the development of a constitution for British END. In their opus to all END supporters, following the May supporters conference, Kaldor and Smith maintained that the "Coordinating Committee had to become more formally accountable to END supporters," and a constitution was needed that defined the "structure of END in a way" that enabled "a much wider participation" and established "real communication and dialogue about END's objectives and strategy."[31] For Smith and Kaldor, a constitution was not simply a formal process. Rather, they argued, the decisions made would "shape END's work in the future":

> Our politics must cross borders. . . . We cannot promote a "line" to be "fed" to the movement or to force a specious unity onto the very diverse disarmament movement of Europe. Nor is there much point in simply conducting the debate inside one elite group . . . [because] the basic idea of END . . . is to promote a debate rather than a "line" . . . [and] END must reflect all this in its own journal . . . [and produce] readable articles which report and reflect the complexity of European politics and the richness of the disarmament movements. . . . As the major public "voice" of END, the journal has to be a voice of discussion.[32]

The Russell Foundation and Thompson saw the push both for the expansion of the END Coordinating Committee and for a new constitution as dismaying developments.[33] Also already embroiled in the crisis over the *END Bulletin*, the Russell Foundation felt that a constitution was the final straw, and they formally split from END.[34] In a public statement the Russell Foundation announced that it was to leave the END Coordinating Committee, maintaining that they could see no value in a "structured British organisation" because, among other things, it would "be a purely British organization, and obviously this can not aspire to direct a European movement."[35]

In many ways, Thompson agreed with Kaldor. Thompson believed that Eastern European activists should be involved in signing the END Appeal and writing for the *END Bulletin* and *End Journal*.[36] Moreover, he had actively encouraged British END to reach out to Eastern Europeans to provide support and to stimulate debate. What is more, Thompson had also encouraged greater professionalism within END. In fact, prior to the Russell Foundation's split with END, Thompson had already withdrawn from the END Coordinating Committee in November 1981, "pending a sort-out of its constitution and finances."[37] However, Thompson was against a new constitution that pursued a democratic agenda and was apprehensive about incorporating grassroots elements. In his letter of protest to the END Coordinating Committee, Thompson denounced any opportunity "for casual supporters with a taste for constitution-mongering to co-opt themselves" and "would not agree to any procedure which allowed a committee of indefinite constitution to make a take-over bid for the assets of END."[38] Moreover, in a letter to Kaldor and Smith, Thompson warned: "This is just the wrong moment to be playing around with too much of that sort of 'democracy' and we think we have been misled by too much 'grass-roots' rhetoric. . . . In no circumstances can some of our work to the East be thrown open to full 'democratic'—i.e. electoral process—however democratic our own internal political discussions on it must be."[39] In fact, in later years, some have argued that Thompson was not, in fact, a major proponent of the concept of politics from below. According to Holland, politics from below was instead "independently central to Ken [Coates]—thus, for example, the Institute of Workers' Control—and independently [important] to Mary. In my view, Edward had no politics from below until END."[40]

Moreover, Mient Jan Faber, head of the IKV, contended that Thompson struggled conceptually with the divergence between his and Kaldor's ideas of grassroots politics. This point grew more salient when Thompson attempted to engage with Eastern Europeans, namely because the principal "natural" partners of an independent peace movement in Eastern Europe were increasingly more aligned with liberal democracy, not socialism. As Faber argued, "it wasn't E. P. for a very specific reason: E. P.—I admire him I must say—but he had a communist background, and he wanted to have a socialist Europe, of course, a free socialist Europe. So socialism was his thing. [But] he basically had no partners to talk to [in Eastern Europe]. The communist officials in the East were, of course, not his partners [either]."[41]

Thompson was at least prepared to debate the notion of détente from below with Faber and Kaldor, and how it should translate into reality.[42] Coates, however, was clearly opposed to the concept. In his letter to Faber, Coates stated:

> I don't think there can be a "détente from below." "Below" and "above" are reasonable categories to use within a State, but relations between different people and different States require a whole mixture of pressures and counter-pressures, diagonally upwards and downwards. There is no way that the independent Moscow peace committee will gather sufficient strength to determine Soviet policy. Indeed, it will be a notorious victory if it gains sufficient support to stay out of prison. . . . It would be far better to talk to governments.[43]

Despite Coates's and Thompson's reservations, the END Coordinating Committee and END supporters continued to pursue the new constitution. The new END constitution was proposed at a special END supporters conference on 23 October 1982 and was formally adopted at a follow-up END supporters conference in July 1983 after consultation.[44] The constitution clearly stipulated that the new *END Journal* would be under the control of the Coordinating Committee and that it would "report on the work of END" and also "promote debate," which included European disarmament and East-West dialogue.[45] The constitution provided for two crucial changes: first, supporters were entitled some input in defining END policy and, second, subscribers to the new *END Journal* were considered "supporters" and given the privileges such status afforded. The constitution also required that representatives participating in the END convention and Liaison Committee who would like to enjoy full participation in the END conventions were now required to provide a signed endorsement of the END Appeal.[46] This implied, perhaps more contentiously, that upon signing the END Appeal, anyone could participate fully in both the END convention and the END Liaison Committee.

Kaldor's approach to solving disputes was further revealed in the way she handled the internal divisions within British END, particularly the debates surrounding the notion of politics from below and the link between peace and human rights. Despite the impasse with Coates and the Russell Foundation,

Kaldor appealed to Coates to allow the Russell Foundation to remain involved in END and sought to bridge the rift.[47] Although she put in enormous effort to maintain good relations with Coates and Thompson, Kaldor continued to actively debated them in a series of letters and meetings.[48]

For quite some time, her efforts seemed to pay off more with Thompson. Thompson's loyalty to Kaldor continued for some time unabated despite their differences.[49] Moreover, when things did go wrong, for instance during some confusion with the release of the US Appeal, Thompson did not believe that Kaldor acted out of "malice"; rather, he believed that it was "the kind of cockup which very intelligent over-confident people make when they try to do difficult things with their left hands in a hurry."[50]

Détente from Below

Whereas Thompson emphasized history from below, Mient Jan Faber, quite independently of Thompson, coined the term *détente from below*, an idea that also influenced Kaldor.[51] Faber, who was then the secretary-general of IKV, had begun in 1977 to establish an East-West grassroots network, most particularly between the Calvinist churches in Holland and church communities in the German Democratic Republic (GDR; East Germany).[52] According to Faber, the END approach appealed to IKV, which had already started a campaign against nuclear weapons. Moreover, Faber argued, the END Appeal was consistent with the view of IKV's partners (nonofficials and independents) in the GDR. Faber suggested, "It was not just about nuclear weapons. It was about the division of Europe. . . . We established these kinds of networks between the GDR and the Netherlands and . . . I was starting to talk about . . . this [as a form of] détente from below."[53] Through fellow activist Eric Olafson, a Norwegian peace activist, Kaldor phoned Faber and invited him to a British END meeting in London in July 1981 to meet with Coates, Thompson, and thirty other supporters.

Thereafter, Kaldor and Faber became close friends and collaborators, bringing END and IKV into a de facto partnership. To accompany the top-down Helsinki process, Mient Jan Faber advocated resistance from below. Ordinary people from Western peace movements and independents from Eastern Europe were to form a civic movement to augment the détente from above.[54] Even much later, Kaldor recalled, "I was really inspired by two people in that context: one is the historian E. P. Thompson who talked a lot about 'history from below'; the other was Mient Jan Faber."[55]

The Politics of Politics from Below

As contestation continued over who should be included in the British END, similar debates were being played out on a larger scale within the Liaison

Committee and within the convention process. The debate threatened to polarize the European peace movement more broadly. Although a central goal behind the END Appeal was to unite Europe, the objective of building a "transcontinental movement of citizens" was, at best, not "widely accepted."[56] At worst, according to Kaldor, it was "bitterly contested."[57]

Ironically, despite the arguments about East-West representation and participation, what did hold the loose coalition of peace groups together at the END conventions and under the Liaison Committee was the END Appeal, albeit with different parts of the appeal being emphasized by different groups.[58] According to one former END member, Patrick Burke, the arguments as to *if* and *how* to engage in East-West relations increasingly divided the convention process and the Liaison Committee between two broad perspectives. Although those who subscribed to each perspective still fundamentally supported a pan-European approach to nuclear disarmament, they viewed the role of independents and officials in Eastern Europe differently.[59]

The first perspective, according to Burke, generally emphasized that contact between East and West be with "official" peace groups in the East, and those who promoted it were skeptical of the value of détente from below. The main proponents of this approach were political party activists and trade unionists, such as members of the Labour Party, the West German Social Democratic Party, and the Transport and General Workers' Union in the UK, as well as groups associated with them that were campaigning for disarmament. Within the convention process, as stated earlier, the Russell Foundation, the West German Social Democratic Party, and the CND were the most sympathetic to this view. Burke maintained that, according to this view, "détente and nuclear disarmament could and should be kept separate from the question of human rights and democracy" in Central and Eastern Europe and the Soviet Union.[60]

The second perspective, and the one Kaldor was sympathetic to, was generally against the Cold War altogether, emphasizing détente from below and the goal of a Europe united "beyond the blocs."[61] Dialogue with "unofficial" or independent groups in the East was the priority. Most adhering to this perspective viewed the initial exclusion of official peace groups, such as the Soviet Peace Committee (SPC), as necessary to establishing any East-West dialogue. Some, however, were adamant that officially sanctioned peace "activists" should not or could not play a major role in the peace movement, nor could they help to overcome the Cold War. Many of the groups subscribed to this view, aside from British END, including IKV and the German Greens.[62]

These debates surrounding whom to engage in Eastern Europe intensified in the lead-up to the second END convention, which was held in West Berlin in May 1983.[63] As END prepared for the convention, heated debates erupted within the Liaison Committee regarding whom should be invited, and under what conditions, from Eastern Europe and the Soviet Union, an argument that threatened to stifle the newly arrived "united" European movement.[64] Up until this stage, the core of the END Liaison Committee had remained small, still consisting of Luciana Castellina, Ken Coates, and John Lambert. However Jürgen Graalfs from the German Greens and Mient Jan Faber from IKV were two recent additions.[65] Upon joining, Faber argued for the "larger expansion" of the Liaison Committee to reflect a greater diversity of views and representation, which mirrored Kaldor and Smith's push within British END and through the *END Journal*.[66] With the expansion, the convention included a greater plurality of views on East-West relations, politics from below, and the link between peace and human rights. Increasingly, representatives of the Liaison Committee reflected less official political representation and a growing grassroots involvement. According to Smith, although Coates had played a key role in initiating the convention process, Smith developed concerns about the ad hoc nature of the way in which Coates conducted the Liaison Committee meetings and explained how the inclusion of other movements helped this situation:

> I mean one of the problems with the sort of ad hoc way of doing things was that Ken could always invite seven extra friends . . . because he was so well networked from different countries and would have a little lobby, in a way, on the [Liaison] Committee. And I remember a discussion in a meeting in Brussels, which I think was after the END convention, discussing whether or not we should somehow change or systematize the representation on the Liaison Committee and arguments being put [forth] that "Well, why change a winning combination? This ad hoc approach works perfectly well." And I think that, over the years that followed, the other movements in Europe took much more ownership over the process of the convention and stabilized or systemized [and] democratized the Liaison Committee much more to make it more genuinely representative.[67]

As the principal organizing force behind the END conventions, the Liaison Committee appealed to other peace groups, and increasingly these other groups attempted to influence the direction of END. For example, following the Brussels convention in 1982, Berlin-based activists argued that the next END convention should be conducted in Berlin, and they gave three reasons: First, 1983 would mark the fiftieth year since German fascism seized power, one consequence of which was the division of Berlin. Second, Berlin was on the boundary of the two blocs, and as a city, more than any other, needed to overcome the bloc system. Third, the convention could influence public debate about the stationing of the planned NATO arms buildup.[68] In reinvigorating the German question, some within the Russell Foundation, such as Bruce Kent, were profoundly anxious about the choice of venue.[69] Nevertheless, it was approved. Given that the next END convention would be in Berlin, the END "German Secretariat" was formed to co-organize the convention. The German Secretariat now began to play a larger role as a section of the Liaison Committee, and the members of the secretariat increasingly defined the themes of the convention, demanding greater attention to the need for East-West dialogue.

To add to the divisions, those new to the Liaison Committee argued that in principle per the new constitution adopted by British END, anyone who signed the END Appeal should be invited to attend the convention as a full participant, including those from Eastern Europe and the Soviet Union. Anyone who had not signed the END Appeal could be invited as observers or guests, with the right to voice their opinion in workshops but not in plenary or international sessions.

Furthermore, Kaldor's (and others') engagement with independent movements and insistence on their involvement in dialogues and conventions were met with resistance, not just within the wider peace movement but also from officials behind the Iron Curtain. Ostensibly, the SPC had planned to become an active member of the END Liaison Committee and to help organize conventions, expecting to be welcomed into the fray as a fellow "peace" committee. The SPC appeared greatly offended when informed that complete participation in the convention required signing the END Appeal, which placed blame for nuclear proliferation "squarely" on the political and military leaders of "East and West."[70] They were also put out that anyone could sign, including the independents within their own states. Moreover, the SPC was pushed past its limits when it discovered that some elements of the peace movement regarded independent representation from Eastern Europe as equal to, or even more legitimate than, the SPC itself.[71] On 2 December 1982, SPC president Yuri Zhukov unveiled a revised hard line against the Western peace movement, charging that END sought to "split the anti-war movement" in order to "infiltrate cold war elements into it" and to "conceal and justify" the aggressive militarist policy of the United States and NATO.[72] Zhukov's 2,000-word tirade against the "Movement for European Nuclear Disarmament" was thought to be his reaction to being "excluded" from the END convention process.[73] But, as Burke argued, Zhukov's letter inadvertently served to reunite the Western peace movement behind the Berlin Convention. In counterprotest, Zhukov prohibited all of the official Soviet and Eastern European peace committees from attending the Berlin Convention, altogether.[74]

On one level, the Berlin Convention was a success. Around 3,000 gathered in the International Conference Center in West Berlin for the three-day convention.[75] Again, Kaldor presented a paper on military conversion, along with other panelists Stuart Holland, Michael Cooley, and Frank Barnaby.[76] Organizing Kaldor's panel was her old SIPRI friend Ulrich Albrecht, together with Reimar Stuckenbrock of the John F. Kennedy Institute, Berlin.[77]

Still, the poor Eastern European participation meant that the convention process did not reflect a genuinely pan-European movement. The absence of the SPC notwithstanding, Eastern European independents still struggled to sign the END Appeal, and some in the END Liaison Committee still equivocated about inviting Eastern European independents to the convention altogether. Furthermore, getting invitations personally to dissidents was difficult as state security frequently intercepted their mail. Finally, even if independents had signed the END Appeal, were invited to speak at the convention, and had actually safely received the invitation, they were frequently unceremoniously blocked from attending by their respective governments. One exception at the Berlin Convention was George Konrád, the Hungarian novelist and independent. Konrád happened to be temporarily living in West Berlin at the time and hence could speak at the opening plenary.[78]

Although independent groups or individuals from Eastern Europe could not attend, many did manage to have statements or letters smuggled out to be read at the convention: for example, Jiří Dienstbier, from Czechoslovakia, wrote on behalf of Charter 77, and statements were received from the PGD in Hungary and the Moscow Trust Group.[79] Although imperfect, a debate between East and West independents, in the context of a wider END convention, had taken seed.

Dialogue with Moscow

Although Kaldor was committed to more participatory forms of democracy and the link between peace and human rights, she did not rule out dialogue with official bodies, such as the SPC. Moreover, Kaldor attempted to understand their position. For example, Kaldor met over tea with Grigori Lokshin, secretary of the SPC, to discuss military conversion. Challenging him on the issue of economic bottlenecks and shortages in the Soviet Union, Kaldor observed that Lokshin remained impervious to any self-critical analysis and would not admit to failures in the Soviet economy. Yet, Kaldor conceded, "maybe we seemed [inflexible] to them."[80]

Kaldor also began to view her political opponents as important and necessary for their ability to foster contestation and debate. They were ordinary people who had the capacity for change. For example, Kaldor, along with Mient Jan Faber and Peter Jarman of Quaker Peace and Service, met with Yuri Zhukov for dinner one evening in December 1983. For Kaldor, possibly the most important insight from conversations with Soviet officials was that her faith in her broader approach to dialogue and intellectual debate was strengthened. So too was Kaldor's view that being challenged by her political opponents was important to her own intellectual and political development, as a means to sharpening her own thinking. In a confidential memo to British END, Kaldor reported on the meeting:

> In future, I think it would be good to see these meetings as occasions for argument and to pursue those discussions to the bitter end. I think what I learned most was that dialogue with our opponents is very important and that these people are as much our opponents as our own establishment. It made

> me realise that we ought to make much more effort to organise this kind of discussion with Conservatives or from the Foreign Office. It's a way of learning and understanding different positions, seeing each other as human beings with faces, and developing our own thinking.[81]

Eastern Independents

During this time, Kaldor also conducted trips across Eastern Europe to engage with independents and nonofficials, most particularly in Hungary. In late November 1982, Kaldor and Faber were invited to Hungary, in the wake of a visit by Thompson, to speak at a number of meetings and debates. They addressed a public meeting held at the Hungarian Academy of Sciences, with an audience of over 150 people, most of whom were from the newly formed PGD.[82] Ferenc Köszegi, founder of the PGD, suggested that he was greatly "influenced" by "Thompson and Kaldor, amongst others,"[83] and that he was inspired by their idea to campaign as a peace movement that was independent of both the regime and the "Democratic Opposition."[84] The PGD was one of the first independent peace movements to emerge in Eastern Europe,[85] and engagement with Western activists was a source of intellectual and moral support. For example, Zoltán Rozgoni, at the time an engineering student at the technical university, was strongly influenced by Kaldor and Faber. Attending a PGD meeting at the Rakpart Club,[86] where around 400 people had assembled, Rozgoni was inspired to political action after hearing both of them speak. Although not a Marxist or politically active, Rozgoni became interested in independent dialogue in Hungary, and soon after became actively involved in independent opposition in Hungary.[87] He described his awakening: "I clearly remember my feelings after that meeting. That's it after all, the thing I've been looking [for] for a long time. . . . I've found it. I think my enthusiasm was partly due to their cautious, non-confronting behaviour, partly the very strong almost unquestionable moral foundation of the whole initiative."[88]

Kaldor along with others at END not only supported Hungarian activists who also envisioned a united Europe but also highlighted the uniqueness of the Hungarian opposition. The PGD provided hope that a genuine Hungarian opposition might emerge, and they were committed to the END idea of making the "free exchange of views a priority."[89] PGD's example had important consequences for nurturing the seeds of Hungarian independence. Two days after the Hungarian Academy of Science's public meeting, the PGD independently held its first public assembly, at which 300 to 400 people gathered to hear other PGD members present their ideas about ways to end the Cold War and the significance of mandating a nuclear-free Europe.[90] By December, the PGD had published and disseminated a leaflet entitled "We Want *Dialogue*!" and by January 1983, the organization had produced the first issue of its journal, *Dialogus*.[91]

Transnational support and alliances formed with Eastern Europe independents had important consequences, particularly in terms of how Soviet officials would respond. Though initially tolerant of the PGD and international peace activists, the Hungarian regime began a crackdown as these individuals became more clearly independent of the government's position. In January 1983, Zhukov visited Budapest and informed Szarkady-Nagy Barna, then secretary-general of the Hungarian Peace Council, that PGD members were "criminals" and ought to be dealt with accordingly. Although Barna responded by maintaining that the Hungarian way to deal with a group like the PGD was not "administratively" but "politically," pressure from Moscow continued.[92] By March 1983, the Hungarian Politburo passed a resolution that meant the PGD's independence would result in its categorization as a threat to the government.[93] Kaldor and many other Westerners were also listed as a threat to Hungarian state security.

In September 1983, upon visiting Hungary, Kaldor maintained that PGD's efforts to sustain an open and public independence movement had been challenged, by both the Hungarian state and Moscow. Following the crackdown by the SPC and the Hungarian Politburo, Kaldor concluded that there was "not much space for independent movements," and so the PGD had been reduced to a "form of personal resistance."[94]

Yet private freedom within Hungarian society, she suspected, would be very difficult to suppress. Younger people were not afraid to debate, and intellectual discussion was very intense, possibly more intense, she argued, than anywhere in Europe. The authorities would probably not be able to reestablish a Stalinist regime of violence and terror, Kaldor argued, a requirement for restoring the political fear that had been instilled in the older generation. Kaldor concluded, "In the end, the question of where you stand in political space is . . . personal and moral. . . . And, as Western peace movements, I do not think we have any moral alternative but to support them."[95]

Kaldor met with Hungarian independents in various ways: through Ferenc Köszegi after he formed the PGD; through Ferenc Miszlivetz, who had spent a year at Sussex University working with Kaldor and later became an important activist in the Hungarian independent movement; through Thompson's contacts with Miklós Haraszti, a writer, activist, and editor of the samizdat journal *Beszelo*; and also through George Konrád.[96] But Kaldor also continued to foster her family connections by frequently staying with her Hungarian cousin, Annamaria, and her uncle, Aurel Varannai.[97] By now in his eighties, Aurel provided Kaldor with background information on dissident intelligentsia, acted as her personal adviser, and introduced her to many other independent activists.[98]

Irrespective of the government crackdown, the independent dialogue between Hungarian dissidents and END had begun, albeit tenuously. Looking back, Hungarian dissident Zoltán Rozgoni believed that the three most significant goals for the independent Hungarian peace movement had already been established by 1984. First, Hungarian dissidents now worked together coordinating underground meetings, dialogues, and samizdat in a genuine exchange of ideas. Second, the movement had self-organized independently of the state, which he believed was "even more important than the issue [of peace] itself."[99] Lastly, international contact, such as with END and the IKV, had also highlighted the differences, rather than just the similarities, of the Hungarian movement to other Eastern European movements. As Rozgoni argued, a dialogue with other Europeans "helped *Dialogue* [PGD] to understand its uniqueness."[100]

Although the PGD as a group began to decline under state pressure, it remained one of the first genuinely independent peace movements in Eastern Europe and played a significant role in laying the foundations for the founding of the Fiatal Demokraták Szövetsége (FIDESZ; Alliance of Young Democrats) in Hungary in early 1988 and for Hungary's subsequent negotiated revolution. As historian Timothy Garton Ash later argued, the establishment of FIDESZ was a decisive moment for the peace movement and played a principal role in the post-Soviet democratization process. Though FIDESZ had only been formally constituted in March 1988, he argued, its formation was embedded in the 1980s politics of independent peace movements and transnational civil society.[101]

East-West Dialogue

In 1983, upon her return from Hungary, adamant that Eastern Europeans should be included in the wider END debate, Kaldor requested to be a formal member of the END Liaison Committee's newly created Relations Extérieures (RELEX; External Relations) subcommittee.[102] RELEX was formed as a transnational group with the primary objective being to promote greater grassroots dialogue between East and West, with Faber as the convenor.[103]

Some in British END were reticent about Kaldor's representing them in both the END Liaison Committee and the RELEX meetings, and, after the Berlin Convention, British END began to distance itself from participating in the Liaison Committee. However, Kaldor continued to attend meetings in Brussels, albeit in an "individual capacity."[104] Many in the END Coordinating Committee were alarmed by what they considered to be the Liaison Committee's increasingly participatory, rather than representative, approach to democracy.

As an individual, Kaldor continued to attend the END Liaison Committee and RELEX meetings, with her emphasis being on East-West engagement through unofficial channels. The Liaison Committee was now widely represented with a mixture of political and, more importantly to Kaldor, grassroots groups from every country in Western Europe. In the lead-up to the next END convention in Perugia, Italy, the importance of having Eastern European participants could not be greater. To increase attendance from this area, the Liaison Committee had formally invited the official, state-sanctioned peace committees, making no delineation between participants and observers. For those on the RELEX subcommittee, this change gave greater impetus to having independents from Eastern Europe participate in the convention, but also hope that, given these concessions, the SPC and other state-sanctioned peace committees would allow independents to attend. RELEX developed a system whereby individuals within RELEX were to report back on the situation in different Eastern European countries so that they could make recommendations to the Liaison Committee to ensure that independents from Eastern Europe would finally participate in the END convention adequately. Initially these individuals included Mient Jan Faber and Wolfgang Muller for Czechoslovakia, Dieter Esche and Walter Grunwald for East Germany, and Mary Kaldor and Mient Jan Faber for Hungary.[105]

The Perugia Splinter

By 1984, the ongoing dispute within the END Liaison Committee surrounding engagement with independents and officials came to a head at the third END convention, held in Perugia.[106] Spilling over from the Berlin Convention, three key Liaison Committee members, Dieter Esche, Walther Grunwald, and Jürgen Graalfs,[107] wrote an open letter to the entirety of the Liaison Committee, arguing that it wrongly continued to prioritize "dialogue with official representatives" as opposed to "the dialogue with our real partners in Eastern Europe, independent peace groups and movements."[108] Moreover, they argued, "some people in the Committee regard independence of blocs as . . . mere rhetoric . . . without relevance for short or medium-term strategies."[109] On the one hand, they argued, some Liaison Committee members "have problems when the discussion turns to subjects such as human rights, social emancipation or national self-determination in Eastern Europe," whereas, on the other, some do "not want to provoke . . . official peace movements in Eastern Europe."[110] Both these position, they argued, had led to inaction, which, they concluded, meant that the Liaison Committee had essentially failed the independent movements in Eastern Europe.

Finally, they contended that the inclusion of their Eastern European partners was fundamentally central to the END Appeal: "We do not follow specific or sectarian interests but refer to the central theme of the *END Appeal*. . . . The *END Appeal* defines the East-West relationship . . . as a structural element."[111] Later, Esche explained that his criticism was aimed at those generally of a "traditional left-wing" or "social-democratic tendency" who emphasized "détente from above" and who avoided a conflict with officials from Eastern Europe in order to safeguard the détente process.[112] According to Esche, the central problem was, "do human rights and peace belong together . . . peace and democracy," or rather, should they be viewed separately, as limited to the realm of "high-level politics" ("*die grosse Politik*").[113]

Although Faber and Kaldor were aware of the open letter, they were not involved in the drafting process, nor did they put their names on it. As Esche later recalled, although Kaldor "sympathized with our document . . . she didn't sign it." Esche suggested, "I think she felt that in Perugia, or next month, or in half a year, there *would* be a split," and Kaldor "wanted to avoid the split. No! Not even that. I think, she would not be *part* of the split."[114]

Ahead of the convention, tensions were already rising. Esche believed that Thompson was disappointed not to be included or consulted in the writing of their open letter. Moreover, as became apparent to Esche and other Berlin-based activists, although the official peace committees had been invited to the Perugia Convention, independents were still not granted permission to attend.[115] Fifty-nine independents from Eastern Europe were invited by the Liaison Committee, yet only two Hungarian independents attended: Miklós Haraszti, from Hungarian Democratic Opposition, and Ferenc Miszlivetz, who was then working with Kaldor at Sussex University. Both Haraszti and Miszlivetz just happened to be on tenure abroad at the time.[116] Esche and others were bitterly disappointed with the fact that Eastern European independents were not granted permission to attend. Moreover, on the opening day, when they saw dozens of peace committee officials from Central and Eastern Europe sitting in the front row, they decided their open letter had not gone far enough. Instead, they decided to "do an action, in typical '68 style."[117] Having attended the Perugia Convention, Burke recalled:

> During the opening session of the Convention, a group of these activists . . . with red cloths tied around their mouths, climbed on to the stage carrying placards on which were printed the names of the Central/East European and Soviet groups and movements whose members had been prevented from attending the Convention. . . . In addition, one activist carried a banner with "Palestine" on it, another with "Turkey," to symbolize the Israeli and Turkish states' refusal to allow two Palestinians from the Occupied Territories and a representative of the Turkish Peace Association, respectively, to travel to Perugia.[118]

Reflecting the divisions already apparent within the END Liaison Committee and the wider peace movements, reactions to the protest were polarized. As the Berlin-based activists entered the stage, many showed their support for the protest by applauding and cheering them on. Conversely, Coates entered the stage demanding that the protesters leave the stage immediately, which also received enthusiastic applause. Offended, the peace committee officials from Central and Eastern Europe and the Soviet Union stood up and left the convention.

Thompson was furious. Denouncing the demonstration and castigating the Berlin-based activists for their offensiveness toward the invited guests, he called for moderation on both sides. As an activist who had led the fight for the END Appeal—and one of the first to initiate engagement with Eastern Europeans—Thompson saw the action as an affront and one that could potentially split an already fragile and tenuous European peace movement.[119] A series of constructive discussions with both officials and independents was the way forward, Thompson argued, without driving further divisions into the "united" pan-European peace project.[120]

This dispute spilled out of the convention and onto the streets of Perugia. According to Esche, Thompson "was very irritated and then very angry and I remember when we met . . . on the streets in Perugia and I went to him to welcome him, and he said, 'Dieter, I don't want to speak with you anymore. You are splitting the peace movement.'"[121] Burke recalled observing the scene: "Dieter walking off in a huff, and then Dorothy [Thompson] making some acerbic remark as he walked away: 'Look at him, *strutting* away.'"[122] For Burke, the heated exchange "was all entertaining from the outside," but he commented that the seriousness of the dispute was not lost on Kaldor.[123] Rather, according to Burke, Kaldor "was trying to make peace between them."[124] Similarly, Esche believed that Kaldor was very much stuck between a multiplicity of positions and serious about smoothing things over:

> Mary . . . was, in this moment in Perugia, in a very difficult situation, because she was sympathetic to us, but she had, of course, for very good reasons, a big loyalty towards Edward. . . . And Mary was a little bit between Edward and Mient Jan and . . . she was between all the lines. . . . We met somehow twenty minutes after this scene in the streets with Edward. And I said [to her], "Can you explain to me what just went on with Edward?" And she tried to explain to me and tried to build the bridge. [And then] she spoke with Edward, but Edward was absolutely [furious].[125]

The rest of the Perugia Convention remained tense, and what was also in contest during the course of the convention was the nature of debate itself. According to Lynne Jones, a member of British END, 300 participants attended the "hot, tense, somewhat gladiatorial atmosphere" of the "East-West Dialogue seminar."[126] During the seminar, Andre Melville, an official from the Soviet delegation, described Kaldor as "totally erroneous" for wanting to discuss "differences."[127] Rather, Melville argued, the emphasis of the dialogue should have been on seeking out commonalities. Somewhat overwhelmed by the intensity of the discussion, Melville contended, "If you call this dialogue, what is a confrontation? We should talk about what unites us, in order to have a dialogue of East and West against nuclear war. We have to accept each other as we are."[128]

Kaldor adamantly disagreed. In response to Melville, Kaldor argued that "a dialogue is where we can discuss our differences, [and] one of the prerequisites for it is self-criticism."[129] Kaldor continued, "How can we accept you as you are, when the USSR [Union of Soviet Socialist Republics] is deploying SS22s and SS23s. We don't expect you to accept us as we are. We accept that we are part of the problem and struggle to change ourselves. Yet I've never heard anyone from the official Eastern peace movement accept any responsibility for this situation."[130] Kaldor's response to Melville was typical of her attitude toward debate. Burke later recalled, "She loves people arguing with her and she doesn't care at all if people disagree with her; that's one of the really nice things about her. But she will be very honest in response."[131]

Notes

1. Dan Smith, interview with author, 4 May 2011.
2. END, "Appeal for European Disarmament," p. 224.
3. Ibid., p. 225.
4. Ibid.
5. Dorothy and E. P. Thompson, *END—Retrospect and Next Steps*, 18 August 1980, PA-MK-END-GEN-3.
6. Bertrand Russell Peace Foundation, "Memo on Relations Between END and the Russell Foundation, with Comments on Dan Smith's Text (Already Circulated)," 23 February 1982, PA-MK-END-GEN-1.
7. According to Ken Coates, the END Appeal and END's goals were a compromise among the cofounders. See Burke, *European Nuclear Disarmament*, p. 48.
8. Stuart Holland, correspondence with author, 1 June 2012.
9. Fernando Claudín left the Communist Party of Spain in 1956 and wrote a book entitled *The Communist Movement: From Comintern to Cominform* in 1975, which influenced Kaldor's thinking. Kaldor also became good friends with Claudín's daughter, Carmen Claudín. Mary Kaldor, correspondence with author, 20 September 2012; see also Burke, *European Nuclear Disarmament*, pp. 43, 121.
10. See Michele Achilli, Norberto Bobbio et al., letter of invitation, 9 October 1981, PA- MK-END-LC/CP.
11. Ken Fleet, letter to E. P. Thompson, 16 October 1981, PK-MK-END-GEN3. The conference was conducted 11–12 November 1982 at the Cenacolo di Vicolo Valdina (one of the halls attached to the Italian Chamber of Deputies).
12. Michele Achilli, Norberto Bobbio et al., letter of invitation, 9 October 1981, PA-MK-END-LC/CP; Draft letter from the Bertrand Russell Peace Foundation to participants in the Rome consultation on 11–12 November 1981, n.d., PA-MK-END-LC/CP. Although the letter is undated, the document was clearly written before 6 November 1981.
13. Burke, *European Nuclear Disarmament*, p. 123.
14. Denis Macshane, "Protest into Policy," *New Statesman*, 9 July 1982. The Brussels Convention was held on 2–4 July 1982.
15. Ibid.
16. Ibid., p. 16.
17. Mary Kaldor, letter to Ken Coates, 23 April 1982, PA-MK-END-GEN-2.
18. Ibid.
19. Ibid.
20. Mary Kaldor, letter to Tony Simpson and Stuart Holland, 16 September 1982, PA-MK-END-GEN-1. For a full list, see "Major European Events, 1981," PA-MK-END-GEN-3; also see, for example, "Draft Agenda for Activist Gatherings to Be Held in Antwerp on December 7th and 8th, 1981," IKV/END, PA-MK-END-GEN-3, and *END Newsletter*, no. 3, December 1981, PA-MK-END-GEN-3.

21. Ulrich Albrecht was an academic friend from SIPRI, a then professor at the Free University. See Burke, *European Nuclear Disarmament*, p. 47.

22. Mary Kaldor, letter to Meg Beresford, 15 October 1981, PA-MK-END-GEN-3.

23. Susan Greensberg, "Means to an END," *New Statesman*, 2 July 1981, p. 3. Kaldor quoted this phrase from Mient Jan Faber. See Dan Smith, "Memo on the Convention of European Nuclear Disarmament," February 1982, PA-MK-END-LC/CP.

24. Mary Kaldor, interview with author, 24 June 2011.

25. Macshane, "Protest into Policy," p. 16.

26. See Alan Johnson, "New Wars and Human Security: An Interview with Mary Kaldor," *Democratiya*, 3 July 2007, online.

27. See, for example, Evans, *In Defence of History;* and Bentley, *Modernizing England's Past.*

28. Apparently, the END supporters conference "called for a working-party to be set up" to develop proposals to modify the structure of END. See Mepham, "END Supporters Conference," pp. 22–23. Dan Smith was the chair of the END supporters conference.

29. E. P. Thompson, letter to Dan Smith and Mary Kaldor, n.d., PA-MK-END-GEN-3. Although not dated, the letter was clearly written prior to the constitution's adoption on 2–3 July 1983.

30. In particular, these concerns were highlighted from the West Yorkshire END branch. See Roger Fieldhouse and Dick Taylor, "For the Attention of the END National Coordinating Meeting on 6 October," 4 October 1982, PA-MK-END-GEN-1. Also see Burke, *European Nuclear Disarmament*, p. 71.

31. See Mepham, "END Supporters Conference," pp. 22–23.

32. Mary Kaldor and Dan Smith, "Shaping the Future: END Supporters Conference," *END Newsletter*, Autumn/Winter 1982, PA-MK-END-GEN-1.

33. The first draft of the new constitution was developed by Dan Smith, as chair of END, amended by the Working Party and the Coordinating Committee, and then was to be presented at the supporters conference on 23 October 1982. See Dan Smith, letter to Tony Simpson and Stuart Holland, 16 September 1982, PA-MK-END-GEN-1. Moreover, in his report, Ken Coates referred to the constitution as "Dan Smith's project for a new constitution." See Ken Coates, "Part II: The London END Committee's Constitution," 2 September 1982, PA-MK-END-GEN-1.

34. Burke, *European Nuclear Disarmament*, p. 86.

35. Bertrand Russell Peace Foundation, "Statement by the Russell Foundation on the Proposed Change of Character of the British European Nuclear Disarmament Coordinating Committee," n.d., London School of Economics Archive END/2/9, London.

36. For example, Thompson appealed to Kaldor, as editor of the *END Bulletin*, to publish an article by Ferenc Köszegi, as he believed doing so was "crucial to our whole E/W [East-West] strategy." E. P. Thompson, letter to Mary Kaldor, n.d., PA-MK-END-GEN-3.

37. E. P. Thompson and Dorothy Thompson, letter to the Coordinating Committee, 7 June 1982, PA-MK-END-GEN-3.

38. Ibid.

39. E. P. Thompson, letter to Dan Smith and Mary Kaldor, n.d., PA-MK-END-GEN-3. Although the letter is undated, it was clearly written prior to the constitution's adoption on 2–3 July 1983.

40. Stuart Holland, interview with author, 23 May 2011.

41. Mient Jan Faber, interview with author, 30 May 2011.

42. In fact, Thompson maintained, "In effect I think you are asking . . . for a new and revised version of the END Appeal of April 1980. I agree that there might be a case

for this. But the necessary consultation and preparation of such a new Appeal would take several months (in the present complex State of the peace movement)." See E. P. Thompson, letter to Mient Jan Faber, 6 March 1983, PA-MK-END-GEN-2.

43. Ken Coates, letter to Mient Jan Faber, 14 March 1983, PA-MK-END-GEN-2.

44. See, for example, END Constitution 1982–1989, London School of Economics Archives END/1/6, London; also see Burke, *European Nuclear Disarmament*, p. 71.

45. Burke, *European Nuclear Disarmament*, p. 71.

46. Ibid., p. 49.

47. For example, in her letter to Coates, Kaldor suggested, "It is a great pity that you will not be able to come to the meeting on Friday as we need to take a decision about the future of the Bulletin. So could you send an answer to this letter . . . in time for the meeting. Basically I feel it is essential that END has its own independent publication . . . accountable to the co-ordinating committee. . . . I would want our cooperation to continue with the Russell Foundation participating both on the coordinating committee and on the editorial collective. . . . It would be much better if this continued to be a cooperative venture." See Mary Kaldor, letter to Ken Coates, 26 July 1982, PA-MK-END-GEN-1, and also Mary Kaldor, letter to Ken Coates, 6 August 1982, PA-MK-END-GEN-1.

48. Mary Kaldor, letter to Ken Coates, 3 September 1982, PA-MK-END-GEN-1.

49. E. P. Thompson, letter to Mary Kaldor, n.d., PA-MK-END-GEN-3. Also see E. P. Thompson, letter to Dan Smith and Mary Kaldor, 21 July 1982, PA-MK-END-GEN-3.

50. E. P. Thompson, letter to Mary Kaldor, 24 August [1983], PA-MK-END-GEN-3.

51. Kaldor maintained that Mient Jan Faber was the first to coin the term *détente from below*, in Mary Kaldor, interview with author, 24 June 2011. See also Mient Jan Faber, "Brief van het IKV-secretariaat aan alle IKV-kernen over Polen kort na 13 December 1981" [Letter from the IKV Secretariat to All IKV Cores on Poland Shortly After 13 December 1981], 133–134, cited in de Gaaf, "Détente from Below," p. 9.

52. Mient Jan Faber, interview with author, 30 May 2011.

53. Ibid.

54. Mary Kaldor, "The Ideas of 1989," p. 75; also see Mient Jan Faber, "Entspannung und Mennschenrechte" [Peace and Human Rights], *Die Nuue Gesellschaft: Frankfurter Hefte* [The New Society: Frankfurter Notebooks] 33 (1986), pp. 740–741.

55. Kaldor, quoted in Schouten, "Theory Talk #30."

56. Kaldor, quoted in Burke, *European Nuclear Disarmament*, p. 184.

57. Kaldor, quoted in ibid.

58. Kaldor, quoted in ibid. See also Paul Anderson, interview with author, 14 June 2011.

59. Specifically, Burke argued that "each implicitly—or, in the period of [Mikhail] Gorbachev's rule, explicitly—framed the political opportunities offered or denied by the regimes in the East differently." See Burke, *European Nuclear Disarmament*, pp. 184–185.

60. Ibid., p. 185.

61. Ibid.; see, for example, Kaldor, "Beyond the Blocs"; Thompson, "Beyond the Blocs."

62. Burke, *European Nuclear Disarmament*, pp. 185–186.

63. The second convention ran 9–15 May 1983 and was held at the International Congress Center in West Berlin.

64. Burke suggested that, for example, questions arose about whether or not only independent activists should be invited. Should only signatories of the END Appeal be invited as full participants, with nonsignatories attending as observers only? Should the presence of officials be conditional on that of "unofficials"? See Burke, *European Nuclear Disarmament*, p. 186.

65. Dan Smith, comments on Liaison Committee meeting, Brussels, 17–18 September 1982, PA-MK-END-LC/CP, London; Ulrich Albrecht and Reimer Stuckenbrock, letter of invitation to Mary Kaldor, 15 December 1982, PA-MK-END-LC/CP, London.

66. Dan Smith, comments on Liaison Committee meeting, Brussels, 17–18 September 1982, PA-MK-END-LC/CP, London.

67. Dan Smith, interview with author, 4 May 2011.

68. Jürgen Graalfs, minutes of the END Liaison Committee held at 3 Boulevard de l'Empereur, Brussels, on 17–18 September 1982, PA-MK-END-LC/CP, London.

69. Burke, *European Nuclear Disarmament*, fn188. Burke asserted that Bruce Kent, the general secretary of CND, in his internal report of a visit to Moscow on 25–27 October 1982, indicated his extreme concern about the choice of West Berlin as a venue for the convention: "Are we not daft—considering all the divisions in the German peace movement and the sensitivity of Berlin—to try to hold a Convention there?"

70. European Nuclear Disarmament, "Appeal for European Nuclear Disarmament," pp. 223–228.

71. The SPC was invited to send participants to the Berlin Convention with "full speaking rights in the workshops . . . but not in the plenary sessions." According to Smith, this solution seemed a "reasonable compromise between the fact that it [the SPC], not surprisingly, has not signed the END Appeal which is the basis of all our activities, and the desire of everybody for a dialogue," in Dan Smith, letter to the *Guardian*, 12 January 1983, PA-MK-END-GEN-2, London. The letter was written in response to an article by Jean Stead ("Nuclear Crusaders Fall Out," *Guardian* [London], 12 January 1983, p. 15).

72. Zhukov, quoted in John Bacher, "The Independent Peace Movement in Eastern Europe," *Peace Magazine*, December 1985, p. 8, online.

73. Burke, *European Nuclear Disarmament*, p. 189.

74. Ibid., p. 188.

75. Europe Section, "European Nuclear Disarmament (END) Convention in West Berlin," *Quaker Peace and Service*, May 1983, p. 1.

76. Program of the convention, END, Berlin, 1983, PA-MK-END-LC/CP, London.

77. Ulrich Albrecht and Reimer Stuckenbrock, letter of invitation to Mary Kaldor, 15 December 1982, PA-MK-END-LC/CP, London.

78. Burke, *European Nuclear Disarmament*, p. 189.

79. Ibid.

80. Mary Kaldor, "Confidential: Impressions of Two Meetings with the Soviet Peace Committee," London School of Economics Archive END /14/20, London.

81. Ibid.

82. Lomax, "The Dialogue Breaks Down"; Mary Kaldor, note to END Finance and General Purposes Committee, 9 November 1982, PA-MK-END-GEN-1, London.

83. Köszegi, quoted in Burke, *European Nuclear Disarmament*, p. 172.

84. Köszegi, quoted in ibid.

85. Chilton, "Mechanics of Change," p. 208. See also Köszegi and Thompson, *The New Hungarian Peace Movement.*

86. The Rakpart Club was created by Miklós Horváth, and Kenney contended that some considered the Rakpart Club to be on par with the famous Petröfi Circle, where political arguments were started in the lead-up to the 1956 Hungarian Revolution; see Kenney, *A Carnival of Revolution,* fn99.

87. Ibid., pp. 99–102.

88. Ibid., p. 99.

89. White, "Open Dialogue in Hungary," p. 15.

90. Burke, *European Nuclear Disarmament*, p. 152.

91. Ibid. Kaldor later maintained that the PGD was not the backbone of the independence movement: "Konrád and . . . other dissidents were the backbone. They were a bit suspicious" of the PGD. Mary Kaldor, correspondence with author, 20 September 2012.

92. Mary Kaldor, memo to END Hungary Group (field notes of Hungary visit 1–19 September 1983), London School of Economics Archive, London, Catalogue of the Papers of European Nuclear Disarmament END/12/6, London.

93. Haraszti, "The Beginnings of Civil Society," p. 76.

94. Mary Kaldor, memo to END Hungary Group (field notes of Hungary visit 1–19 September 1983), London School of Economics Archive, London, Catalogue of the Papers of European Nuclear Disarmament END/12/6, London.

95. Ibid.

96. Mary Kaldor, correspondence with author, 31 October 2010.

97. Ibid.

98. Kaldor, quoted in Johnson, "New Wars and Human Security."

99. Zoltán Rozgoni, quoted in Kenney, *A Carnival of Revolution*.

100. Ibid.

101. Chilton, "Mechanics of Change," p. 209.

102. Mient Jan Faber, letter to Julian Harber, 21 December 1983, PA-MK-END-LC/CP, London. At this point, the Liaison Committee had three subcommittees, Finance, Program, and External Relations.

103. Ibid.

104. Mary Kaldor, memo to the END Coordinating Committee, n.d., PA-MK-END-GEN-2, London. Although the memo is undated, it was clearly in mid-July 1983.

105. Ibid.

106. The Perugia conference was conducted 17–21 July 1984.

107. The authors of the letter were members of a West Berlin group called Initiative for an East-West Dialogue, founded shortly after the END convention held in West Berlin in May 1983. See Burke, *European Nuclear Disarmament*, p. 188.

108. Dieter Esche, Jürgen Graalfs, and Walther Grunwald, "Some Remarks About the Controversy Concerning the East-West Dialogue," *Listy: Documents of Independent Peace Movements East-West* 2, 27 February 1984, London School of Economics Archives, London, quoted in Burke, *European Nuclear Disarmament*, p. 190.

109. Burke, *European Nuclear Disarmament*, p. 190.

110. Ibid.

111. Ibid.

112. Dieter Esche, quoted in ibid.

113. Ibid.

114. Dieter Esche, interview with author, 31 March 2011.

115. Ken Coates and Mient Jan Faber, general invitation to END Convention in Perugia, 16 March 1984, PA-MK-END-Perugia, London.

116. Kenney, *A Carnival of Revolution*, p. 140; Ferenc Miszlivetz, interview with author, 18 February 2011.

117. Kenney, *A Carnival of Revolution*, p. 103.

118. Burke, *European Nuclear Disarmament*, p. 191.

119. See Kenney, *A Carnival of Revolution*, p. 104.

120. See, for example, E. P. Thompson, letter to the *Guardian*, 26 September 1985, PA-MK-END-GEN-2, London.

121. Dieter Esche, interview with author, 31 March 2011.

122. Patrick Burke, interview with author, 10 May 2011.
123. Ibid.
124. Ibid.
125. Dieter Esche, interview with author, 31 March 2011.
126. Lynne Jones, "Tentative Dialogue in Perugia," *New Statesman,* 3 August 1984, p. 16.
127. Andrew Melville, quoted in ibid., p. 16.
128. Ibid.
129. Kaldor, quoted in ibid., p. 17.
130. Ibid.
131. Patrick Burke, interview with author, 10 May 2011.

6

Independent Civil Society

I think the experience of END . . . during the 1980s ended up having a massive impact on all the work [Mary Kaldor] did on civil society, and its role in international relations, during the 1990s and up to today.[1]

AS KALDOR TRAVELED BEHIND THE IRON CURTAIN, HER ENGAGEMENT with Eastern European independents further contributed to her understanding of the concept of civil society. Many Eastern Europeans, particularly the Czechs, learned Greek in order to reread all the classical authors on democracy and civil society. According to Kaldor, "I felt they were articulating ideas that expressed what we were trying to do in the peace movement but which we hadn't had the language for—they gave us *antipolitics, civil society*, and even *globalization*, which George Konrád was talking about back in 1982. It was a terrific education for me."[2]

One Eastern European with whom Kaldor collaborated academically was Ferenc Miszlivetz, a Hungarian independent who was then involved in a college in Hungary that was only partially sanctioned by the state. Upon meeting with Kaldor in Budapest in 1982, Miszlivetz recalled, "I understood that this was someone of Hungarian origin interested in local democratic initiatives, opposition activities, in a *very* genuine way."[3] After receiving a Leverhulme Trust Scholarship, Miszlivetz took the opportunity to study at Sussex University in 1983. While there, Miszlivetz worked closely with Kaldor at the Institute for Development Studies on a number of projects on East-West dialogue. Through his previous discussions and debates with dissidents in Hungary and across Eastern Europe, Miszlivetz began to appreciate the conceptual importance of civil society:

> When this notion of civil society came I immediately understood what it was, but that was not the case within Western academia. I remember I was giving

> a few seminars at Sussex in '83 and '84 . . . and [used] this phrase civil society and everyone was kind of surprised. . . . They understood it, and they didn't at the same time. These early theories [in Eastern Europe] already suggested that the new agent of democratization will be civil society, not political parties or clandestine political movements, but kind of open-ended and open networks of civil society.[4]

The concept of civil society increasingly informed Kaldor's and Miszlivetz's scholarly work. During his time at Sussex, Miszlivetz participated in endless debates and seminars with Kaldor, and other colleagues at Sussex, which further sharpened his ideas regarding civil society. As Miszlivetz later recalled, "I remember talking to Mary and some other colleagues on a daily basis, so we had seminars in the afternoon and dinners in the evening."[5]

For Miszlivetz, this practice was a stark contrast to debates in Eastern Europe, which were often discreet and subterranean: "For me it was fantastically interesting, because it was the first time I participated in that kind of political activity going from small meetings in the country side, some small peace circles, you know, neighborhood people."[6] In early 1984, Miszlivetz presented a paper at Sussex chaired by Kaldor on the subject of civil society, which led to Kaldor and Miszlivetz's collaboration over a series of months on an article entitled "Civilisational Crisis" published in early 1985.[7] Miszlivetz later maintained that the article was "kind of a breakthrough in a way, because it went against the conventional academic wisdom," which emphasized change through electing a new government or implementing a new foreign policy.[8] Kaldor and Miszlivetz argued in their article:

> The aim is not to capture state power, for a radical social movement would find it just as difficult as current political parties to escape the rules and constraints of the current inter-state system. Rather, the aim is to redefine the relationship between states and between states and civil society, to change the circumstances of power. Anti-systemic movements win when their ideas are implemented, not when their people form a government.[9]

Kaldor also employed the term in her activist and journalist writing, such as her END field trip reports,[10] and Kaldor was not the only one who used it. Other activists had adopted the term from their associations with Eastern European dissidents.[11] Yet, according to Patrick Burke, E. P. Thompson in particular was utterly "dismissive" of the term: "[Thompson's] interest faded in the mid-eighties and Mary's influence became stronger in that field [of East-West dialogue], and she began to use phrases like *civil society* at about that point, which Edward was allergic to."[12]

Use of the term, or not, also reflected the distance between Ken Coates's, E. P. Thompson's, and Mary Kaldor's visions of how the left could solve the problem of engagement with Eastern Europe. As Richard Falk, a fellow activist and scholar, later reflected, Kaldor was often at odds with her END peers who held a more rigid left position:

> Mary was never a part of what one could call either the ideological or dogmatic left. She was eager to establish her credentials as an independent intellectual citizen, with relatively good connections with the establishment, both in Europe and in the United Kingdom. . . . She felt that was the way to be effective and exert influence. She had these two ideas, of the role of civil society on the one side, but, on the other side, the importance of dialogue with the elites.[13]

Moreover, some in the Western peace movement questioned the value independents could play in changing intrastate and interstate dynamics altogether. Robert Borosage, US director of the Institute for Policy Studies, argued: "Given the limits on political freedoms in the East it is very unlikely that an independent peace movement there will play much of a role in the peace effort. Therefore the prospects and the fate of the peace movements in the West should not be made dependent upon the growth and health of the independent peace groups in the East."[14]

Although Kaldor began to use the term *civil society* academically in the mid-1980s, Paul Anderson, then deputy editor of the *END Journal,* later argued that her ideas regarding civil society were still undeveloped and only took shape from the mid- to late 1980s. Moreover, even though Kaldor was engaged in many of these intellectual debates regarding civil society and other concepts with Eastern Europeans, by the mid-1980s she had scaled back her academic writing. Anderson observed:

> Actually she wasn't doing that much in the way of writing beyond the kind of journalist stuff or occasional journal articles. She had made her reputation initially with *The Disintegrating West,* which was . . . very, very well received, and it was one of those books that everyone in international relations read as a very radical kind of counterpoint to . . . the realist accounts of international relations, and then *The Baroque Arsenal.* Those two books which, I think, had established her intellectual reputation at that time. She was obviously involved in all sorts of other things, and I think the experience of END . . . during the 1980s ended up having a massive impact on all the work she did on civil society and its role in international relations during the 1990s and up to today. But . . . I don't think that her ideas about civil society and international relations were fully formed at the time that we worked together during the 1980s.[15]

Civil Society in the East

Although Kaldor continued to explore the idea of civil society during the 1980s, not until much later did she reflect more broadly on the concept in her academic writing. Even though the original concept of civil society can be traced back to Aristotle, Kaldor argued that early modern thinkers recognized no division between civil society and the state.[16] For John Locke, civil society was a society governed by the rule of law, based on the principle of equality, with everyone being subject to the law, including the ruler. A government's legitimacy depended on the consent of the people, and if the government lost this consent, the ruler or government could, in principle, be overthrown. Essentially, Locke's view, although nothing short of radical for its time, meant that civil society was limited to a social contract primarily between the state and society.[17] Georg Hegel later broadened the concept of civil society to include the immediate space between the family and the state, in which the individual becomes a public person active within the micro and macro aspects of civic life, yet, for Hegel, civil society remained dependent on the state.[18] Hegel's characterization of civil society incorporated the economy and was employed by Karl Marx and Friedrich Engels, who considered civil society the "theatre of history."[19]

In the twentieth century, the definition of civil society was refined again as the realm not just between the state and family but as the space outside the state, market, and family, generally meaning the space of political debate, culture, and ideology. The intellectual most associated with this concept of civil society is Antonio Gramsci, the Italian Marxist. Gramsci posed the question of why a communist revolution would, in all probability, occur in Russia before it would occur in Italy. Civil society, Gramsci had argued, was the key: in other words, "in Russia, the state was everything, [and] civil society was primordial and gelatinous," whereas in Italy, "there was a proper relation between state and society and, when the state trembled, a sturdy structure of civil society was at once revealed."[20] For this reason, Gramsci's recommendation for the Italian Communist Party was that it implicitly and explicitly become involved in civil society, taking up positions in civil society, including in the media and universities, and making itself present in public discourse, with the intention of being able to challenge the cultural power of the bourgeoisie and the commonsense assumptions of everyday life that support the existing structures of economic and political power.[21]

Although the narratives changed, Kaldor insisted, all the preceding definitions of civil society maintained a rule-governed society based on the consent of the people or a "society based on a social contract among individuals."[22] The evolving definitions of civil society reflected the different ways that consent was formed within different periods. According to Kaldor's interpretation to this point, civil society was "the process through which individuals negotiate, argue, struggle against or agree with each other and with the centres of political and economic authority."[23] For this reason, in the early modern period, the primary concern was civil rights, or the freedom from fear. What defined the "civil" in civil society was that physical coercion had been replaced with laws, and the actors in civil society were the emerging bourgeoisie. In the twentieth century, the primary actors challenging the state were the workers, with the contestation surrounding social and economic emancipation, a contestation that Kaldor argued further refined the concept of civil society.[24]

Also at the core of earlier concepts, Kaldor argued, was the inextricable link between civil society and the state. States that exemplified civil society were differentiated from others that were still characterized by violent coercion, such as the empires in the East. Most particularly, civil society was in distinct contrast with relations between states that, due to the absence of a single authority, were distinguished by anarchy and the state of nature. Indeed, many of its proponents thought civil society within the home state was correlated to a propensity for war abroad, as the ability to organize and unite against what was considered to be a common enemy enabled a civil society to be possible.[25]

Kaldor's connection between militarization and civil society could be found in older philosophers. Like other proponents of Scottish Enlightenment, Adam Ferguson sought to produce a scientific approach to the study of social trends, and he argued that this study had to be undertaken through empirical examination of other societies. To better understand the developments in society, after studying the Scottish Highlanders and American Indians, Ferguson concluded that contemporary society had resulted in the decline of natural empathy toward others and a dwindling sense of community. Using the example of Sparta, he maintained that a pervasive martial spirit and sense of patriotism were one way to mitigate the risk of an individualistic society.[26] Hegel held a somewhat stronger viewpoint. He believed that war was not only important but necessary for the "ethical health of peoples. . . . Just as the movement of the ocean prevents the corruption which would be the result of perpetual calm, so by war people escape the corruption which would be occasioned by a continuous or eternal peace."[27] Nevertheless, not all theorists took this position on civil society.[28]

Perhaps the thinker who most influenced Kaldor's thinking on civil society was Immanuel Kant. Kant believed that the optimum constitution for the state was, in fact, not at war or through patriotism but the opposite. For Kant, civil society could only be achieved through nonviolent means and within the context of what he referred to as universal civil society.[29] Kaldor concluded that Kant saw establishing a functioning civil society as "subordinate to the problem of a law-governed external relationship with other states, and cannot be solved unless the latter is also solved."[30] Kant viewed war and anarchy between states as impediments to civil society, Kaldor argued, and for this reason a "functioning civil society was not possible except in the framework of what we would now call a global civil society."[31]

For Kaldor, the social contract becomes the key feature in Kant's notion of universal civil society. Within the global context, the central contract between the state and individual, although still important at the state level, is also being expanded beyond the nation-state. In the same way that the social contract mitigated anarchy and war within states, according to Kaldor, individual social contracts must expand beyond the state, thus preventing war between states. In the same vein, Kaldor viewed civil society as "the medium through which one or many social contracts between individuals, both women and men, and the political and economic centres of power are negotiated and reproduced."[32] And Kaldor viewed these contracts as global. Kaldor later declared, "I certainly would not object to being called a Kantian. . . . Kant . . . believ[ed] that the perfect constitution of the state could be achieved only in the context of a universal civil society."[33]

According to Kaldor, the concept of civil society was reinvented both in Eastern Europe and Latin America during the 1970s and 1980s, through activities completely independent of the state.[34] Kaldor argued that this reinvention of civil society was a response to the failure of revolutions, or, more precisely, the failure of the violent overthrow of regimes. Furthermore, as many Eastern European dissidents now argued, society in Eastern Europe had to be altered by the people, and doing so meant civil society had to be decoupled from the state. For example, in his article first published in 1978, Polish dissident Adam Michnik argued that attempting to invoke violent change (such as the Hungarian Revolution in 1956) or change from above (such as the Prague Spring in Czechoslovakia in 1968) had failed. The only plausible strategy was to induce change from below nonviolently.[35] For Michnik, Kaldor pointed out, this change meant shifting the relationship between state and society toward a civil society based on independence, autonomy, and the ability to maintain self-organization separate from the state.[36] In this respect, Michnik drew on Alexis de Tocqueville's notions of civil society and freedoms of association and movement. De Tocqueville believed that civil society was the domain of the private sphere, which was regulated by a civil code or private contract law augmented by the state. Yet de Tocqueville also conceded that a vibrant civil society functioned independently of the state.[37] Michnik insisted that de Tocqueville "contributed so much to our thinking about politics."[38]

De Tocqueville's concept of a civil society as independent of the state was picked up by many Eastern European dissidents and reinterpreted as a means to renegotiate the space currently occupied by the state and as the precondition to transitioning away from authoritarian or totalitarian government by democratic and nonviolent means. For example, Czech activists, particularly in Charter 77, began to focus on the withdrawal of dissidents from the state and on creating space for civil engagement. This process began, according to Václav Havel, with simple, day-to-day actions of ordinary people. In *The Power of the Powerless*, Havel wrote that the origins of Charter 77 exemplified the nonviolent approach, demonstrating that in a posttotalitarian system, the preconditions for movements that gradually assumed political significance did not require overt confrontations or political events between different forces or concepts. Primarily, these movements originated in what Havel termed the "pre-political," the space "where living within a lie confronts living within the truth, that is, where the demands of the post-totalitarian system conflict with the real aims of life."[39] Given the complexity and manipulation of the posttotalitarian system, Havel also argued:

> Every free human act or expression, every attempt to live within the truth, must necessarily appear as a threat to the system and, thus, as something which is political par excellence. Any eventual political articulation of the movements that grow out of this "pre-political" hinterland is secondary. It develops and matures as a result of a subsequent confrontation with the system, and not because it started off as a political program, project, or impulse. Once again, the [Prague Spring] of 1968 confirm[s] this. . . . The extent to which it is a real political force is due exclusively to its pre-political context.[40]

For Hungarian independents, such as Miszlivetz, their experience and understanding of the reconceptualization of civil society was not dissimilar. According to Miszlivetz, the 1956 Hungarian Revolution was considered the last revolution of the conventional type, and independents in Hungary began to consider alternatives, which involved developing "democracy to get more freedom by *avoiding* violence."[41] Initially Hungarian dissidents examined the ideas of István Bibó, in particular his concept of small circles developed in the 1950s and 1960s. Miszlivetz maintained that Bibó emphasized the importance of small circles of freedom, which included family or friendship groups, where one could "speak out, and you say what you think, [and where] you feel free."[42]

Over time these small circles would, in theory, increase in number, connect with other circles, and eventually overlap. In 1983, Tamás Fellegi and István Stumpf, both Hungarian independents who were influenced by their associations with Solidarity in Poland, took the idea of small circles and introduced university classes at Eötvös Loránd University in Budapest that were conducted outside the official curriculum. Inspired by the Poles' form of self-organization independent of the state, Fellegi and Stumpf formed an only partially sanctioned college, later called Bibó College, with one of the first year-long courses being on the Hungarian Revolution of 1956.[43] Miszlivetz was asked to become professor of sociology at Bibó College. He argued that, although Bibó "didn't use the word *civil society*," the concepts of small circles and civil society were combined to produce Bibó College, which became the nucleus for Hungarian independent civil society.

According to Miszlivetz, Hungarian independents also gained insights from other experiences of nonviolent resistance, such as the work of Martin Luther King, Jr., and the US civil rights movement, including "acts of solidarity" and "white people demonstrating with black people," which showed "that solidarity should be established between different players."[44]

Even though the idea of civil society was an "ancient" concept, with several reiterations by Locke, de Tocqueville, and Gramsci among others, Kaldor and Miszlivetz insisted that it was reinvented by the Polish group Solidarity. Miszlivetz later suggested that the idea of civil society was "mostly [reshaped] by Michnik and [Jacek] Kuroń. . . . It is a very rich concept because it is based on the recognition or the understanding that the old political game is not going to bring results . . . this old communist autocratic way of thinking, or that you need a clandestine centralized committee who decides. . . .

We *don't* need to agree about everything. We *want* a free, open, democratic society."[45]

Kaldor embraced the concept of civil society as it was reinvented by Eastern Europeans for two key reasons. First, the new interpretation of civil society, unlike that of Gramsci and his predecessors, explicitly proposed independence and autonomy between civil society and the state, a position that aligned with Kaldor's advocacy of participatory democracy and politics from below. Second, unlike traditional forms of revolution, which were facilitated by violence to enable a change in regime, the modern concept of civil society focused on the change in, and maturity of, the society, progressing toward democratic and liberal debate. Unlike Thompson, who relied on representative democratic principles of political involvement, Kaldor pursued the interpretation of civil society that was advanced by Eastern European dissidents because it challenged not only the relationship between society and state but, more importantly, the concept of political representation itself.

During her fieldwork in Hungary in 1985, Kaldor started to articulate the emergence of small "civil society" groups among students as the most remarkable new development in Hungary. Organizing themselves around former PGD dissidents and radical faculty members, they would meet regularly in groups of six or seven in private houses to discuss philosophical or peace issues and to debate. In addition, the development of the Hungarian green movement was equally compelling. In response to a major hydroelectric scheme on the Danube near the borders of Czechoslovakia and Hungary, the Hungarian green movement produced its own magazine and played an independent role similar to that of the PGD a few years earlier. Moreover, under pressure, Hungary had just introduced a new electoral law that, in theory, allowed candidates who were not officially sanctioned to be elected, though in practice much effort was invested by the regime to ensure votes were misrepresented or falsified. Nevertheless, students openly discussed appealing the outcomes.[46]

Kaldor observed that the PGD had taken on a myth-like quality among young Hungarian students.[47] She also reported that "they feel that there is a kind of hidden civil society and the problem is how to expand its sphere of influence and how to push what can be done to the limits of tolerance. For them *Dialogue* [PGD] has become an idea to which they aspire."[48] Later, some of the people leading these civil society groups went on to found West-East Dialogue, who organized the 1987 meeting at Eötvös Loránd University in Budapest, paving the way for Hungary's negotiated revolution.[49]

The Negotiated Revolutions

Kaldor believed that the new approach to civil society created "islands of civil engagement" in Eastern Europe. These important spaces, she argued, were made possible by two factors. First, like-minded dissidents in Eastern Europe had forged links with Western European peace and human rights groups, which supported them materially; publicized their experiences, such as in the *END Journal* or through the Helsinki Watch Committee or Amnesty International; and played a role in putting pressure on institutions and governments. Second, the existence of international legislation, such as the Helsinki Final Act, which Eastern European governments signed, provided a human rights platform for emerging dissident groups such as Charter 77 and the Polish Komitet Obrony Robotników (Committee for the Defense of Workers) to hold their governments to account.[50]

Kaldor also contended that ideas about civil society contributed to the underlying premise for the Velvet Revoluion in Czechoslovakia and the negotiated revolutions in Poland and Hungary. Although the revolutions of 1989 did not explicitly produce new ideas, the dissident activities and debates developing throughout the 1980s did produce new thinking that was critical to the way the 1989 revolutions unfolded.[51]

Dissidents such as Miszlivetz supported this view. The civil society discourse was a means to change the relationship between the state and its people, not just in a repressive regime but also in the West. Framing the relationship in terms of civil society, Kaldor argued, meant that a dissident became an ordinary person with the right to participate in the political process. As Kaldor later recalled, "it was a way of saying, 'Actually we're respectable citizens, we're civil society . . . [but] we're not *dissidents*' . . . [and] I think it's very hard for people to realize now how difficult it was to be a peace activist in the eighties."[52]

Even though civil society was interpreted in the context of a decoupling of society from the state within Eastern European nations, a wider process of globalization also added to Kaldor's interpretations of civil society. Civil society, in this sense, was a type of globalization from below. The ideas that most influenced Kaldor's thoughts on globalization initially were from George Konrád, a Hungarian dissident and writer at the Eötvös Loránd University. In 1982, Konrád wrote in *Anti-Politics* that of the social changes that had taken place in the twentieth century, one of the most interesting was the emergence of an international network, facilitated by the "global flow of information," which lends from so many different technical and institutional levels. Konrád argued, "The individual, whether a transmitter of messages or a receiver, can no longer live within a purely national context even if he wants to. . . . Globalisation has gone furthest in the natural sciences. . . . Today an international network of intellectual institutions is being formed, independent of governments."[53] According to Miszlivetz, being connected to a transnational civil society became "very important after [the Hungarian Revolution of] '56."[54] Using his associations with END as an example of a loose consortium of groups and individuals that supported Eastern European independents in the lead-up to the 1989 revolutions, Miszlivetz maintained:

> Thanks to the END—because END was the kind of cosmopolitan part of the British peace movement, which Mary and E. P. Thompson were actually leading figures of—I participated in the Perugia Convention that was in '84. And that was exactly the moment when Dieter Esche and Jürgen Graalfs said, "Why don't we make this rather blurred END a bit more political," and started with an initiative they called European Network for East-West Dialogue. I heard the word network, and I was fascinated, and I, of course, joined, and, ever since 1984, it was very active. It was very small, not very known, but I think it played a very important role because it was able to mobilize East European intellectuals, students, so-called opposition circles, even if most of them were not very sympathetic with the peace movement.[55]

Although a pan-European or global civil society was the goal, questions regarding European nationalism and identity remained. For example, during Kaldor's trips to Hungary, the question of national identity was debated in Eastern European independent circles. Konrád, for instance, was particularly interested in the meaning of nationalism and the question of identity, particularly European identity and the future of "Europe." In her field notes sent to the END Coordinating Committee, Kaldor maintained that the issues of identity raised by independents such as Konrád should be addressed: "I think it is very important that we start to address these issues—what we mean by European identity—are we interested in such issues, or are we afraid of what this implies?"[56] This question of identity became more important after the fall of the Berlin Wall with the breakup of the Balkans and the Caucasus in the 1990s.[57]

Even though Kaldor and many others would debate the terms *civil society* and *global civil society* throughout the late 1980s and 1990s,[58] for former dissidents, such as Miszlivetz and Michnik, civil society remained a conceptual framework that enabled democratic transition in Eastern Europe, with the support of their transnational counterparts. After working with Kaldor at Sussex University, Miszlivetz returned to Hungary and later initiated the Hungarian Network for East-West Dialogue in 1987, which was the founding platform for the Hungarian political party FIDESZ, led by the young Viktor Orbán, the future prime minister of Hungary.[59]

Although Eastern European dissidents influenced Kaldor, they were also influenced by her. As Miszlivetz wrote in "Understanding Civil Society Before and After 1989," "Kaldor draws our attention to the fact that the emergence of social movements and citizen groups was global."[60]

Notes

1. Paul Anderson, interview with author, 14 June 2011.
2. Mary Kaldor, quoted in Johnson, "New Wars and Human Security."
3. Ferenc Miszlivetz, interview with author, 18 February 2011.

4. Ibid.
5. Ibid.
6. Ibid.
7. Kaldor and Miszlivetz, "Civilisational Crisis."
8. Ferenc Miszlivetz, interview with author, 18 February 2011.
9. Kaldor and Miszlivetz, "Civilisational Crisis," p. 61.
10. For example, in her field report after a trip to Hungary for END in 1985, Kaldor maintained that unofficial "circles" and independents "feel that there is a kind of hidden civil society and the problem is how to expand its sphere of influence." See Mary Kaldor, memo to END Hungary Group: field notes of trip to Hungary, 10 May 1985, London School of Economics Archive END/12/6, London.
11. Ferenc Miszlivetz, interview with author, 18 February 2011.
12. Patrick Burke, interview with author, 10 May 2011.
13. Richard Falk, interview with author, 13 May 2015.
14. Borosage, quoted in Gordon, "From the Other Shore," p. 408.
15. Paul Anderson, interview with author, 14 June 2011.
16. See, for example, Kaldor, "The Idea of Global Civil Society."
17. See Locke, *The Two Treatises of Civil Government.*
18. See Hegel, *The Philosophy of Right.*
19. Kaldor, "The Idea of Global Civil Society," p. 584.
20. See Gramsci, *Selections from the Prison Notebooks.*
21. Kaldor, "The Idea of Global Civil Society," pp. 584–585.
22. Ibid., pp. 584–585.
23. Ibid., p. 585.
24. Ibid.
25. Ibid.
26. Ferguson, *An Essay on the History of Civil Society.*
27. Hegel, *The Philosophy of Right*, p. 331.
28. Kaldor, "The Idea of Global Civil Society," p. 585.
29. Ibid. See Immanuel Kant, "Perpetual Peace."
30. See Kaldor, *Global Civil Society.*
31. Ibid..
32. See ibid.
33. Kaldor, "The Idea of Global Civil Society," p. 583.
34. See ibid. See also Kaldor, *Global Civil Society.*
35. Michnik, *Letters from Prison and Other Essays.* See also Havel, *The Power of the Powerless*; and Haraszti, "The Beginnings of Civil Society."
36. Michnik, *Letters from Prison and Other Essays.*
37. De Tocqueville, *Democracy in America.*
38. Adam Michnik, "The Rebirth of Civil Society," paper presented at "Ideas of 1989" public lecture series, London School of Economics, London, 20 October 1999, online.
39. Havel, *The Power of the Powerless*, p. 27.
40. Ibid.
41. Ferenc Miszlivetz, interview with author, 18 February 2011.
42. Ibid.
43. Kenney, *A Carnival of Revolution*, pp. 137–140.
44. Ferenc Miszlivetz, interview with author, 18 February 2011.
45. Ibid. Jacek Kuroń was a Polish activist and cofounder of the Workers' Defense Committee (KOR).
46. Mary Kaldor, memo to END Hungary Group: field notes of the trip to Hungary, 10 May 1985, London School of Economics Archive END/12/6, London.

47. The ongoing repression caused a split in PGD. One splinter group formed a new peace group that was authorized by the National Peace Council, named 6-4-0 (after the numbers of years Hungary spent in the first two world wars and the hope that a third war will not arise). The organization sought to reach youth who were turned off by the stuffy style of the National Peace Council, though the council's policies on peace, however, were accepted.

48. Mary Kaldor, memo to END Hungary Group: field notes of trip to Hungary, 10 May 1985, London School of Economics Archive END/12/6, London.

49. Kenney, *A Carnival of Revolution*, pp. 99–102; Mary Kaldor, correspondence with author, 31 October 2010.

50. Kaldor, "The Idea of Global Civil Society."

51. Ibid.

52. Mary Kaldor, interview with author, 20 June 2011.

53. Konrád, *Anti-Politics*, p. 210.

54. Ferenc Miszlivetz, interview with author, 18 February 2011.

55. Ibid.

56. Mary Kaldor, memo to END Hungary Group and END Coordinating Committee: field notes of trip to Hungary, 17–26 October 1984, London School of Economics Archive END/12/6, London.

57. Makarchuk, Pakula, and Alton, "HCA," p. 5; Spencer, "Helsinki Citizens' Assembly," p. 24.

58. For *civil society*, see, for example, Arato and Cohen, *Civil Society and Political Theory*; Keane, *Civil Society and the State*; and Ignatieff, "On Civil Society." For *global civil society*, see, for example, Keane, *Global Civil Society?*; Kaldor, *Global Civil Society*; Walzer, *Toward a Global Civil Society*; Lipschutz, "Reconstructing World Politics"; de Oliveira, *Citizens*; and Wapner, "Environmental Activism and Global Civil Society."

59. Kenney, *A Carnival of Revolution*, p. 140; Ferenc Miszlivetz, interview with author, 18 February 2011.

60. Miszlivetz, "Understanding Civil Society Before and After 1989," p. 102.

7

Dealignment, Helsinki Citizens' Assembly, and Moscow

> *At least in my understanding and my perception, [Kaldor] was, in the whole process of the END convention, the leading representative of END. Absolutely! . . . So she was really a key person . . . [and she] was quite an important person inside END, and then in the whole process [she] guided us to the Helsinki Citizens' Assembly. She was not a simple activist. . . . In the Helsinki Citizens' Assembly she was very, very strongly involved. By her intellectual presence also: she wrote a lot of documents and contributions to the discussion. She was really one of the leading persons. Absolutely!*[1]

THE REAL VALUE OF END WAS THAT IT OPENED UP A SITE TO EXPLORE and debate the issues of both representation and the link between peace and human rights in the context of a greater European forum, however imperfect the process. Challenging the limits of solidarity within the mainstream Western peace movement, these debates at the Perugia Convention were a tipping point for both British END and the loose coalition of groups across Europe. For the Western peace movement, these arguments were often centered on the legitimacy of representative democracy in contrast to participatory or direct democracy. Consequently, Eastern European dissidents emphasized liberal democracy, civil liberties, and civil society, as opposed to a revised Marxist agenda or the change of regime or government.

After she had allowed the dust to settle from the storm of Perugia, Kaldor continued to encourage debate within the newly expanded, but divided, END Liaison Committee. For example, Kaldor attempted to stimulate debate on what the end of the Cold War would look like and how security could be thereafter redefined across Europe. During a follow-up END Liaison Committee meeting, Kaldor proposed the theme for the next convention in Amsterdam as "the end of the post-war period—[a] new security system for Europe."[2] However, Kaldor's proposal was not adopted. Although she conceded the difficulties the END Liaison Committee would face in debating, much less challenging, the status quo in Europe, she believed that debate was an indispensable process. Kaldor appealed to her colleagues to reconsider what she felt to be rigid positions regarding East-West engagement. Furthermore, she conveyed her concerns over what she considered to be a "kind of factionalism (there is a sort of rigid aggressive way of arguing) [that] could paralyse all our work."[3]

In the past, to circumvent the END Liaison Committee's paralysis, Kaldor had ensured that independents were invited to conventions and seminars directly. For example, during a field trip to Hungary in late 1984, Kaldor noted that members of the PGD were disappointed not to have received invitations to the Perugia Convention and that they suspected the END Liaison Committee of cooperating with the Soviet officials.[4] To ensure they were included in the next convention, she wrote a number of invitations during her field trips in 1984.

Now in 1984, Kaldor was also inviting Hungarian dissidents to become involved in preparations for the upcoming END convention in Amsterdam.[5] That independents knew they were invited was important in producing a pan-European solidarity, irrespective of whether or not they were blocked from attending by their own governments. Furthermore, this simple act of inviting them to attend and to become involved in the planning was important in its own right. As Patricia Chilton, a fellow activist, discovered, "many of the most significant contacts were not meetings at all, but invitations."[6]

Within British END, a debate also ensued regarding British END's association with the newly formed European Network for East-West Dialogue (ENEWD), which was led by Dieter Esche. Between autumn 1984 and early 1985, the END Coordinating Committee through a process of consultation debated whether British END should become a member of the ENEWD, concluding finally that the organization would not join nor send an official representative to the upcoming Yalta Seminar in Berlin in February 1985. The event was referred to as the Yalta Seminar because it marked the fortieth anniversary of the Yalta Conference, which had defined Europe's post–World War II arrangements. According to E. P. Thompson, the decision was "a painstaking and democratic consultation process, which involved much time, much fringe discussion, much travel . . . and [was] an illustration of how END can work as a responsible political collective."[7] Although Kaldor was sympathetic to ENEWD, many in the Coordinating Committee were skeptical of the group. In particular, Thompson considered the group to be a radical initiative, which would divide the Western peace movement. Thompson argued:

> It has since become evident that a more serious political operation is intended, one stage of which is the "Yalta" seminar in Berlin. . . . It has been widely discussed in Europe that a new alignment is coming into being, linking up "radical" sections of the Western peace movement with "dissident" intellectual groups in the East—elements in KOS, Charter 77 and among Hungarian opposition intellectual circles. It has been reported in a major Warsaw

> Solidarnosc [Solidarity] paper that an "anti-Yalta" group was formed at Perugia, whose object is either to take over the leadership of the Western peace movement or to split it, between "anti-Yalta" and pro-Soviet sections.[8]

Despite the END Coordinating Committee's decision, Kaldor and three members of END decided that they would attend the ENEWD's Yalta Seminar, as individuals and not as representatives of END, and that they would join the group as individual members.[9] One of the END members attending with Kaldor, Paul Anderson, then deputy editor of the *END Journal*, insisted that "we weren't representing anyone apart from ourselves, [and] we made that entirely clear."[10]

Nonetheless, British END was alarmed by their attendance. Thompson was particularly outraged. Anderson recalled that Thompson considered their attendance at the Yalta Seminar "to be a provocation, [and] that led to a certain amount of bad blood really between people around Mary (including myself) and the Thompsons, which was never really completely resolved."[11] END employee and member Patrick Burke, who also attended with Kaldor and Anderson, elaborated:

> The best known person at END (apart from Thompson), Mary Kaldor, went. So it looked like an official delegation. And both Thompsons—Edward and Dorothy—went ballistic when they heard about this. There was an awful Coordinating Committee [meeting] after we got back. [Edward and Dorothy] refused to come, [and] they resigned from END, which they did a couple of times, but still, they meant it: "We don't want anything more to do with END" . . . [and] "Mary shouldn't become [a] full member of the Network." They were very angry with what Mary had done. That I did attend didn't matter so much. But Paul Anderson and Fiona Weir and I (three officeworkers) plus Mary were all there and [it looked like] it was kind of an official visit. [Thompson] was very angry.[12]

From Thompson's perspective, that Kaldor and three END members attended the ENEWD meeting in Berlin appeared to call "into question the whole operation of END" and the nature of END as a democratic collective.[13] Thompson argued:

> It was the clearest possible political recommendation that END should not be officially associated [with ENEWD]. And what was the result? I understand that Mary Kaldor, editor of *END Journal* and END's best-known officer in Europe, addressed the introductory plenary session in Berlin (attended by the press) and that three END staff, including our Organising Secretary, went with her. This makes a mockery of any democratic consultative process within END. It will be assumed in Europe either that END is split in half, or the delegation will be taken as an official representation presence. . . . It is likely to be widely reported in East Europe that END is represented in the new "anti-Yalta" formation.[14]

Despite the controversy, Kaldor and a few of the members of British END continued to attend the ENEWD activities, albeit as individuals and not as representatives of END. With various attempts made to smooth things over with the Thompsons and the END Coordinating Committee, END increasingly began to work in parallel with ENEWD, though often as an opposing force. Burke recalled:

> The END Coordinating Committee wrote what could only be described as a grovelling letter [to the Thompsons]. At the time I thought, "This is so English." I sort of imagine[d] this wouldn't happen in Dieter Esche's group . . . or the Greens. Then it all just kind of faded away, and we didn't join the Network [ENEWD]. Edward and Dorothy came back to END. . . . Mary wrote a reconciliatory or conciliatory letter about a month later saying, "Let's not get too worked up about all this," [and] you know, "We don't have to join," to the Coordinating Committee. Sort of signaling that she wasn't going to make a big issue out of it, which is very much Mary's style, I think. She certainly is very strong in her arguments, but she also likes for people to get on with each other. And then Mary or someone from END went to many, if not all, of a large number of Network meetings from then on as an "observer"—as de facto members, not de jure. So officially we weren't members, but we took part in all the meetings. And that was the compromise that was reached.[15]

The Independent Scholar

During the course of the 1970s and 1980s, Kaldor remained an academic at Sussex University. Keen to maintain her research independence, Kaldor had supported her work financially through an array of research grants and teaching. Nevertheless, by the mid-1980s, Kaldor had still not received a tenured position (nor any other permanent academic appointment). According to one of her colleagues, then also at Sussex, Kaldor's activism was considered problematic. Zdenek Kavan observed that the issue was not about being political or not being political. Rather, it was about "how."[16] Kavan recalled:

> At the time there was certainly quite a lot of prejudice that you can't be a serious academic if you are devoting so much time to political causes. . . . Political activism was indeed perceived as something that academics don't do. . . . [Later] I certainly remember, [when I was on an] appointments committee, that was certainly the question that [was] raised [about Kaldor], which is, is she going to be sufficiently committed to the job. She had to battle it in that sense with this prejudice until . . . the early nineties.[17]

During this time, Kaldor also found securing external funding for her research increasingly difficult. Although during the 1970s, Kaldor had remained attached to Sussex University and other centers and institutes and had relied on various grants and funding arrangements to supplement her work, by the mid-1980s funding sources became scarce. While Christopher Freeman was director of SPRU, Kaldor's unorthodox approach to her academic work was supported, even celebrated. However, SPRU's new director, Geoffrey Oldham, was vastly less enthusiastic. Suddenly her career as an academic, which had seemed so successful to that point, was in question. Kaldor later recalled:

> Suddenly I became a "dissident," and it became much, much more difficult. . . . I remember going to the Ford Foundation, and they said, "We all know the difference between the old Mary Kaldor and the new Mary Kaldor," so [finding] funding was difficult. I think I went through a period of not having enough funding. Then when Geoff Oldham took over [SPRU], he didn't want me to work on these issues. IDS [Institute for Development Studies], where I also had a fellowship, didn't want me to work on Eastern Europe. . . . [Then] I made this Labour Party broadcast with Robin Cook. . . . The vice chancellor [of Sussex Univeristy] rang up and was furious that the University of Sussex was on a Labour Party broadcast. And then we tried all kinds of ways to raise money for our projects and our programs . . . and it was just impossible to get funded, and then we had Rowntree Funding to set up a little Disarmament Unit in SPRU, and then Geoff Oldham wanted to get rid of it and said it was too political.[18]

Even though Kaldor seriously considered giving up on academia, she maintained that she felt that she could never withdraw from her intellectual interests and her advocacy approach. For a moment in her life, Kaldor considered continuing her work through a different role, such as a full-time activist or as editor of the *New Statesman*. Kaldor recalled: "On the contrary, there was lots of times when I thought, 'Should I become a full-time activist, like Mient Jan [Faber]? Should I run the END office? Or something?' . . . That was my main thought: 'Maybe I *should* just be doing this full-time rather than be an academic.' . . . I never thought [of giving up]. I mean, I *loved* what I was doing, and I thought I was doing the right thing."[19]

In the end, however, Kaldor did not relinquish her academic career. She decided that although she battled with Oldham and the vice chancellor, academia still ensured greater intellectual and political independence. Martin Albrow, British sociologist and colleague, later observed that Kaldor's resolve to remain in academia and negotiate her research funding revealed her determination for independence as well as her entrepreneurial approach to academia:

> She's never had to follow anybody else's agenda, which is very unusual for any academic. It's partly because she worked in a center outside the mainstream for so long in this outfit called SPRU, and she was there for her work. . . . She had to go out and get the money to work on the research and so on. In that sense, she is very much a self-made academic, self-made intellectual. . . . That's how she has had to survive. . . . It's always been her own efforts that get the money. . . . The vast majority of academics work within a program which they don't invent.[20]

Despite the difficulties of academia, Kaldor continued to develop a network consisting of activists, scholars, politicians, and practitioners, both as friends and colleagues. Daniele Archibugi, who had started his PhD at Sussex University, recalled Kaldor's intellectual circle, which included people passing through from all around the world, such as Richard Falk, Viktor Orbán, Ferenc Miszlivetz, and Italian intellectual Lino Pertile. In addition to E. P. Thompson and Stuart Holland, "there was a convergence of common friends at Sussex . . . and therefore everybody [who] was in the neighborhood would came down" to Kaldor's flat for dinner or lunch".[21] Although Archibugi and Kaldor would later collaborate on a series of edited books in the 1990s, he maintained that the informal discussions and debates with Kaldor defined him. They would meet in Brighton, in London, or on occasion at her parents' house in Cambridge. Archibugi recalled:

> [Formal] collaborations have always been less important in my view than the collaboration we get during a conversation at dinner or by meeting with Mary's friends. . . . I met Richard Falk at Mary's house—that was back in the mid-eighties—and many other people. It's been very helpful. Mary has been very generous in giving me the opportunity to meet quite a lot of her colleagues, and I'm very grateful to her for that. I mean it wasn't something formal, but she brought together people socially [from] everywhere, in Sussex, London, or in Cambridge.[22]

Kaldor also continued to merge activism and policy in her academic writing. For example, as a result of the conference "Dealignment for Western Europe" held jointly by the Transnational Institute and the United Nations University in Amsterdam in 1983, Kaldor teamed up with Richard Falk to put together an edited collection of essays entitled *Dealignment: A New Foreign Policy Perspective,* which was finally published in 1987.[23] Unlike the policies of nonalignment and neutrality, which remained strictly limited to agreements between the blocs, dealignment was a policy developed to transcend the bloc system. Although initially advocating using the term *nonalignment*, as ideas were refined and debated, Kaldor soon abandoned it for the term *dealignment*.[24] The concept of dealignment was utilized in an attempt to create space for new political forces and more democratic power structures, both between and within states, outside the Soviet-US axis. The process of dealignment would be a gradual process of moving away from the requisite common positions of each bloc and establishing a new consensus built on a respect for pluralism.[25]

Kaldor believed that democratization in Eastern Europe was a crucial element to dealignment. If the "Atlantic alliance" between Western Europe and the United States was about internal cohesion and not about a Soviet threat, then the first priority was to reconsider the internal unity of the "West." The Soviet-US divide combined a set of international arrangements with domestic politics, entrenched in a set of social, economic, and military institutions. By emphasizing a bipolar model of the world, the status quo was characterized by the permanent state of confrontation between Western democratic and Eastern totalitarian systems. Dealignment meant withdrawing from the bloc status quo or bloc system and therefore relinquishing the undemocratic international and domestic arrangements it supported.[26]

For Kaldor, Hungary was an important site for exploring and testing the concept of dealignment. In 1985, during a field trip to Hungary, Kaldor observed that many of the independents were interested in the idea of dealignment. Although the director of the Hungarian Institute for International Relations maintained that the time was not right for such ideas in Eastern Europe, Kaldor disagreed, arguing that the opportunities for dealignment were strong in the Hungarian independence movement, but that everything depended on what happened in the Soviet Union. If Mikhail Gorbachev maintained a tough stance, then Hungary, she guessed, would fall into line. However, if Gorbachev held to a progressive line, she proposed that Hungary would begin to play a significant, more independent role in the region. In her field report, Kaldor highlighted the developments of the Hungarian Institute for International Relations, which had begun studying any possible room for maneuver in Hungarian foreign policy and openly discussing the need to pursue Hungarian national interests, as opposed to Soviet interests.[27]

Yet Kaldor's debates concerning dealignment and nonalignment extended past Hungary. As Dieter Esche later remarked, "in the whole British-American discussion, [Kaldor] was a key person for the whole nonalignment peace discourse."[28] As in the 1970s, Kaldor continued to develop connections with, and lecture or consult for, other universities. For example, she was the European coordinator at the United Nations University Subprogram on Peace and Global Transformation from 1982–1988. She conducted the Bertrand Russell Peace Lectures at McMaster University in Hamiliton, Ontario, Canada, in January 1987. She was a consultant with the World Institute for Development Economics Research program on militarization and the world economy at the United Nations University in 1987 as well as coconvenor of the US/European Summer Schools on Global Security and Arms Control with the University of California, San Diego, in 1987 and 1988. Through Falk, Kaldor became guest lecturer at the Woodrow Wilson School of Public and International Affairs, Princeton University, during the mid-1980s. One of her students was the young David Petraeus, later commander of US Military Central Command and director of the CIA.[29]

"As If" a United and Pacific Europe

The development of the HCA was the outcome of an amalgamation of ideas, meetings, dialogues, academic texts, appeals, and debates in response to the END Appeal. In 1983, Jiří Dienstbier, a Czech dissident with Charter 77, wrote a letter to the second END convention in Berlin agreeing with the END Appeal's concept of an "as if" stance on the East and West acting together. Quoting from the appeal, Dienstbier called for "the two superpowers to withdraw all nuclear weapons from European territory," and he suggested that all Europeans "must commence to act as if a united, neutral, and pacific Europe already exists."[30]

Although the concept seemed an overly idealistic and aspirational one, dissidents and peace activists who were committed to a united and independent Europe and emphasized direct democratic participation began to consider ways in which the "as if" concept might be implemented. For example, in March 1985, Charter 77 wrote the Prague Appeal, which was launched at the END convention in Amsterdam in July. Written in response to the END Appeal's original approach of détente from below, the authors of the Prague Appeal retained the concept of "as if" as a core normative belief, binding the independent East-West peace movements to a common objective.[31] The Prague Appeal was a call to "overcome the structure of the power blocs through an association of free and independent nations . . . within a democratic and self-governing all-European community living in friendship."[32] The authors of the Prague Appeal advocated that "the Helsinki Final Act . . . did not represent simply a confirmation of the status quo . . . [but that] this process has firmly established the idea of the indivisibility of peace—not only in relations among states, but also between state and society and between the citizens and the authorities."[33] Unlike previous communications, statements, or declarations issued by Charter 77, the Prague Appeal contained a detailed mandate for how Europe would work within the framework of the "Conference on Security and Cooperation in Europe and its Final Act signed in Helsinki."[34] For many Western activists, in particular END, committed to working with independent dissidents in the Eastern bloc countries, the Prague Appeal was confirmation that Charter 77 was starting to seriously engage with the END Appeal and the wider END movement, despite the ongoing debates across the wider END movement concerning who should be involved in the convention process.[35]

Similarly, the Helsinki Memorandum: Giving Real Life to the Helsinki Accords was written as a further continuation of the END Appeal and the Prague Appeal to unite Europe. The Helsinki Memorandum, written by ENEWD and of which Kaldor was a signatory, was delivered at END's Évry Convention in France in 1986. The authors of the document declared: "For us, the three 'baskets' of the Helsinki Final Act are interdependent. We oppose any tendency to play off peace against freedom or vice versa. A lasting détente cannot be bought at the cost of civil liberties and human—political and social—rights. Peace and security, détente and cooperation, basic rights and self-determination of people have to be achieved all together."[36]

According to Burke, the Helsinki Memorandum was important for three reasons. First, it was a concrete step to progressing and expanding the East-

West dialogue. Unlike the previous appeals, statements, and letters, which were unilateral, the Helsinki Memorandum was produced by a broader circle of activists from both sides of the Iron Curtain and so established a unified position. Second, it inspired further practical steps in the East-West dialogue, such as the seminars at Żytnia Street, Warsaw, and Eötvös Loránd University, Budapest. Third, it was an important process that led to the establishment of the HCA.[37]

The Helsinki Memorandum was then also presented at the Helsinki Review Conference in Vienna in November 1986, the third review conference by the OSCE signatories of the Helsinki Final Act in 1975.[38]

The East-West Debate

In 1987, arguments in END concerning East-West representation and participation at END conventions continued unabated. During a Liaison Committee meeting in May 1987, Ken Fleet of the Russell Foundation was recorded as expressing concern about the Polish group Freedom and Peace. Fleet commented that "Freedom and Peace have not signed the *END Appeal*. They are therefore *not* direct partners of ours."[39] Coates wrote that Freedom and Peace "does not really fit into the European peace movement" as "it seems to make the disarmament of other countries [i.e., the West] conditional on a change in the political regime in Poland."[40] Although Freedom and Peace delegates could certainly attend the END conventions, Coates argued, it "was absolutely wrong to invite this organization to provide a speaker in the closing plenum at Coventry."[41] Therefore, he argued, inviting Freedom and Peace member Konstanty Radziwiłł to contribute a speech "did not represent the consensus of the European peace movements, and indeed had very little to do with the overall objective of European Nuclear Disarmament."[42] Nevertheless, by the end of the hotly contested Liaison Committee meeting, the committee approved Freedom and Peace as a participant in the plenary, and Radziwiłł delivered the closing END convention plenary speech.

Yet, for some on the Liaison Committee, the argument surrounding this incident confirmed that the convention process had now become redundant in relation to the question of East-West dialogue. One British END member argued that the convention process was now more engrossed in the question of who should represent the peace movement than the action of East-West dialogue itself.[43] Moreover, many of the ENEWD members, if not all, had left the Liaison Committee in frustration. One member of the END Liaison Committee, Fiona Weir, even argued that the Liaison Committee "does NOT represent the peace movement. . . . On East-West issues, the fact that the majority of [ENEWD] contacts have pulled out has shifted the political balance enormously," and that the "mood among the peace movements" within the Liaison Committee is one of "a growing sense of revolt."[44] Weir maintained that "conditions are there for a serious consideration of withdrawing from the process" by many of the major players, leading to a dissolution of the convention process altogether.[45]

Although many major peace groups did not withdraw, the fact that ENEWD had largely split away from END was a serious blow to the END convention process. In her report on the next END convention, held in Lund, Sweden, in 1988, Kaldor, then still a member of the END Liaison Committee and a de facto member of ENEWD, described the separation frankly: "The Liaison Committee . . . is unworkable, given the irreconcilable division between political parties and peace movements. Further still, the Liaison Committee is unable to reach a united position on East-West questions."[46] In many respects, by then the ENEWD had superseded the END Liaison Committee's broader role of facilitating East-West dialogue.

Although the END convention process remained fractured, the signing of the Intermediate-Range Nuclear Forces (INF) Treaty in 1987 had proven a source of political optimism for END and for Kaldor personally. Although only 1,200 activists attended the Lund Convention and despite the internal friction within END, the themes of the convention demonstrated an exuberance in response to the signing of the INF Treaty and Gorbachev's reforms, with topics such as "new opportunities for détente," "détente and the third world," and "new tasks for the peace movements."[47] For Kaldor, the INF Treaty was not just a political development but also a personal experience. In August 1988, Moscow invited Kaldor as an independent observer to the Kazakhstan steppe to watch as SS-12 missiles, which were formerly directed at China, were destroyed as a part of the INF Treaty.[48]

As confidence in the INF Treaty swelled, interest in END steadily declined. Increasingly, the European peace movement lost its raison d'être, and, with it, the British END transitioned into what became European Dialogue in 1989, and the Moscow Convention in 1991 was the final END convention, just as the Strategic Arms Reduction Treaty I (START I) came into effect.

United Citizens

Irrespective of the Liaison Committee and the convention process, the East-West network was moving toward greater Eastern European engagement. Although the END Appeal, Prague Appeal, and Helsinki Memorandum paved the way for a conceptual approach to a kind of Helsinki process from below, the meetings at the Żytnia Street and the Eötvös Loránd University confirmed that assemblies between East-West could happen.

The meetings on Żytnia Street in Warsaw conducted in the Church of God's Mercy, entitled "International Peace and the Helsinki Accords," set a precedent within the peace movement. However, not everything went as planned. Mary Kaldor, Mient Jan Faber, and Jan Minkiewicz, as well as a dozen others from East Germany and Czechoslovakia, were blocked from entering Poland en route to the event, scheduled 7–9 May 1987.[49]

Nevertheless, those who crossed the Polish border undetected experienced a rare occasion when a truly East-West dialogue was conducted, more surprisingly, in Poland. Much relied upon the courage of one priest who welcomed the 200 delegates from fifteen countries into his church under the watchful eyes of Western cameras. This international attention and the fact that more than twenty Western peace delegates had already been detained along the border accounted for the authorities' volte-face on a previous plan to storm the meeting. Zbigniew Romaszewski, a leading figure in Solidarity, remarked, "All of a sudden a totally international event is held and people from East and West speak freely, and no one stands up to say 'no, you can't do it.'"[50] The Żytnia Street meeting was also important because, although discussions were often heated, a sense of a greater unity could be found between East and West. Richard Bloom, a participant, described the meeting: "Everybody was united in a sense that the dialogue was worthwhile, that they wanted to continue it and that they had found in each other natural allies and future partners."[51]

The follow-up meeting in Hungary was equally important, and this time Kaldor was not blocked from attending. As the principal organizer of the meeting, Miszlivetz was determined to conduct the meeting as an open dialogue.[52] Students from the College of Social Science and Law at the Eötvös Loránd University of Budapest, along with other Hungarian independents and ENEWD, organized the meeting, which took the name "Conference on Human Rights and Democracy" and was held on 21–22 November 1987. Meetings that seemed impossible to hold either in the West with activists from the East or in the East at all could now be held in Hungary, and the networks made full use of this opportunity. Miszlivetz later recalled:

> So we said, "It's a real discussion. It's a dialogue." It was fantastically successful, and there were attempts, as I said, to intimidate the university. . . . It's true that a lot of Western journalists came. There was a very high [international] scrutiny: Reuters and AP [Associated Press] and others. And that was a good moment because it was young people, mostly from the countryside, [who] joined this elite movement—this so-called democratic opposition and the Western peace movement and other networks. It was a kind of European moment in '87 and '88.[53]

This meeting was significant for two reasons. First, it created a formal mandate for East-West activists to work together on a commitment for democratic change. A statement issued by the attendees declared that "we the undersigned" agree to "articulate and to clarify common values in search of an all-European democratic movement."[54] Moreover, the participants committed to "work[ing] together to enlarge the space for an active civil society through Europe, where the rights of the individual are guaranteed, respected, and not subordinated to the power of the state," including "the right of citizens to form independent groups, associations and organisations."[55]

Second, the meeting served as the genesis for the first independent political opposition in both Hungary and across Eastern Europe. Shortly after the seminar, Miszlivetz and some of the other Bibó College students formed the Circle of the Network for East-West Dialogue at the college, thus creating the basis for an independent opposition and laying the foundation for the political group, FIDESZ.[56]

Also at this meeting, Kaldor met her future cochair of the HCA, Sonja Licht, a graduate of the University of Belgrade and a Yugoslav dissident.[57]

A Citizens' Framework for Helsinki

By June 1988, the basic outline for a European citizens' assembly project was produced at a three-day seminar in Prague entitled "Prague 88," although not without some confrontation with state authorities.[58] The principal organizers of the event were Jan Kavan (activist and later Czech foreign minister) and Jaroslav Šabata, a member of Charter 77.[59] During the course of the three-day seminar, police constantly interrupted proceedings, insisting on arresting and interrogating participants. On the second day, several activists, including Kaldor and Christopher Hitchens, then a British journalist who was covering the story for a US magazine, were arrested and jailed by Czech police for meeting representatives of Charter 77 at Jan Urban's home, a member of Charter 77.[60] Hitchens, detained in a cell in Prague with Kaldor, described their treatment: "We were told we were enemies of the state and were denied the right to telephone our embassy. They [the police] were very rude and insulting and we were told this was punishment."[61] By the end of the three-day seminar, the entire preparatory team of the HCA, including thirty-four foreigners and the majority of the Charter 77 members present, had been arrested.

Although deemed enemies of the state by Czechoslovakian officials,[62] the members of the seminar produced the foundation for establishing the HCA.[63] As Kaldor and her cell mates were incarcerated and smuggling "news of their capture to Western reporters, they were still hatching plans for the 'European Citizens' Assembly' to link progressive movements and monitor human rights."[64] Padraic Kenney maintained, "This idea would carry the movement through to the revolution. And if they suspected it before, now they knew for sure that 'Europe' looked a lot different from a Prague jail cell . . . than from a convention hall in Amsterdam, Coventry, or Berlin."[65] In police stations and airport lounges, the HCA preparatory team still managed to issue a press release calling for a citizens' assembly, resolute in their efforts, irrespective of arrests.

After the Czech police broke up the seminar and expelled the foreigners, the HCA civil society project was syndicated through a broader coalition across Eastern and Western Europe, including through participants of the END convention held in Lund in July 1988, a seminar in Kraków, Poland, in August 1988, and a seminar organized by ENEWD in Nijmwegen, Holland, in September 1988. Kaldor believed that participants responded positively to the "Prague 88" proposal and that their ideas were beginning to take form. She wrote, "The project is assuming ever more concrete features."[66] By the follow-up meeting in Budapest, keen to make their point that politics from below mattered more than the political arrangement of the Cold War, the HCA preparatory team ambitiously planned its first major international launch to be conducted in Prague in 1990.[67] Timothy Garton Ash wrote in the *New York Review of Books* that "for the first time in decades, the primary limits to political change in Eastern Europe are not external but internal" and that a socialist state acting independently of Moscow seemed possible.[68]

Although the HCA was a collaborative enterprise between activists from Eastern and Western Europe, Kaldor, utilizing her experiences in END, played a central role in shaping its conceptual formation. Nevertheless, Kaldor maintained that HCA was a joint-led project between herself and Faber. According to Kaldor, she and Faber drew on the experiences of END and IKV, respectively, utilizing the many forms of political organization and activism they had become familiar with, such as the forum, debate, the assembly, and building grassroots networks, to create a politics from below: "[HCA] was a sort of intellectual partnership between me and Mient Jan. . . . I think END was really Edward's baby, and, as END developed, I became a key thinker in it. But, you know, that kind of politics was new to me at that stage so I was learning from people like him. Whereas with HCA, I was really taking the lead and shaping it."[69] Miszlivetz corroborated Kaldor's claim:

> I think Mary's contribution was absolutely essential in this. Without Mary, it would not have happened. We had these great guys like E. P. Thompson, but E. P. Thompson would have never—he came and he met with some Dialogue [PGD] people, but he did not have this personal attachment and he didn't, I don't think, have the knowledge and the commitment, and the others, the same. So Mary, because of her Hungarian origin, because of her emotional intelligence, her openness . . . she had a better touch, a better kind of sense of East and Central Europe—Hungary especially—but also Poland and relations with Václav Havel and [Adam] Michnik.[70]

Fall of the Berlin Wall

After the collapse of the Iron Curtain, Kaldor's influence widened to include the newly established HCA. In Kaldor's view, the HCA was to be an OSCE that transcended official boundaries.[71] Like END, HCA became the transnational umbrella organization that united Western European peace activists and former Central and Eastern European dissidents but also included activists from Canada and the United States. By October 1990, HCA was officially launched in Prague and first chaired by Šabata and Faber. Havel, the new Czech president, was key speaker to the assembly.

HCA's charter was nothing short of ambitious, declaring that "overcoming the division of Europe is the job, especially, of civil society, of citizens acting together in self-organized associations . . . across national boundaries," where the "Helsinki process from above has to be complemented by an equally significant Helsinki process from below."[72] Supporting the new charter, over 700 people attended the first HCA convention from twenty-five European countries, in addition to the Soviet Union, Canada, and the United States. For Kaldor, the convention drew together a new international organization that was dedicated to the defense of both peace and human rights: "a pan-European security system that would supplant the military blocs and find ways of solving conflicts in Europe without reliance on military force . . . and [would provide for] the creation of a trans-European civil society."[73]

Although Kaldor was optimistic that civil society had a critical role to play, she did not consider the HCA to simply speak for civil society. In her speech to the closing session of the HCA launch, Kaldor reflected her predilection for direct or participatory democracy, arguing,

> We are not representative of civil society. We are a part of civil society. If we were representatives of civil society, we would be no different to a parliament. . . . We are ready to discuss with everyone. . . . In fact, we don't represent anyone. . . . In many cases, we represent no one but ourselves. And our power rests not on who we represent but in what we do: in what we say, in our ideas, in our quest for truth, in the projects we undertake.[74]

Many who attended the 1990 Prague launch of the HCA and were actively involved in its establishment went on to become significant political leaders in their own right. For example, Václav Havel became Czech president, Jiří Dienstbier became Czech foreign minister and later UN special rapporteur for human rights in the former Yugoslavia, Jan Kavan became Czech foreign minister and president of the UN General Assembly, Martin Palouš became permanent representative to the United Nations for the Czech Republic, Viktor Orbán became prime minister of Hungary, and Pascal Milo became foreign minister of Albania.[75]

Although HCA members focused on all aspects of Europe, the growing discontent throughout the Balkans caught their attention. Another attendee of the HCA meeting was George Papandreou, Jr., later foreign minister and then prime minister of Greece.[76] George Papandreou recalled that at the launch of the HCA, in Prague, they began making contact with the Balkan countries through nongovernmental organizations (NGOs) and new civil society groups in an effort to support them against the rising nationalistic tendencies:

> [This process] was very important, and it so happens that out of this a number of us became ministers, while the rest of us responded to other callings. But it became very important to create a counterbalance to the more nationalistic fears that grew out of the lack of knowledge, or the vacuum of contact. . . . One of my central points is that this civic experience of civil society, having already been so important, will continue to be important—and increasingly so—as we move ahead towards a globalised society.[77]

In many respects, the HCA became the conceptual successor to END and ENEWD, and for its members its establishment was a significant benchmark of END's success and the implementation of the END Appeal. Burke reflected, "A final measure of success, perhaps, for END and other activists involved in the East-West Dialogue, was the creation of the Helsinki Citizens' Assembly (HCA). The post–Cold War pan-European alliance of citizens had been just an idea; by the end of the decade the alliance was strong enough to give birth to a successor that did indeed span the continent."[78]

Moscow

Although profoundly involved in encouraging the grassroots shaping of the HCA, Kaldor also played a role in bringing Eastern European dissidents directly into the Russian foreign affairs arena. In 1989, Eduard Shevardnadze, then Soviet minister of foreign affairs, decided to open the doors of the Moscow State Institute for International Relations (MGIMO) for the first time. As the high-level training center for the Soviet Ministry for Foreign Affairs, MGIMO was an enigma.[79] In the spirit of glasnost, Shevardnadze decided to conduct a two-week conference on the subject of international relations at MGIMO, 10–24 July 1989, a conference that would include Western academics and practitioners. To assist with the organization of the conference, Shevardnadze approached the University of California, San Diego, with which Kaldor was affiliated. In 1987, the Armament Disarmament Information Unit at the University of Sussex and the Institute for Global Conflict and Cooperation of the University of California, San Diego, had begun coordinating a number of East-West seminars on armaments and arms control. Together, they assisted Moscow in organizing the conference. In principle, MGIMO elected three regions to participate: the Soviet Union, Europe, and the Americas. While Kaldor selected and organized the European delegation to the conference, James Kelly from the Institute for Global Conflict and Cooperation was responsible for the Americas.

For Kaldor, Europe included both East and West. One of the delegates was Geneviève Schméder. Schméder recalled,

> Mary was the one responsible for inviting Europeans . . . from both sides of the Iron Curtain. From the East side, there were all the dissidents, which after became famous, but at that time they were not, like Miszlivetz, and on the West side, Mient Jan. She invited Pierre Lellouche, who is very right wing, but a very clever person and a good specialist on security issues, et cetera, and me, who were the two French [representatives].[80]

Schméder recalled that the atmosphere of the Moscow seminar appeared in stark contrast to the final decades of the Cold War. Discussions between dissidents or nonofficial Westerners and Soviet officials, which would have been considered fantastical before, were now being conducted within an elite training center and at the homes of high-ranking officials from the Committee for State Security [Komitet gosudarstvennoy bezopasnosti; KGB]:

> So here we were in Moscow in June '89 discussing European security, and it was just crazy. It was just unbelievable! We had these discussions in the flat of the high official of the KGB, where Polish attendees were discussing what they think of the government. You had Lellouche improvising a German reunification in front of Russians, and Americans completely titillated. You had this Pakistan guy [Eqbal Ahmad] who was supposed to talk about the reverse picture of Afghanistan, so there was a morning or afternoon on Afghanistan. There was the Russian convenor who was the political commissioner in the Russian Embassy in Kabul at the time of the coup, which was the very beginning of the war—the first Afghan war. There was a meeting that I went to with Mary . . . where there was a minute of silence with everybody standing silently for one minute in memory of the last tsar [laughing].[81]

According to Kaldor, the meeting was an incredible opportunity for former dissidents and military officers alike from Eastern Europe to meet with MGIMO, but also with people in Gorbachev's administration. For example, Kaldor said that she contacted the Hungarian Foreign Ministry and requested that George Konrád and Miklós Haraszti as well as a Hungarian army officer attend the MGIMO conference, which required the Hungarian Embassy in Moscow to provide permission to MGIMO. Kaldor also invited Adam Michnik, which presented an enormous test for MGIMO and the Ministry of Foreign Affairs:

> And MGIMO said, "No way. We will never allow Adam Michnik to step inside this place," and I said "Look—" (It had just been after the elections where Solidarity and Adam Michnik had been elected as members of parliament.) And I said, "You know, he might be the next foreign minister of Poland." And they said, "We'll never allow him." It was the time George Bush [Sr.] was visiting Eastern Europe, and so Adam Michnik put out a press release saying he had cut short his meeting with Bush in order to attend an East-West seminar in Moscow. And so I said to them, "Look, if you don't allow him in, it's going to be all over the Western press, and you have been ordered by Shevardnadze to be open to the West, so you must allow him." So

> this went on and finally they agreed. They refused to send a car to the airport to meet him, so I went by taxi to the airport to meet him, and it was just a huge thing. . . . They had a huge press conference in Moscow and [Michnik] met with all the people around Gorbachev's [administration]. So it was actually really important in terms of legitimizing Solidarity.[82]

The Moscow seminar marked a shift in Schméder's thinking concerning the limits of the Cold War. Upon her return, Schméder reconsidered both the dynamics of the Cold War and the prospect of now collaborating with Kaldor, something that before had been out of the question for her:

> When we came back, we were really thrilled. We were really excited. I came back here to Paris saying, "The Cold War is over. The Cold War is over." And everybody said, "You poor, stupid . . ." And I said, "No, no, I'm talking seriously." But of course nobody took it seriously, and I was so infuriated and cross that I decided that now the time had come for me to work on this issue, because now things were completely changing. But in France it took years before people began to realize that. So I [began to] work with Mary and that was the beginning of our professional collaboration. . . . And we never stopped working together.[83]

The MGIMO seminar provided Kaldor and Schméder with just enough intellectual common ground to begin collaborating on their first project. The following year, they were awarded a commission by the United Nations University to start the program "Restructuring the Global Military Sector," a series of studies that would lay the groundwork for Kaldor's "new wars" thesis.

Notes

1. Dieter Esche, interview with author, 31 March 2011.
2. Mary Kaldor, Liaison Committee Report, 9 November 1984, PA-MK-END-LC/CP, London.
3. Ibid.
4. Mary Kaldor, memo to END Hungary Group and END Coordinating Committee: field notes of trip to Hungary, 17–26 October 1984, London School of Economics Archive, London, Catalogue of the Papers of European Nuclear Disarmament, END/12/6, London.
5. Ibid.; Mary Kaldor, memo to END Hungary Group: field notes of trip to Hungary, 10 May 1985, London School of Economics Archive END/12/6, London.
6. Chilton, "Mechanics of Change," p. 200.
7. E. P. Thompson, letter to the END Coordinating Committee, 9 February 1985, London School of Economics Archives END 3/9, London.
8. Ibid.
9. Patrick Burke, interview with author, 10 May 2011.
10. Paul Anderson, interview with author, 14 June 2011.
11. Ibid.
12. Patrick Burke, interview with author, 10 May 2011.

13. E. P. Thompson, letter to the END Coordinating Committee, 9 February 1985, London School of Economics Archives END 3/9, London.

14. Ibid.

15. Patrick Burke, interview with author, 10 May 2011.

16. Zdenek Kavan, interview with author, 1 July 2011.

17. Ibid.

18. Mary Kaldor, interview with author, 24 June 2011.

19. Ibid. Kaldor also remarked that she wanted to arrange her working life around her children: "I suppose the other thing that worried me was rushing around all the time and what impact that was having on the children. . . . I think I never traveled for more then about a week, occasionally a bit more than a week, and so I was never really away from the children for very long. . . . I think that was always my total priority. . . . I mean I notice now. . . . It's funny. Again, it's not something I ever said to myself, that children matter more than anything else. I realize now that the sacredness of my [day spent with my grandchild] is exactly how I felt about my children. I think it's just that it's such a pleasure, and it is the nicest thing in life actually. . . . They were so sweet, my little boys." Ibid.

20. Martin Albrow, interview with author, 8 June 2011.

21. Daniele Archibugi, interview with author, 22 June 2011.

22. Ibid.

23. Kaldor and Falk, *Dealignment*.

24. Kaldor, "Beyond the Blocs."

25. Kaldor and Falk, *Dealignment*, p. 13.

26. Kaldor, "The Atlantic Technology Culture," in Kaldor and Falk, *Dealignment*, p. 143.

27. Mary Kaldor, memo to END Hungary Group: field notes of trip to Hungary, 10 May 1985, London School of Economics Archive END/12/6, London.

28. Dieter Esche, interview with author, 31 March 2011.

29. David Petraeus, correspondence with author, 19 April 2011.

30. Chilton and Dienstbier, "The European Citizens' Assembly."

31. See Dienstbier, Šabata, and Kaldor, "The Helsinki Citizens' Assembly"; see also Jiři Dienstbier, "The Helsinki Process 'from Below,'" *END Journal* 37 (1989), insert; and Mary Kaldor, "Letter: Labour's Assistance to Its New Colleagues in Eastern Europe," *Independent* [London], 27 April 27 1990, p. 18..

32. Dienstbier, Kanturkova, and Sustrova, "The Prague Appeal." See also Jiři Dienstbier, Eva Kanturkova, and Petruska Sustrova, "Introduction: The Prague Appeal (Building a Peaceful Europe)," *END Journal* 15 (April–May 1985), p. 34.

33. Ibid.

34. Burke, *European Nuclear Disarmament*, p. 218.

35. Ibid., p. 169.

36. "Helsinki Memorandum: Giving Real Life to the Helsinki Accords," Network for East-West Dialogue, April 1987, PA-DE, Berlin.

37. Burke, *European Nuclear Disarmament*, p. 199.

38. US Helsinki Watch Committee, *Violations of the Helsinki Accords*, pp. i–iv.

39. Fleet, quoted in Burke, *European Nuclear Disarmament*, p. 194.

40. Coates, quoted in Burke, *European Nuclear Disarmament*, p. 194.

41. Burke, "European Nuclear Disarmament," p. 194.

42. Ibid.

43. Patrick Burke, "Report of Feb 14/15 1987 Liaison Committee Meeting," London School of Economics/END Archive, London.

44. Fiona Weir, "Liaison Committee Report, 23/4 May 1987 Coventry," London School of Economics/END Archive, London.

45. Ibid.
46. Kaldor, "From Gloom to Surprise," p. 21.
47. Burke, *European Nuclear Disarmament*, p. 137.
48. Neil Ascherson, "What Will Cop Blame Now?" *Sydney Morning Herald*, 20 September 1988, p. 17.
49. Kenney, *A Carnival of Revolution*, p. 115.
50. Romaszewski, quoted in Bloom, "Provoking Peace in Poland," p. 5.
51. Ibid., p. 5.
52. Kenney, *A Carnival of Revolution*, p. 140.
53. Ferenc Miszlivetz, interview with author, 18 February 2011.
54. "Hungarian Meeting a Success," p. 8.
55. Ibid., p. 8.
56. Kenney, *A Carnival of Revolution*, p. 140.
57. Sonja Licht, correspondence with author, 4 May 2010.
58. "Helsinki Citizens' Assembly, the European Civil Centre for Conflict Resolution," in International Helsinki Federation, files of the executive director, Open Society Archives 318-0-1, Box 3, Budapest.
59. Czechoslovak Helsinki Committee Prague, *Human Rights in Czechoslovakia*, US Helsinki Watch Committee, and the International Helsinki Federation for Human Rights, Washington, DC, and Vienna, March 1989, pp. 7–8.
60. Chilton, "Mechanisms of Change," p. 210.
61. Christopher Hitchens, quoted in McEwen, "Home Truths for Prague?"
62. Ibid.
63. Czechoslovak Helsinki Committee Prague, *Human Rights in Czechoslovakia*, p. 8.
64. Kenney, *A Carnival of Revolution*, p. 117.
65. Ibid.
66. "Helsinki Citizens' Assembly, the European Civil Centre for Conflict Resolution."
67. Chilton, "Mechanisms of Change," p. 210.
68. Timothy Garton Ash, quoted in Ascherson, "What Will Cop Blame Now?" p. 17.
69. Mary Kaldor, interview with author, 24 June 2011.
70. Ferenc Miszlivetz, interview with author, 18 February 2011.
71. Mary Kaldor, "Closing Session of the Helsinki Citizens' Assembly," speech presented at the Founding Session of the Helsinki Citizens' Assembly 19–21 October, Prague, 21 October 1990, PA-MK-HCA-Brighton.
72. HCA, Helsinki Citizens' Assembly Founding Document, Prague, 1990, http://www.hyd.org.tr/?pid=180.
73. Kaldor, quoted in Wittner, *Confronting the Bomb*, pp. 406–407.
74. Kaldor, "Closing Session of the Helsinki Citizens Assembly."
75. George Papandreou, Jr., "Panel on the Influence of the Ideas of 1989 on Foreign Policy," paper presented at "Ideas of 1989," Centre for Global Governance, London School of Economics, 2000, online.
76. Ibid.
77. Ibid.
78. Burke, *European Nuclear Disarmament*, p. 217.
79. On MGIMO, see, for example, Tickner and Wæver, *International Relations Scholarship Around the World*; also see Ilyumzhinov et al., *Articles on Moscow State Institute of International Relations*.
80. Geneviève Schméder, interview with author, 1 June 2011.
81. Ibid.
82. Mary Kaldor, interview with author, 11 May 2011.
83. Geneviève Schméder, interview with author, 1 June 2011.

8

The Problem of Intervention to Stop War

> *I joined the Caravan of Peace, and we went to Armenia. I always feel Mary's shelter. . . . I remember it was dangerous for me. If they tried to shoot me, and they missed, they could have shot her, but she was courageous. I was sitting by Mary on the bus. [The paramilitary] stopped our bus . . . [during] a time when there is a lot of unofficial troops. So it was a danger. [The paramilitary] became very angry, and they entered the bus, and they thought they may take me from there. Mary laughed and Mary talked with them, just to distract their attention from me. . . . [Then], the soldiers went back off the bus. After that I saw Mary's face: she was as white as a ghost, because she was afraid for me.*[1]

AS THE COLD WAR DREW TO A CLOSE, EUPHORIA SWEPT ACROSS THE former Soviet Bloc and US alliance states alike, renewing hopes for a more peaceful and secure world order. Mikhail Gorbachev's speech to the UN General Assembly served as a pretext for this optimism: "Today, further world progress is possible only through a search for universal human consensus as we move forward to a new world order. . . . The idea of democratizing the entire world order has become a powerful socio-political force."[2] President George H. W. Bush opined that the end of the Cold War marked the "new partnership of nations" and a "historic period of cooperation," during which a "new world order can emerge. A *new* era: freer from the threat of terror, stronger in the pursuit of justice, and more secure in the quest for peace."[3] In *The End of History and the Last Man,* Frances Fukuyama concluded that the new world order would see a universal shift by states toward embracing liberal democracy, as no other political system now stood to contest this change.[4]

The fall of the Berlin Wall also spurred the very real possibilities for greater European unification. Hans-Dietrich Genscher, then West German foreign minister, declared that German unification would serve to "heal a deep wound, namely the division of Europe."[5] Inspired by Jean Monnet, a political economist who supported European integration, Valéry Giscard d'Estaing, former president of France, and Helmut Schmidt, former chancellor of West Germany, maintained that the Franco-German axis had already played a critical role in advancing European unification. Therefore, d'Estaing and Schmidt asserted, "we do believe that, at the beginning of an entirely new era in Europe, France and Germany must act jointly to overcome the dangers and to seize the opportunities as they did daringly through the pooling of resources in the 1950s."[6] Indeed, the European Parliament declared that "in the spirit of the Helsinki Final Act, all the peoples of Europe . . . are entitled, both now and in future, to live in security within their present borders."[7]

Kaldor was optimistic about the future of Europe, yet she also voiced concern. In 1990, Kaldor conveyed her enthusiasm for the unification of Europe in the *New Left Review*: "Everyone now agrees that unification is inevitable. It is already taking place at the level of society."[8] But she was not entirely positive: "What is taking place, in the aftermath of 1989, is a political struggle for the future of Europe." She questioned "on whose terms" unification would be negotiated.[9] Moreover, as capitalism was increasingly interpreted as the winning ideological force after the fall of communism, Kaldor warned that "the 1990s may well go down in history as the moment when Europe (and the world) took the wrong direction because of a commitment to capitalist orthodoxy."[10] Kaldor conceded that socialism had, in many respects, been discredited, but she argued that socialist ideals, such as Fabian principles of egalitarianism and social justice, along with liberal ideas advanced by John Maynard Keynes, were being wrongly eclipsed by the perceived supremacy of capitalism. Just as importantly, she argued, no space had been left to debate the limitations and failings of capitalism:

> [Socialism] does contain the notion of a strategy for social justice, a method of social organization that replaces capitalism. Because socialists failed to address the problem of state power, the portrayal of statist forms of economic organization as "socialist" does have some truth. And yet, the absence of an appropriate word with which to pursue the goals of material equality and economic democracy, the absence of a framework within which to discuss problems of ownership and control, uneven development and social policy leaves a vacuum. These concerns will become ever more important in the coming years and we need to be able to conceptualize and articulate them.[11]

Fred Halliday, one of Kaldor's contemporaries when studying at Oxford University, was vastly less optimistic than Kaldor. In the same issue of the *New Left Review*, Halliday maintained that, although both sides of the former Iron Curtain proclaimed the end of the Cold War and that the world was "entering an epoch of greater security," in reality, new dangers lay ahead:

> The least that can be said is that if we are to return to a pre-1914 world then there are some obvious dangers. It was that world of inter-capitalist conflict undistracted by the existence of a socialist rival that gave rise to decades of colonial plunder and the great war itself. . . . Indeed if one of the hallmarks of the late 1980s has been the ending of cold war, the other has been the resurgence of nationalist sentiment.[12]

Although Halliday and Kaldor were both critical of the left for their ambivalence toward authoritarianism in Soviet and Eastern blocs, they held vastly different views on the dynamics of the Cold War. As Stephen Howe, professor of history at Bristol University, later maintained, the difference between Kaldor and Halliday "reflected Fred's greater tendency . . . to see the Cold War as a genuine and profound clash of ideologies and social systems, as opposed to Kaldor's view of the superpowers as having the rather similar and in important ways complementary aim of dividing the world between them and shutting out any 'third-way' option."[13] Furthermore, although both were skeptical of the role capitalism could play in delivering a new world order, Halliday was the first to recognize the resurgence of chauvinist nationalism.

Kaldor's initial euphoria began to dissolve in the face of the First Gulf War.[14] In August 1990, Saddam Hussein invaded Kuwait with 120,000 troops and 850 tanks, resulting in the UN commitment to military intervention and sanction during Operation Desert Storm.[15] The newly formed HCA was divided on the subject of intervention in Iraq. Many of the Czech members supported military intervention and drew parallels to Munich in 1938. Conversely, some were adamantly against war in the Gulf, including members from France, Britain, and Hungary, as well as Kaldor herself. Kaldor argued, "To be against war (as I was) meant coming to terms with the uncomfortable fact that without war, sanctions may not have worked and the Kuwaitis might have continued to suffer occupation, torture and execution."[16] Yet Kaldor also conceded at the time that "to be for war, meant condoning the terrible slaughter of thousands of Iraqis, the disintegration of Iraq and Kuwait, the legitimation of military methods, the economic costs, and above all, the new political divisions."[17]

Kaldor also questioned the social organization of violence against Iraq, presented as a state of exception in which liberal discussion between state and society was suspended or marginalized. In the United Kingdom, Kaldor argued, politicians led the discussion on war in Iraq, and opposition in Parliament was thinly debated or sidelined altogether. Media debates failed to include the views of ordinary people on if, or how, intervention should be conducted. Moreover, Kaldor argued, Western foreign policy toward Iraq appeared, at best, inconsistent: not only had the West failed to condemn Saddam Hussein's aggression toward Iran, but Western leaders had, in fact, supported Iraq in its final years of the Iran-Iraq War. Furthermore, the West did not introduce sanctions against Iraq when it used chemical weapons against both Iranians and the country's own Kurdish population.[18] Just as importantly, Kaldor maintained, war dangerously oversimplified politics:

> [War] reduces complex political situations to a zero-sum game, good versus bad, our side versus their side, democracy versus barbarism. Those who oppose this war, whether they like it or not, are at worst identified with barbarism and, at best, accused of naivety, of not understanding the true nature of Saddam Hussein's rule of fear. . . . To take into account people and not just states, to think about the future of democracy in the Middle East as a whole, then it may turn out that the simple good-bad characterization is something we shall deeply regret for decades to come. . . . Democracy can never be imposed. In the end it was the peoples of Eastern Europe who overthrew their governments, not Western military might. If we are really serious about democracy, the most we can do is to act consistently to further the cause of democracy and self-determination. . . . If this war goes on to the bitter end, then [we] have a responsibility to explore the full consequences of what is happening, to try to understand the world from different perspectives, the perspective of ordinary people and their actual experiences, not the abstractions of right and wrong personified in states.[19]

Closer to home, Kaldor argued, prospects for greater European integration were also marked by new divisions within—and in some instances disintegration of—the state. Czechoslovakia had divided into two nation-states, the Soviet Union was collapsing, and Albania had descended into anarchy, causing the mass exodus of around 18,000 refugees mainly to Bari, in southern Italy.[20] At the same time, the rise of violent nationalism in Yugoslavia and the Caucasus threatened to engulf those regions in war.[21] These latter conflicts would increasingly consume her activist work and, in turn, become the focus for her scholarship.

Campaigns in the Balkans

After thirty-five years of peace in Yugoslavia, Josip Broz Tito died in 1980, ending his long and controversial career as head of state. On his death, President Jimmy Carter said, "During that period he and his peoples faced many challenges, but met them with a resolute determination to maintain Yugoslavia's independence and unity, and its own unique approach to domestic and foreign policies."[22] Tito had been celebrated for his ability to maintain so many disparate republics within the one nation-state.

However, by 1990 some within Yugoslavia were negatively comparing Tito with "Lenin, Stalin, Nicolae Ceausescu and other longtime icons of European communism."[23] Sonja Licht, a member of HCA who was based in Belgrade, maintained that, rather than resolve ethnic tensions, the Tito regime had engendered a "totalitarian state of mind."[24] Following Tito's death, the 1980s saw Yugoslavia experience declining financial power, widened social insecurity, and increased political violence.[25] Despite all that was happening, still many never expected war in Yugoslavia. Gwynne Dyer, military historian formally at the Royal Military Academy Sandhurst, confidently declared that "nobody is going to let the shiny new Europe be spoiled by an ugly civil war in the Balkans."[26]

When Kaldor and Licht took over as cochairs of the HCA in 1991, they believed that the idea of a united and peaceful Europe had become untenable.[27] Yet both believed that HCA could still play an important role in Europe. Licht suggested that the "main role" of the HCA "was to promote citizens to get involved in European affairs; the main goal was . . . to integrate Europe from below, meaning for citizens to have a say" in the future of Europe.[28]

For Kaldor, if peace, human rights, and democracy were to be developed in Europe, then new types of political arrangements had to be introduced. In an article for the HCA newsletter, Kaldor wrote that despite the difficulties confronting European civil society, events in the Balkans were not predetermined, and the HCA still had an important role in influencing the outcome of political events.[29] Although social contracts were still required between state and society in the form of traditional nation-based political organizations, she continued, they needed to be supplemented by new international institutions such as the Commission on Security and Cooperation in Europe, the European Community, or the Council of Europe to guarantee human rights, to regulate economic and ecological cooperation, and to provide a common security policy. Yet the legitimacy of these institutions relied upon the "existence of a horizontal civil society, a genuine transnational political culture."[30] Kaldor therefore concluded that the "challenge for HCA" was to "try to construct that political culture, to preserve shared human values against the onslaught of new fundamentalisms and particularisms, to discuss and develop creative ideas about Europe's future."[31] With the fragmentation of Yugoslavia viewed largely by HCA members as inevitable, they saw civil society and politics from below as more important then ever to curtail the slide into nationalism and ethnic division.

Not everyone was as optimistic about the role HCA could play in solving European security problems. Jaroslav Šabata, HCA member and former Charter 77 dissident, maintained that the HCA could be a good way to support the development of civil society in countries where civil society was endangered or underdeveloped. Concurring with Kaldor, Šabata maintained that HCA was not, strictly speaking, a section of civil society. Rather it was one project that could "facilitate the change from an 'immature' civil society to a 'mature' one."[32] Šabata observed, "The image of the HCA itself as a part of civil society can lead to overestimating its possibilities."[33] Irrespective of their differing views, HCA members saw the value of supporting civil society to counter the populist politics and nationalist divisions curtailing the possibilities for a pluralist and democratic society.

The HCA in Belgrade

As political violence in the Balkans increased, HCA members responded by attempting a series of grassroots public campaigns. In their open letter entitled "Yugoslavia Needs Help from Outside," Licht and Kaldor denounced the use of military armored units by Yugoslav federal police, who had fired at civilians demonstrating at Terazije Square in Belgrade on 9 March 1991.[34] While Belgrade sought to declare a national state of emergency, which the other republics rejected, Belgrade officials maintained that the military's role was to restore peace. During the course of the week, knowing which civilian authority ultimately commanded the military became increasingly difficult.[35]

European and Western governments should, Kaldor and Licht pleaded, denounce political violence and support a peaceful and democratic process.[36] They argued that the demonstration was "in favour of democracy" and that "democratisation cannot be based on tanks and guns."[37] The demonstration had included students of Belgrade University, Serbian opposition parties, and the ordinary citizens of Belgrade who, they argued, demanded an end to government ownership of Serbian media by the Socialist Party of Serbia, particularly TV Belgrade and Politika Publishing House.[38]

With a network as wide as the former END convention process and the ENEWD,[39] the HCA consortium of members began writing letters to newspapers, conducting public meetings and conferences, and lobbying their governments and European ministries to apply political pressure on the Yugoslav republics to seek a political solution and to support debates on nonofficial levels.[40]

Yugoslav activists had played a key role in the ENEWD in the 1980s. They had supported Eastern European dissidents in the lead-up to the nonviolent revolutions and were involved in the preparatory stage of the HCA. Indeed, the first press conference announcing HCA's Founding Assembly was in Ljubljana, Slovenia.[41] Like their Eastern European counterparts during the 1980s, the Yugoslav branch of the HCA began to garner support from other activists and groups, both within the Balkans and internationally. In May 1991 an HCA collective was established in Sarajevo, and by the start of June, seventeen other HCA offices had been established in cities across Yugoslavia.[42] To encourage further debate from below, HCA conducted press conferences in seventeen cities throughout Yugoslavia in the same month in order to foster solidarity between national, religious, and ethnic groups.[43] Similarly, to encourage international solidarity and public debate, a series of meetings and conferences were organized across Europe and the United States, in cities such as London, Kiev, New York, Bratislava, Athens, Prague, Padua, and Paris.

Kaldor finally concluded that the collapse of Yugoslavia could not be stopped, not even with international intervention; instead, protecting and supporting civil society were of utmost importance. In an article in the

Guardian, Kaldor argued that only at the civil society level could the Balkan republics survive the crisis of fragmentation through a demand for political responsibility and the "development of a more profound sense of what it means to be a citizen," rather than the current superficial sense of citizenship based on ethnicity.[44]

The support of civil society became more challenging as military activities escalated. As the Yugoslav federal army moved troops and artillery forces toward the Slovenian border in late June 1991, Licht telephoned Kaldor from Belgrade to discuss her concerns but also to discuss what actions could be taken by HCA. Having already scheduled an HCA leadership meeting the following week in Romania, they decided to move the meeting to Belgrade and to invite additional participants so as to reflect a plurality of views from across all the Yugoslav republics and across the globe.[45]

As one of the first large scale meetings in Europe on the subject of the disintegration of Yugoslavia, the aim of the emergency HCA conference was to debate the implications of the fragmentation of Yugoslavia, to develop strategies for political plurality and greater European integration, and to discuss the very serious possibility of a protracted war in the Balkans. The event, entitled "Disintegration of Yugoslavia—Integration of Europe," was conducted on 5–7 July 1991 in Belgrade, a week after Licht's initial phone call to Kaldor. Over 150 participants attended from all over Yugoslavia but also from other countries such as Germany, Italy, Great Britain, and Hungary.

As cochairs, Kaldor and Licht led participants in debates about nationalism, civil society, and international intervention. The key question was, what could HCA do to stymie the escalation of violent tensions? Participants included grassroots activist groups, such as IKV, and famous dissidents such as Adam Michnik and Milovan Đjilas, the latter being the former vice president of the Yugoslav Federal Republic, expelled from the party in 1954 and later imprisoned for criticizing what he considered a corrupt and privileged regime.[46] Given the limitations of civil society in the Balkans, HCA members saw supporting grassroots politics as key. George Papandreou, an HCA member and future prime minister of Greece, pointed out the "weak fabric of NGOs in the Balkan countries due to the authoritarian regimes that have existed for so many years. We are called to develop such structures from the bottom up. A Balkan conference would not only be a forum for discussing the problems facing the Balkans, but focus on strengthening non-governmental structures."[47]

Prior to the HCA conference, the European Community troika, consisting of Luxembourg foreign minister Jacques Poos, Italian foreign minister Gianni De Michelis, and Dutch foreign minister Hans van der Broek, met with Yugoslav officials in an attempt to halt the political violence. Slovenia and Croatia had both conducted referendums for independence on 23 December 1990 and 19 May 1991, respectively, and, on 25 June 1991, Slovenia abruptly declared its independence, provoking Belgrade to reject the declaration and begin mobilizing its armed forces to secure the Slovenian border.[48] The troika left Yugoslavia empty-handed. At the same time, Austria sent several thousand troops to its southern border and requested an explanation for the "extraordinary military activities," which included the apparent violation of Austrian airspace by the Yugoslav Air Force. Austria also requested a meeting at the Conflict Prevention Centre of the Commission on Security and Cooperation in Europe to convey its concerns.

Determined to resolve a European problem with European diplomacy, the European Community troika members got back on the plane to Belgrade to secure a final peace agreement with its Yugoslav partners. En route to the Balkans, Jacques Poos quipped, "This is the hour of Europe. . . . It is not the hour of the Americans."[49] On 30 June 1991, the troika arrived in Yugoslavia, and this time triumphantly secured their cease-fire agreement.[50]

Several days prior to their conference, HCA members were keen to explain the dynamics of political violence and their concerns for what they believed was just the start of a terrifying and enduring war and, to that end, requested a meeting with the troika in Belgrade. The troika declined their invitation. No less then two days after the European Community's troika departed from Belgrade, the cease-fire was broken. On 2 July 1991, the Jugoslovenska Narodna Armija (Yugoslav People's Army) bombed the Slovenian city of Ljubljana and other regions of Solvenia, particularly Krško. War had begun.[51]

While war raged in Slovenia, the HCA conference, chaired by Licht and Kaldor, continued in Belgrade as a series of heated debates. Warning of the dangers of associating culture and ethnicity with borders, Ernest Gellner, the British-Czech professor of social anthropology at the University of Cambridge, argued that the unqualified pursuit of self-determination through the exercise of force would represent a "tidying-up of the ethnic map."[52] However, former dissident Adam Michnik maintained that there was "no difference between communism with a xenophobic face and anticommunism with a Bolshevik face."[53] Conversely, Marko Hren, of the independent Ljubljana Peace Group and a coauthor of the Helsinki Memorandum in the 1980s, insisted that there was indeed "a difference—not judging but differentiating—between Slobodan Milošević, Franjo Tuđman and Milan Kučan."[54] Hren also argued, "One can't just throw them all in the same basket."[55] From still another angle, Montenegrin-born Milovan Đjilas argued that the impending war was not so much a war between Yugoslav citizens as a war between its "ruling nationalist elites."[56] Moreover, Đjilas delivered a prescient warning of what lay ahead, particularly for BaH:

> That war would not only be a war between the states, it would also be a religious war, especially in Bosnia and Herzegovina. The radical groups, which are tolerated by the [Yugoslav] legal authorities, would cause massacres on a

> large scale. Internationalization of the conflict cannot be avoided, the uprising of Albanians in Kosovo would bring Albania into it, while the Muslim countries would assist Bosnia.[57]

The HCA also debated the politics of international political and military intervention in the Yugoslav conflict. Although many within the HCA viewed the disintegration of Yugoslavia as unavoidable, they argued that, at the very least, separation should be administered nonviolently and that each of the republics should show support for multiethnic civil society. The breakup of Yugoslavia therefore required a negotiated, democratic process, they argued, such as was seen during the Velvet Revolution and other negotiated revolutions in Eastern Europe. Some HCA members, who were pacifists, were adamantly against a military intervention.

The HCA's approach was to support the resolution of the conflict by political means. Encouraging former Yugoslavians to resist political violence and highlighting the need for political intervention from external government actors became, broadly speaking, the initial focus of the HCA.[58] Licht argued that Yugoslavia must, therefore, "be dissolved in a civilised way."[59] Dušan Janjić, a lawyer and coordinator of the Forum for Ethnic Relations in Belgrade, maintained that the departure of Slovenia and Croatia out of the Yugoslav federation represented the "first violent change of borders since the Helsinki Accords."[60]

Conversely, others argued that the time had come to take sides and to use military force. According to Tomaz Mastnak, a coauthor of the Helsinki Memorandum, Serbia was the aggressor, and force was required to stop the Yugoslav People's Army. Mastnak asserted that an anti-Serbian position "was the only, at least consistent, anti-war position I can imagine. There is no symmetry between Serbia and Croatia; they are anything but [in] an equal position. To condemn all violence is therefore fallacious; it means siding with the aggressor."[61] In direct reply to Mastnak, Mient Jan Faber argued that to view Serbia as a solitary aggressor supported an invalid assumption, which is to accept the self-determination of Croatia (and other republics) predicated on the idea that statehood should be defined on the basis of a purified ethnicity. In so doing, Faber argued, Mastnak was effectively saying, "It is acceptable to declare the right of self-determination for an ethnic group even if the territory is inhabited by a mixed population. To be sure it is the federal army, backed by Milosevic, that is shelling towns and villages in Croatia, but the *casus belli* was the conflict between Croatia and the Serbian minority."[62]

Possibly the most ominous forewarning came from Zdravko Grebo, then professor of law at the University of Sarajevo. Consistent with Đjilas's view, Grebo maintained that the disintegration of Yugoslavia would also spur a division within, and the disintegration of, BaH as a republic. An ensuing war in BaH, he concluded starkly, would be "hell."[63] Licht remembered that at the end of the conference, they composed a message:

> Mary was as usual the principal author of that statement, and the first sentence of the statement started with "the disintegration of Yugoslavia may prove to be a major challenge for the integration of Europe," which of course proved to be true. This is the paradox: . . . the politicians pretended that things can be business as usual, [and] it is enough to come and to visit and to discuss a little bit. . . . And there was us, who were representing civil society [groups] sending a completely different message, in fact sending a panicked message saying, "Look this is serious. One has to do something very, very seriously here."[64]

A number of initiatives emerged from the HCA emergency meeting in Belgrade, but three key ones would play an important role in forming Kaldor's experiences of war and her later conceptualization of it. The first was the emergence of the *Yugofax* publication established in September 1991. The initial idea was to send civic observers from the HCA to areas of potential conflict, to bear witness to military activities and political violence, and then to publish the observations as weekly monitoring reports for both a Yugoslav and wider international audience. Initially, Licht and her husband coordinated the monitor reports via a fax machine from their home in Belgrade.[65]

Yugofax became a formal publication, with the aim being both to provide a cross section of views from across Yugoslavia to counter the notion that all Yugoslavians were nationalists and ethnically divided and also to raise awareness of the violence and political unravelling occurring on the ground.[66] At a time when information and the media were controlled by the Yugoslavian state, *Yugofax* was viewed as a type of "citizen monitoring" system to counter the government's nationalist propaganda and to provide some level of transparency and accountability.[67] *Yugofax* gave a voice not only to formal members of the HCA but also to nonmembers whose views were marginalized in the Serbian press, such as Natasa Kandic, the Serbian human rights activist and founder of the Humanitarian Law Centre.[68] Later *Yugofax* became the *Balkan War Report* and then finally a formal organization, the Institute for War and Peace Reporting, which still exists today.

The second initiative was the Peace Caravan, also called Citizens for Peace. Beginning on 25 September 1991, 400 activists started a four-day march from Trieste, Italy, and Skopje, Macedonia, traveling through Croatia, Vojvodina, Serbia, and BaH. From the very beginning, those in the Peace Caravan faced a difficult trek, as political tensions were running high. As they passed through Rijeka in western Croatia, for example, houses were garrisoned with sandbags, and placards were directed at the group, warning, "Traitors, Out of Croatia."[69] Arriving in Sarajevo on 29 September, 10,000 people formed a human chain around a mosque, Orthodox church, Catholic church, and synagogue. The Peace Caravan demanded an "immediate ceasefire, a peaceful solution through negotiations, the right of civil society to intervene to protect human rights, the right of resistance to laws that violate human rights, including the right of soldiers to desert, and respect for the right of self-determination."[70] The group included local activists from all the republics of Yugoslavia, peace activists from across Europe, and members of the European Parliament.

Although the Peace Caravan appeared enthusiastic and determined, no one really had any illusions that the war would stop. Vedran Vucic, an activist from Split, Croatia, working with the HCA, suggested, "No-one imagined the caravan could stop the war. . . . But the goal was not just to hear everyone say the same thing. The caravan was symbolic of the idea that it is possible to oppose the war."[71] Similarly, Licht maintained that the main idea of these initiatives, including *Yugofax* and the Peace Caravan, was to change the narrative increasingly driven by nationalists to divide the federation but also to persuade Yugoslavs to devise political rather than violent solutions. Licht explained that those participating hoped "to convince the citizens of Yugoslavia to endure in their anti-war activities. . . . We were also hoping to generate more genuine interest in the outside world for the dangerous developments unfolding in the Balkans."[72] Kaldor later recalled: "I think the key importance of the caravan was that it established a network of activists that was extremely important during the war, both in offering solidarity as well as developing ideas and proposals."[73]

The third initiative that informed Kaldor's thinking in relation to civil society and organized violence was the role of peace zones, peace areas, and safe zones, a subject that will be explored in Chapter 10.

Wars of the South Caucasus

Unlike in the Balkans, many of the contacts in the South Caucasus were made after the launch of HCA. Following the attendance of several activists from Georgia, Armenia, and Azerbaijan at an HCA meeting in Moscow in 1991, HCA began to consider broadening participation to all the South Caucasus. With the assistance of Svetlana Gannushkina, a veteran human rights activist and Russian dissident from Memorial, a Russian historical and human rights society,[74] additional activists from the South Caucasus were identified, and the group Transcaucasus Dialogue was officially started at HCA's second convention in Bratislava in March 1992. Soon after, HCA committees in Armenia, Georgia, Azerbaijan, and Nagorno-Karabakh established their own HCA offices in the region, and those offices worked closely with the HCA offices in Turkey, which were established by Murat Belge, a Turkish journalist and activist.[75] Among the new collective was Anahit Bayandur and Natalya Martirosyan, activists from Armenia; Arzu Abdullayeva and Bashir Safaroglu, from Azerbaijan; Alexander (Sasha) Rusetsky, from Georgia; and Karen Ohanjanyan, an activist from Nagorno-Karabakh and founding member of the revolutionary Karabakh Committee.[76]

Just as the wars in the South Caucasus ignited in 1992, Kaldor and Faber were invited by the new HCA Caucasus collective to conduct a field trip to the region. Arriving in Tbilisi, Georgia, on 8 August 1992, the HCA members hoped to raise international awareness of the ensuing wars across the South Caucasus and to provide support for the local HCA activists. In support of the new HCA offices, they embarked on a series of Peace Caravans around the South Caucasus, groups that included activists from each of the South Caucasus states, including Nagorno-Karabakh, traveling around the region by bus or helicopter together, holding press conferences, and consulting government officials in an act of solidarity. The HCA members' visit to the region coincided with the week that Eduard Shevardnadze, then acting Georgian head of state, launched the invasion of Abkhazia, and Azerbaijan ordered troops into Armenia. As in the Balkans, HCA activists were concerned about the rise of ethnic nationalism in the region.

Initially, Kaldor's response to war in the South Caucasus was a sense of unreality and confusion about the objectives of those waging the war, aptly reflected in her field notes. She recorded that at a dinner, Faber gave a toast, announcing that he could not understand the war. In reply an Armenian officer, dressed in a makeshift green and white uniform and sneakers, sitting beside Kaldor, answered, "We, none of us, understand this war."[77] She described her feelings:

> [There] is a pervasive sense of unreality. I often had the disturbing feeling that we were war tourists—rich, larger than life Westerners, who fly in for a week and then return to their nice clean, well-stocked safe homes. . . . It didn't occur to any of us, I think, to be afraid when we flew back from Nagorno-Karabakh with the wounded in a helicopter as darkness fell and bombing began. It was only when we saw the relief on the faces of our friends when we got back that we knew.[78]

A key issue that Kaldor became aware of when she arrived in Baku, Azerbaijan, was the hostage situation. According to Arzu Abdullayeva, another HCA activist, hundreds of Armenians and Azerbaijanis had been taken hostage by various paramilitary factions and exchanged for weapons and rations.[79] These exchanges included the bodies of the deceased. The discussion within the Azerbaijan HCA was a pragmatic one: the war had grown so complicated that the scope of their strategies was limited to activities that would serve to de-escalate the war rather then halt it. Both Abdullayeva and Sasha Rusetsky believed that HCA could play a role in facilitating the release of hostages as one such method of de-escalation.

Thereafter, one of the meeting's outcomes was for Mary Kaldor and Radha Kumar, the Executive Director of HCA in Prague, to write a letter on behalf of the group to both the Azerbaijan and Armenian presidents and to Georgia's Shevardnadze requesting support for their strategy for the hostages, and calling for the immediate unqualified unilateral cease-fire and release of hostages on all sides. They hoped if everyone agreed to release the hostages, the cycle would be broken whereby hostages were taken as a way of negotiating the release of the other side's hostages. In the Kazakh-Echevan region on their way to Armenia, the caravan scouted out a particular KGB officer, well known for hostage exchange negotiation, who made an impression on Kaldor:

> Within minutes, he arrived in person—a caricature of an agent—small and dark, lean and fit, not an ounce of fat, fatigues, gun and green sunglasses. At first, he was reluctant to answer questions. We pressed him to help us, to release Alimov's son or, if he had no power, to mediate for us. We gave moralistic speeches about the awfulness of the practise of exchanging hostages. Eventually he revealed that he was negotiating a deal involving ten families. . . . Alimov's son was part of the deal and could be released on Monday. As he became more forthcoming, he explained that all the hostages were kept by separate families not by the Armenian authorities. The only power he had was to act as mediator. He had a list of 429 hostages he was negotiating deals for. While we talked to him, ten more names were added. One of the strangest things at the dinner was to see Arzu, Sasha and the KGB officer closeted together exchanging names of hostages.[80]

Arriving in Stepanakert, the de facto capital of the self-declared state of Nagorno-Karabakh, Kaldor and the HCA team attempted to engage with activists as well as government officials and the militia to discuss ways of mitigating the violence. While in Stepanakert, Kaldor met with Nagorno-Karabakh's prime minister, deputy prime minister, the chair of the Commission for Human Rights, and members of the Karabakh Committee, a "group of intellectuals recognized by many Armenians as their *de facto* leaders," largely seen as responsible for starting the war between Armenia and Azerbaijan.[81] The prime minister was dismissed from his post the following Saturday. Kaldor also observed how war legitimized particular actors through the use of political violence to form an army. For example, Kaldor met with Serzh Sargsyan, Nagorno-Karabakh's chief of security and later president of Armenia. According to Kaldor, he maintained that he was "trying to create a regular army and that this was much easier now that there is 'real war.' In a real war with tanks and helicopters, formerly independent military forces are willing to join together."[82] While Kaldor was on the tarmac with injured soldiers awaiting medical airlift back to Yerevan, Karen Ohanjanyan, a former member of the Karabakh Committee, was asked, "Do you regret having founded the Karabakh Committee?" Ohanjanyan replied, "Don't ask me now. Ask me when the war is over."[83]

For Kaldor, as could be expected from her relationships with dissidents during the 1980s, the political and personal were intertwined. The HCA chairs in each of the republics across the South Caucasus felt Kaldor and Faber to be their "friend," along with many others in the HCA network.[84] Moreover, HCA activists felt that all the HCA members expected and enjoyed debate, and Kaldor and Faber took them seriously as equal partners.[85] In particular, members of the HCA in the South Caucasus reported that Kaldor would not allow others to address them disrespectfully.

This protective approach also extended to how other activists treated the new members of HCA's South Caucasus branches. For example, after the 1992 South Caucasus trip, Peter Jarman, former member of END and the Quaker Peace and Service, wrote his own report, which he intended to circulate to all the relevant HCA people involved, and which was rather critical of activists in the HCA from the South Caucasus. In her response, Kaldor wrote a letter to Jarman, maintaining that she felt him to be patronizing and judgmental and that his words further fueled antagonism among the South Caucasus HCA members. Indeed, Kaldor told Jarman:

> I asked you to chair the final sessions both because I felt you had been rather left out and I wanted to give you a more central role. The problem was that you treated the people present not as citizens trying to work together, but as official parties to a conflict which you were trying to negotiate. . . . You kept steering the discussion towards their disagreements about the causes of the conflict instead of just letting them talk. What they wanted to talk about was the positive things they could do together. Radha and I, in fact, restrained ourselves from interrupting. . . . The same misunderstanding applies to the meeting with Shevardnadze. The HCA people in all three republics had requested that we put their projects to Shevardnadze. . . . Both Anahit [from Armenia] and Arzu [from Azerbaijan] were thrilled by what we said at the meeting with Shevardnadze. . . . You may not have appreciated how incredibly difficult [it] is to be responsible for a very diverse group of people, in a dangerous situation. . . . Let me know if you plan to circulate [your report] as I should like them to see this letter as well.[86]

Abdullayeva suggested that Kaldor's concerns extended to Abdullayeva's personal safety within an authoritarian regime. Much later, when the Azerbaijan government began to crack down on dissidents, Abdullayeva argued that the international HCA network and, in particular, her relationship with Kaldor became critical to her personal survival. She later reflected:

> Why I say she is really a friend is because you know our situation in our country, not only in Azerbaijan, . . . but in the world where conflict exists. . . . People live under a big threat. . . . There was a situation when I started to be persecuted in this country because of my Armenia-Azerbaijan relations. . . . It was a difficult time. . . . I could even be kidnapped—there was an attempt to do this. . . . Once our office got a fax from the United Kingdom Embassy telling me that [Foreign Secretary] Jack Straw "shared his concern about the persecution of Arzu Abdullayeva, and we give all our support to this human rights and peace activist." He had asked our government to "take care of this person" . . . of me! I was so surprised. . . . Jack Straw asked about me! I am a simple person here, somewhere far away. So I immediately think, this is

> something Mary did! . . . And she didn't say anything. . . . No, she just did it. . . . It's a guarantee in some ways that they will not kill me.[87]

Yet these interactions reflected Kaldor's attempts not only to manage and negotiate complex environments but also to act on a multiplicity of levels. To move between confident international diplomat and humble ally permitted Kaldor greater access, both from the top down as well as from below. Having worked closely with Kaldor since the 1980s, Faber believed that Kaldor's approach mirrored her parents' politics: "On the one hand, like her father, very cosmopolitan. . . . And on the other hand, there is her mother who was down to earth. And she moves in between them—she moves from one side to another side—all the time. That's my experience with her. And that makes it *interesting*."[88] From Kaldor's perspective, her style of engagement did reflect her family milieu to some extent: "The point is that my mother's politics were very grassroots, and my father was much more engaged with the political elite. And I have always tried to do both."[89]

Upon her return to the United Kingdom, Kaldor's engagement as an activist during the war in the Caucasus triggered a shift in her thinking toward the legitimacy of international intervention. On one hand, traditional notions of conventional war were conceptually linked to clear political objectives. On the other, Kaldor viewed war as the fundamental absence of genuine political debate and more legitimate democratic forms of politics, such as politics from below. In the case of the wars in the South Caucasus, Kaldor was disturbed that liberal political debate was stifled, but more concerning to her was the absence of clear political objectives. Kaldor observed, "War is organised. It is an activity of states with definable political goals. It can be ended by political solutions. This is disorganised, endemic and pervasive. This part of the post-Communist world is characterised not so much by freedom but by free for all, not by democracy and markets but by a kind of laissez-faire violence."[90]

Kaldor found extraordinary the fact that no one seemed to have anticipated the consequences of the breakdown of the communist system. Introducing democracy into societies that had never experienced multiple political parties, free association, social movements, or even political debate now appeared ambitious and naive, at best. Indeed, free elections, in and of themselves, could not produce nor constitute a liberal participatory democracy. In the absence of civil society and the rule of law and during a state's descent into unmitigated violence, intervening by force may, Kaldor argued, be required:

> There have to be talks with as many parties to the conflict as possible, but force may have to be used, UN or CIS [Commonwealth of Independent States] peacekeeping forces for example. But if force is used, it has to be done in such a way as to re-establish authority and confidence at all levels of society. But force cannot be used one-sidedly, it has to be used against all those who are breaking the norms of humane behaviour. Otherwise, the

> peacekeeping forces will be dragged into the mire. And it has to be accompanied by the reconstruction of institutions—administration, justice, public infrastructure—just as the allies did in post-war Germany.[91]

Up until this point, Kaldor had remained largely against the concept of military intervention. However, now she revealed a more ambiguous stance, indicating that military intervention may be a necessary means to reestablishing authority and protecting society from the debilitating effects of war. Although this stance indicated the start of a critical shift in her thinking, not until after her experiences in BaH did Kaldor decide that her mind was changed. Over the next few months she formed a clear position on the need for military force to stop violence.

Further debate on the legitimacy of intervention within HCA was spurred by the Battle of Vukovar in Croatia in August 1991, which was characterized by ethnic cleansing orchestrated by the Yugoslav People's Army and the Serbian paramilitary forces.[92] Kaldor recalled that during the HCA debates, "we were endlessly discussing it at the time of the ethnic cleansing in Croatia, and I remember even Sonja [Licht] saying maybe we need UN peacekeeping forces, and then there was this whole argument with the Slovenes and the pro-Slovenes people who felt we should be supporting independence, and sometime at that point I felt that [the emphasis] should be a military force to protect [people from] ethnic cleansing."[93]

In response to her experience of contemporary war, Kaldor began the process of solving what she considered to be a series of ontological problems in the way war, violence, and intervention were framed, not simply within the context of the nation-state but, more importantly, within the realm of civil society, grassroots politics, and peace and human rights.

Two key problems began to dominate Kaldor's thinking. First, she could not reconcile her experience of war with her conceptual understanding of "conventional" warfare. Although violence was disorganized in the conventional sense of war, it nonetheless stemmed from an organizing principle anchored by a narrative of nationalist identity. Second, Kaldor believed that not only was civil society unable to curtail ethnic violence once it started but also civil society could not survive in a situation of violence, and military intervention was required to defend civilians and to uphold the rule of law. Kaldor's views on violence and humanitarian intervention continued to evolve through her experiences as an activist in BaH.

Notes

1. Arzu Abdullayeva, interview with author, 29 March 2011. Abdullayeva was an HCA activist, and the incident related took place during the Armenian-Azerbaijani War in 1992.

2. Mikhail Gorbachev, address to the 43rd UN General Assembly Session, 7 December 1988, http://legacy.wilsoncenter.org/coldwarfiles/index-34441.html.
3. George H. W. Bush, "Towards a New World Order," speech presented before a Joint Session of Congress, 11 September 1990, http://bushlibrary.tamu.edu/research/public_papers.php?id=2217&year=1990&month=9.
4. See Fukuyama, *The End of History and the Last Man.*
5. Hans-Dietrich Genscher, quoted in "German Unification Good for Europe, Minister Says," *Globe and Mail*, Toronto, 30 April 1990, p. A8.
6. Valéry Giscard d'Estaing and Helmut Schmidt, "Franco-German Role in Unification of Europe," *San Francisco Chronicle*, 14 February 1990, p. 1.
7. European Parliament Resolution of 23 November 1989 on the recent developments in Central and Eastern Europe, OJ C323 of 27 December 1989, pp. 109–110.
8. Kaldor, "After the Cold War."
9. Ibid.
10. Ibid.
11. Ibid.
12. Halliday, "The Ends of the Cold War."
13. Howe, "Son of the Bani Tanwir."
14. See, for example, Kaldor, "Editorial," *Helsinki Citizens' Assembly, News Bulletin.*
15. See Bush, "Towards a New World Order."
16. Kaldor, "Editorial," *Helsinki Citizens' Assembly, News Bulletin*, p. 2.
17. Ibid.
18. See, for example, Ismael and Ismael, *The Gulf War and the New World Order.*
19. Mary Kaldor, "Death Blow to Democracy," *Times*, London, 26 January 1991, p. 7.
20. Henckaerts, *Mass Expulsion in Modern International Law and Practice*, p. 104.
21. See, for example, Kaldor, "Editorial," *Helsinki Citizens' Assembly, News Bulletin.*
22. Jimmy Carter, "Josip Broz Tito: Statement on the Death of the President of Yugoslavia," 4 May 1980, http://www.presidency.ucsb.edu/ws/?pid=33364.
23. Joseph A. Reaves, "Tito's Image Is Taking a Tumble in Yugoslavia," *Chicago Tribune*, 7 December 1990, p. 6. See also Mazower, *The Balkans.*
24. Sonja Licht, quoted in Mary Kaldor, "Long Divisions of the Balkan Mind: Nobody Wants War, but Nobody Can Agree," *Guardian* [London], 21 June 1991, p. 5.
25. Julijana Mojsilovic, "100 Years After His Birth, Tito's Land in Ruins," *Houston Chronicle*, 26 May 1992, p. 7.
26. Gwynne Dyer, "Europe Won't Allow Civil War to Erupt in Yugoslavia," *Kitchener-Waterloo Record*, 13 June 1991, p. A9.
27. Kaldor had met her cochair, Belgrade-based Sonja Licht, during the Eötvös Loránd University seminar in Hungary with Viktor Orbán in 1987 (see previous chapter).
28. Sonja Licht, interview with author, 22 February 2011.
29. Mary Kaldor, "A Bumpy Ride," in *Helsinki Citizens' Assembly, Prague News Bulletin*, Fall 1991, International Helsinki Federation, files of the executive director, HU OSA 318-0-1, Box 3, Budapest.
30. Ibid.
31. Ibid.
32. Jaroslav Šabata, quoted in "From Cold War Division to Europe of the Regions: A Conversation with Jaroslav Šabata (Interview by Fred Abrahams)," *Helsinki Citizens' Assembly, Prague News Bulletin*, Spring–Summer 1991, International Helsinki Federation, files of the executive director, HU OSA 318-0-1, Box 3, Budapest.
33. Ibid.
34. Mary Kaldor and Sonja Licht, "Letter: Yugoslavia Needs Help from Outside, Editorial," *Independent* [London], 20 March 1991, p. 28.

35. Graff, "Mass Bedlam in Belgrade."

36. Kaldor and Licht, "Letter: Yugoslavia Needs Help from Outside," p. 28.

37. Ibid., p. 28.

38. Ibid.

39. By spring and summer 1991, the HCA network extended to the following countries and countries in transition: Austria, Belgium, Bulgaria, Czech Republic, Canada, Denmark, Finland, France, Corsica, Germany, Greece, Hungary, Ireland, Italy, Netherlands, Norway, Poland, Romania, Spain, Sweden, Switzerland, Turkey, England, Scotland, United States of America, Soviet Union, Ukraine, Azerbaijan, Estonia, Latvia, Lithuania, and Yugoslavia (which at that stage included activists in Belgrade, Ljubljana, and Split). See *Helsinki Citizens' Assembly, News Bulletin*, Spring–Summer 1991, 12, International Helsinki Federation, files of the executive director, HU OSA 318-0-1, Budapest.

40. See, for example, Kaldor and Licht, *Yugofax Breakdown*.

41. According to Licht, the Yugoslav groups consisted of "an alliance of various individuals, representing civic and academic organizations across former Yugoslavia." Sonja Licht, correspondence with author, 4 May 2010. Kaldor, however, maintained mainly Slovenians were involved in these groups: "Radmila Nakaradha was someone involved in my UNU [United Nations University] project, and I invited her to reply to an article the Slovenes wrote in the *END Journal*. Radmila introduced me to Sonja, and Sonja became involved in the Hungarian meeting in 1987." Mary Kaldor, correspondence with author, 25 October 2012.

42. Mary Kaldor, correspondence with author, 25 October 2012.

43. Mary Kaldor and Sonja Licht, "Letter to Friends (Helsinki Citizen Assembly Members)," 1 July 1991, 1, International Helsinki Federation, files of the executive director, HU OSA 318-0-1, Box 3, Budapest.

44. Kaldor, "Long Divisions of the Balkan Mind," p. 5.

45. Ibid.; Mary Kaldor, interview with author, 24 June 2011.

46. Sonja Licht, correspondence with author, 4 May 2011. See also Kaldor, "A Decade of Humanitarian Intervention," p. 116; Davorka Zmiarevic, "Fix the Politics Not the Borders," *Yugofax*, 28 December 1991, p. 4.

47. George Papandreou, "National Committee Updates: Greece," in *Helsinki Citizens' Assembly, Prague News Bulletin*, Spring–Summer 1991, International Helsinki Federation, files of the executive director, HU OSA 318-0-1, Box 3, Budapest.

48. Blaine Harden, "Yugoslav Military Attacks Slovenia," *Austin American Statesman*, 28 June 1991, p. A1.

49. Jacques Poos, quoted in Alan Riding, "Conflict in Yugoslavia; Europeans Send High-Level Team," *New York Times,* 29 June 1991, online.

50. Bethlehem and Weller, *The "Yugoslav" Crisis in International Law,* p. xxvii.

51. Ibid., p. xxvii.

52. Gellner, quoted in Baker, "The Actions of the HCA," p. 65.

53. Michnik, quoted in ibid., p. 65.

54. Hren, quoted in ibid., p. 65. Slobodan Milošević was president of Serbia, Franjo Tuđman was president of Croatia, and Milan Kučan was president of Slovenia.

55. Hren quoted in ibid., p. 65.

56. Đilas quoted in ibid., p. 65.

57. Milovan Đjilas, "Disintegration of Yugoslavia, Integration of Europe," Belgrade Meeting, 7 July 1991, in *Helsinki Citizens' Assembly, News Bulletin*, no. 2, Fall 1991, 9, International Helsinki Federation, files of the executive director, HU OSA 318-0-1, Box 3, Budapest.

58. Baker, "The Actions of the HCA," p. 65.

59. Licht, quoted in ibid., p. 65.
60. Janjić, quoted in ibid., p. 65.
61. Mastnak, quoted in ibid., p. 65.
62. Faber, quoted in ibid., p, 65.
63. Quoted in Kaldor, "A Decade of Humanitarian Intervention," p. 116.
64. Sonja Licht, interview with author, 22 February 2011.
65. Ibid.
66. Ibid.
67. See, for example, Silvano Bolcic, "Citizens Sans Frontiers," *Yugofax*, 28 December 1991, 7, International Helsinki Federation, files of the executive director, HU OSA 318-0-1, Box 3, Budapest.
68. Natasa Kandic, interview with author, 22 February 2011.
69. Peter Annear, "Difficult Road for Yugoslav Peace Caravan," *Green Left Weekly* 33, 30 October 1991, online.
70. Ibid.
71. Ibid.
72. Sonja Licht, correspondence with author, 4 May 2011.
73. Mary Kaldor, correspondence with author, 25 October 2012.
74. Svetlana Gannushkina, correspondence with author, 30 April, 15 May, and 5 June 2011; Mary Kaldor, "Field Notes: A Week in the Caucasus: August 1992," PA-MK-HCA-SC, London. For further information on Gannushkina, see, for example, Politkovskaya, *A Russian Diary*; and "Human Rights Defender in Russia: Svetlana Alekseevna Gannushkina," Amnesty International, 9 December 2008, online.
75. Murat Belge founded the Turkish HCA, and although he was not part of the Caucasus group, he was deeply involved in establishing Turkish-Armenian relations between civil society groups. Mary Kaldor, correspondence with author, 25 October 2012.
76. Natalya Martirosyan, interview with author, 17 March 2011; Karen Ohanjanyan, interview with author, 21 March 2011; Alexander Rusetsky interview with author, 24 March 2011; Arzu Abdullayeva, interview with author, 29 March 2011; Kaldor, "Field Notes: A Week in the Caucasus"; Anahit Bayandur, correspondence with author, 27 November 2010.
77. Kaldor, "Field Notes: A Week in the Caucasus," p. 4.
78. Ibid., p. 1.
79. Ibid.
80. Ibid., pp. 6–7.
81. Keller, "Armenian Capital Is Roused by Calls for New Freedoms," p. 2.
82. Kaldor, "Field Notes: A Week in the Caucasus," p. 1.
83. Ibid., p. 9.
84. Natalya Martirosyan, interview with author, 17 March 2011; Karen Ohanjanyan, interview with author, 21 March 2011; Alexander Rusetsky, interview with author, 24 March 2011; Arzu Abdullayeva, interview with author, 29 March 2011.
85. Ibid.
86. Mary Kaldor, letter to Peter Jarman, 24 September 1992, 1–2, PA-MK-HCA-Brighton.
87. Arzu Abdullayeva, interview with author, 29 March 2011.
88. Mient Jan Faber, interview with author, 30 May 2011.
89. Mary Kaldor, correspondence with author, 20 September 2012.
90. Mary Kaldor, "Conflict in the Caucasus," *Guardian* [London], 21 August 1992, p. 16.
91. Ibid., p. 16.
92. See, for example, Woodward, *Balkan Tragedy*.
93. Mary Kaldor, interview with author, 20 June 2011.

9

The Politics of Violence

> *For me, especially coming from a journalist background, I always thought that academia often can be too isolated. I remember listening to some lectures about the Yugoslav war at Cambridge [University], and I just felt these people haven't really "smelt" the war. I had just come from that situation, and I just couldn't really relate to it, and that's why I was really skeptical about academia. Mary, for me, demolished that myth because she really knows what it's like.*[1]

THE WAR IN THE SOUTH CAUCASUS TRIGGERED THE SHIFT IN MARY Kaldor's thinking, but the war in BaH brought Kaldor to an understanding of why military intervention could at times be necessary. Moreover, as in the Caucasus, Kaldor was influenced not just by her experiences on the ground but by the relationships she developed throughout the war. In response to ethnic divisions in Yugoslavia, both Mary Kaldor and Sonja Licht, as cochairs of the HCA, had joined activists in BaH to launch their first branch of the HCA in Sarajevo in May 1991.[2] The newly launched group consisted of a consortium of individual activists and groups based in Sarajevo and was headed by Zdravko Grebo, a law professor at the University of Sarajevo.[3]

Over the next several years, Kaldor believed that the constant debate and dialogue with HCA activists in the former Yugoslavia, such as Grebo and Licht, and her collaboration with them served to change her stance on intervention:

> I think I was anti-intervention at the beginning of the Bosnian war, and then just witnessing what was happening made me realize I was for intervention. . . . People like Zdravko were hugely influential—absolutely!—and their experiences. . . . I think if I had been watching [the war on] TV, I don't know if I'd have changed; I think it was actually meeting people and seeing what it was like in that situation that made a huge difference. I mean that's my view, always.[4]

These relationships were very much reciprocated. For example, Grebo later maintained that Kaldor was significant in supporting his role as an activist within BaH. He believed that Kaldor had more influence not only because her academic position but also her "celebrity status," making her well known across Europe to the political elite, the media, and multilateral organizations such as the United Nations. But Grebo also maintained that Kaldor was important because "we were friends."[5]

Kaldor's experiences of war and ethnic nationalism were also reflected in her activist articles and academic scholarship. She gradually shifted away from focusing on the economics of military technology to writing about multiethnic civil society, identity and violent nationalism, and the political economy of war. She began responding to a radically different, unfamiliar context, compared to her experiences of the Cold War. In effect, her activism was leading her to address a field of political study that was new to her.

Was Kaldor out of her depth? Kaldor felt so. Through her work at SIPRI and SPRU and as a policy adviser for the Labour NEC, she had proven herself an expert on the arms trade and the economics of military industry. But she was not an expert in war. In fact, she was attempting to learn about war in the midst of one: "All of this was completely new stuff for me. I had been writing about nuclear deterrents and military technology, and suddenly I was writing about nationalism and civil society . . . and sort of trying to catch up."[6]

During the course of the events of 1992, Kaldor's experiences of war and her involvement with HCA activists influenced her stance on the subject of intervention, as reflected in her writing. For example, initially Kaldor cowrote an article in *Yugofax* with Licht entitled "Nationalism and War, Civil Society and Peace," in which they argued that "it was in part by default that nationalism became the new mobilising ideal."[7] To "invent" a Croat, Slovene, or Serb was to provide a pure, unadulterated identity.[8] Countering nationalism required an emphasis on a liberal political debate concerning the legitimacy of war: "The only solution is to build a politics from below."[9] Yet, by the end of 1992, Kaldor wrote an article in the *New Left Review* in which she concluded that the implementation of UN protectorates and military intervention to protect civil society was necessary.[10] Kaldor argued:

> One important proposal put forward by peace and human rights activists in the Former Yugoslavia, especially in Bosnia-Herzegovina, is multi-ethnic international protectorates or protected zones. The idea is that local authorities should be able to demand international protection in order to preserve or restore multi-ethnic communities. Political authority would be replaced until the atmosphere of fear has been removed; in other words, political solutions would be considered only after the fighting has stopped. Protected zones would, of course, require an extensive international commitment, not only in terms of peace-keeping troops, but also for economic, social and

civil reconstruction. A bottom-up approach alone cannot stop war, at least not in the short run.[11]

Throughout the war in BaH and the Caucasus, Kaldor wrote a series of essays exploring intervention to protect civil society in the context of organized violence. Combined with her work at the United Nations University, these essays formed the foundation of the ideas that she would explore more fully in *New and Old Wars*.

Civic Protests

According to Kaldor, when war started in Yugoslavia, Grebo was deeply concerned that the disintegration of the country would see the situation in BaH degenerate into a horrific, protracted war.[12] Unlike Slovenia, Serbia, and Croatia, BaH began as a genuinely multiethnic and secular society. According to a census conducted in 1991, Muslims accounted for 44 percent of the population, with Serbs at 31 percent, and Croats 17 percent.[13] Whereas Slovenian and Croatian independence seemed clearly based on ethnicity, BaH appeared neutral and accepting of ethnic diversity. The first multiparty elections were held in BaH, conducted on 18 November 1990, which resulted in a coalition government formed by the three ethnically represented, communally based parties.[14] Interethnic marriage and interethnic neighborhoods were the norm rather than the exception, Grebo remarked, and this intermixing made partition not just ethically unpalatable but, practically speaking, impossible without terrible violence.

Very early on, Grebo began to consider ways to protect civilians and to retain a multiethnic civil society.[15] Although strategies were constantly debated with all the HCA activists from BaH throughout the duration of the war, Grebo's ideas laid the basis for many of HCA's activities within BaH. Kaldor later reflected, "I remember him saying if Yugoslavia falls apart then Bosnia will be 'hell.' . . . I mean in a way all the proposals that we came up with [were] actually put forward by Zdravko in 1991 at that meeting in Belgrade."[16]

For example, one of the main proposals Grebo put forward was the concept of "peace zones."[17] Although Mary Kaldor and Mient Jan Faber were regarded as the first to propose and popularize the idea of UN protectorates or "safe havens" in BaH at the start of the Yugoslav war,[18] both Kaldor and Faber attribute the idea's origins to Grebo.[19] HCA and Grebo also raised the idea of peace zones or safe havens at the International Municipal Peace Conference in Budapest, which endorsed the peace zone concept in November 1991. Attended by a number of HCA activists from Yugoslavia, the conference saw the idea of peace zones gain interest especially among representatives from cities, such as Subotica in northern Serbia and Zenica in BaH, and the plan was endorsed by the Council of Europe.[20] Stephanie Baker, an HCA officer based in

Prague, remembered, "The HCA began working on a comprehensive project to support zones of peace—an initiative for cities and municipalities to declare themselves in favour of non-violent resolution of conflicts."[21]

From Political Violence to War

By 1992, as a vote for independence drew near, ethnic violence across BaH increased. On the weekend of 29 February and 1 March, the referendum was conducted with armed Serbian vigilantes at major Sarajevo intersections. As a vote for independence became more likely, many expected reprisals from Bosnian-Serb nationalists. In defense, Muslims armed themselves in the center of Sarajevo. The majority of Sarajevo's police were Serbian, and many were seen positioned near Parliament, making no attempts to stop vigilantism or to uphold the rule of law.[22] According to one vigilante, a World War II–era Serbian nationalist emblem fastened to his black beret, "the referendum was illegitimate; we do not accept leaving Yugoslavia."[23] The majority of Serbs boycotted the vote and declared a "Serb Republic of Bosnia-Herzegovina," threatening to secede if the United Nations and European Community recognized BaH as an independent republic.[24] Moreover, with the majority of Yugoslav defense industries based in Bosnia, the federal army heavily resisted BaH secession. According to Branko Kostic, the acting chairman of the presidency of the Socialist Federal Republic of Yugoslavia and the federal army's self-declared commander in chief, federal troops would never withdraw from BaH.[25]

Despite the threats, on 3 March, with 99.7 percent of voters in favor of independence,[26] Alija Izetbegović, the chairman of the presidency for BaH, declared on a televised broadcast, "We can now say that Bosnia is a sovereign and independent state."[27] Sixty percent of BaH's territory was, at this stage, controlled by Serbian nationalists, and in response to Izetbegović's announcement, this group warned they were ready to defend themselves with arms. At the same time, fatigued by an eight-month war in Croatia, many of Yugoslavia's armed factions voiced support for a UN peacekeeping operation planned that month, revealing the fractured nature of the warring forces.[28]

Izetbegović, playing down fears of ethnic violence, held that "there may be a few isolated incidents, but a general armed conflict will not erupt."[29] His assurance, perhaps, reflected the misplaced confidence of BaH's international partners (namely, the European Community and the United States), rather than the views of the political elites in BaH. As both the European Community and the United States had promised to recognize BaH should a referendum achieve independence, the BaH government felt assured that they had robust international support. On this basis, Haris Silajdzic, BaH's foreign minister, claimed that he was confident the federal army would accept the decision and would ensure a peaceful transition.[30]

Irrespective of the BaH government's confidence, many Bosnians, including Grebo, were unconvinced that US and European Community recognition of the referendum would guarantee a nonviolent transition. Following Izetbegović's declaration of independence, Grebo, on an independent radio station, called for people of all ethnicities and nationalities to join him in peaceful protest on the streets of Sarajevo, to walk through the militants' heavily armed blockades, and to tear down the barricades erected by Muslim and Serbian paramilitary groups dividing the city ethnically.[31] Over the next few days some 200,000 people responded, assembling in the streets of Sarajevo. Serbs, Muslims, and Croats were chanting, "We want peace," in an effort to avert war in BaH, and demanding the establishment of an international protectorate.[32] Thousands more had traveled by bus to join the protests from Tuzla, Zenica, and Kakanj but were blocked from entering Sarajevo by the Bosnian Serb nationalist paramilitary.[33] The demonstration attempted to show that the majority of Sarajevo's population was against the ethnic-based division of BaH into a series of minirepublics or for Sarajevo itself to be divided by a Berlin Wall–style partition.[34] In response, the BaH government released a statement addressed to the Croats, Muslims, and Serbs in support of the protesters, stating, "This country is the property of all of you and you all should defend it together."[35]

Yet, as the European Community and the United States declared their recognition of the newly formed BaH on 6 and 7 April 1992, respectively, the Bosnian Serbs started their forewarned offensive within the newly recognized nation-state of BaH. On Wednesday, April 8, the Bosnian war started when nationalist Serb snipers fired upon the civilian demonstrators, which Grebo had played a role in mobilizing. As promised, a Serb self-styled parliament based in Banja Luka declared its "secession" from BaH, and the Republika Srpska (Serbian Republic) was established,[36] with Radovan Karadžić elected as president. Appointed as chief of staff of the Army of the Serbian Republic, General Ratko Mladić had both the support of the Serbian Republic Parliament and, just as importantly, the support of Slobodan Milošević, whose government provided military and political assistance.[37]

As the Serbian Republic's new army organized assaults within BaH in response to the recognition by the European Community and the United States of BaH's independence, the United Nations and the European Community initiated a series of diplomatic efforts that would exemplify the countless attempted negotiations, sanctions, peace processes, and plans to resolve the conflict over the next three years.[38] The US Department of State asserted, "We are looking at future steps we and others might take to bring the international community's concerns to bear."[39] Lord Peter Carrington and Joao de Deus Pinheiro, both European Community diplomats, were offered as negotiators to visit Yugoslavia in order to "make their contacts" initially in Sarajevo and then in Belgrade and Zagreb.[40] By May, the siege of Sarajevo, which would represent the longest siege in modern warfare of a capital city, had begun when a mortar shell fired from a Serb position in the hills of Sarajevo killed sixteen people waiting in line for bread. In response, the United Nations imposed sanctions on the Serbian Republic.[41]

As war enveloped the newly formed nation-state of BaH, both Kaldor and the greater part of HCA across Europe, Canada, and the United States were drawn into what would be the greatest challenge of HCA's very short history.

Notes

1. Denisa Kostovicova, interview with author, 9 June 2011. Kostovicova was a journalist and then a lecturer at London School of Economics.

2. See "Proposal: HCA Office in Sarajevo," Helsinki Citizens' Assembly, fax, 23 November 1993, 1–11, PA-MK-HCA-Brighton.

3. Not long after, following BaH's independence, Grebo would write the first draft of the BaH constitution based on the principles of a multiethnic civil society, and he would play a major role in the campaign for "safe areas" during the course of the war. Sonja Licht, interview with author, 22 February 2011.

4. Mary Kaldor, interview with author, 11 May 2011.

5. Zdravko Grebo, interview with author, 7 March 2011.

6. Mary Kaldor, interview with author, 20 June 2011.

7. Kaldor and Licht, "Nationalism and War, Civil Society and Peace," p. 8.

8. Kaldor and Licht argued, "A successful career nearly always meant collaboration with the old regime while those dissidents who had resisted the system provided an unwelcomed reminder of those who had remained complicit. With the exception of Bosnia and Herzegovina . . . , the 1990s elections across Croatia and Serbia had overwhelmingly voted for ethno-nationalist leaders." Nationalism, Licht and Kaldor argued, "was an attractive proposition for those aspiring to assume new identities, and who nevertheless were loath to renew ideas of class and unwilling or unable to go through the difficult process of developing a dialogue on citizenship and civil society." Ibid., p. 8.

9. Ibid., p. 12.

10. Kaldor, "Yugoslavia and the New Nationalism."

11. Ibid., p. 112.

12. Zdravko Grebo, interview with author, 7 March 2011; Mary Kaldor, interview with author, 10 July 2011.

13. Ogata, *The Turbulent Decade,* p. 51.

14. For example, in the BaH elections, the Muslim Party of Democratic Action (led by Alija Izetbegović), the Serbian Democratic Party, and the Croatian Democratic Union together won 202 of the 240 seats in the two houses of parliament. In contrast with the Croatian and Serbian elections, and with the exception of Radovan Karadžić, cofounder of the Serbian Democratic Party, Bosnians elected moderate politicians, with nationalist Croats voting for the moderate Stephan Kljuic and Bosnian Muslims voting along both ethnic and secular lines. Fikret Abdic, a Bosnian Muslim, regarded as a pragmatist, received the most votes, overshadowing Izetbegović by 150,000 votes. However, Izetbegović gained leadership when Abdic declined the position and stood down. As the new president, Izetbegović was the only president of a Yugoslav republic who was never a communist. BaH as an independent state was founded on the basis of neutrality and secularism, and for this reason, when the wars in Slovenia and Croatia

began, the UN High Commission for Refugees (UNHCR) and the UN Protection Force (UNPROFOR) established their headquarters in Sarajevo in 1991 and 1992, respectively. Ogata, *The Turbulent Decade,* p. 51; Kumar, *Divide and Fall?* p. 42; Chuck Sudetic, "Turnout in Bosnia Signals Independence," *New York Times*, 2 March 1992, p. A.3.

15. Kaldor, "A Decade of Humanitarian Intervention," p. 117; Zdravko Grebo, interview with author, 7 March 2011.

16. Mary Kaldor, interview with author, 24 June 2011. Later regarded as a hero in Sarajevo, Grebo gained access to international and local media within BaH, including radio stations, and soon after set up his own radio station, called Radio Zid (Radio Wall). Playing modern music and news programs and producing provocative debates on air, Grebo attempted to maintain Sarajevo's "urban style and civilised environment" and was known for his honesty and irreverence (Gjelten, *Sarajevo Daily,* pp. 154, 202). Throughout the duration of war, radio became a primary communication tool as access to electricity was intermittent, and the production of television broadcasts and newspapers was contingent on sieges, the availability of resources, and logistics.

17. Zdravko Grebo, interview with author, 7 March 2011; Mary Kaldor, interview with author, 11 May 2011. During the Cold War, "zones of peace" were demilitarized municipalities or countries. A local constituency would lobby the mayor, local councilor, or state officials to declare the area a peace zone. According to David R. Mares, "in the 1980s, South Americans borrowed the Zone of Peace concept from Australia and New Zealand in an effort to keep the Cold War from undermining regional security . . . and [their effort] was directed at the superpowers, not the states within the region." Mares, *Violent Peace*, p. 49. Also see Kacowic, *Zones of Peace in the Third World.*

18. James Cusick, "Safe Havens Urged for War-Torn Cities; Briton's Plan for Sarajevo Resurrected," *Independent* [London], 17 September 1993, p. 3. Also see Mary Kaldor and Jeanette Buirski, "Letter: Step-by-Step to Lasting Peace in Bosnia," *Guardian* [London], 8 April 1993, p. 23. Safe areas had already been introduced in previous conflicts, such as in the first Iraq war and in Somalia, but those in BaH formed the most ambitious proposed package. As high-profile international activists, Kaldor and Faber were key to campaigning for safe havens and, in the process, refined and popularized the idea across Europe. Yet, because Faber wrote mainly in Dutch, Kaldor insisted she more often received the credit, even when she did not deserve it; Mary Kaldor, correspondence with author, 10 July 2010.

19. Mary Kaldor, interview with author, 20 June 2011; Mient Jan Faber, interview with author, 30 May 2011.

20. See Baker, "Citizens' Movement," pp. 64–68.

21. Ibid., p. 67. The concept also included pairing cities with other municipalities throughout Europe to provide moral support (such as supporting peace, human rights, and plurality) and material support (such as democratic institution building), with cities in Italy, Spain, Holland, and Norway already expressing interest at the beginning of the process. The peace zones concept was also outlined in a joint *Yugofax*-HCA publication edited by Licht and Kaldor entitled *Yugofax Breakdown: War and Reconstruction in Yugoslavia.* After declaring Subotica a peace zone, Mayor Josef Kazsa announced that founding peace zones would help "[to] prevent further pressures on our ethnic peace and to stop the mobalisation of those citizens [for war] who do not want to participate in war." See ibid. Moreover, the HCA proposed the idea of developing peace zones to the meeting of the Council of Ministers of the Commission on Security and Cooperation in Europe, conducted in Prague in January 1992, for other cities in the former Yugoslavia and possibly in troubled Nagorno-Karabakh. Local HCA branches, in partnership with HCA members across Europe, initiated the lobbying with officials of the

UNHCR. Moreover, as Grebo was involved with several programs on broadcast radio at the time, the notion of peace zones or safe havens could be found not just within the HCA but across BaH airwaves. See ibid.

22. Carrol J. Williams, "Bosnia Violence After Vote on Independence," *San Francisco Chronicle*, 2 March 1992, p. A.1.

23. Quoted in ibid., p. A.1.

24. Ibid.

25. Ibid.

26. Nohlen and Stöver, *Elections in Europe*, pp. 330, 334.

27. "World-wide: Bosnia-Herzegovina Moved Nearer to Independence from Yugoslavia," *Wall Street Journal*, 2 March 1992, p. 1-1; Sudetic, "Turnout in Bosnia Signals Independence," p. A.3.

28. Williams, "Bosnia Violence After Vote on Independence," p. A.1.

29. Alija Izetbegović, quoted in Sudetic, "Turnout in Bosnia Signals Independence," p. A.3.

30. "World-wide," p. 1-1.

31. "Serb Rebels Leave Sarajevo Barricades: Militants Fire on Marchers, Then Retreat," *Star Tribune*, 3 March 1992, p. 2.A.

32. Y. Chazan, "Battle Lines Tense in Bosnia," *Guardian* [London], 8 March 1992, p. 8; "Thousands in Bosnia Hold Tallies for Peace," *Boston Globe*, 6 March 1992, p. 7; Kaldor and Licht, "Nationalism and War, Civil Society and Peace," p. 11; Kaldor, "A Decade of Humanitarian Intervention," p. 116.

33. "Thousands in Bosnia Hold Rallies for Peace," p. 7.

34. Gjelten, *Sarajevo Daily*, p. 9.

35. Ibid., p. 42.

36. See "The Amendments VII and VIII to the Constitution of the Republika Srpska" (in Serbian), *Official Gazette of the Republika Srpska* 1, no. 15 (29 September 1992), p. 569.

37. D. B. Ottaway, "U.N. Plan for Peace Rejected by Serbs," *Austin American Statesman*, 6 May 1993, p. A.1.

38. See Gow, *Triumph of the Lack of Will*.

39. "A Tragedy of Errors," *Guardian* [London], 23 April 1992, p. 22.

40. Ibid.

41. Charlie Connelly, "The New Siege of Sarajevo," *Times* [London], 8 October 2005, online. See also Dizdarevic, *Sarajevo*.

10

Safe Havens and Protectorates

I think that you should call David Reilly, and maybe even [Tony] Land, to see if everything is OK with meetings, and [blue] ID cards. It would be better if you will do it, instead of me. . . . Some of the UNHCR [UN High Commission for Refugees] guys are really behaving with us Bosnians and ex-Yugoslavians with [a] special kind of disrespect. Sometimes I have a feeling that for people like Tony I am either labour force [like] secretaries in his office, or "warring side" you should keep distance with. Anyhow, someone who is not the most appropriate problem-solving person. They will listen [to] you with more respect, so your phone-call will help with our delegation and Sarajevo office.[1]

BY AUGUST 1992, BAH HAD REACHED A CRITICAL POINT AS THE CYCLE OF political violence escalated. A report by Helsinki Watch documented several incidents of mass executions, carried out by the Serbian paramilitary and linked to Serbian president Slobodan Milošević.[2] However, the group also maintained that horrendous acts of violence were being perpetrated on all sides. Furthermore, as nationalist politics surged, the paramilitary was experiencing a rise in influence, coinciding with an increased presence of organized crime and criminal syndicates.[3]

One of a number of paramilitary groups was the Arkan's Tigers, which pioneered the "ethnic cleansing" that later characterized the Balkans conflict.[4] Led by Željko Ražnatović, former hitman from the Yugoslav Ministry of the Interior, their strategy for "ethnic cleansing" was later adopted by other Serbian paramilitary groups, including the Scorpions.[5] The modus operandi of Arkan's Tigers was to encircle a small town or village, block all the main exits and entrances, and advance into the village. Proceeding to each house, the paramilitary would order civilians into the main street, separating men from the women and children. After robbing them, they would force the women and children to leave the village, and their houses would be plundered and burnt. The men were murdered, forced into labor, or directed into improvised prison camps.[6] The paramilitary generally carried a list of prominent Muslim leaders and, upon identifying them, would ensure that leaders were the first to be killed.[7] According to Radha Kumar, executive director of HCA and then based in Sarajevo, the Arkan's Tigers effortlessly transitioned from small-time mafia or criminals to paramilitary and remained an effective force throughout the conflict.[8]

A year earlier, in April 1991, safe havens had been established in Iraq to protect the Kurdish population from ethnic cleansing during the First Gulf War under operation Provide Comfort.[9] Now, the concept of safe zones was being expanded to areas protected by a third party, in particular the UN Protection Force (UNPROFOR). In 1992, the HCA requested the establishment of

> protected zones both for the whole of Bosnia-Herzegovina and for the UNPA [UN Protected Area] areas of Croatia and for individual municipalities. The basic idea is where authority has broken down, the international community should take over civil authority and carry out a programme of demilitarisation, restoration of order and justice, economic and social reconstruction, and so on, so that refugees can return to their homes, the atmosphere of fear can be removed, and a process of democratisation can begin in which the future status of the area can be determined. Such protected zones would be administrated by international institutions in co-operation with civic movements, NGOs, municipalities, and so on.[10]

As cochairs, Mary Kaldor and Sonja Licht were involved in a broader HCA campaign to debate the need for protected zones with activists, NGOs, peacekeepers, the United Nations, intellectuals, and politicians. For example, the safe zones proposal was debated on Bosnian radio and within NGOs and multilateral institutions (including with the UNHCR in Sarajevo), the Council of Europe, and the European Community.[11] Moreover, as international diplomacy and high politics failed to arrive at a peaceful settlement, the HCA continued to campaign for safe zones in BaH.

The initial idea of protected zones was further developed during the "Citizens and Municipal Peace Conference" held in Ohrid, Macedonia, 5–8 November 1992. The Ohrid conference was jointly organized by HCA and the Standing Conference of Local and Regional Authorities in Europe and supported by the European Community as a means of building greater solidarity and networks between groups in the Balkans. Moreover, the conference provided a site for producing further strategies for preserving civil society. During this meeting, arguments arose regarding how to protect multiethnic civil society, resulting in the origin of an agreed official position of the safe havens approach, which incorporated a UN protectorate across the entire nation-state of BaH and, with it, the inception of HCA's international campaign for safe havens. HCA, in association with the Council of Europe, also met with President Alija Izetbegović and other members of government (including the deputy prime minister, minister for social affairs, minister for health, and director of the State Agency for Humanitarian Aid), the mayor, religious leaders, international aid agencies (including the UNHCR), and the International Press Centre, including journalists based in Sarajevo, to advocate for the establishment of protected zones.[12]

Kaldor continued to work with the HCA to build a general consensus with the broader public through various international campaigns. For example, in December 1992, Mary Kaldor and Mient Jan Faber wrote an appeal for safe havens within BaH, using similar language as that to develop safe zones for the Kurdish people, and HCA branches across Europe called on the United Nations to extend its mandate to include safe havens or UN protectorates across BaH.[13] The HCA "safe haven postcard" program was one such high-profile component of the campaign. Much of the international campaign centered on pressuring national governments and international diplomats, under the Geneva Convention to declare UN protectorates and pressuring the wealthier countries to accept refugees. To raise the profile of the campaign, the HCA garnered support from members of the European Parliament and key public figures such as Paddy Ashdown, a British politician and later high representative for BaH.[14] Around 300,000 postcards signed by individuals across Europe were sent to negotiators and governments all over Europe. Almost 30,000 of the postcards were sent directly to David Owen, former British foreign secretary, and Cyrus Vance, former US secretary of state, who were attempting to negotiate an accord. The postcards called for safe havens and for UN protection of multiethnic communities as a primary step for ensuring a pluralist civil society in BaH.[15]

Kaldor also tried to engage with Vance and Owen directly to present the concept of protected zones for the entire BaH state and for the UN protected areas of Croatia.[16] Zdravko Grebo recalled that he traveled with Mient Jan Faber, Mary Kaldor, Sonja Licht, and Žarko Puhovski (an activist and lecturer in political science at the University of Zagreb) to Geneva to meet with Vance and Owen:

> We spoke with Cyrus Vance, who was at the time old and exhausted. The meeting lasted no more than fifteen minutes, and it was ten o'clock in the morning, and he fell asleep. But the meeting with Lord Owen was really something. I think—I'm sure—that Mary was behind the whole idea. And of course, Mary having a personal, family, academic biography, she was a personal friend of Lord Owen. . . . It was really something. Mary was very tough—and Lord Owen was very tough.[17]

Kaldor's recollection of the meeting was less enthusiastic than Grebo's. According to Kaldor, Owen was not interested in the meeting. As foreign secretary, Owen had selected Kaldor as panel adviser for arms control and disarmament at the Foreign Office in the 1970s, and they had remained friends since. Kaldor remarked that she organized the delegation of activists from each of the three warring republics—Croatia, Serbia, and BaH—to advise Owen personally:

> What we were very excited about was that outside [Owen's] room there were all our postcards; there was a man counting our postcards! . . . Mient Jan said to him, "You may have noticed that we have sent you a lot of postcards. Are you going to reply to all the people who sent [one]?" And [Owen] said, "I think this is the silliest campaign I've ever heard of, and they go straight into the wastepaper basket. And if you want to influence me, you either do it through my friends," with a little nod to me, "or through important people I can't ignore." Isn't that awful? And what I found that was terrible was that he just lectured us the whole time. He even said, "Zdravko, do you know . . ." And I thought, "It's incredible; here are these brilliant people." I thought, "He's seeing them as a favor to me, not because he's truly interested in what they [think]. . . . These are truly independent intellectuals who could really help him."[18]

Owen maintained that he was initially interested in the concept of a UN protectorate. However, his concern was one of practicality:

> The reason why Cy Vance and I were against safe havens is well documented in the archives. . . . I was very interested in the concept of a UN protectorate in September and October 1992, but the more we looked at it, the more impossible it was to envisage. Again one of the problems was that there was not the capacity to run a UN protectorate. Vance . . . [was] never able to get sufficient troops to man the borders of Bosnia and Herzegovina or to even keep open crucial supply lines, let alone [protect] the safe havens.[19]

Ethnic Partition and the Failure of Diplomacy

Although the United Nations declared the BaH conflict to be an issue of international security, it remained ambivalent toward the establishment of safe areas and protecting civilians by force.[20] Sadako Ogata, the high commissioner for the UNHCR, maintained that the idea of safe havens would be "difficult to implement" and required further research.[21]

More concerning was the comment of one of Ogata's officials, who stated that the Bosnian war was nearly over anyway, with ratification of the Vance-Owen accord now likely. Radovan Karadžić, leader of the Bosnian Serbs, suggested a "compromise" on the BaH constitution. Although agreeing to the human and minority rights provisions of the constitution outlined in the UN peace accord, Karadžić argued that an independent state for ethnic Serbs should be established within the "former" BaH. Thereafter, Karadžić unashamedly reassured, Muslims and Croats could create as many states as they liked with what was left.[22]

Finally, the UN Security Council took the next step. On 13 August 1992, it declared that "the situation in Bosnia and Herzegovina" constituted a "threat to international peace and security," and that the "provision of humanitarian assistance in Bosnia and Herzegovina is an important element in the Council's efforts to restore international peace and security in the area."[23] Adopting Resolution 770, the Security Council called "upon States to take nationally or through regional agencies or arrangements all measures necessary" to ensure the "delivery by relevant United Nations humanitarian organizations and others of humanitarian assistance to Sarajevo and wherever needed in other parts of Bosnia and Herzegovina."[24] Nonetheless, on the ground the lack of political will to utilize "all means necessary" precluded intervention by force to protect civilians from physical violence (or the imminent threat of violence) and in many instances failed to ensure that humanitarian aid was facilitated by force.[25]

Despite attempts to seek a diplomatic peace agreement with Radovan Karadžić and Slobodan Milošević, the Vance-Owen accord languished. In an effort to retain the territorial integrity of BaH, international mediators Vance and Owen announced a plan to split Bosnia into ten autonomous provinces under the jurisdiction of a weak central administration, with nine out of the ten provinces controlled by one of the three ethnic-national groups. With severely limited powers, the central government would have no army, and its authority would also be limited in other administrative areas, including monetary policy, health, education, and policing. In essence, the administration of BaH would effectively be split among the three ethnic groups, with no overall governing powers.[26]

For Kaldor, the proposed accord was nothing short of reckless and endorsed the violent division being achieved on the ground, giving the warring elites a signal that they were in a position to legitimately negotiate the terms and conditions while committing war crimes. By November, General Ratko Mladić, chief of staff of the Army of the Serbian Republic, reportedly gave UN officials in Sarajevo his ultimatum, to the effect that if the tens of thousands of Muslims continued to resist surrender in Bosnian enclaves, he would "starve them out."[27]

Kaldor was not alone in her concerns. Initially, Izetbegović rejected the Vance-Owen plan, maintaining that the plan accepted the ethnic cleansing in Bosnia and also left Bosnia without an army to defend itself upon the United Nations' departure. When journalists asked Izetbegović why he refused Owen and Vance's call for him to meet again with Karadžić face-to-face, Izetbegović declared, "They forced me to sit at the same table with a man who inspired all these terrible crimes. Despicable is not too strong a word."[28] Izetbegović continued:

> In practical terms, the people who made this plan would reward the aggressors for their "ethnic cleansing," by leaving them in control of the territories they have taken. What they should have done was exactly the opposite. They should have punished the aggressors and given back the "ethnically

cleansed" territories to the Bosnian Government, to the Bosnian people and to the state of Bosnia and Herzegovina.[29]

Nevertheless, as the Vance-Owen plan failed, many diplomats and academics increasingly accepted that ethnic division as the only realistic option.[30] For example, John J. Mearsheimer and Robert A. Pape, both at the University of Chicago, saw division as the only practical solution to end the war in BaH.[31]

In June 1993, a new plan devised by David Owen and Thorvald Stoltenberg, who had replaced Cyrus Vance, explicitly divided BaH into three ethnic districts under a "Union of Bosnia i Herzegovina,"[32] which would retain the territorial integrity of the state, with Sarajevo as a multiethnic capital.[33] The plan was presented by Owen and Stoltenberg in Geneva to Karadžić, now president of the Bosnian Serb administration,[34] Milošević, president of Serbia, and Izetbegović, president of BaH, along with Franjo Tuđman, president of Croatia. While meeting with Milošević and peace negotiators in the morning, Karadžić described the plan as unrealistic, maintaining that the key to lasting peace was a division of BaH into three separate ethnic states, which he argued had already largely been attained by force. Karadžić asserted, "The reality is we already have three entities. If they are not delineated properly, then let's do it by negotiation and not by fighting."[35] At the meeting, Tuđman showed a composed and conciliatory approach. Yet, on the ground, the Croation Defense Council (Hrvatsko vijeće obrane), who were originally fighting alongside the Muslims against the Serbs, had shifted policy and begun their own ethnic-cleansing operation against Muslims, which added another series of state or quasi-state actors carving up the BaH map along ethnic lines.[36]

Yet, although Kaldor was critical of those such as David Owen for what she saw as their elitism and policy impotency, the hesitation of Western governments to intervene politically and militarily in BaH revealed a much broader lack of political will. Humanitarian intervention, particularly after the US failure during the Second United Nations Operation in Somalia, remained a hotly contested concept.[37] Moreover, in autumn 1993, in response to the US intervention into Somalia, Samuel H. Huntington, a well-regarded conservative US political scientist, famously quipped: "It is morally unjustifiable and politically indefensible that members of the [US] armed forces should be killed to prevent Somalis from killing one another."[38] Huntington was not alone.[39] Following the botched US involvement in Somalia, US officials would find gaining support for another intervention to be nothing short of a challenge.

The failed Somali intervention was not the only experience that made governments wary. Argument also surrounded the sovereign rights of the state to conduct a "civil war" without the interference of other states. South African justice Richard Goldstone, a former judge and later chair of the Kosovo Commission, received this insight from a conversation with Edward Heath, former British prime minister, who stated frankly what was the general, even if unspoken, consensus among politicians at the time. Goldstone recalled his shock when Heath opined that "if people wished to murder one another, as long as they did not do so in his country, it was not his concern and should not be the concern of the British government."[40]

Also the ill-fated notion that long-standing, irresolvable mutual dislike based on religious and ethnic lines played a role in spurring violence in the Balkans also discouraged intervention. David Owen was influenced by Rebecca West's book *Black Lamb and Grey Falcon*.[41] Owen explained that he "had dipped into, rather than re-read, Rebecca West's account of her travels through Yugoslavia in the late 1930s," asserting that "on every page I had found a labyrinth of history, weaving a complexity of human relations that seemed to bedevil the whole region."[42] Sympathetic to West's view, Owen argued that "history points to a tradition in the Balkans of a readiness to solve disputes by the taking up of arms and acceptance of the forceful or even negotiated movement of people as the consequence of war."[43] Similarly, journalist Robert D. Kaplan argued in *Balkan Ghosts* that the wars in that region were fueled by "ancient hatreds."[44] Kaplan's book was said to have influenced Bill Clinton's initial decision, as US president, against military intervention in the Balkans.[45] In this way, Western governments could view any political or military intervention as going against the "historical grain" or as "pusillanimous realism."[46]

Yet some argued that these books offered very little in the way of meaningful context for understanding contemporary war in the Balkans. Richard Holbrooke, who later brokered the Dayton Accords, argued that *Black Lamb and Grey Falcon* and *Balkan Ghosts* were both examples of "bad history," and that things would have looked quite different if Clinton had read either Warren Zimmermann's *Origins of a Catastrophe: Yugoslavia and Its Destroyers* or Noel Malcolm's *Bosnia: A Short History,* the latter of which was published later, in 1994.[47] For Kaldor and Licht, Clinton simply needed to engage with local Bosnian or Herzegovinian human rights activists and refugees, whose security was the source of political legitimacy, rather then rely on travel memoirs or the warring elite to inform policy.[48]

Last Campaign for a Multilateral Authority

Not until March 1993 did the United Nations begin to seriously discuss the establishment of safe havens in the Security Council after a series of events brought the plight of Srebrenica to their attention. General Philippe Morillon, UNPROFOR commander, and Larry Hollingworth, UNHCR chief of operations in Sarajevo, had decided to lead a convoy to Srebrenica to deliver humanitarian aid, concerned with depleting rations and the increase in refugees from neighboring towns and villages. Upon delivering the aid, the contingent, in particular Morillon, was prevented from leaving by a crowd of women. The United Nations was their protection, the women argued, and their last chance for survival. If the contingent left, they pleaded, the city would fall to the Serbs in a matter of days, if not hours. The next morning Morillon made an impromptu announcement to the people of Srebrenica and to Western media: "I am placing you under the protection of the United Nations." The crowd erupted into cheering and clapping.[49]

Within the UN Security Council, debate ensued. UN ambassadors in New York awoke to breaking news that UNPROFOR had declared Srebrenica a safe zone and thus began nervous conversations with governments concerning the protection of BaH civilians. Sadako Ogata, UN high commissioner for refugees, was, in principle, sympathetic to intervention for the protection of civilians, and she began to lobby the UN Security Council to adopt a resolution for the official establishment of UN safe areas.[50] Hollingworth recalled,

> While we slept New York was awake. And in a flurry. The actions, the words and the decision of *mon General* had slung the cat into the bird cage. The feathers of Boutros Boutros-Ghali were ruffled. . . . Ambassadors were explaining to their countries the nuances of what they had signed up to do; the UNPROFOR General . . . was defining to the press the connotations of "safe" as in "havens" and "areas."[51]

Kaldor and the HCA were elated that a grassroots call for a UN protectorate had been heard and that UN troops were supporting the safe haven declaration and campaigned to support of the citizens of Srebrenica. In their letter to the *Guardian*, Mary Kaldor and fellow HCA member Jeanette Buirski called for "extensive UN intervention in Bosnia-Herzegovina" to protect civilians. Kaldor and Buirski argued that, although the potential dangers of military intervention could be easily discerned, "the risks of doing nothing are even greater."[52] They went on to say,

> Along with many in the besieged cities, and now Mrs Ogata of the UNHCR, we call for Srebrenica and Sarajevo to be declared UN protectorates—to remove political legitimacy from the warlords, to disarm the paramilitaries, . . . [and] possibly through the creation of a wider UN transitional authority, to create the economic, social and civic conditions throughout Bosnia-Herzegovina in which law and order can be restored and refugees returned to their homes. Plans for ethnic cantonisation are repellant and unworkable. We call for support for the restoration of multi-ethnic communities in Bosnia-Herzegovina as a political objective. . . . The authority of the UN should be used to close detention camps and stop atrocities, to give legitimacy to those opposition voices who share our objectives, and to bring those responsible for war crimes to justice. The future of Bosnia-Herzegovina has to be decided, not by the warmongers hiding behind "negotiations," but by all its citizens through a democratic process. This process can only be established once hostilities cease, law and order is restored and the

> atmosphere of fear removed. As long as we stick to principles of human values there is no compromise acceptable on ethnic purity so closely connected with territorial claims. There is only one message to the warlords: we will not join in, even if our politicians are inclined to do so.[53]

Responses to their article were mixed. Tom Gallagher, at the Department of Peace Studies, Bradford University, criticized HCA, and Kaldor specifically, for their passivity and for not going far enough. Gallagher argued that, as the HCA had been established to support peace, democracy, and a European civil society, it had failed in its mission. Paralyzed in the face of a Yugoslavian civil war, HCA stood, not unlike the governments and international organizations it criticized, wholly ineffectual. Criticizing Kaldor for drawing distinctions between levels of military intervention and then opting for a "gradual approach," Gallagher insisted that organizing civil society protests were, at best, a "minimalist" approach. To prove its worth, he suggested, the HCA should recognize the principle of the peace movement regarding the "use of force in cold war times" as wholly obsolete in the face of potentially millions of civilians being slaughtered. Furthermore, Gallagher argued, HCA's response should have been to mobilize those who sympathized with its aims to pressure governments to take prompt, measured actions of a military and nonmilitary kind, to stop the slaughter.[54]

In another letter, K. W. J. Barnham agreed in principle with the ideas Kaldor and Buirski proposed regarding the UN intervention. However, Barnham suggested that the "how" was much more complicated without an actual military invasion, which he conceded the United Nations would reject.[55] Martin Shaw, a lecturer at Sussex University, in a letter, contended that any UN safe haven as proposed by Kaldor and Buirski would in reality need a UN military force to defend the havens against the Serbian military and concurred with Kaldor and Buirski's claim that no government would act unless public opinion demanded it.[56]

In their letter of reply in May 1993, Kaldor and Buirski were more explicit about the use of force. Appealing again to citizens throughout Europe, they asked that citizens demand action from their governments. Because the Vance-Owen plan was rejected by the Bosnian Serb Parliament and could not stem the ongoing ethnic cleansing, the West must act with a new strategy. They suggested that a UN civil administration should be established in BaH to manage the humanitarian aid, and an international force deployed to stop the shelling and ethnic cleansing. A political-military solution was required from the United Nations to immediately establish safe zones for those areas under immediate danger and for the safe passage of relief convoys. A UN transitional authority was needed to restore the rule of law and would require a clear mandate to protect civilians in BaH, they argued, not just to protect that state.[57]

Following this exchange, Kaldor began to develop a more comprehensive concept of safe havens, envisaging more than peacekeeping. Rather she emphasized a UN civilian-led administration augmented by law enforcement. In 1993, Kaldor developed a plan, which she outlined in *A UN Authority for Bosnia-Herzegovina*. Her proposal provided a political and military solution to the conflict. Compared to diplomats and negotiators, Kaldor saw the problem as more nuanced: How does a country ensure that the link between peace and human rights, or between politics from below and civil society, is not just retained but thrives? The Vance-Owen plan, Kaldor argued, was a political solution to stop the fighting. However, she continued, political solutions could be established only once the fighting had ceased: "Instead of trying to find a political solution in order to stop the fighting, the aim would be to find a political solution only after the fighting had stopped," and then "a democratic process can be established."[58]

The plan also reflected Kaldor's shift toward cosmopolitan politics to solve the problem of organized violence and genocide. The political objective of the proposed UN authority was for "extensive international civil involvement until the atmosphere of fear has been removed,"[59] so that, thereafter, citizens could begin the process of deciding their own future, rather than being forced to allow warring political elites, the army, or the paramilitary to decide it for them. The role of the temporary UN administration was to take over civil political authority until the rule of law and a democratic framework were sufficiently developed. The UN authority would not recognize the recent ethnic demarcations, and the civil administration would be supported, Kaldor declared, "through full-scale military intervention."[60]

Rather than the traditional objectives of crushing the enemy or forcing them to the negotiating table, as in classical notions of war and diplomacy, the political objective of the intervention force would be to stop the violence and guarantee the protection of ordinary Bosnians and Herzegovians, not unlike domestic civil policing. It would also ensure the territorial integrity of BaH, uphold a cease-fire, and provide immediate assistance to besieged towns. Kaldor suggested that refugees and peace and human rights groups within BaH would support the proposal for a UN transitional authority. Moreover, she added, these ideas had been proposed by those living within Yugoslavia since the beginning of the war:

> Essentially the task of the UN authority would be to supervise the restoration of order and to establish the conditions in which elections could be held for a constituent assembly which would approve the constitution. . . . A UN authority could enhance the legitimacy of the international community. . . . The Vance-Owen maps could undermine its legitimacy; however sincere and energetic the efforts to stop war by finding an acceptable compromise among the warring parties, the maps ultimately confirm the status quo established by the fighting and reward those who engage in ethnic cleansing.[61]

However, Kaldor's shift toward the protection of civilians by force remained a minority position both within the broader international HCA group and across the international community more generally. Licht maintained that HCA never "advocat[ed] for military intervention, at least, not as an organization."[62] British policymakers still had very little appetite to intervene. Douglas Hurd, then British foreign secretary, argued that, at an international level, "no one favoured standing aside from Bosnia completely. [However,] no one was ready to stop the killing by taking the country over and imposing a just solution. Everyone favoured limited intervention."[63] In his article in the *Guardian*, Hurd insisted that, although events in Yugoslavia were nothing short of tragic, few were advocating military intervention by force:

> "Something must be done" is the cry of columnists. . . . [Yet] very few specifically recommend comprehensive military action. There is certainly no member of NATO talking in those terms; and indeed no government which is prepared to send its own troops to fight and stay in Bosnia for that purpose. Yet that is the only logical means of practising what they preach. . . . What we are doing in Bosnia is not abdication, but sense.[64]

Later, Hurd maintained that at the heart of limited intervention was a realist approach to the war in BaH. Referring to a group of critics who reminded him of Otto von Bismarck's alleged statement that the Balkans were "not worth the bones of a single Pomeranian grenadier," Hurd concluded that "the instinct of the realist was to stay out."[65] Added to this was the very real belief that intervention could not—and would not—stop the war. Hurd commented later, "If the firm and rapid use of military force would have stopped the fighting (let alone brought peace with justice) we would have agreed to it. . . . But professional advice allied to common sense repeatedly indicated that this was a hallucination."[66]

As further international attempts to arrive at a peace settlement continued, Kaldor and the HCA founded "The Last Chance" campaign in June 1993. The Last Chance Appeal asked leaders around the world to "have the courage to start again with a new political approach: lifting the siege of Sarajevo, establishing administration there, and [making preparations] for a UN Authority for the whole of Bosnia Herzegovina."[67] Local branches of the HCA organized a series of protests against the siege of Sarajevo and the war in BaH. These were held in Sarajevo, Zagreb, Belgrade, Istanbul, The Hague, Kishinyov (Moldova), Prague, Paris, Copenhagen, Rome, Sofia, and many places in Britain. Over 6,000 signatures were presented to the European Community, the United Nations, and the G7 heads. The authors and signatories of the Last Chance Appeal demanded that the siege of Sarajevo be lifted and a UN transitional authority be implemented across all of BaH.[68] The appeal was the subject of media campaigns, parliamentary debates, and municipal resolutions.

Kaldor lobbied government ministers directly. For example, she sent the Last Chance Appeal to Hurd, asking him to press for intervention. Hurd remained reticent about the use of force. In reply to Kaldor, Hurd wrote that "we all want to see an end to the tragedy that has been inflicted on Bosnia-Herzegovina for the past 15 months," and he stated that international efforts were being made to reach a "negotiated settlement":

> The European Council in Copenhagen on 21–22 June supported the renewed efforts of Lord Owen and Mr Stoltenberg to promote a fair and viable peace acceptable to all three parties. This would have to be based on the principles established by the London Conference, including maintenance of the territorial integrity of Bosnia-Herzegovina. With the situation in Sarajevo and elsewhere deteriorating, we must do everything to encourage a negotiated settlement. I am sure that there will be a fine discussion of this at the Tokyo Summit.[69]

Kaldor was not satisfied with Hurd's response. In her letter of reply, Kaldor requested a meeting with Hurd. She stated that she wanted to discuss the Last Chance Appeal. She also wanted to negotiate between Hurd and General Morillon to lift the siege in Sarajevo. After fifteen months under siege, she argued, Sarajevo had begun to divide ethnically. Despite UN resolutions that permitted UNPROFOR to use all means necessary to ensure humanitarian aid, the political will, warned Kaldor, remained grossly inadequate:

> The situation in Sarajevo is desperate. When I spoke to General Morillon, he said that lifting the siege of Sarajevo was militarily feasible even with the troops now available in Sarajevo. I think it could change the whole role of the international community if the siege were lifted. If we allow the Serbs to get away with preventing fuel supplies from reaching Sarajevo, how do we honestly expect a "fair and viable peace"?[70]

Kaldor also continued her campaign in the form of newspaper articles and public debate. She emphasized that to establish the safe havens required not only UN forces on the ground defending civilians and stopping the fighting but also a political objective. Kaldor maintained that "a civil administration would be the key to restoring legitimacy and authority in the former Yugoslavia."[71] Civil society was still alive in BaH, though underground. But now, more than ever, it desperately needed international support.

The UN Security Council finally declared a number of cities in BaH to be safe havens. Security Council Resolution 819 (April 1993) and 824 (May 1993) declared that Srebrenica, Sarajevo, Tuzla, Goražde, Bihać, and Žepa and their surroundings should be designated safe areas and be safeguarded from military assault. Resolution 836 (June 1993) authorized UNPROFOR "to take necessary measures, including the use of force, to reply to bombardments against the safe areas by any of the parties or in the event of any deliberate obstruction in or around those areas to the freedom of movement of UNPROFOR or of protected humanitarian convoys."[72]

Despite the declaration being sanguine and confident, UN Secretary-General Boutros Boutros-Ghali qualified the defensive nature of the safe havens. In his statement, Boutros-Ghali explained that troops on the ground would not "guarantee the defence of the safe area, but would provide a basic level of deterrence, assuming consent and cooperation of the parties."[73] What made this statement particularly dispiriting was that Serbian troops were not known for consenting to, or cooperating with, an international agreement during the course of the war. In fact, they had consistently gone against such agreements. Moreover, if the political objective was not to defend safe havens, then what was the objective? And what purpose was there in sending often ill-equipped and underresourced forces that could only deter an army that was of a cooperative and consenting nature?

Safe havens had been established in northern Iraq precisely because Saddam Hussein's regime proved a threat to the Kurdish population, both in the past, with the use of chemical weapons, and at the point of establishing the safe haven when 1.5 million Kurds had fled their homes and moved toward the Turkish border. Moreover, the Kurdish safe haven had succeeded in its objective because British and US forces guaranteed the defense of the safe haven, irrespective of the consent of Saddam Hussein, and, when called upon, had defended the Kurdish minority when attacked by Iraqi forces. But the protection of northern Iraq was not a UN-mandated mission. This mandate, and the execution of this mandate, had been determined outside the UNSC.

Blue Cards

Following the implementation of UN safe havens, the HCA was given the status of an "implementing agency" by the UNHCR, which Secretary-General Boutros-Ghali declared the "lead agency" in the effort to establish safe havens.[74] As an implementing agency, the HCA, and by extension Kaldor, were provided access to and mobility between the siege lines by the possession of a blue ID card issued by the United Nations.[75] The blue ID card allowed Kaldor to move around the country during the war in support of local HCA activists. As a partner of UNHCR, HCA members could travel on UN planes and with UN convoys. While on the advisory committee for the HCA Sarajevo office, along with Zdravko Grebo, Mient Jan Faber, and others, Kaldor became increasingly involved in HCA projects in BaH.[76] These projects included delivering blankets gathered from HCA affiliates across Europe, collecting books for the national and university libraries in Sarajevo,[77] conducting summer schools and courses at universities in Mostar and Tuzla,[78] providing legal aid and civil monitoring of humanitarian aid,[79] and hosting human rights workshops with attendees that included the Bosnian prime minister and government officials, representatives from the United Nations, members of the military, lawyers, representatives of NGOs, embassy representatives, and academics.[80]

Now as UNHCR partners, Kaldor and Faber, as the more high-profile faces of HCA, continued to push for a more comprehensive UN transitional authority to be established across BaH. The primary objective would be to provide military and civil assistance, with the aim of reestablishing full Bosnian sovereignty as soon as possible.[81] In September 1993, the HCA developed a proposal that detailed a UN protectorate in Sarajevo and a European Community protectorate in Mostar, to be established immediately. This proposal would provide civil administration and oversight for police and enforce the rule of law with military intervention. This safe haven plan would be then widened to all of BaH.[82]

Although Kaldor and Faber were key figures, many Bosnian HCA activists supported this proposal or, as in Grebo's case, had been major proponents since the start of the war. By this stage, Zdravko Grebo and Haris Pasovic, the director of Sarajevo's main artistic theater working with HCA, believed that "the UN and the world [had failed] to quell the violence in Bosnia,"[83] and that inaction had led to the current situation. In his own proposal, entitled "Appeal from Sarajevo to the European Council Meeting in Copenhagen," Grebo advocated for an "EC [European Community] (or UN) Sponsored Transitional authority":

> [It] would be set up for a given period of time, say ten years. All Bosnians would thus at last be given the time and opportunity to reflect on what their new, independent, civil institutions should be, and to call on the advice from outside for this purpose. . . . The situation is now such that security cannot be entrusted to any one of the three warring parties . . . ; it must be left to outsiders to provisionally ensure this essential aspect of social life. The proposal would call for the long term deployment of EC military and civilian personnel.[84]

Yet, while activists in HCA, such as Grebo, were constantly engaged with officials concerning how to solve the problem of violence in BaH, he, like many others, depended upon his more famous colleagues, such as Kaldor, to get his views across and to have his concerns heard. During the war, while working with HCA and the UNHCR, Kaldor traveled to BaH more frequently in support of the HCA's operations but also to raise the profile of activists and awareness of conditions on the ground. For example, Kaldor conducted civic monitoring in Mostar and drove from Split to the besieged city of Tuzla as part of the "Open City" project. She also stayed in Sarajevo for extended periods to support the HCA office. On one occasion, having arrived on the UNHCR's monthly rations plane, Kaldor was stranded in Sarajevo after the airport was shelled and temporarily closed in July 1993. While in Sarajevo, Kaldor worked with Grebo and continued to gain some insight into life in a besieged, militarized city. Later, Kaldor wrote of her experience in the *Progressive*:

> It is dangerous to walk the streets. . . . There are thirty-six different armies in town and crime is rife. There is no water, no coal, no electricity. Humanitarian aid is completely inadequate. . . . Monthly rations . . . consisted of one kilo of flour, half a kilo of rice, half a litre of oil, one can of beef, three bars of soap and a packet of biscuits for those over sixty. The black market flourishes. . . . Zdravko is respected because of his integrity, because of his consistent anti-nationalist stance, and because unlike the politicians, he shares the privations of life in Sarajevo—the exposure to sniper fire and shelling, the lack of food, water and fuel.[85]

Although Kaldor often deferred to HCA activists, such as Grebo, for options and problem solving on the ground, she, in turn, was relied upon to support the same activists who felt increasingly disempowered by the experience of war. Mary Kaldor, Mient Jan Faber, and Igor Blazevic (then HCA Balkan project coordinator based in Sarajevo and Prague) organized a meeting with David Reilly, then heading the Bosnian program at the UNHCR in Zagreb, and also with Tony Land, head of the UNHCR office in Sarajevo.[86] Yet, although Blazevic was the Bosnian project coordinator for HCA and from Bosnia, he felt unable to present his ideas to the UNHCR directly and relied on both Kaldor and Faber to engage with the UNHCR on his behalf. As war deepened, in many ways Bosnians became a restricted subclass within their own state.[87]

Although Blazevic worked with HCA in the assistance of humanitarian monitoring, he, like most Bosnians, found moving around BaH and some parts of Sarajevo impossible, even with a blue ID card. Given the dangers of the occupied Bosnian Serb areas and Croat Serb areas, foreigners were safer than the local Bosnians in traversing BaH, even under the auspices of the United Nations. Faber also observed this dynamic. In his report, Faber remarked that "initially, we have to send Radha [Kumar] to Sarajevo for assisting the establishment of a network of civic activists. As a foreigner she probably was able to pass borders which couldn't easily be passed by locals."[88] In short, local activists who wanted to participate in their own civic monitoring were stymied by the fact that although they should not need a blue ID card to safely move throughout their country, foreigners could do so more safely. As Blazevic told Kaldor, "it is a little bit stupid that I am asking [for a blue] ID card for me as well."[89]

For Bosnians, such irony was not simply confined to blue cards and civic monitoring but was also apparent in the limits of civil society and civilization in a war zone. By November 1993, the failure of political action to stop the war, Kaldor maintained, meant that civil society was now in crisis and dissolving fast in the face of abject violence. Consequently, as enmity increased, many Bosnians were beginning to lose their appetite for defending a multiethnic state.[90] As Haris Pasovic, an HCA colleague and friend of Kaldor's, declared, "Welcome to the Twenty-first Century. Come and see the beginning of the end of Western civilization."[91] Hirvo, a writer, quipped, "[Francis] Fukuyama talked about the end of history. This is it." For Hirvo, Sarajevo was the "future."[92]

Ethnic Division and the End of Civil Society

By the end of 1994, the HCA project to create safe havens had failed; in fact, the UN havens had become the most dangerous places in Bosnia.[93] The UN safe zones left civilians exposed as targets because they were increasingly segregated by ethnicity and often undefended. In one instance, Serb fighter jets used napalm on the Muslim enclave of Biha , which was a UN-declared safe haven. The United Nations claimed that the napalm bomb did not detonate. Nevertheless, the attack on the UN safe area was affirmation that the Serbs were intensifying their assaults as winter approached and that the United Nations was either unwilling or unable to use force to protect the Bihać safe haven.[94] In another instance, Kaldor described the situation after the first massacre in Sarajevo's safe haven: "In Sarajevo the ceasefire is holding. But nobody is celebrating. It is partly because it was achieved through a massacre. It is partly caution. And it is partly because it has come too late."[95]

The violence in the safe havens was a predictable outcome of two factors. First, the United Nations relied upon indiscriminate military air strikes against enemy targets to control the violence rather than using troops on the ground to more specifically protect civilians. Second, UN forces often were not granted the permission to return fire unless fired upon themselves. As a result, civilians in the safe havens who were unarmed could not defend themselves, and, given the order not to fire unless fired upon, in some incidents, the UN forces were made to be passive witnesses to the violence as they continued to receive conflicting mandates from the United Nations and their respective governments.[96]

Kaldor believed that without the political will to intervene by force to stop the war, the UN approach was now to partition and separate the ethnic groups to curtail the violence; two years of Sarajevo's siege had effectively destroyed the Bosnian people's desire for multiethnic coexistence, and a divided city and country where the inevitable end result. Protracted inertia by the UN Security Council had compounded the ethnic divide beyond repair: the "most likely outcome . . . [was] a city divided under international military protection, the continued siege of Sarajevo, with the only access remaining restricted to the air, making it impossible for Sarajevo's population to leave."[97] The presence of French troops on, "ironically, the 'Bridge of Brotherhood and Unity' that divided the now Serb-held Goražde from the rest of the city exemplified the expected outcome of the conflict.[98]

The critical point for the war in BaH came on 11 July 1995, when around 1,500 Serbian troops began their assault on the safe haven of Srebrenica, overrunning the small contingent of lightly armed Dutch peacekeepers. Hajrudin Avidic, mayor of Srebrenica, could be heard describing the situation on Radio Sarajevo: "The town is being pounded with everything you care to name . . . [and] UNPROFOR has withdrawn." He went on to warn, "At the moment tanks are moving in, and if the international community does not intervene, the people in this town will suffer a catastrophe."[99] The siege of Srebrenica caused US secretary of defense William Perry to question the United Nations' ability to continue its humanitarian mandate within its restrictive political objectives.[100]

Four days after the offensive began, the UN command threatened military intervention. Despite two successful NATO air strikes on Serbian artillery inside the enclave, Dutch defense minister Joris Voorhoeve requested that air strikes be suspended after receiving threats that the Serbian military would execute the thirty Dutch soldiers held hostage by them. After the fall of Srebrenica, the Serbian military proceeded to murder 8,000 Muslim men. Having effectively seized Srebrenica, the Serbian chain of command then had their sights set on overrunning the nearby safe haven of Žepa.

When military intervention was finally authorized to stop the war, and the aggression quickly drew to a close after foreign soldiers arrived, an earlier claim that outside military intervention in the Balkans was futile was repudiated.[101] The war in BaH ended on 12 October 1995 when Richard Holbrooke, US assistant secretary of state, brokered an enforceable cease-fire agreement. The General Framework for Peace in Bosnia and Herzegovina (or "Dayton Accords") was formulated in Dayton, Ohio, on 21 November 1995 and signed in Paris on 14 December 1995.[102]

For someone whose agenda was not only to protect the people of BaH but also to retain multiethnic civil society, Kaldor regarded the intervention as too little, too late. Moreover, the war in BaH ended after the populations had already been "ethnically cleansed," with around 150,000 people killed and almost two-thirds of the population displaced.[103] Kaldor conceded that Western air strikes against Serbian positions, in addition to French and British ground forces, had lifted the siege of Sarajevo. However, she argued, the West had, through diplomatic arrangements, including the Dayton Accords, "legalised what had happened on the ground: the partitioning of Bosnia into separate Serb, Muslim, and Croat parts."[104] The negotiators had continued to give warring elites political legitimacy through the process of negotiating the accords. To add further insult to injury, many of these elites who negotiated the borders and the Dayton Accords were later subject to a series of indictments for war crimes, including Rodovan Karadžić, Ratko Mladić, and Slobodan Milošević.[105] This turn of events served to underscore the complicit role of diplomacy. It also reflected the limited tools available to negotiators when dealing with warring leaders who are accused of war crimes.

War had changed Kaldor. The transformation was not just an intellectual or professional one but also a deeply personal one. Kaldor saw war in the Balkans and Caucasus not only through her own eyes but through the eyes of her friends and fellow activists. Kaldor was not the same person, because neither were Grebo or Abdullayeva, or others she had worked with during the course of the wars in the Balkans and Caucasus. As cochair of the HCA, she had been a proponent of a united Europe, one that supported civil society, the link between peace and human rights, and politics from below. But in many respects, that project had failed.

Up until the wars in the Balkans and South Caucasus, Kaldor's intellectual and activist preoccupations were focused on moving away from a war-based system dependent on a military industrial complex in the Western and Eastern blocs. Her work at SIPRI, her book *The Baroque Arsenal,* and her work on conversion were all products of these preoccupations. The Cold War, as Kaldor had argued, had been an "imaginary" war but, nonetheless, framed in classical conceptions of war: states against states, supported by classical ideas of armies against armies, both preparing for a nuclear war. Unlike the Cold War, the wars of the Balkans and Caucasus were executed by state and quasi-state actors, within their own state, and explicitly against their own people. In her response to wars in the Caucasus and Balkans, and as an activist in HCA, Kaldor began to consider the problem of political violence in the post–Cold War era and to influence public debate surrounding the role of international norms to protect civilians in the context of war. Both her thinking and her approach adapted to events as they unfolded on the ground.

For Kaldor, the nature of war was not new, but the character of war was. Over the next four years, Kaldor developed the notion of "new wars" and, with this new insight, the proposition of "cosmopolitan law enforcement."

Notes

1. Igor Blazevic, "'Urgent' Letter to Mary Kaldor," 4 February 1994, PA-MK-HCA-Brighton.

2. T. Rowe, "'We Have Evidence of Bosnian Genocide': Rights Group Wants War Crimes Investigation of Serbian President," *Hamilton Spectator*, 13 August 1992, p. A.1.

3. See, for example, Andreas, *Blue Helmets and Black Markets.*

4. See Stewart, *Hunting the Tiger.*

5. Gjelten, *Sarajevo Daily*, pp. 88–89; Stewart, *Hunting the Tiger*, pp. 80–90.

6. Owen, *Balkan Odyssey*, p. 84. Owen maintained that this tactic was more effective than traditional warfare, stating that the "medieval siege, putting citizens under barrage and psychological pressure but not launching a frontal attack" was also used in Sarajevo.

7. Silber and Little, *Yugoslavia*, pp. 244–247.

8. Kumar, *Divide and Fall?* p. 40.

9. On Operation Provide Comfort, see the Statement of Lt. Gen. John M. Shalikashvili, US Commander, Operation Provide Comfort, House of Representatives, Committee on Armed Services, Defense Policy Panel, presided over by Rep. Les Aspin, chairman of the panel, Washington, DC, 4 September, 1991. Also see Gordon W. Rudd, *Humanitarian Intervention.* Although UN Security Council Resolution 688 did not explicitly authorize US, French, and British forces to secure safe havens for the Kurdish population in northern Iraq, given the constraints of the UN Security Council, an indirect approach provided the most viable solution to ensuring the protection of the

population. The threat to civilians did not qualify as a "threat to international security" as outlined in Chapter VI of the UN Charter, "Pacific Settlement of Disputes." In particular, Article 37 read, "If the Security Council deems that the continuance of the dispute is in fact likely to endanger the maintenance of international peace and security, it shall decide whether to take action under Article 36 or to recommend such terms of settlement as it may consider appropriate." See United Nations, "Chapter VI: Pacific Settlement of Disputes," Charter of the United Nations, online. Given that China would invariably veto any suggestion to declare Iraq's treatment of the Kurds and Shias as a "threat to international peace," the British and French establishment of safe havens and monitoring of no-fly zones was therefore executed without specific Security Council authorization (although sympathetic to the policy indications adopted earlier by the Security Council). See Rosalyn Higgins, Memorandum to the Foreign Affairs Committee, "The Expanding Role of the United Nations and Its Implications for United Kingdom Policy," 17 February 1993, and Foreign Affairs Committee, 17 February 1993, Q.390.

10. Stephanie Barker, Helsinki Citizens' Assembly Report, 1992, PA-MK-HCA-Brighton.

11. Faber, "Human Security from Below."

12. In November 1992, the HCA and the Standing Conference of Local and Regional Authorities led a joint delegation to Sarajevo to discuss the proposals at the Ohrid conference with civic movements, government officials, and international groups. The delegation included several participants from Sarajevo, including Zdravko Grebo, who hosted the delegation, and Ibrahim Spahić, then at the International Peace Centre. They also met with writers, film directors, and artists. Local HCA branches in partnership with HCA members across Europe continued to lobby UNHCR officials. The campaign was then expanded to mobilize the European Community and United Nations directly. Proposals were also presented to the Commission on Security and Cooperation in Europe at its Council of Ministers meeting held in Prague. See Radha Kumar, report on Sarajevo, 26–29 November 1992, 2 December 1992, 1-5, MK-PA-HCA-Brighton.

13. See "Proposal: HCA Office in Sarajevo," Helsinki Citizens' Assembly, 23 November 1993, 1-11, PA-MK-HCA-Brighton.

14. Paddy Ashdown, correspondence with author, 30 June and 4 July 2011.

15. *The Balkan Peace and Integration Programme, 1991–Present*, n.d., European Dialogue, p. 4; Kaldor, "A Decade of Humanitarian Intervention," p. 117.

16. Zdravko Grebo, interview with author, 7 March 2011; Mient Jan Faber, interview with author, 30 May 2011; Mary Kaldor, interview with author, 10 July 2011. Also see Igor Blazevic, "HCA Office in Sarajevo: Proposal Submitted to the HCA ICC Meeting," Prague, 4–7 March 1994, 1-33, PA-MK-HCA-Brighton.

17. Zdravko Grebo, interview with author, 7 March 2011.

18. Mary Kaldor, interview with author, 20 June 2011.

19. David Owen, correspondence with author, 19 September 2012. Kaldor later stated: "Owen made this point at the time. We thought the situation was too dangerous to be pragmatic. He ought to have been making the argument for more troops rather than opposing safe havens." Mary Kaldor, correspondence with author, 25 October 2012.

20. "The Search for a Safe Haven in the Kingdom of Death," *Economist* 325, no. 7786, 21 November 1992, pp. 59–60.

21. Ogata, quoted in ibid., p. 59.

22. Ibid.

23. UN Security Council Resolution 770, online. Moreover, the Security Council demanded that "unimpeded and continuous access to all camps, prisons and detention

centres be granted immediately to the International Committee of the Red Cross and other relevant humanitarian organizations and that all detainees therein receive humane treatment, including adequate food, shelter and medical care." Finally, the resolution evinced a commitment to an intervention mandate, as opposed to humanitarian assistance and peacekeeping.

24. Ibid.

25. While negotiations between the three states and the newly formed Serbian Republic continued, winter approached and conditions worsened across BaH. Electricity, gas, and water services became sporadic in Sarajevo, and UN humanitarian convoys continuously blocked by Serb forces struggled to deliver aid to Muslim enclaves in central Bosnia, now overcrowded with refugees or internally displaced peoples. See Rieff, *Slaughterhouse*; and Gow, *Triumph of the Lack of Will.*

26. John F. Burns, "Bosnians Plead for a Chance for Unity," *New York Times*, 3 February 1993, p. A.8.

27. "The Search for a Safe Haven in the Kingdom of Death."

28. Izetbegović, quoted in Burns, "Bosnians Pleads for a Chance for Unity," p. A.8. Moreover, Izetbegović maintained that, although he respected Vance and Owen and believed that they were trying to "square the circle," he argued that violence orchestrated by nationalistic state and quasi-state forces was nothing short of criminality. Izetbegović argued that Karadžić was not a legitimate political actor to be negotiated with but rather a criminal to be indicted.

29. Izetbegović, quoted in ibid., p. A.8. Kaldor later stated: "A very important argument was that Izetbegović was the elected president. They [Bosnian-Serbian quasi-state actors] were not and he felt they should not be treated as equals." Mary Kaldor, correspondence with author, 25 October 2012.

30. Initially, Milošević and Karadžić accepted the Vance-Owen peace plan, but it was later rejected by the Bosnian Serb Parliament. See D. B. Ottaway, "U.N. Plan for Peace Rejected by Serbs," *Austin American Statesman*, 6 May 1993, p. A.1.

31. Mearsheimer and Pape, "The Answer," p. 24. Mearsheimer and Pape recognized that Bosnians remained reticent about the idea of further ethnic division and continued to support a multiethnic state; despite the citizens' preferences, however, they concluded that partition was the way forward.

32. Cyrus Vance resigned after the failed Vance-Owen plan. Replacing him on 1 May 1993 was Thorvald Stoltenberg, former Norwegian minister of foreign affairs and former UN high commissioner for refugees. See Rogel, *The Breakup of Yugoslavia and Its Aftermath.*

33. According to Mirko Pejanović, the Owen-Stoltenberg peace plan had four main points: (1) As demanded by the United States, the BaH would be a UN member state with internationally recognized boundaries; (2) the Bosniak territorial areas would be no less than 32 percent of the total area of BaH; (3) Bosnia would have legal access to the sea from Neum to Brčko within its legal borders; and (4) Sarajevo would remain physically unpartitioned and be the capital city of BaH. The United States also demanded that the population be allowed to return to the territory from which they had been expelled by force before and during the war. See Pejanović, *Through Bosnian Eyes*, pp. 177–178.

34. On 13 May 1992, Karadžić was voted president of Bosnian Serb administration, which was based in Pale, following the dissolution of the Socialist Federal Republic of Yugoslavia. Throughout the time he assumed his position, Karadžić held de jure powers, as per the constitution of the Bosnian Serb administration, which included commanding control of the Bosnian Serb army.

35. Karadžić, quoted in Paul Lewis, "2 Leaders Propose Dividing Bosnia into Three Areas," *New York Times*, 17 June 1993, p. A.3. One of the sticking points of the Geneva meeting was that Karadžić wanted to also carve up Sarajevo. Karadžić already

had control of several suburbs of Sarajevo and had installed a type of "Berlin Wall." See also Pejanović, *Through Bosnian Eyes*.

36. The International Criminal Tribunal for the Former Yugoslavia (ICTY) later indicted several political and military leaders from the self-proclaimed Croatian area of BaH, in the Lašva Valley case, for ethnic cleansing and war crimes committed against Bosniak civilians. For example, see Kordić and Čerkez, ICTY (IT-95-14/2); Prosecutor v. Tihomir Blaškić Judgement, ICTY (IT-95-14); Prosecutor v. Miroslav Bralo Judgement, ICTY (IT-95-17).

37. See, for example, Bowden, *Black Hawk Down*, p. 114; Weiss and Hubert, *The Responsibility to Protect*; UN Security Council Resolution 794 (1992), para. 3, online.

38. Huntington, "New Contingencies, Old Roles," p. 42.

39. Hurd, *In Search for Peace*, p. 131.

40. Heath, quoted in Goldstone, *For Humanity*, p. 74. See also the Independent International Commission on Kosovo, *The Kosovo Report*.

41. See West, *Black Lamb and Grey Falcon*. West believed that it was "impossible to think of the Balkans as gentle and lamb-like" (p. 21), and she considered violence to be the Balkan way of resolving conflict, particularly in relation to politics. Furthermore, West's book was largely considered to be pro-Serbian.

42. Owen, *Balkan Odyssey*, p. 6.

43. Ibid., p. 3. Owen maintained, "It points to a culture of violence within a crossroad civilization where three religions, Orthodox Christianity, Islam, and Roman Catholicism, have divided communities and on occasions become the marks of identification in a dark and virulent nationalism" (p. 3).

44. Kaplan, *Balkan Ghosts*. Kaplan used West's book as his guide as he traveled through Yugoslavia. In *Balkan Ghosts*, Kaplan claimed, "I would rather have lost my passport and money than my heavily thumbed and annotated copy of *Black Lamb and Grey Falcon*" (p. 8).

45. See, for example, Michael T. Kaufman, "The Dangers of Letting a President Read," *New York Times*, 22 May 1999, online.

46. For "historical grain," see Hodge, *Britain and the Balkans*, p. 3. For "pusillanimous realism," see Gow, *Triumph of the Lack of Will*.

47. Kaufman, "The Dangers of Letting a President Read"; Holbrooke, *To End a War*. Malcolm's book argued that Bosnia was indeed cosmopolitan and multiethnic and that the Bosnian war in 1992 was the result of populist, elitist politicians who were essentially criminals (Malcolm, *Bosnia*). Holbrooke suggested, "It was, of course, undeniable that the ethnic groups within Yugoslavia nursed deep-seated grievances against one another. But in and of itself, ethnic friction, no matter how serious, did not make the tragedy inevitable—or the three ethnic groups equally guilty" (p. 23).

48. See Kaldor and Licht, *Yugofax Breakdown*.

49. Morillon and Hollingworth had decided to lead a convoy to Srebrenica, which they knew was in danger of falling to the Serbs. Bringing along a medical doctor from the World Health Organization, journalists, and Canadian soldiers, they did not request permission from Sadako Ogata, UN high commissioner for refugees, or the United Nations in New York. Upon entering Srebrenica after a nine-month siege, they found dire conditions. Seeing the conditions and heeding the pleas of the women, overnight Morillon devised a plan. The next morning Morillon requested a megaphone, a UN flag, and a radio (to allow the Serbs to listen in) and requested Hajrudin Avidic, mayor of Srebrenica, to gather the people of the town. Leaning outside a window several stories above the crowd, Morillon made an impromptu announcement to the crowd down below: "I came here voluntarily to be with you. I have decided to stay. I am placing you under the protection of the United Nations." At his cue, Hollingworth pushed the pole

with the UN flag out the window, and the crowd responded enthusiastically. Journalist Tony Birtley, having realized he had just captured a world exclusive on his camera, asked General Morillon, having now unilaterally placed the city under the protection of the United Nations, if the safe haven would work. Morillon replied, "Of course." Hollingworth, *Merry Christmas, Mr Larry*, pp. 184–209.

50. See Ogata, *The Turbulent Decade*.

51. Hollingworth, *Merry Christmas, Mr Larry*, p. 203.

52. Mary Kaldor and Jeanette Buirski, "Letter: Step-by-Step to Lasting Peace in Bosnia," *Guardian* [London], 8 April 1993, p. 23.

53. Ibid.

54. Tom Gallagher, "Finding a Policy of Peace," *Guardian* [London], 14 April 1993, p. 19.

55. K. W. J. Barnham, "A Show of Force That Could Save Bosnia," *Guardian* [London], 10 April 1993, p. 20.

56. Shaw, "Finding a Policy for Peace," p. 19.

57. Mary Kaldor and Jeanette Buirski, "The Search for a Solution for Bosnia," *Guardian* [London], 7 May 1993, p. 21.

58. Mary Kaldor, *UN Authority for Bosnia-Herzegovina*, n.d., 1, PA-MK-HCA-Brighton. Although the report is undated, it was clearly written just prior to 9 May 1993.

59. Ibid.

60. Ibid.

61. Ibid.

62. Sonja Licht, correspondence with author, 4 May 2010.

63. Hurd, *The Search for Peace*, p. 131.

64. Douglas Hurd, "Keeping Our Heads in a Nightmare," *Guardian* [London], 1 July 1993, p. 22. Hurd's article was attached to a reply letter to Kaldor for her reference. Not satisfied with Hurd's reply, Kaldor's campaign to lift the siege of Sarajevo took symbolic gestures to the door of the British prime minister's official residence at Downing Street. Kaldor and others, including Michael Ignatiff, then editorial columnist for the *Observer*, Susannah York, British actor, and several British MPs, including Michael Meacher and Calum MacDonald, delivered sewage to the door of Downing Street. In an open letter in the *Independent*, the group explained that UN Resolution 770, passed on 14 August 1992, authorized the United Nations to stop the siege and to use "all necessary means" to get humanitarian supplies to the people of BaH. Moreover, they argued, UN Resolution 815, adopted 30 March 1993, expanded authorization of UN troops to act "without the agreement of all parties, under Chapter VII of the Charter of the UN," explicitly enabling the regaining of control in BaH by force. Despite the UN resolutions, the group argued, families in Sarajevo were boiling sewage to extract drinking water, and after fifteen months of a gruelling siege, "now the Serbs are refusing to allow UN convoys carrying fuel supplies to enter the city. The fuel is needed to operate the pumps that clean the water. Surgeons cannot wash their hands before performing operations. The first cases of typhus have already been reported. The WHO [World Health Organization] is predicting imminent epidemics of typhus, dysentery and cholera." They also argued that General Morillon agreed that stopping the siege of Sarajevo was feasible, concluding the article with the following: "While we all acknowledge that the situation is complex and difficult, we cannot accept that the only alternative is to do nothing. We call upon our government, through its voice in the UN and its influence in Europe, to lift the siege now. This would not only bring relief to the people of Sarajevo, it would save a multi-ethnic and multi-cultural community which has resisted ethnic division and which symbolises the values of the UN Charter. It could also create a space where diplomatic and political initiatives would not be entirely dic-

tated by might over right." Pam Giddy, Lesley Absela, Lisa Appignanesi, Beryl Baincridge, Jeanette Buirski, Sarah Dunant, Lisa Jardine, Michael Ignatiff, Mary Kaldor, Julia Neuberger, Claire Rayner, Michelle Roberts, Natalie Speir, Susannah York, Michael Meacher, Calum MacDonald, Liz Lynne, Frank Field, Harry Barnes, and Lady Wynne Jones, "UN Has the Authority to Relieve Sarajevo," *Independent* [London], 17 July 1993, p. 15.

65. Hurd, *The Search for Peace*, p. 97.

66. Ibid. However, despite the initial European and national show of leadership and the diplomatic keenness demonstrated at the beginning of the war, the West hesitated on a clear strategy of action as war in Yugoslavia ensued. According to Hurd, there was never a member of Whitehall "sitting down calmly" who would conclude that providing economic aid or deploying British troops to Bosnia was in Britain's interest. Of course, Hurd insisted, Britain had a broader interest to avert Balkan war and to prevent a significant fall out between the West and Yeltsin's transforming Russia. Hurd later argued, "[The final test] to be applied in a democracy is public opinion. Realists and idealists have to concur on this. Public opinion cannot lead, neither can it be ignored. . . . Although public opinion could not force a government to undertake an enterprise against its better judgement, it can powerfully influence that judgement. On Bosnia no such influence was exerted. . . . It seemed possible that the general indignation and the individual advocacy of particular measures might fuse into powerful pressure for intervention. It never happened" (pp. 128–131).

67. The Sarajevo and international HCA branches started the Last Chance Appeal on June 21. See Igor Blazevic, "HCA Office in Sarajevo: Proposal Submitted to the HCA ICC Meeting, Prague," 4–7 March 1994, PA-MK-HCA-Brighton.

68. Mary Kaldor, "Bitter Lessons of Hiroshima," *Guardian* [London], 6 August 1993, p. 19. In the article, Kaldor encouraged people to take part in Hiroshima Day when an all-day vigil would be held in Trafalgar Square and other places in Britain. She also requested readers to send a fax of support to the Sarajevo HCA and contact their MPs to ask for Parliament to be recalled in order to demand that Sarajevo be saved.

69. Douglas Hurd, letter to Mary Kaldor, 5 July 1993, 1, PA-MK-HCA-Brighton.

70. Mary Kaldor, letter to Douglas Hurd, July 1993, 1, PA-MK-HCA-Brighton.

71. Mary Kaldor, quoted in James Cusick, "Safe Havens Urged for War-Torn Cities; Briton's Plan for Sarajevo Resurrected," *Independent* [London], 17 September 1993, p. 3.

72. Security Council Resolution 819 (1993), Security Council Resolution 824 (1993), Security Council Resolution 824 (1993), all available online.

73. Boutros Boutros-Ghali, cited in Gordon, "A Recipe for Making Safe Areas Unsafe," p. 213.

74. Boutros-Ghali began to refer to the UNHCR as the "lead agency" in May 1992. See "Secretary-General's Report," S/23900, 12 May 1992, para. 16. As Michael Pugh and S. Alex Cunliffe argued, the UNHCR ran into two key operational problems, largely because by spring 1992, for the first time in history, the UNHCR was effectively operating in the midst of a war zone. In the summer of 1991, the UNHCR appointed a special envoy, Jose-Maria Mendiluce, who established a separate office in Sarajevo before BaH declared independence. Beginning with nineteen staff for the entire former Yugoslavia at the end of 1991, by 1995 the UNHCR had 738 local and international staff assigned to twenty-nine offices. Pugh and Cunliffe, "The Lead Agency Concept in Humanitarian Assistance"; Pugh and Cunliffe, "The Politicisation of the UNHCR in the Former Yugoslavia"; and Minear et al., *Humanitarian Action in the Former Yugoslavia*. Yet, in the context of profound civil insecurity and the absence of any consistent impartial law enforcement, the UNHCR had become the lead organizing agency by default. Francois Fouinat, coordinator of the UNHCR task force for the for-

mer Yugoslavia, concluded, "It is not simply that the UN's humanitarian efforts have become politicized. It is rather that we've been transformed into the only manifestation of the international political will." Fouinat, quoted in Minear et al., *Humanitarian Action in the Former Yugoslavia*, p. 7. Over the duration of the war, the lack of decisive international actors, in effect, served to delegitimize the United Nation's role.

75. Andreas, *Blue Helmets and Black Markets*, p. 48.

76. See, for example, Igor Blazevic, "HCA Office in Sarajevo," Helsinki Citizens' Assembly, 4–6 March 1994, PA-MK-HCA-Brighton.

77. Ibid.; Igor Blazevic, "Library Project: Project for the Restoration of the University Library in Sarajevo," Helsinki Citizens' Assembly, n.d., 1-7, PA-MK-HCA-Brighton.

78. See, for example, Mary Kaldor, "Report on Trip to Mostar and Tuzla," September 1994, 1-5, PA-MK-HCA-Brighton.

79. See, for example, Igor Blazevic, "HCA Office in Sarajevo," Helsinki Citizens' Assembly, March 4–6, 1994, 1-8, PA-MK-HCA-Brighton.

80. See, for example, "Helsinki Citizens' Assembly Sarajevo—Second HCA Workshop—Human Rights, Minority Rights and Collective Rights," Sarajevo, 6 May 1994, PA-MK-HCA-Brighton.

81. Mary Kaldor and Mient Jan Faber, "A UN Transitional Authority for Bosnia-Herzegovina," *HCA Newsletter,* no. 7, Summer 1993, PA-MK-HCA-Brighton.

82. "UN/EC Protectorate for Sarajevo and Mostar," Helsinki Citizens' Assembly, The Hague, 2 September 1993, 1-6, PA-MK-HCA-Brighton.

83. Zdravko Grebo and Haris Pasovic, "Hiroshima Commemoration Day: 6 August 1993," 31 July 1993, PA-MK-HCA-Brighton.

84. Zdravko Grebo, "Appeal from Sarajevo to the European Council Meeting in Copenhagen," Helsinki Citizens' Assembly, Sarajevo, 17 June 1993, PA-MK-HCA-Brighton. In the same document, Grebo also articulated how this legally might be implemented.

85. Kaldor, "Sarajevo's Reproach," p. 21. Kaldor maintained in the same article, "All this [humanity] has been preserved, to some degree, despite the war and the siege. Every day people are killed and wounded; in one recent week, thirty-one people were killed and 194 wounded. Since the beginning of the siege, 8,871 people have been killed in Sarajevo, including 1,401 children, and 16,660 people wounded. It is dangerous to walk in the streets—not only because you might get killed but also because you might be picked up by one of the more fearsome Bosnian commanders to dig trenches while exposed to Serbian fire" (p. 21).

86. Igor Blazevic, letter to UNHCR Zagreb, "Programme SO BH, UNHCR Zagreb, Attention: David Reilly," 3 February 1994, 1-2, PA-MK-HCA-Brighton.

87. See, for example, Andreas, *Blue Helmets and Black Markets*.

88. Mient Jan Faber, note to the advisory committee for Sarajevo office—Zdravko Grebo, Mary Kaldor, Josep Palau, and Mient Jan Faber, Helinki Citizens' Assembly, The Hague, 14 July 1994, PA-MK-HCA-Brighton.

89. Igor Blazevic, "'Urgent' Letter to Mary Kaldor," 4 February 1994, p. 1-1, PA-MK-HCA-Brighton.

90. Kaldor and Faber argued, "In the HCA, we have always stressed the importance of civil society, the role that civic groups can play in preventing war and building democracy. What has become clear over the last year is that this is not enough, even with support or European institutions. . . . We need a new set of policies that are directed towards the enforcement of universal human rights, that are designed to protect individuals against violence and not states. In essence what is needed is a transnational rule of law. This is collective security in the broadest sense and not just collective defence." Kaldor and Faber conceded, "In wars or in highly polarised situations, the space

for civil society is squeezed. We also need to press European institutions to adopt a new political approach that could provide an enabling framework in which the sources of insecurity can be confronted." Mary Kaldor and Mient Jan Faber, *The Crisis of European Institutions, in Conflicts in Europe: Towards a New Political Approach*, Helsinki Citizens' Assembly Publication Series No. 7, Prague, 1993, PA-MK-HCA-Brighton.

91. Quoted in Kaldor, "Sarajevo's Reproach," p. 21.

92. Ibid. See also Fukuyama, *The End of History and the Last Man*.

93. See Gow, *Triumph of the Lack of Will*; see also Rieff, *Slaughterhouse*.

94. "Bosnia Snipers," *Prime Time News—CBC Television*, broadcast transcript, Southam Inc., Toronto, 18 November 1994.

95. Mary Kaldor, "Partition Cannot Sustain Peace; the UN May Keep the Streets of Sarajevo Calm, but Not Indefinitely," *Independent* [London], 17 February 1994, p. 20.

96. In the aftermath, in an action that would further add to the confusion of UN peacekeeper roles, Dutch peacekeepers were held liable for not protecting the citizens of Srebrenica. Two examples of explicit civil actions brought against them by Bosnian survivors in The Hague are as follows: First, Van Diepen Van der Kroef, a Dutch law firm, represented eleven plaintiffs including the Mothers of the Enclaves of Srebrenica and Žepa, which consists of 6,000 relatives of the victims. They charged that the State of the Netherlands and the United Nations failed in their obligation to prevent genocide, as per the International Genocide Convention, and are therefore both liable. In July 2008, the court ruled that although it has no jurisdiction in the case against the United Nations, the court can rule against the State of the Netherlands. Since then, the plaintiffs have appealed the UN immunity. See Association "Mothers of Srebrenica" and ten individual plaintiffs (the Association et al.) v. State of the Netherlands and the United Nations (UN) LJN: BD6796, Rechtbank-Gravenhage, (295247 / HA ZA 07-2973); see also The Hague District Court, Judgment in the incidental proceedings, The Hague, 10 July 2008, http://zoeken.rechtspraak.nl/resultpage.aspx?snelzoeken=true&searchtype=ljn&ljn=BD6796&u_ljn=BD6796. Second, in two combined cases against the State of the Netherlands, consisting of a claim by Hasan Nuhanović, a former UN interpreter, as well as the family of an electrician who was employed by the United Nations at Srebrenica, Rizo Mustafić, both the plaintiffs maintained that Dutch battalion troops within their peacekeeping role were responsible for ensuring the security of the UN-protected zone and allowed troops from the Army of the Serb Republic to murder their relatives (Nuhanović's entire immediate family including father, brother, and mother and Mustafić, a husband and father). The premise of the case was that the Dutch government, in particular the minister of defense, had de facto command of the Dutch battalion as per the Dutch Constitution (Article 97[2]), which enables the government ultimate command over all operations of the Dutch military forces. Initially the court maintained that the Dutch government would not be held responsible as they were under a UN mandate. Nevertheless, following an appeal by the plaintiffs in July 2011, the Court of Appeal held that the Dutch government was indeed responsible for, and actively organized, the evacuation during the fall of Srebrenica. For this reason, the Dutch state was responsible for the decision to evict Mustafić and Nuhanović's father from the Dutch battalion compound. Moreover, the court maintained that this decision was wrong given that Dutch soldiers would have known the dangers (namely that the people under their protection would be tortured or killed). In this case, plaintiffs were eligible for compensation. See Nuhanović v. the Netherlands, DC: 265618/ HA ZA 06-1672 (200.020.174/01), and Mustafić-Muji et al. v. the Netherlands, DC: 265618/ HA ZA 06-1672 (200.020.173/01); also see Nederlandse Staat aansprakelijk voor dood drie Moslimmannen na val [Srebrenica Dutch state liable for death of three Muslim men after the fall of Srebrenica], Supreme Court of the Netherlands, 5 July 2011, www.rechtspraak.nl.

97. Kaldor, "Partition Cannot Sustain Peace," p. 20.

98. Ibid. Furthermore, by August 1994, both Kaldor and Faber explicitly identified with cosmopolitan principles, particularly in relation to the safe havens in the Balkans. Arguing in the *Independent* that the "protectorates could provide an umbrella for the reconstruction of cities in Bosnia-Herzegovina along cosmopolitan principles," both Kaldor and Faber began to ask for further military intervention. They claimed, "'Widening' protection of safe heavens would require additional ground troops; if the international community is unwilling to provide them, the alternative is air strikes, which are notoriously ineffective without follow-through on the ground. . . . The proposal for international administration should be implemented straight away. There are already UNPROFOR troops in the 'safe areas'—Gorazde, Zepa, and Srebrenica—the roads (corridor) connecting them are regularly used by UN-protected convoys. This kind of protecting should, however, be upgraded substantially. NATO forces should take over the role of UNPROFOR, since they are better armed and equipped and, if given a mandate, could really function as a counterthreat." Mary Kaldor and Mient Jan Faber, "Back to War or Forward to Cities of Hope; a Cosmopolitan Bosnia Offers the Best Chance of Peace," *Independent* [London], 1 August 1994, p. 13.

99. Avidic, quoted in Robert Block, "A Passive West Seals Town's Fate: Bosnian Serbs Gave Warning," *Independent* [London], 16 July 1995, online.

100. "Serbs Overrun UN 'Safe Haven,'" BBC Online, 11 July 1995, online.

101. For example, in 1999, Kofi Annan, in his report on the fall of Srebrenica, lamented: "With the benefit of hindsight, one can see that many of the errors the United Nations made flowed from a single and no doubt well-intentioned effort: we tried to keep the peace and apply the rules of peacekeeping when there was no peace to keep. We tried to eschew the use of force except in self-defence, which brought us into conflict with the defenders of the safe areas, whose safety depended on our force." Annan, *Report of the Secretary-General.*

102. See "Dayton Peace Accords on Bosnia," USA State Department, 30 March 1996, http://www.state.gov/www/regions/eur/bosnia/bosagree.html; Holbrooke, *To End a War*, pp. 185–214.

103. Estimated casualties and population displacement during the BaH war are still in dispute. See Haydon, "'Ethnic Cleansing' and 'Genocide.'" Also see Jan Zwierzchowski and Ewa Tabeau, "The 1992–95 War in Bosnia and Herzegovina: Census-Based Multiple System Estimation of Casualties' Undercount," paper presented at the International Research Workshop on the Global Costs of Conflict, 1–2 February 2012, http://www.icty.org/x/file/About/OTP/War_Demographics/en/bih_casualty_undercount_conf_paper_100201.pdf.

104. Kaldor and Beebe, *The Ultimate Weapon Is No Weapon*, p. 23.

105. For example, see Prosecutor v. Milošević ICTY (IT-02-54); Prosecutor v. Karadžić, ICTY (IT-95-5/18-PT); and Prosecutor v. Mladić, ICTY (IT-09-92-I).

11

New Wars

I can't think of any war in history where there has been a clinical war of battlefields away from people, which [Kaldor] talks about as "conventional war." And we were complicit in that because we still talk about conventional war. I get wound up in front of a constant number of audiences, and, in fact, I'll be speaking this afternoon to the staff college [about it]. And I think that that's a complete misunderstanding of the history of warfare. And in the military we put capital letters on things, which makes it even worse: capital C for Conventional War.[1]

KALDOR'S EXPERIENCE IN THE 1990S IN THE BALKANS AND THE CAUCASUS shaped her understanding of contemporary war. By the end of 1999, Kaldor had begun to formulate her ideas on two key issues: First, rather than "conventional war," what had been happening in the Balkans was emblematic of a new type of war, what Kaldor came to describe as "new wars."[2] Second, the need for humanitarian intervention by force was critical under situations of abject violence, but the approach taken by the United Nations and NATO was vastly inadequate because it was not aimed at maintaining the security of the civilian population on the ground. More precisely, she argued, what the people of BaH needed was not "peacekeeping" but "cosmopolitan law enforcement."[3] Kaldor was attempting to reframe the questions and adapt the language in both the political and analytical observation of war, but she was also attempting to advocate a different conceptual framework to change the way that politicians, academics, and the general public understood war.

As a response to the end of the Cold War and the prospect of a new world order, Mary Kaldor along with scholar Daniele Archibugi, among others, began both to explore the idea of how international organizations can be more democratic and to consider the concept of cosmopolitan democracy.[4] Although cosmopolitanism was not a new concept, Archibugi wrote the first article exploring the term *cosmopolitan democracy*. In "The Reform of the UN and Cosmopolitan

Democracy: A Critical Review," Archibugi examined how the United Nations could be reformed in accordance with Immanuel Kant's notions of cosmopolitism, league of nations, and cosmopolitan law.[5] Reflecting on what inspired him to consider the concept of cosmopolitan democracy, Archibugi recalled:

> I think that the driving force to do that was to see how, after the collapse of the Soviet Union, it was possible to link countries into democratic union which will reflect human rights, so I was heavily influenced by the historical moment. . . . The term *cosmopolitan* was important, because I never believed that it was possible to move towards a world federal state, so we needed to find an international organization, which was looser and which would include the possibility for citizens to participate.[6]

As in the 1980s, Archibugi was in constant debate and discussion with Kaldor. These discussions increasingly included David Held, Richard Falk, Luigi Bonanate, and Norterto Bobbio, all prominent academics. In 1995, all six scholars contributed to the second text relating to the term *cosmopolitan democracy*, edited by Archibugi and Held, entitled *Cosmopolitan Democracy: An Agenda for a New World Order*.[7]

Even though Kaldor was exploring ideas for a cosmopolitan political democracy, she still resisted a top-down approach to politics. Rather, she continued to see cosmopolitanism as a way of strengthening and protecting politics from below. David Held pointed out that, although he emphasized a "global policy," or top-down approach, Kaldor emphasized the grassroots aspects of cosmopolitan democracy.[8] Similarly, Archibugi maintained that Kaldor's notion of cosmopolitan democracy continued to emphasize the role of civil society:

> Mary and I were always discussing this. Mary's more inclined to believe in informal participation [and] global civil society toward [cosmopolitan democracy]. While I also believe it's important to have some sort of institutional content for that . . . Mary has always been more interested in, if you like, the movement side rather than in the actual organization. But I continue to regard the two things as struggles for the same aim.[9]

As the initial euphoria of the post-Soviet era dissipated, and during the course of her experiences in the Balkans and Caucasus, Kaldor's focus was on how cosmopolitism could address or counter resurgent nationalism and organized violence. In her chapter in Archibugi and Held's edited book, Kaldor maintained that far from demonstrating participatory democracy or cosmopolitan norms, European institutions remained preoccupied with the security of the nation-state, and, consequently, the security of the BaH citizens had been a secondary concern.[10] According to Kaldor, the war in the former Yugoslavia revealed the contradictions of modern war as much as those of the modern state: "It cannot be described as a classic inter-nation-state war on the Clausewitzian [conventional] model. But nor can it be described as a civil war."

Rather than involving a conflict within a state between two opposing forces, the war "is fought by private armies and is about the fragmentation of territory."[11] In the case of the Balkans and the Caucasus, more than two sides were competing for power, with a mixture of military, paramilitary, vigilanties, and criminal gangs, not all necessarily aligned to a single side or to a common cause. Furthermore, Kaldor argued, in solving the Yugoslav crisis, diplomats had remained focused on nation-states, and consequently, the warring elites as representatives of the states and quasi-states remained the dominant actors, whereas cosmopolitan or democratic norms were sidelined:

> Policy options were the result of internal compromises among the EC [European Community] states rather than the result of the actual situation in Yugoslavia. They only envisaged a solution based on nation-states, and the choice they opted for—a unitary state or a collection of new ethnically based states—depended on their own internal biases. Initially, the European Community took a pro-federation position which seemed to legitimise the role of the Yugoslav army in Slovenia and Croatia. Then, under German pressure, the European mediators concentrated exclusively on politicians, indicating their inter-governmental myopia and their scepticism about the role of citizens; [and] they were rather unwilling to meet with [these citizens].[12]

United Nations

At the same time as Kaldor was reflecting on cosmopolitan norms as a counter to nationalism and ethnic violence, she was also working as a consultant for the United Nations University, examining how the United Nations might prepare for the future of war. Although Kaldor had worked for the United Nations University's World Institute for Development Economics Research (WIDER) program since 1985, the emphasis of the program had shifted following the end of the Cold War.[13] In response, Mihály Simai, then director of the WIDER program, initiated a new project entitled "Restructuring the Global Military Sector," after consultations with Boutros Boutros-Ghali, then Secretary-General of the United Nations. Although Boutros-Ghali was then working on his Agenda for Peace initiative,[14] Simai decided that Boutros-Ghali's agenda did not reflect the changing contemporary political and military landscape:

> I realized that there was no research on such issues [as] what will be the role of the defense sector, the armies, arms trade, defense technologies in the post–Cold War era. Everybody was talking only about the "peace dividend." I understood that while the dangers of a global nuclear war have been radically reduced, a new era of small wars was coming. The [Secretary-General] asked me to help him in restructuring peacekeeping operations and [to] prepare the UN for the future wars.[15]

Simai selected Kaldor to head the program. In addition to recognizing her research and activist experience, Simai, being a fellow economist and of Hungarian dissent, was well acquainted with Kaldor and her family: "I appreciated not only her research work but also her participation in the European Nuclear Disarmament. I also sounded out the views of my predecessor, Lal Jayawardena [former director of WIDER], and he firmly supported my idea. In my view it was an excellent choice, and she and the group did original and good work."[16]

Although the title of the project was "Restructuring the Global Military Sector," Simai found Kaldor's proposed title for the book, "New Wars," "more interesting and appealing."[17] It would be published as *New Wars* in 1997, coedited by Kaldor and Basker Vashee.

As research director for the project, Kaldor's mandate was to explain "what is new about contemporary wars."[18] In the introduction to the book, Kaldor maintained that, for all intents and purposes, the era of "conventional" war had existed only for a fleeting historical period, principally confined to Europe, and that period was drawing to an end. For this reason, an era of new wars lay ahead. By coining the term *new wars*, Kaldor was attempting to answer the question, what is new about contemporary war? Certainly her aim was to identify what was different about the wars in the Balkans and Caucasus. Yet, at the same time, she was also struggling to change the way that people thought about war. Reflecting on how she developed the term, Kaldor later explained:

> I was never completely sure what I was going to call them. Was I going to call them new wars, postmodern wars, private wars, civil wars? Civil wars is the word that has become very popular. But I was always very unhappy about civil wars too, because these wars don't take the classic form of government versus rebels. Although, sometimes they do, like in the [Muammar] Qaddafi case, were rebels are also involved. [New wars] are very "global," was one of my points, and they have something to do with weak states and globalization . . . a kind of predatory political economy. . . . So I felt civil wars was a kind of misnomer, and the problem with the term civil wars is that people still see wars in much the same way as a classic contest of wills between two legitimate sides. . . . I mean the word I used (but it's a bit too conspiratorial) is a mutual enterprise. Very much the same argument I made about the Cold War. That these were people we found using violence and—actually in many ways they had a shared interest—in creating a violent situation. So . . . my goal was to make people understand that these were completely different and that the classic ways of dealing with wars, which was to be either on one side or the other, [and] to do "conflict resolution," was inappropriate.[19]

Moreover, Kaldor attempted to argue that the wars in the former Yugoslavia and the South Caucasus shared a new model. In each case, the nation-state had experienced development and industrialization, but nationalism or ethnic division had, as a cyclical effect, triggered an unravelling of the nation-state anyway. In a chapter she coauthored with Vesna Bojicic, entitled "The Political Economy of War in Bosnia-Herzegovina," they maintained:

> What happened in Yugoslavia was the disintegration of the state both at a federal level and, in the case of Croatia and Bosnia-Herzegovina, at a republican level. If we define the state . . . as the organisation which "successfully upholds the monopoly of legitimate organised violence," then it is possible to trace first the collapse of legitimacy and, secondly, the collapse of the monopoly of organised violence. . . . The emergence of virulent nationalism, which did indeed construct itself on the basis of certain traditional social divisions and prejudices—divisions which by no means encompassed the whole of contemporary Yugoslav society—has to be understood in terms of the struggle, on the part of increasingly desperate elites, to control the remnants of the state.[20]

Kaldor's proposal of a new model, with Bojicic, remained entirely normative: Who *should* legitimately control the state in BaH, for instance, rather than who *gained control* through force and violence? The chapter was also framed within a constructivist view: For example, whose interest did these wars serve? These questions in large part explain the difference between the theories of the well-known war theorist Carl von Clausewitz and Mary Kaldor. Clausewitz was a keen observer of war, but Kaldor's key concern was not simply to observe or to write the definitive book on war. Even so, Kaldor's intention was not to cast Clausewitz aside but to reflect a normative assessment of organized violence anchored in a constructivist approach to war. Her point was to change the prevailing discourse and, therefore, how we respond to war.

In new wars, Kaldor and Bojicic advised, the need for involvement of the international community becomes greater, rather then less, to safeguard international norms. They explained, "What was needed, in effect, was not peace keeping but humanitarian law enforcement."[21] Although conceding this sort of international policing presented several challenges, new strategic thinking was required regarding countering ethnic cleansing and developing and supporting democracy and politics from below, allowing the people to rule the state. New rules of engagement and norms of behavior, as well as different resources, command structures, and forms of organization were required to support intervention.[22] Bojicic and Kaldor concluded, "If Bosnia has become the paradigm of the new type of warfare . . . , it could also become a model for a new type of humanitarian reconstruction and a symbol of a new Europeanism or internationalism."[23] Kaldor would later reframe "internationalism" in terms of cosmopolitan norms, augmented by a global civil society.

Shifting Parameters of Intervention

After the publication of *New Wars*, Kaldor continued to explore the theme of new wars and to engage wider public discourse on the way that the international community responds to contemporary organized violence. During

Kaldor's involvement in the conflicts in BaH and the South Caucasus, she wrote several articles and now compiled them together as a series of collected essays to form a book. To gauge the book's accessibility, Held suggested that the draft be sent for review to Jonathon Steele, foreign correspondent for the *Guardian*.[24] Although Kaldor intended to produce only a small book of essays, Steele suggested that the text be revised and rewritten to create a more coherent, broader argument regarding Kaldor's ideas on new wars,[25] which she did, and in 1999, Kaldor published her seminal book *New and Old Wars: Organised Violence in a Global Era*.[26]

As with *New Wars*, a major objective of *New and Old Wars* was to change the way ordinary people and policymakers thought about war and ethnic violence, except this time the text was aimed at a much broader audience. Academia had resisted explaining the ethnic tension in the Balkans as solely "ancient hatreds."[27] However, the idea of ancient hatreds remained a dominant theme in media coverage and policy during the course of the war. Many journalists and practitioners described the wars in the Balkans as "Balkanization" or "tribalism," maintaining that the "civil war" was the result of ancient ethnic feuds.[28] Governments, such as the those under George H. W. Bush and, in its early years, Bill Clinton, embraced this notion to avoid humanitarian intervention.[29] Conversely, Kaldor, along with historian Noel Malcolm and other outspoken critics, publicly challenged the ancient feuds or ethnic war proposition.[30] Kaldor explained:

> My objective was that I felt people looked at the wars as though they were old wars, and, in particular something that I've started to articulate much more recently . . . [people] treated the wars as though each side had legitimate goals, and it was a matter of finding a resolution that would satisfy the warring parties. Whereas if you understood that the warring parties were themselves illegitimate and were actually marginal in their society, and the wars were a way of making them more important, then it leads you to a completely different approach to how you deal with those wars. So I wanted to show that the wars of today are completely different . . . from the wars in the minds of politicians. That was really the goal. It was to make people see war in a different way.[31]

In *New and Old Wars*, Kaldor also explored the role of nationalism. Instead of regarding nationalism as a tool for nation building and fostering brotherhood, Kaldor argued that nationalism had been reconstructed as a tool by the elites to facilitate political mobilization, to presage social and ethnic division, and to then control what was left of the fragmented state. For BaH, the result was the undermining of the legitimate authority of the state in the eyes of the people and therefore a weakening of the state's monopoly on organized violence. The social organization of violence, unhinged from the state, then came under an organizing principle of exclusion and ethnic identity. As the social contract between the people and the state declined, and the country unravelled, organized crime by both quasi-state and nonstate actors thrived.[32] Black markets and organized crime reigned supreme.

For this reason, Kaldor argued that new wars, as a political rather than a military challenge, was about the decline of political legitimacy and therefore required a very different international policy response. Unlike the classic modern war economy, which mobilized the population as a unit and was production oriented, the economy based on new wars paralyzes the state, rips apart the population, and is parasitic. Indeed, the new form of warfare was what she termed "a predatory social condition." It not only damaged the warfare zone itself but seeped into neighboring regions, heightening identity-based politics, scattering refugees, and encouraged black market profiteers. It created "bad neighborhoods" in the world economy and global society, regional clusters such as the Balkans, the Horn of Africa, the Caucasus, Central Africa, Central Asia, West Africa, and parts of the Middle East.

According to Kaldor, the new-war economy, in which a range of armed groups—repurposed national armies, paramilitary groups (often financed by governments), self-defense units, mercenaries, and international troops—became involved to perpetuate violence, including committing systematic genocide, expelling a population forcibly, and rendering areas uninhabitable, either through violence or the threat of violence.[33] In this way, Kaldor argued, the role of nonstate actors and state actors in the new wars had changed. Moreover, whereas earlier in the twentieth century, over 80 percent of casualties were members of the military in these contemporary wars, she pointed out, approximately 80 percent of causalities were civilians.[34] This figure remains a source of controversy. Yet, the point that Kaldor attempted to make was that traditional concepts of war focused on the role of state-based armies. During World War II civilians were targeted to end the war, such was the case in Dresden, Nagasaki, and Hiroshima. But, in new wars, civilians were targeted as a central feature of war and were likely to be targeted by nonstate or quasi-state actors. Furthermore, the key objective was to continue the war rather than to end it.

Cosmopolitan Law Enforcement

To address the issue of new wars, Kaldor argued, required a new cosmopolitan model. Cosmopolitanism is a set of principles and a positive political vision, tied to the rule of law. Cosmopolitans are found in democratic countries, but, Kaldor insisted, they can also be found within the local communities at the heart of the violence, as "islands of civility," where identity politics has not seduced the people. Real cosmopolitanism is therefore not about bargaining agreements between warring factions; rather, it is about pluralist notions of civil society, which foster democratic debate.

Kaldor drew on a number of thinkers in devising the term *cosmopolitan law enforcement*. For example, Kaldor's notion of cosmopolitan law enforcement, in some respects, was a continuation of thinking along Fabian terms regarding the state and society, augmented by cosmopolitan norms. But it was also anchored in John Locke's notion of citizenry as the source of the state's legitimacy.[35] In Kaldor's case, legitimacy is not limited to representative democracy but rather based on civil society and participatory democracy, whereby the legitimacy of the leader rests with the people. She also borrows from Hannah Arendt's ideas that power rests on legitimacy and not on violence. Kaldor explained, "By legitimacy, I mean both consent and even support for political institutions, as well as the notion that these institutions acquire their authority on the basis of operating within an agreed set of rules—the rule of law."[36]

Kaldor also takes a very particular notion of Jean-Jacques Rousseau's *The Social Contract*, that people must "be forced to be free" and that the law that is created by the people does not represent the constraints on private individual freedom but, rather, reflects an expression of individual liberty.[37] Enforcing the rule of law, which includes criminal law, is not a limit on individual liberty because as a citizen and as an individual, participants in democracy are unequivocally contracted with the state to be constrained if, as an individual, they do not respect their own will as expressed in the general will of the law. In this way, laws articulate the constraints of civil freedom but in doing so enable citizens to arise from a "state of nature" to establish a civil society. Kaldor interspersed these ideas with cosmopolitan notions of the social contract and Lockean concepts that liberty depends on a rule of law.[38]

For Kaldor, cosmopolitanism emphasized diversity. Kaldor draws on Kantian ideas of the stranger as a guest, deserving of our hospitality, rather than being forced to assimilate. Kaldor remarked:

> What I found interesting about the term [cosmopolitanism] was the way it combined assumptions about human equality and human principles with a celebration of human diversity—the different ways of being human. I think the idea of promoting a cosmopolitan politics as the basis for political legitimacy was at least as important as law enforcement. Or, to put it another way, was a condition for international law enforcement.[39]

At the same time, the sovereign is not above the law. Drawing on Arendt's notion of liberal debate and the social contract, the state, therefore, cannot permit the social organization of violence outside the acceptable limits of violence agreed by law. In other words, contrary to Clausewitz's notions of the political character of war, where politics and violence coexist, as a liberal, Kaldor believed that violence is anathema to politics.

In this way organized violence is not a legitimate continuation of politics. Rather, for Kaldor, war, in modern times, is all about the politics of fear, and it is a symptom of the absence of liberal politics or genuine debate. For this reason, states still have an essential role to play in enforcing the law, as permitted by the social contract, and that authority explicitly allows for the use of force to uphold the rule of law. In the same vein, the state, which is to say individual state actors who represent the state, must abide by the same laws. In this respect, there are no collective criminals, simply individual criminals who face the same retribution in the view of the law, equally.

The physical protection of ordinary people from violence is not enough, Kaldor argued. Rather, the state should also protect their right to hold a political view, to openly disagree, to debate, and to thrive in a civil society. But this protection, Kaldor argued, requires enforcing cosmopolitan norms of behavior: "The analysis of new wars suggests that what is needed is not peacekeeping, but enforcement of cosmopolitan norms; i.e., enforcement of international humanitarian and human rights laws."[40] For Kaldor, "cosmopolitan law-enforcement is somewhere between soldiering and policing."[41] Yet, consistent with Kaldor's notion of politics, the objectives of cosmopolitan democracy and cosmopolitan law enforcement are to protect grassroots politics and civil society in order to maintain the social contract. In this way politics from below—rather than politics from above—remains the source of legitimacy.

Just as civil society plays a crucial role in informing the role of law enforcement in domestic society, Kaldor maintained that global civil society augments cosmopolitan law enforcement. When governments fail to protect their citizens' human rights and to uphold the rule of law within their own states, Kaldor argued, that other governments around the world who have diplomatic relations with the United Nations or NATO that are responsible for upholding universal human rights. In addition, all citizens of the world are active participants. Therefore, when organized violence or war breaks out, from a cosmopolitan perspective, we are all responsible. When the question arises of whether Westerners should be involved in other people's wars, Kaldor concluded, "I think we *are* involved whether we like it or not. I don't think there is really a choice. The question is *how* are we involved?"[42]

Straw Man or Window into the Future of War?

When Kaldor published *New and Old Wars*, it was met with a broad array of responses from scholars, former guerrillas, revolutionaries, activists, military practitioners, and policymakers alike. Criticisms of Kaldor's book largely focused around three key concerns.

First, were "new wars" really new?[43] Brigadier Andrew Sharpe, former head of land and research strategy at the Defence Concepts and Doctrine Centre within the British Ministry of Defence, explained, "I'm always slightly suspicious of people who think things are new. . . . Kaldor always talks about things like detention, torture, rape, and targeting of the civilian population as a new aspect of war. I think that is *profoundly* and *fundamentally* flawed."[44] Similarly, some scholars, such as Mats Berdal, saw nothing especially new about violence targeted at civilians, adding that a "one-sided attention to economic motives and global character of conflict also runs the risk of creating a distorted picture for what is driving actors to violence."[45]

Second, was the concept of new wars casting classical, particularly Clausewitzian, notions of war aside, and if so, had Kaldor misinterpreted Clausewitz? Hew Strachan and Andreas Herberg-Rothe, for instance, questioned Kaldor's interpretation of Clausewitz's theories.[46] They argued that Kaldor was a "sophisticated and nuanced critic of Clausewitz," particularly in relation to her observation that "Clausewitz was fond of pointing out that 'war is a social activity.'" Strachan and Herberg-Rothe noted that this "observation . . . goes to the heart of what exactly Clausewitz meant by policy and politics."[47] Nevertheless, Strachan and Herberg-Rothe contended, Kaldor did not always consider the context in which Clausewitz used the German word *Politik*. They argued that, contrary to what Kaldor proposed, Clausewitz's notion of the *Politik* could encompass both policy and politics. Therefore, dependent on the context, Clausewitz may have referred to foreign policy or to the social upheaval of the French Revolution, which could include state and nonstate actors. Strachan and Herberg-Rothe believed that Kaldor had overlooked these nuances. For this reason, they concluded that Kaldor had misinterpreted Clausewitz's notion that war was an "act of violence to compel our opponent to fulfil our will" to incorrectly mean only in relation to states.[48] Given that Kaldor's main case study was Bosnia, where nonstate actors were key to orchestrating violence, they suggested that Kaldor mistook Clausewitz to be an observer of "old wars" rather than an analyst of war more broadly. As a result, his theories could easily be applied to the situation in the Balkans as well, if his work was more broadly interpreted.[49]

Third, did new wars, or contemporary wars, really experience a higher civilian death rate than other wars in history? Psychologist Steven Pinker, who wrote much later, would maintain that civilian deaths due to conflict, in historical terms, have actually declined significantly over the course of history.[50]

Aside from analytical criticisms, Ken Booth noted the confidence and certainty with which Kaldor presented her arguments in *New and Old Wars*.[51] Booth commented, "In her latest book, Mary Kaldor seems to have no doubt. That is its strength."[52] Nevertheless, Kaldor's arguments went too far, he explained, and "this is its weakness."[53] Booth also made a further observation. Kaldor's prescription for cosmopolitan law enforcement marked a departure from her previous ideas of politics from below: "This top-down perspective on how to deal with the world's ghetto wars is a major departure from Kaldor's inspirational advocacy of 'détente from below' in the 1980s. . . . As was the case then, cosmopolitan values—which include the delegitimatisation of violence—are best promoted by cosmopolitan means."[54]

Yet some also posited that *New and Old Wars* aptly articulated a new era, and understanding, of war.[55] Martin Van Creveld, an Israeli military historian at Hebrew University, pointed out, "Putting the so-called revolution in military affairs firmly to one side, Mary Kaldor has provided us with a window into the future of war."[56] David Cortright, peace activist and scholar at the University of Notre Dame, argued that Kaldor's book "*New and Old Wars* was one of the very best accounts of the changing social relations of war."[57]

Interestingly, the new wars concept appealed to people outside of academia. Joaquin Villalobos, a former Salvadoran guerrilla and later consultant, concurred with Kaldor's *New and Old Wars*, arguing that the result is not the victory of one side but the fragmentation of society and the privatization of violence. Villalobos wrote, "In Latin America . . . we face what some describe as a continental civil war against organized crime, street gangs, common crime and social violence." Previously, political violence was an agent of change, Villalobos argued, but revolutionary violence could no longer be an "agent for change" within the context of new wars. For example, the revolutionaries in Colombia, he argued, had transitioned from "ideological fundamentalism" to "the world's top cocaine syndicate."[58] Karen Ohanjanyan, one of the original founders and former secretary for the Karabakh Committee, the revolutionary group that started the war in the South Caucasus, also supported Kaldor's book.[59] Narcís Serra, Spain's former minister for defense, also agreeing with Kaldor, suggested that interstate war has become "too costly to be a rational business."[60] Besides, states had lost the legitimate monopoly on violence as actors in international relations by using war as an extension of policy. Military officers have also concurred with Kaldor's new wars concept, including General Klaus Reinhardt, who commanded the German Army Command, NATO Joint Headquarters Centre, and Kosovo Force, and Major-General Andrew Salmon, former commandant general of the Royal Marines, former commander of Coalition Forces in Basra, and former director of force generation and force readiness at Supreme Headquarters Allied Powers Europe, NATO.[61] Both Reinhardt and Salmon went on to work with Kaldor on human security policy for the European Union.

Debates on Clausewitz

Characteristically, Kaldor's response to criticisms of *New and Old Wars* reflected her confidence in debating in the public sphere. Kaldor had already begun to refine her ideas on new wars through debates with activists, scholars, politicians, civilians, and military and policy practitioners throughout the wars in BaH and the Caucasus. Moreover, Kaldor continued to debate the ideas advanced in her new wars proposition and to respond to her critics through the publications of a second and third edition of *New and Old Wars* in 2007 and 2012, respectively. Kaldor suggested that her main objective was always to challenge perceptions of contemporary war: "I agree in a sense that many of the features of new wars existed in previous wars although I do think there are some real new features. But let's say for the sake of argument that nothing is really new. . . . Rather than to show there is a historical break . . . my point really was to make people *think* differently."[62]

Forcing people to question if today's wars are new, old, or, indeed, have ever been very conventional could arguably be Kaldor's greatest contribution. It stimulated debate on the *idea* of war, bringing to the fore the question about the legitimacy of force and organized violence by and within states and society. As academic Jacob Mundy argued, the key to Kaldor's work on new wars was essentially to move the debate beyond traditional notions of war.[63]

Moreover, even those most critical of Kaldor's work argued that she set the agenda for the debate surrounding contemporary war. Berdal, for example, argued that Kaldor's book "helped to stimulate" a broader conversation "about the nature of contemporary war," whereas Strachan maintained that *New and Old Wars* served as a conceptual "straw man" for contemporary security discourse.[64]

Some argued that Kaldor precipitated a more sophisticated debate on Clausewitz's work. Strachan and Herberg-Rothe stated that prior to Kaldor's *New and Old Wars*, critics of Clausewitz were guilty of both understanding *On War* "through the lens of its later interpreters" and exaggerating Clausewitz's focus on war and policy. The "denouement to these trends," Strachan and Herberg-Rothe argued, was Mary Kaldor's book.[65]

Whether they agreed with Kaldor or not, both practitioners and academics alike emphasized the need to challenge preexisting views of war. Kaldor's work did that. Michael Howard, who cotranslated Clausewitz's *On War* and founded the Department of War Studies at Kings College, stated that he was "immensely impressed and stimulated" by *New and Old Wars*.[66] Howard explained that he admired Kaldor "immensely for her moral courage, and intellectual honesty."[67] He added that even at times when he did not see her point of view, he felt Kaldor, and scholars like her, should be "constantly challenging existing concepts of war and formulating new ones."[68] Sharpe concurred that conventional notions of war should be challenged, including the ideas about conventional war that are taught at military colleges.[69]

Kaldor believed the debate on the legitimacy of organized violence should extend past academic literature. When Kaldor asked Major-General Salmon to advise her on the writing of two high-level security reports, Salmon explained, she "asked me to talk about how we use militaries and how we link it [defense] to police law and order issues. . . . So I delivered this work which was *quite* controversial, and that was *exactly* what Mary wanted because she wanted to start bringing different actors together to look at what we need to do differently in the future."[70] David Petraeus, former director of the CIA and commander of US Central Command, concurred: "I've been acquainted with Mary Kaldor since . . . I was in grad school . . . [and] I've admired her energy, drive, and some of her ideas—though, as you would expect, I haven't agreed with all of her ideas—though . . . she's one of those who is truly stimulating."[71]

Although she had posited a new war paradigm, Kaldor did not cast Clausewitz aside entirely. Rather, she had begun the process of building upon his work. Her interpretation of new wars was post-Clausewitzian, but not for the reasons Strachan and others suggested, which is to say that Clausewitz was no longer relevant. She agreed that Clausewitz's *Politik* could be interpreted as both policy and politics.[72] But she was post-Clausewitzian in the literal sense of extending Clausewitz's methodological approach by building on his understanding of the dialectic between the real and the ideal and his emphasis on combining theory, experience, and empirical study.[73]

Kaldor also suggested that the new wars argument accepted that particular key propositions posed by Clausewitz, including the "Trinitarian conception of war as reason, chance and emotions" along with "the primacy of policy and politics and the instrumentalisation of war," remained extremely relevant, dependent on their interpretation.[74] Yet, she argued, the "new wars" of the twenty-first century can only be defined in contrast to what went before, and an understanding of what went before depends heavily on what one learns from reading *On War*.[75] And what one can learn from Clausewitz largely comes down to how one interprets Clausewitz.

Although Kaldor agreed that violence is a form of political mobilization, she still questioned the concept of conventional war. Indeed, she thought that a realistic interpretation of Clausewitz was counterproductive to ending violence in contemporary war and in determining appropriate mandates for military forces. If for Clausewitz, Kaldor argued, the aim of "[conventional] war is external policy and political mobilisation the means, [then] in new wars it is the other way round."[76] The objective of war was now the "mobilisation around a political narrative and external policy," and that "policy *vis-à-vis* the proclaimed enemy was the justification" for the violence.[77] The definition of war, she argued, needed to be reformulated. Kaldor took Clausewitz's work and recast it to start to re-create her own definition:

> War is an act of violence involving two or more organised groups framed in political terms. According to the logic of this definition war could either be a "contest of wills" as is implied by Clausewitz's definition or it could be a "mutual enterprise." A contest of wills implies that the enemy must be crushed and therefore war tends to extremes. A mutual enterprise implies that both sides need the other in order to carry on the enterprise of war and therefore war tends to be long and inconclusive. . . . In new wars, the aim is not the overthrow of the enemy. New wars need enemies.[78]

At the beginning of the wars in the Balkans and Caucasus, Kaldor had viewed war as the absence of politics. Nevertheless, through the experiences of war, Kaldor drew from Clausewitz's insights, and her new wars argument acknowledged that violence was framed in political terms. Yet, although Kaldor concluded that violence in new wars was political and that these wars were a continuation of politics, as Clausewitz had argued, Kaldor maintained that violence was not a legitimate form of politics. Rather, legitimate politics was the combination of the rule of law and the capacity for ordinary citizens to be involved in a liberal debate without fear of violence.

Simultaneously, as the debate on new wars evolved, Kaldor was appointed professor at the London School of Economics, a move supported by Anthony Giddens, then director of the institution. Giddens was keen to hire Kaldor: "I was very much in favor of attracting Mary to the school because I admired her ability to mix first-rate scholarship with an orientation to practical problems."[79]

Although challenging the idea of war and arguing a case for why intervention was necessary occupied Kaldor's scholarly work, *New and Old Wars* was published just as a war in Kosovo loomed, a war that would serve to further challenge Kaldor's ideas on intervention.

Notes

1. Andrew Sharpe, interview with author, 6 July 2011. Brigadier Sharpe is the former head of land strategy in the Development, Concepts and Doctrine Centre of the UK Ministry of Defence.
2. According to Stephen Reyna and Herfried Münkler, in 1997, Kaldor was the first to coin the term *new wars*. See Reyna, "Taking Place," p. 293; and Münkler, *The New Wars,* cf 57, p. 144. See Kaldor and Vashee, *New Wars*; and Kaldor, *New and Old Wars*.
3. See Kaldor, *New and Old Wars*, p. 66.
4. Daniele Archibugi, interview with author, 22 June 2011.
5. Archibugi, "The Reform of the UN and Cosmopolitan Democracy," p. 301.
6. Daniele Archibugi, interview with author, 22 June 2011.
7. Archibugi and Held, *Cosmopolitan Democracy*.
8. David Held, interview with author, 18 May 2011.
9. Daniele Archibugi, interview with author, 22 June 2011.
10. Kaldor, "European Institutions, Nation-States and Nationalism."
11. Ibid., p. 91.
12. Ibid., p. 93.
13. Although the Finnish government was not directly involved in the project, Finnish officials had been interested in WIDER's work on Russian political and economic transformation and the extent to which the Russian military sector would be restructured, if at all. A major component of WIDER's research had addressed the Leningrad and Murmansk region, and the Finnish government was keen to establish contact within the Russian military R&D sector. Mihály Simai, correspondence with author, 26 January 2011.

14. See Boutros-Ghali, *An Agenda for Peace.*

15. Mihály Simai, correspondence with author, 26 January 2011. The term *peace dividend* was used at the end of the Cold War, particularly by US president George H. W. Bush and UK prime minister Margaret Thatcher in the early 1990s, ostensibly to explain the economic benefits of cutting defense spending. See, for example, Gupta et al., "The Elusive Peace Dividend."

16. Mihály Simai, correspondence with author, 26 January 2011.

17. Ibid. According to Simai, *New Wars* was significant. Of the book's impact, Simai remarked, "For at least a decade, the book was a standard work in the profession. When I was lecturing for the high-ranking officers of NATO, they knew about the project and the books."

18. Kaldor and Vashee, *New Wars*, p. xi.

19. Mary Kaldor, interview with author, 24 June 2011.

20. Bojicic and Kaldor, "The Political Economy of War in Bosnia-Herzegovina," p. 140.

21. Ibid., p. 167.

22. Ibid.

23. Ibid., p. 169.

24. Mary Kaldor, interview with author, 20 June 2011.

25. Ibid.

26. See Kaldor, *New and Old Wars.*

27. For example, see Hobsbawm, *Age of Extremes*; and Đilas, *The Contested Country.*

28. For a journalistic example, see Kaplan, "The Coming Anarchy." For an example of a practitioner's take, see Charles G. Boyd, "Making Peace with the Guilty: The Truth About Bosnia," *Foreign Affairs*, September/October 1995, online. For discussion of how journalists influenced policymakers in the debate, see Wimmer et al., *Facing Ethnic Conflict.*

29. For discussion of how the Bush administration believed that the conflict in Yugoslavia was fueled by ancient hatreds and how this perspective influenced their decision to avoid humanitarian intervention, see Western, "Sources of Humanitarian Intervention."

30. See Malcolm, *Bosnia*; and Malcolm et al., "Appease with Dishonour: Faulty History."

31. Mary Kaldor, interview with author, 24 June 2011.

32. Kaldor, *New and Old Wars*, pp. 69–79.

33. Ibid.

34. Ibid.

35. See Locke, *Second Treatise of Government.*

36. Kaldor, *New and Old Wars*, p. 114.

37. Rousseau, *Oeuvres complètes*, III, p. 364; Rousseau, *The Collected Writings of Rousseau*, IV, p. 141.

38. Kaldor, "The Idea of Global Civil Society," p. 583.

39. Ibid.

40. Kaldor, *New and Old Wars*, pp. 124–125.

41. Ibid., p. 125.

42. Mary Kaldor, interview with author, 20 June 2011.

43. For example, see Berdal, "How 'New' Are 'New Wars'?"; Newman, "The 'New Wars'"; Malešević, "The Sociology of New Wars?"; Melander et al., "Are 'New Wars' More Atrocious?"; Kalyvas, "'New' and 'Old' Wars"; Reyna, "Taking Place," p. 293; Brzoska, "'New Wars' Discourse in Germany"; Drake, "Sociology and the New Wars in the Era of Globalisation."

44. Andrew Sharpe, interview with author, 6 July 2011.
45. Berdal, "How 'New' Are 'New Wars'?" pp. 489–490.
46. Strachan and Herberg-Rothe, "Introduction."
47. Ibid., p. 10.
48. Ibid.
49. Ibid..
50. Pinker, *The Better Angels of Our Nature*.
51. Booth, "New Wars for Old."
52. Ibid., p. 163.
53. Ibid.
54. Ibid., p. 170.
55. For example, see Münkler, *The New Wars*; Duffield, *Global Governance and the New Wars*; and Shaw, "The Contemporary Mode of Warfare?"
56. Van Creveld, quoted in Kaldor, *New and Old Wars*, back cover; Van Creveld, correspondence with author, 13 April 2010.
57. David Cortright, correspondence with author, 31 May 2011.
58. Joaquin Villalobos, "Nuevas guerras y viejas izquierdas," *El Pais* [The World], 29 September 2007, online.
59. Karen Ohanjanyan, interview with author, 21 March 2011.
60. Narcís Serra, interview with author, 25 May 2011.
61. Klaus Reinhardt, interview with author, 13 May 2011; Andrew Salmon, interview with author, 19 May 2011.
62. Mary Kaldor, interview with author, 10 July 2011.
63. Mundy, "Deconstructing Civil Wars."
64. Berdal, "How 'New' Are 'New Wars'?" p. 478; Hew Strachan, interview with author, 8 July 2011.
65. Strachan and Herberg-Rothe, "Introduction," p. 10.
66. See Clausewitz, *On War*; Michael Howard, correspondence with author, 27 May 2014.
67. Michael Howard, correspondence with author, 27 May 2014.
68. Ibid.
69. Andrew Sharpe, interview with author, 6 July 2011.
70. Andrew Salmon, interview with author, 19 May 2011.
71. David Petraeus, correspondence with author, 19 April 2011.
72. Kaldor, "Inconclusive Wars."
73. Ibid., p. 271.
74. Ibid.
75. Ibid.
76. Ibid.
77. Ibid., p. 278.
78. Ibid.
79. Anthony Giddens, correspondence with author, 7 June 2011.

12
Rethinking Intervention

Issues of legality versus legitimacy have roiled the international law community ever since the Kosovo Commission declared that the NATO intervention in Kosovo was "illegal but legitimate."[1]

MARY KALDOR'S IDEAS OF NEW WARS AND COSMOPOLITAN LAW enforcement evolved simultaneously as she attempted to explain why the international community should be involved in the social organization of violence, irrespective of state sovereignty. She also endeavored to challenge the way conventional war is thought about. The proposition of cosmopolitan law enforcement reflected Kaldor's normative aspirations for the creation of an international obligation to uphold the rule of law and protect civilians threatened by organized violence. Her ideals became particularly salient in her support for the military intervention in Kosovo and the subsequent NATO-led intervention Operation Allied Force in 1999.[2] During the course of the war in Kosovo, through her relationships, activism, scholarly work, and involvement with the Independent International Commission on Kosovo (hereafter Kosovo Commission), Kaldor's thinking on how intervention should be conducted was further distilled.

In the lead-up to the war in Kosovo, Kaldor attempted to support various forms of participatory democracy and civil society in Kosovo. Initially, she encouraged dialogue between various nonstate actors within Serbia and Kosovo. Encouraging these exchanges often involved traveling to Kosovo, frequently with others such as Natasa Kandic, a Serbian human rights activist. Kandic related: "I remember very vividly that I traveled with Mary. It was before the war in Kosovo, around 1997–98. She was very focused on Kosovo, and we traveled together from Belgrade. She wanted to visit Mitrovica and I traveled to Pristina. It was summer, very hot, and she traveled to meet some people to see how to start some dialogue between the Serbs and the Albanians."[3]

As violence escalated into war, Kaldor believed that force should be used not only to stop the war between Serbia and Kosovo but specifically to protect civilians. As she had done in the Balkans and the Caucasus, Kaldor attempted to connect prodemocratic civil society activists in Kosovo with key policymakers in Europe. For example, as a component of Britain's EU presidency in 1998, Kaldor convinced Robin Cook, then foreign secretary under Tony Blair, to host the People's Europe Conference, a civil society meeting that augmented the European Council and provided the Council with recommendations.[4] Led by Kaldor, with the assistance of Paul Anderson, a former fellow END activist, the People's Europe Conference was held in June at the London School of Economics. Kaldor had invited Kosovar Albanians from the HCA to attend, and during the course of the conference, the Kosovar Albanians met with Cook personally. According to Anderson, this interaction at the conference played a role in shaping the way that Cook thought about intervention in Kosovo:

> The People's Europe [Conference] in 1998 was her [Kaldor's] idea. . . . Mary had met Robin [Cook] and said, "Why don't we have a big civil society conference as part of Britain's presidency of the European Council?" And Robin [agreed] . . . but that was the time when [the war in] Kosovo was beginning to kick off, and through the Helsinki Citizens' Assembly, we got quite a few young Kosovars over who met Cook and in a sense came to dominate proceedings. . . . There is a case for saying that through this, Cook changed his mind about Kosovo, because he'd been very much against any kind of military intervention. But through the contacts, not only through People's Europe, but through Helsinki Citizens' Assembly, there was very definitely a shift in Cook's position. I mean Blair takes all the credit for the whole thing but in fact he was pressed by Cook.[5]

As violence escalated in Kosovo, the United Nations was under increasing international pressure to respond. The UN Security Council adopted Resolution 1199 in September 1998, invoking Chapter VII of the UN Charter, demanding an immediate cease-fire by all parties in Kosovo and the Federal Republic of Yugoslavia (Serbia and Montenegro).[6] Yet many governments within NATO had grown wary of the United Nations, particularly following the failure of intervention in BaH, most particularly the British and French. However, the day after the UN resolution passed, the North Atlantic Council of NATO released an "activation warning," which meant that NATO had increased its level of military preparedness "for both a limited air option and a phased air campaign in Kosovo."[7]

Even before the failure of the Rambouillet Accords, which attempted to broker a peace deal but failed,[8] Kaldor attempted to engage a wider public debate to protect noncombatants in Kosovo. In her article in the *Independent,* Kaldor reported that when Veran Matic, director of the independent Belgrade radio station B92, met with Richard Holbrooke, US special envoy to the Balkans, he asked Holbrooke why he continued discussions with Slobodan Milošević.[9] Apparently Holbrooke responded by saying Serbia had no opposition leader, leaving Milošević as the only authority. In reply, Matic argued what was critical was not catering to individual frontrunners but rather providing support for a broad spectrum of democratic initiatives to foster an alternative public debate. In her article, Kaldor explained that war suppressed democratic groups who advocated peaceful approaches to solving conflict. Although Kosovar Albanians had maintained ten years of nonviolent resistance to Serbian repression, they had failed to gain international support. Within Kosovo, as Serbian violence increased, the nonviolent resistance by Kosovar Albanians appeared to lose legitimacy. As the Kosovar Liberation Army continued to arm themselves against Serbian police, the task of negotiating a political solution became increasingly tenuous and problematic. Binary political positions became entrenched as violence increased and war ensued, causing a circular effect of reprisals and retaliations. Kaldor stated that the use of force by the international community was, therefore, now necessary:

> Talks should focus on establishing a meaningful ceasefire enforced by peacekeeping troops under OSCE auspices who would also be responsible, as in Bosnia, for controlling weapons stores and for demilitarisation. The forces should be commanded by Europeans, probably British or French. There should be a token Russian presence to satisfy the Serbs and, if possible, a token US presence to satisfy the British who do not want to commit ground troops without this. At the same time, the "extraction force" that is currently based in Macedonia, under NATO auspices, should be expanded and renamed a "deterrent force" to intervene in the event that the ceasefire breaks down.[10]

Kaldor was particularly skeptical about the use of air support to protect civilians. Air strikes were notoriously counterproductive, Kaldor maintained, especially without the support of ground troops. Moreover, air strikes provided justification for a crackdown on the opposition and fueled extremism. The threat of air strikes, the year before, had, Kaldor argued, provided justification for closing down independent media and introducing repressive university laws, as well as making aid delivery difficult for NGOs. Rather, ground troops should be mobilized with a clear mandate toward enforcement of international norms, rather than the pursuit of an "enemy."

Referring to the British military experience in Northern Ireland as an example, Kaldor argued that a law enforcement mandate was entirely feasible. The emphasis in Northern Ireland had been on ground troops, over air support, and political discussions with the Irish Republican Army were considered only after a cease-fire had been convincingly established. A similar approach, Kaldor argued, should be taken in Kosovo:

> European governments have been pioneering a new approach to peace-enforcement that contrasts with the American preoccupation with bombing. The British Defence Review is innovative in the way that it reorients British armed forces to contingencies of the Bosnia and Kosovo type. Moreover, this kind of thinking is not confined to the British. The Danes developed their own strategic concept during the Bosnian war and were very effective at enforcing humanitarian corridors and even eliminating Serbian tanks. A strategy of this kind has to be combined with a political effort to support and build up democratic alternatives in Serbia as well as Kosovo and indeed in the whole Balkan region. Milosevic needs to be isolated, not courted, by the international community, and indicted by the war crimes tribunal. The indictment of Radovan Karadzic did help open up new political perspectives in Bosnia. The international community needs to talk to and support the democrats, whoever they are and however marginal they appear today.[11]

On 15 January, the day after Kaldor's article was published, the Račak massacre transpired. Around forty-five Kosovar Albanian farmers had been "rounded up" and murdered.[12] Discovered by OSCE monitors, including William Walker, head of the Kosovo Verification Mission, and foreign news correspondents, the bodies were a stark reminder of the genocide witnessed in BaH.[13] Although Belgrade denied the killings, Račak was the latest of a series of reprisals by the Kosovo Liberation Army and Serbia, which had escalated over the winter of 1998–1999.[14]

For many, Račak marked a turning point in the war. As the Rambouillet Accords and diplomatic efforts appeared to fail, Javier Solana, as secretary-general of NATO, began to assume an important role in building the international consensus required for a NATO-led intervention.[15] As academic Ryan C. Hendrickson, argued, the turning point for Solana's influence "came when UN Security Council Resolution failed to achieve military-authorisation akin to Bosnia."[16] The political result was that the United States and Britain then "shifted their primary diplomatic activities to NATO," and in doing so, Solana's influence increased "as the North Atlantic Council became the principal diplomatic forum for resolving the conflict."[17] As the United Nations failed to provide a clear mandate, NATO governments under the direction of Solana elected to bypass the UN Security Council and use force to end the violence in Kosovo.[18]

Although Kaldor attempted to inform public opinion during the Kosovo War, she was also being influenced by the debates. For example, she and Mient Jan Faber attended the Hague Appeal for Peace Conference.[19] There they argued a case for the legitimacy of intervention in Kosovo. Even though they conceded NATO aerial attacks in the name of human rights were shameful, they argued that the absence of any outrage at the conference for the ethnic cleansing of Kosovars was equally disturbing:

> There were passionate demands for an end to NATO bombing. But what made one feel uncomfortable was that they did not seem to express the same

> energy and concern about the plight of the Kosovar Albanians. . . . They were not particularly interested to hear the views of Kosovar Albanians; indeed at the session where Kosovar Albanians spoke about their experiences, some participants said that this was a waste of time since they could hear these sorts of stories on television. And there was very little discussion about how to stop ethnic cleansing.[20]

Kaldor and Faber's stance was very much the minority position at the conference. Yet, for some, their arguments did open up debate about the use of force in preventing genocide. David Cortright, activist and professor at Notre Dame University, who also attended the Hague conference, recalled that Kaldor was adamant that protecting civilians by force, as in the case of Kosovo, was an international obligation. According to Cortright, she argued her case in the face of vehement opposition. Cortright maintained that he did not agree with Kaldor at the time and was uncertain about the legitimacy of the NATO bombing. Nevertheless he admitted he was forced to reexamine his own thinking:

> I remember vividly the scene . . . , when [Mary Kaldor], Mient Jan Faber, and a few other brave souls were defending the NATO intervention against the Milošević regime in a jam-packed and contentious informal session in the basement of the main conference hall . . . from the simplistic knee-jerk opposition, the usual default peace movement position against any and all use of force, and acknowledged that in some instances, [and] overcoming Milošević's tyranny would certainly qualify, force may be necessary.[21]

Independent International Commission

Arguably, the most important way that Kaldor got her views across to a wider audience was through her contribution to the Kosovo Commission. The *Kosovo Report*, the ultimate product of the commission, was an initiative of Swedish prime minister Göran Persson in 1991. Persson was "concerned by the absence of independent analysis of the conflict in Kosovo and of any real attempt to research the lessons to be learned from the conflict."[22] Endorsed by Kofi Annan, then Secretary-General of the United Nations, the twelve-month study was cochaired by Justice Richard Goldstone, a former judge in South Africa, and chaired by Carl Tham, a former Swedish member of parliament. Upon its completion in 2001, the study was presented to Annan. Both Goldstone and Tham selected the members of the commission, one of whom was Kaldor. Tham recalled:

> We tried to get a broad and very qualified commission, [consisting of] members with different experience, views, and positions. We also tried to get a truly global commission, with members also from Asia and Russia. And of

> course a reasonable gender balance. In fact, that is also what we got. All members—except for our Russian friend—participated actively. The commission was unique [in that] the members wrote the text themselves, including Mary. . . . There were at the beginning very different opinions in the commission, especially regarding the NATO war, but we succeeded—through hard work—to get a common view. The members were truly intellectuals: they had respect for analysis, facts, and arguments.[23]

As the cochair of the Kosovo Commission, Goldstone maintained that Kaldor's relationship with the Balkans influenced her thinking in the report. In his opinion, Kaldor provided "outstanding input with regard to all important issues referred to in the report."[24] He also noted Kaldor's merging of the political and the personal, particularly in the sense that she had "a long-standing relationship with the region and tremendous empathy for the plight suffered by the people there."[25]

Tham explained that at the start of the Kosovo Commission, members often disagreed on the role of intervention and NATO, particularly Richard Falk, a member of the commission from the United States.[26] Later, when Falk reflected on the commission's debates, he explained that initially he was vehemently at odds with Michael Ignatieff, from Canada, who, or so he believed, wanted to downplay any criticism of NATO's role, particularly its decision to bomb from high altitudes, which would mean more civilian casualities. Falk believed that Ignatieff was also opposed to any consideration that the United States and NATO were avoiding a potential diplomatic solution and that they had not engaged in any serious diplomatic effort at Rambouillet in the lead-up to the war.[27] Yet he observed that, although Kaldor was keen to debate the issues and was critical of NATO, she was also interested in how to solve the problem of intervention:

> Mary played an important role in articulating the guidelines for this kind of unauthorized intervention, use of military force, [in the report]. She was definitely more in touch, through her work in Helsinki Citizens, with human rights activists and other activists in Kosovo and in Serbia, as well as Bosnia. And she was much more ready to be critical of NATO. . . . In recent years she has been quite close to Solana, the head of NATO [during the Kosovo intervention], and this is part of this two-tier strategy of hers, which is that the way you are effective in politics, in the kind of politics she wants to pursue, is to encourage constructive civil society initiatives, but also to be ready and receptive to dialogue with the elite, the policymakers.[28]

Through these debates, the commission members drew some important conclusions.[29] The commission concluded in the *Kosovo Report* that the NATO intervention into that country, which was not sanctioned by the UN Security Council, was "illegal, but legitimate." The commission was especially critical of some aspects of the intervention, particularly the use of air strikes.[30] At the same time, the authors of the report contended that intervention to protect civilians was consistent with international human rights laws and norms. However, the authors went on to state:

> Experience from the NATO intervention in Kosovo suggests the need to close the gap between legality and legitimacy. The Commission believes that the time is now ripe for the presentation of a principled framework for humanitarian intervention which could be used to guide future responses to imminent humanitarian catastrophes and which could be used to assess claims for humanitarian intervention. It is our hope that the UN General Assembly could adopt such a framework in some modified form as a Declaration and that the UN Charter be adapted to this Declaration either by appropriate amendments or by a case-by-case approach in the UN Security Council. We also suggest a strengthening of the level of human rights protection contained in the UN Charter—aware of course of the political problems of implementing such a change.[31]

After the Kosovo War, Kaldor continued to support international involvement in Kosovo, particularly the notion of cosmopolitan law enforcement. For example, Kaldor pointed out that when violence broke out in Mitrovica, in northern Kosovo, during 2000, the UN police were outnumbered, and Danish troops came to their assistance to provide extra law enforcement to augment the role of the police. Operating on their own individual initiative, the Danes responded to the situation by demonstrating international norms. The objective of the Danes was, in a practical sense, much like civil policing, to enforce UN policy, whereby they disarmed all those exchanging fire and bearing arms in order to protect civilians from violence. According to UN police, the Danes were outstanding.[32] Kaldor asserted:

> Humanitarian intervention has to be understood as a new phenomenon, not simply in terms of goals but also in terms of methods. The idea of overriding state sovereignty in defense of human rights marks not just a conceptual break with a state-centered view of the world but a practical break from traditional forms of warfighting. . . . Conventional war between states has become an anachronism.[33]

Although controversial, Kaldor and her colleagues' involvement in the Kosovo Commission reflected their attempt to stimulate debate concerning the obligations to provide cosmopolitan law enforcement among a broader audience. As Cortright contended, the report that Kaldor and others aided in drafting was equally controversial in judging the NATO campaign to be morally justified. Nevertheless, Cortright argued, *The Kosovo Report* crystallized the dilemma over how to protect civilians persecuted by brutal and violent regimes. The report, he argued, helped to make people more thoughtful about the process of humanitarian intervention and contributed to the advent of the "responsibility to protect" principle.[34]

Kosovo Report

The *Kosovo Report* contributed to debate in three ways. First, it caused people to reconsider the nature of intervention. For example, critics such as David Chandler argued that "the liberal preoccupation today with genocide, war crimes, and barbarism has little to do with either the genocide and ethnic cleansing of the Holocaust or with the recent civil conflicts in Africa and the Balkans."[35] Instead, these critics saw intervention as a means for Western governments to legitimize their power after the fall of communism through a moral foreign policy agenda.[36] Although socialists, such as John Pilger and Tariq Ali, criticized humanitarian intervention in Kosovo as nothing more than a continuation of the Western Imperialist agenda,[37] others, such as Nicholas Wheeler, maintained that military intervention to save lives is a necessary and legitimate action by states and a duty of the international community.[38] From an academic viewpoint, the *Kosovo Report* also challenged the discourse surrounding the moral and ethical legitimacy of humanitarian intervention and the role of international norms in securing both peace and human rights.[39] Ken Booth argued:

> [The Kosovo Commission] follows a tradition of similar bodies inaugurated by Willy Brandt [former German chancellor] several decades ago. Some have produced important work (notably Olof Palme's Commission on common security); others have been somewhat forgettable. The Kosovo Commission is one of the former; those with something important to say, even if—like me—you do not agree with the findings.[40]

Second, the *Kosovo Report* represented a significant challenge to international law.

Third, the *Kosovo Report* was a significant challenge to the United Nations itself. For example, in response to the report, Annan launched a series of reports providing a comprehensive view "about the way forward" for collective security. In March 2000, Annan convened a high-level panel, chaired by Lakhdar Brahimi, former minister for foreign affairs for Algeria and UN special representative to South Africa and Haiti. The panel's objective was to undertake a review of UN peace and security activities, and the findings were later detailed in *The Report of the Panel for United Nations Peace Operations* (referred to as the *Brahimi Report*). Key to the *Brahimi Report* findings was the need for the United Nations to be prepared to defend civilians from violence. Moreover, the report suggested the United Nations may be held accountable for that protection: "The Security Council has . . . established, in its resolution 1296 (2000), that the targeting of civilians in armed conflict and the denial of humanitarian access to civilian populations afflicted by war may themselves constitute threats to international peace and security and thus be triggers for Security Council action. If a United Nations peace operation is already on the ground, carrying out those actions may become its responsibility, and it should be prepared."[41]

In response to the *Brahimi Report*, a select UN high-level panel prepared a report entitled *A More Secure World: Our Shared Responsibility,* which addressed how states can work collaboratively to address organized violence.[42] It effectively established that the United Nations, an organization first established for the security of the nation-state, must now subordinate the state to the security of individuals within the state. Moreover, they determined that legitimacy and legality were equally important when accessing the primacy of humanitarian intervention, effectively transforming the premise of humanitarian intervention. Anne-Marie Slaughter, then director of the International Legal Studies Program at Harvard Law School and later director of policy planning under Secretary of State Hillary Clinton, argued:

> The important point is that the [UN] high-level panel moved the goalpost. It assumes that the criteria of legitimacy will be applied by the Security Council itself, thereby assuming legality. The question thus becomes not whether it is illegal but legitimate, but rather whether it is legal and legitimate. The legitimacy inquiry becomes a second filter on the decision to use force. . . . The Security Council not only must establish the presence of a breach of the peace, threat to the peace, or act of aggression under Article 39, but also must determine that the use of force in response would satisfy the five criteria of legitimacy.[43]

Both reports were presented at the September 2005 World Summit, convened at the UN headquarters in New York, to address the possible reform of the UN approach to intervention. Although not all the reform recommendations were enacted, one in particular was: the "responsibility to protect," a formulation of the "right of humanitarian intervention" developed by the UN commission and proposed by Annan's *In Larger Freedom* reform package. At the High-Level Plenary Meeting at the 2005 World Summit, held 14–16 September, the UN General Assembly agreed to the "responsibility to protect," which involved "clear and unambiguous acceptance by all governments of the collective international responsibility to protect populations from genocide, war crimes, ethnic cleansing and crimes against humanity."[44]

Civil Society in a Global Era

In 2000, following the war in Kosovo, Kaldor returned to exploring the concepts of civil society, politics from below, new wars, and cosmopolitan law enforcement in light of the wars in the Balkans and Caucasus. In particular, she became preoccupied with the idea of a global civil society. Just as civil society had linked citizens within and across states in Europe during the

Cold War and during the wars in the Balkans and Caucasus, global civil society linked citizens internationally. In particular, Kaldor began the development of a yearbook on the subject. Like the yearbooks Kaldor had worked on at SIPRI at the start of her career, the objective of the new series of yearbooks was to promote debate: instead of being a collection of data on the exchange of weapons, the yearbook would provide a survey of the exchange of ideas on "global civil society." Initially edited by Mary Kaldor, Marlies Glasius, and Helmut Anheier, the first yearbook included articles from journalists, activists, business consultants, policy advisers, and scholars. In the first edition of the yearbook, Kaldor wrote a chapter entitled "The Decade of Intervention," in which she reflected on the 1990s and assessed the interrelationship between global civil society and intervention. The launch of the yearbook, entitled *Global Civil Society 2001*, was supposed to be held in New York and included praise for the yearbook from former US president Bill Clinton among other notables.[45] Nonetheless, the official launch of the first yearbook was canceled. In September 2001, the same week that the yearbook was to be released, four commercial passenger jets were hijacked by members of al-Qaeda's Hamburg cell. Two were intentionally flown into the Twin Towers in New York, another crashed into the Pentagon, and the fourth was unsuccessful in its attempt to hit the White House. In response, the United Kingdom and the United States launched Operation Enduring Freedom in October 2001 in Afghanistan, after demanding that the Taliban extradite Osama bin Laden and oust al-Qaeda. By December, the United Nations had sanctioned the International Security Assistance Force to establish stability in Kabul.

However, the world was set for an altogether different course when George W. Bush unveiled the *National Security Strategy of the United States of America* in September 2002, outlining the administration's doctrine of preemption for intervention in Iraq.[46] Unlike the intervention in Afghanistan, the United Nations was unlikely to sanction an intervention in Iraq. Nevertheless, Tony Blair, then prime minister of Britain, increasingly aligned himself with Bush's position and pressed the British people toward forming a coalition with the United States and going to war in Iraq. In response, Cook, then leader of the House of Commons, resigned from Blair's cabinet in protest.

Although Kaldor would continue to produce the global civil society yearbook annually, the concepts of humanitarian intervention and civil society were set for a perilous course over the next decade. Like Cook, Kaldor was against the intervention in Iraq. Rather than an opportunity "to establish a new agenda for the world" and to negotiate a "new social contract" globally, the September 11 attacks were, Kaldor argued, used by her government and the United States to mark what she described as the beginning of the "Great Divide."[47]

Notes

1. Slaughter, "Security, Solidarity, and Sovereignty," p. 626. Anne-Marie Slaughter is a former director of policy planning for the US State Department under Secretary Hillary Clinton.

2. Mary Kaldor, "We Must Send in Troops to Stop the Killing in Kosovo," *Independent* [London], 14 January 1999; Mary Kaldor, "Comment: Kosovo Crisis: Bombs Away! But to Save Civilians We Must Get in Some Soldiers Too," *Guardian* [London], 25 March 1999.

3. Natasa Kandic, interview with author, 22 February 2011.

4. See Kaldor, "Eastern Enlargement and Democracy"; Mary Kaldor, "A New Forum for Europe," *Times Higher Education*, 5 June 1998, online.

5. Paul Anderson, interview with author, 14 June 2011.

6. "Security Council Demands All Parties End Hostilities and Maintain a Ceasefire in Kosovo," UN Security Council press release regarding Resolution 1199 (1998), SC/6577 3930th Meeting, 23 September 1998, online.

7. "Statement by the Secretary-General Following the ACTWARN Decision," press release, NATO, 24 September 1998, online.

8. For Rambouillet Accords, see Weller, "The Rambouillet Conference on Kosovo."

9. Kaldor, "We Must Send in Troops to Stop the Killing in Kosovo," p. 4.

10. Ibid.

11. Ibid.

12. Julius Strauss, "Massacre That Started Long Haul to Justice," *Daily Telegraph* [London], 30 June 2001, online.

13. Jon Silverman, "Racak Massacre Haunts Milošević Trial," BBC Online, 14 February 2002, online.

14. The incident was immediately condemned by the UN Security Council and later would serve as the basis for laying charges of war crimes against Milošević and his top officials. See "Report of the EU Forensic Team on the Račak Incident," 17 March 1999, quoted in Weller, *The Crisis in Kosovo 1989–1999*.

15. Hendrickson, "Javier Solana and the Operation Allied Force."

16. Ibid., p. 94.

17. Ibid.

18. "Under Orders: War Crimes in Kosovo Report," Human Rights Watch, 2001, online.

19. A global civil society summit entitled the Hague Appeal for Peace Conference in 1999 was conducted during the time NATO was intervening in Kosovo. The summit gathered 10,000 participants from around the world and included several representatives from various governments. The theme of the assembly was "Another world is possible." See Pianta, *UN World Summits and Civil Society*, p. 14fn.

20. Kaldor and Faber, "What Is Humanitarian Intervention?"

21. David Cortright, correspondence with author, 29 April 2010.

22. Independent International Commission on Kosovo, *The Kosovo Report*, p. 5.

23. Carl Tham, correspondence with author, 4 July 2010.

24. Richard Goldstone, correspondence with author, 2 May 2010.

25. Ibid.

26. Carl Tham, correspondence with author, 6 July 2010.

27. Richard Falk, interview with author, 13 May 2015.

28. Ibid.

29. Carl Tham, correspondence with author, 4 July 2010.

30. Kaldor and others were against air strikes and argued that the objective of such nonprecise violence was to bring down the Milošević regime rather than defend the ordinary civilians. See, for example, Regehr, "Defence and Human Security"; and Oberleitner, "Human Security," p. 194.

31. Independent International Commission on Kosovo, *The Kosovo Report*, p. 5.

32. Kaldor, "Humanitarian Intervention."

33. Ibid., p. 25.

34. David Cortright, correspondence with author, 29 April 2010.

35. Chandler, *From Kosovo to Kabul,* p. 220.

36. Ibid.

37. John Pilger, "Humanitarian Intervention Is the Latest Brand for Imperialism as It Begins Its Return to Responsibility," *New Statesman*, 28 June 1999, online. See also Ali, *Masters of the Universe?*

38. See Wheeler, *Saving Strangers.*

39. For further discussion of the debates surrounding the legitimacy of Kosovo and humanitarian intervention, see Booth, *The Kosovo War*; Wheeler, *Saving Strangers*; Voon, "Closing the Gap Between Legitimacy and Legality of Humanitarian Intervention"; and Muggleton, "The Doctrine of Humanitarian Intervention and the NATO Air Strikes Against the Federal Republic of Yugoslavia."

40. Booth, "Book Review," p. 336.

41. The panel's report to the Secretary-General is attached to "The Identical Letters Dated 21 August 2000 from the Secretary-General to the President of the General Assembly and the President of the Security Council," UN Doc. A/55/305–S/2000/809, 21 August 2000.

42. See United Nations, *A More Secure World.*

43. Slaughter, "Security, Solidarity, and Sovereignty," p. 626. Annan also submitted his own follow-on report entitled *In Larger Freedom: Towards Development, Security and Human Rights for All.*

44. General Assembly Resolution 60/1, World Summit Outcomes Document (2005), p. 31, http://www.who.int/hiv/universalaccess2010/worldsummit.pdf. See Annan, *In Larger Freedom.* See also "Annan Calls for Endorsement of Responsibility to Protect," Human Security Policy Division, Human Security and Human Rights, Bureau of Foreign Affairs Canada, http://www.iciss.ca/menu-en.asp. Also see, for the full document, "60/1. 2005 World Summit Outcome," United Nations, online (particularly the section entitled "Responsibility to Protect Populations from Genocide, War Crimes, Ethnic Cleansing and Crimes Against Humanity," Sections 138, 139, 140).

45. Bill Clinton, in relation to Anheier, Kaldor, and Glasius, *Civil Society Yearbook 2004/2005*, quoted on http://www.uk.sagepub.com/books/Book227013.

46. See *National Security Strategy of the United States of America*, White House, Washington, DC, 17 September 2002, http://georgewbush-whitehouse.archives.gov/nsc/nss/2002/.

47. Kaldor, quoted in Oretga, "El 11-S, Una ocasion desperdiciada," p. 6.

13
Human Security

I was very pleased to read your commentary, "A human security doctrine for Europe and beyond," in the International Herald Tribune. . . . *I have been long waiting for such a study on human security. During my ten-years serving as United Nations High Commissioner for Refugees, I was constantly confronted with the challenges of how to protect people displaced by war. . . . Neither protection of individuals nor long-lasting state security can be achieved without first ending the violence. I cannot agree with you more to emphasize the "how" to intervene rather than endlessly arguing the "whether" when gross abuses on civilians are taking place.*[1]

ALTHOUGH MARY KALDOR SUPPORTED THE KOSOVO INTERVENTION IN principle, even if not NATO's tactical air strikes, she was entirely against the intervention in Iraq. Kaldor believed in an approach that protected individuals rather than states and felt that humanitarian intervention could only be legitimate within a cosmopolitan law enforcement framework, not in the realm of conventional warfare. Unsanctioned by the United Nations, the first phase of the Iraq intervention commenced in March and April 2003. The conflict was conventionally fought and mostly consisted of UK and US troops, with the key mandates being to disarm the regime, removing any weapons of mass destruction, particularly nuclear weapons, and to bring about regime change. Although they rapidly disposed of the government of Saddam Hussein, the coalition forces soon discovered that the regime did not have an active nuclear weapons program. Moreover, coalition partners began to observe the dangerous consequences of a political vacuum after Paul Bremer, administrator of the Coalition Provisional Authority of Iraq, sacked the Baath Party and, consequently, caused the rise of a nebulous insurgency that threatened to unravel order in not just Iraq but neighboring countries across the Middle East.

For Kaldor the issue with the Iraq intervention was related to one of political objective. First and foremost, a genuine humanitarian intervention in

Iraq, Kaldor argued, would have meant being serious about human rights provisions listed in the 1991 UN Security Council resolutions. A humanitarian intervention would, therefore, have meant sending in weapons inspectors but also would have included human rights monitors. Second, deploying troops on the border might have been necessary to put pressure on the Iraqi regime to comply with the resolution, but the objective of those troops would not have been invasion and regime change. Rather their purpose would have been to protect civilians in the event that the government decided to crush an uprising, as had happened, for example, to the Kurdish population in 1991, when troops were deployed to provide a safe haven in northern Iraq.[2]

At this point, one could argue that Kaldor's opposition to the Second Gulf War was wholly inconsistent, particularly given her support for the NATO intervention in Kosovo, which, like the intervention in Iraq, had been illegal and not sanctioned by the United Nations. Yet, in Kaldor's view, the intervention in Iraq was not only illegal but also illegitimate. The legitimacy of the Kosovo intervention lay with its political objective, which, she argued, was to protect citizens and to stop the genocide. The authors of the *Kosovo Report* had concluded that a dangerous gap had remained between legality and legitimacy, a gap that needed to be addressed by identifying the conditions for humanitarian intervention. Regrettably, she contended, that gap had never been closed, and its existence provided those who supported a war in Iraq the political currency to push for what was essentially classical warfare on the basis of "humanitarian" grounds.

She did not believe regime change qualified as a legitimate reason for intervention. In this way, she argued, Tony Blair, the British prime minister, had confused "pre-emptive war with humanitarian intervention," borrowing the language of humanitarianism to incite a war and to legitimate the use of organized violence.[3] Kaldor reflected later: "One interesting aspect to all of this is the idea of liberal interventionism that Blair was so keen on, the idea that we do have the right to intervene to bring about human rights. This is a very human security inspired idea. What he couldn't understand is that you cannot violate human rights to bring about human rights, you cannot have *wars* for human rights."[4]

At the time, Kaldor was not alone in her thinking. Many of her coauthors on the *Kosovo Report* were also against the intervention in Iraq. For example, Carl Tham, a cochair of the Kosovo Commission, argued that the Iraq War was illegal:

> Few dispute that—and it was not legitimate in the sense of the Kosovo war. The idea to expand the very restrictive idea of humanitarian intervention into a general license for war against repressive regimes is, I think, very dangerous. Even more so is the concept of preventive action, which can be used at random as an argument for war. It will in fact erode the whole idea of an international legal order as expressed in the UN Charter and its prohibition of the use of force.[5]

Another member of the Kosovo Commission, Richard Falk, concurred with Tham and Kaldor. For him, the administration of George W. Bush had been "uninterested in the pursuit of humanitarian goals for their own sake" and abused such goals "as a cover for imperial objectives," creating a situation that "is dangerous for world order and undermines international law and the UN."[6] Both Tham and Falk argued that the possible threat of weapons of mass destruction—which was the primary argument brought by the United States to the UN Security Council—had no relationship to nor bearing on humanitarian intervention.

Kaldor observed that many who initially started as peace activists and who became passionate about human rights found not flipping to a neoconservative position difficult. She saw those who began political life on the left, who had been apologetic about communism, had merged their positions with lifelong neoconservatives, such as Richard Perle, chairman of the Defence Policy Board Advisory Committee and advocate of regime change during the Bush administration. As a minority in the peace movement who linked peace and human rights and thought of them as having equal status, as in the Helsinki Accords, Kaldor maintained that this position in the peace movement in the 1980s caused her to think differently about the grounds for intervention: "It holds you back when it comes to things like bombing. And this is the real problem. The neocons on the one hand are passionate about human rights but on the other hand they think bombing is legitimate in support of human rights."[7]

For Kaldor, more work had to be done to define how humanitarian intervention should be conducted. Kaldor favored ground forces over bombing, which she viewed as indiscriminate and inaccurate in protecting the rights of ordinary people on the ground from genocide and war crimes. This point, for Kaldor, was critical:

> I was very unhappy about [bombing] at the time, and I am even more so in retrospect. I was in favour of intervention in Kosovo but I was very unhappy with the use of air-strikes. I just think it's unacceptable. . . . The problem with the liberal internationalists and their alliance with the neocons is that they believe in wars for human rights so they have flipped over to the human rights side instead of holding peace and human rights together.[8]

Kaldor was responding to political events unfolding in Europe and increasingly beyond. Her experiences as an activist in Eastern Europe in the 1980s and the Balkans and Caucasus in the 1990s, her role in the Kosovo Commission, and now her response to September 11 and the consequent interventions in Iraq and Afghanistan informed many of the ideas in her book *Global Civil Society: An Answer to War*.[9]

But a book on global civil society seemed futile. In response to what Kaldor considered to be an abominable position for the Labour Party, she attempted to encourage public debate through conducting workshops with activists, scholars, journalists, and policymakers; writing articles for newspapers and journals; and engaging and supporting individuals and groups in Europe focusing on civil society. Increasingly, these debates began to include her activism experiences on the ground in Iraq and Afghanistan, and Kaldor continued to view the roles of scholarship, academia, and activism as intertwined.

Javier Solana and the European Security Capability Group

As the US executed President Bush's national security strategy in late 2002, Europe remained divided over the legitimacy of intervention in Iraq. Although the European Union had attempted to develop their own security strategy in 2003, which would reflect the "Petersberg tasks," a list of security and military priorities incorporated into the Common Security and Defence Policy (CSDP), it lacked the detail and mandate necessary to translate their vision into a clear, united foreign policy response to the events unfolding in Iraq and Afghanistan. Moreover, a British Labour government had instigated the rift, and Kaldor found herself fundamentally at odds with some prominent governmental figures.

Kaldor attempted, by various means, to stimulate debate and to solve the problem of a coherent foreign and security policy across Europe. Perhaps her most concerted efforts were in the form of collaboration between her and Javier Solana, then high representative for common foreign and security policy for the European Union. Solana asked Kaldor to convene a group of academics and practioners to examine the European Union's security capabilities.[10] According to Narcís Serra, former defense minister of Spain who served at the same time that Solana was that country's minister for foreign affairs, Kaldor was really the driver for the project: "No, no, it was Mary. I helped her. The leader is *always* Mary, because she has the strength, the vision, the vitality."[11]

Kaldor and Solana formed a study group that would change the way that European policymakers and the European public more broadly responded to war, humanitarian disasters, and organized violence. Together with Serra, Solana and Kaldor assembled the European Security Capability Group (ESCG), with Kaldor as the convener. According to the coordinator of the study group, Marlies Glasius, a scholar in international human rights law, the ESCG was formed in a concerted attempt to unify European security policy:

> It was very much born out of Iraq and how not to do things. . . . I think what Solana wanted (because there was such a complete breakup [in Europe]) was some sort of unifying vision. And he thought that Mary was a good person to go and supply that, and I think eventually we did do that. . . . He wasn't very clear what the vision was meant to be. One of the things he said to her at the time was "So make it very concrete . . . tell us what sort of materials we need, what sort of troops." . . . That's why he called the study group "European Se-

> curity Capabilities." [It was] this whole notion that it shouldn't just be philosophical and abstract. It should tell them what they should train for. What they should buy.[12]

From the onset, Kaldor decided that a diversity of views, experiences, and expertise was important to shaping the group's vision. Although Kaldor included people with whome she had worked before, such as Ulrich Albrecht and Sonja Licht, she also included people who were controversial and who would stimulate debate within the group. For example, Christine Chinkin, scholar and barrister, did not agree with the findings of the *Kosovo Report*. Chinkin believed that any intervention must be legal. Moreover, she did not believe that the approach taken by NATO with regard to the intervention in Kosovo was appropriate: "What did they do? They take the human rights monitors away before the bombing campaign started. That *does* seem to be slightly inconsistent [from a human rights viewpoint]."[13]

Another example of Kaldor's attempt to foster debate in the ESCG was the inclusion of Andrew Salmon, an officer in the Royal Marines. Salmon recalled his first meeting with Kaldor while he was the director of plans for the Coalition Military Advisory Training Team on assignment in Baghdad. Based in "The Republican Palace" in 2003, which served as the US headquarters during its occupation of Iraq, Salmon was preparing the training plan for the new Iraqi armed security forces. Salmon recalled, "Mary interviewed me [in Iraq], and we were having a conversation in the Green Cafe in Baghdad when we were rocketed, and we sort of hid under the table and we carried on the interview there."[14] Salmon explained, "That's when she asked me to get involved in this project on future European security capabilities, and I *really wasn't* interested and said, 'No, thank you. Don't bother.' And so she kept asking me."[15]

After his assignment in Iraq, Salmon returned to the United Kingdom for a brief assignment at the Royal College of Defence Studies for a four-month foundation term. Kaldor asked Salmon again to be involved in the project, this time to deliver a paper at her first ESCG workshop, explaining his view on the use of the military in support of law enforcement and his experiences in operations in the Balkans. As Salmon maintained later, Kaldor "asked me to talk about . . . how we use militaries and how we link it [defense] to police law and order issues. . . . So I delivered this work which was *quite* controversial, and that was exactly what Mary wanted."[16]

Keen to make their findings accessible to the public and to policy advisers alike, she encouraged the group members to use less academic terms in their writing. Instead of *cosmopolitan law enforcement* and *politics from below*, they used the term *human security* to emphasize the transition away from state-based, classical notions of security. Not until sometime into the ESCG study did Kaldor begin to use *human security* as an umbrella term to articulate the group's work. Glasius recalled: "*Human security* was not the initial rubric at all. There was a notion that European security ought to be distinct. There was a notion that bottom-up ought to play a role, that we were going to look at what sort of responses new wars required. . . . But the specific notion of human security we ended up with quite late in the day in the development of writing that report."[17]

The idea of using the concept of human security to underpin international or foreign policy was not new, the term being first popularized in the UN Development Programme report entitled *Human Development Report 1994: New Dimensions of Human Security.*[18] And by the late 1990s, countries such as Canada and Norway had pursued human security as a key feature in their foreign policy agendas. Japan also used the term and concept, a move championed by Sadako Ogata, then UN commissioner for refugees. The Japanese government and the UN Secretariat launched the UN Fund for Human Security in 1999. With the support of Kofi Annan, and at the advent of the Millennium Declaration in 1999, they established the Commission on Human Security, which was cochaired by Sadako Ogata and economist Amartya Sen. It was this report that influenced Kaldor to change the name to *human security.*

As Glasius relayed:

> I think we might have been six months or a year in before we picked that particular term. And I can remember where it came from: Mary had read the report *Human Security Now,* which I think must have just come out at the time. . . . But she just got hold of the report probably because she has a connection with Amartya Sen. And I remember her calling me up on the weekend and saying, "Yeah, well we need to think some more about this notion of human security. I've been reading this report." And that's how we stole the term.[19]

Similar to how Canada, Norway, and Japan had forged a human security foreign policy in their own state, the ESCG was working to design and implement a human security policy for the European Union in what would become known as the European Security and Defence Policy (ESDP). During the course of the year, the ESCG consulted with a vast array of people outside the study group, they commissioned papers and studies, and they conducted interviews and workshops, which all served to shape the final report that was presented to Solana.

Activism in Iraq and Afghanistan

As before, Kaldor's involvement was also driven by her relationships with other activists. One activist with whom Kaldor worked in Iraq was Yahia Said. During the 1990s, Said was based at the HCA office in Prague. Later, he studied with Kaldor at Sussex University, and he followed Kaldor to the London School of Economics when she moved. Said's family was Iraqi and had been forced to flee Hussein's regime. After the initial invasion of Iraq, Said and Kaldor attempted to support Iraqi activists in the same way they had supported activists in the Balkans. Kaldor recalled her initial visits to Iraq with Said:

> It was very like Bosnia actually. I mean it was so moving. . . . First of all, we met all Yahia's relations. . . . [And then] wherever we went, everyone knew Yahia's father: people who had been in the underground, who had been threatened, they all cried when they saw him. It was just so unbelievable. So in fact Iraq was very, very similar, and we made really good friends. . . . [When] I went to Iraq, I went with Yahia.[20]

One of the first field trips that Kaldor and Said conducted in Iraq was during October and November 2003, during which they were keen to support grassroots democratic elements. They also wanted to stimulate greater debate in the United Kingdom about the role of British forces in Iraq. Kaldor and Said produced a discussion paper to highlight their findings, entitled "Regime Change in Iraq: Mission Report," and they identified a very real risk of a "weak state scenario."[21] For Kaldor and Said, Iraq was "characterised by weak rule of law," "entrenched local particularist political fiefdoms," and "low-level but pervasive violence."[22] "In such a scenario," they argued, "the former regime and the Islamic fighters would become just another element in a particularist mosaic."[23] According to Kaldor and Said, the only way to interrupt this trajectory was "for Iraqis to establish their own democratic institutions" and for other nations to allow them to "take ownership of those institutions."[24]

Kaldor's involvement in Afghanistan was quite a different journey. She became involved in the conflicts in that country when asked to undertake research by several organizations, including the United Nations. Given that she had had no previous contact with activists in Afghanistan, she got in touch with the Open Society, who referred her to Dr. Mohammad Saeed Niazi, director of the Civil Society Development Centre in Afghanistan, former chair of Faryab Province Veterinary Committee, and a former member of the mujahedeen. Thereafter, Kaldor and Niazi formed a research partnership through their respective centers—the Centre for Global Governance and the Civil Society Development Centre—that extended over several years.

One of the key reports that Kaldor undertook concerning the war in Afghanistan was a collaboration with Marika Theros, formally an activist at the Humanitarian Law Centre in Belgrade and an instructor in journalism for the Crimes of War Project. Theros was at one point based in Kabul, and Kaldor and Theros were commissioned by the Century Foundation to write a report on Afghanistan, in particular the role of the international community. They entitled the report *Task Force on Afghanistan in Its Regional and Multiregional Dimensions*, and the cochair of the project was Lakhdar Brahimi, the former UN special representative for Afghanistan. To conduct the study, Kaldor and

Theros worked in partnership with Niazi and researchers from his center. When asked why Kaldor and Theros's paper was interesting, Brahimi replied:

> Most people go to Kabul for two days. They meet the same people (I call them "the fifty people who speak English"). . . . Everyone speaks about civil society, and that you have to involve the people, and that you have to listen, local ownership, and so on. But when you look at what they have done, they have spoken to those fifty people who speak English . . . and they say, "We have spoken to the people of Afghanistan." . . . I think [Kaldor and Theros] did a little bit more than that. They made sure that they saw people who didn't speak English. Old people. Young people. Women. From the capital. From the regions. From the north. From the south. I think that they really came much closer than most people to the very, very diverse views of the people of Afghanistan. They spoke to former mujahedeen, religious people, people close to the Taliban, people that are violently anti-Taliban, and so on. Also there were people, women in particular, whom they also spoke to, and who have not met with foreigners.[25]

A Split in a European Defense Agenda

As the destabilizing effects of the interventions in Iraq and Afghanistan were being realized, those involved in setting the European defense agenda remained split as to how to define and solve the problem of international security. Kaldor's team had set out their ideas in a report, *A Human Security Doctrine for Europe: The Barcelona Report of the Study Group on Europe's Security Capabilities* (*Barcelona Report*),[26] which was officially unveiled at the Universal Forum of Cultures in Barcelona ("Barcelona Forum") in September 2004. The *Barcelona Report* advocated seven operational measures: "the primacy of human rights, clear political authority, multilateralism, a bottom-up approach, regional focus, the use of legal instruments, and the appropriate use of force."[27]

September 11 and the invasion of Iraq remained dominant themes of the Barcelona Forum, not only because these events had caused a split in the European defense agenda but also because the legitimacy of humanitarian intervention was now under question more than at any time before. At the launch of the report, Solana maintained that the European Union had already incorporated some of the ideas presented therein following the various meetings that the key members of the ESCG had held with EU foreign policy officials, and these ideas would be further "discussed in various political committees" of the European Union.[28]

Solana supported the recommendations of the *Barcelona Report*. He argued that, although the European Union was withdrawing from many peacekeeping missions in countries still experiencing political and military turbulence for political reasons, the European Union "must begin to consider that perhaps we have to play a global role."[29] To show his support for the *Barcelona Report*, Solana included a copy of the report on the European Union's External Affairs website, and he also set up a civil-military planning division in the European Union's External Affairs Office.[30]

The *Barcelona Report* was controversial in a number of ways, most particularly because the authors challenged European countries to develop a cohesive foreign and defense policy. Such a policy would mean integrating their own defense and intelligence capabilities. For example, one of the key recommendations of the report was the Multilateral Rapid Response Team, consisting of 15,000 people, of which one-third would be civilian personnel (including human rights monitors, police, development specialists, and humanitarian specialists).[31] The authors also recommended a new legal framework to administer and oversee the decision to intervene and manage operations on the ground. The multilateral task force would utilize the domestic laws of host and sending states, international human rights law, international criminal law, and international humanitarian law.

For many, despite its intention to detail capability and to outline the practical requirements to execute human security policy, the *Barcelona Report* was considered terribly idealistic and unworkable. For example, when David Petraeus, who was then commander of US Central Command and oversaw the compilation of the *U.S. Army Counterinsurgency Field Manual*,[32] read the *Barcelona Report,* he decided that a multilateral force was an "unrealistic recommendation."[33] Concurring with Petraeus was Brigadier Andrew Sharpe, then head of land and research strategy at the Defence Concepts and Doctrine Centre within the British Ministry of Defence. Sharpe contended that he "would tend probably to come down on the side of Petraeus" not only because a task force on standby would be expensive but also because the politics of an EU task force still represented a domestic political challenge.[34] Asked if NATO already acted as a multilateral force, Sharpe replied:

> You don't really have nations with different skills. Well, you do, and you don't. What NATO hasn't done—but there is a lot of talk about it, because it would save money—has given role specialization to people [or nations] and said [for example], "You do logistics, I will do policing, he'll do the administration, he can do transport, [and] he can do war fighting," because people simply don't trust that to happen. And what if, for example, NATO was to agree to do—to pluck an example out of the air—Libya? And let's say the Germans were the ones that we'd agreed [would] provide strike aircraft, and German politics said, "Well, I'm not joining in this time?" Then NATO can't do it.[35]

However, others in the military believed that with the right leadership a multilateral task force could be possible, such as Chris Henwood, who was a group captain based at NATO Allied Joint Force Command in Naples. As a

Royal Air Force officer with military experience in Bosnia, who has written doctrine for counterinsurgency and peace support operations, Henwood argued that, although developing a formal structure within the European Union might not be possible at this time, given the lack of political will, "individuals can make a difference." Henwood argued that Paddy Ashdown's role in Bosnia offered an example of what a "well-networked individual leader . . . with the right power and the right connections" can achieve "with a number of disparate organizations."[36] Civilian leadership did in this instance, he insisted, lead a multilateral civilian-military task force.[37] Salmon, concurring with Henwood's viewpoint, concluded that Ashdown's objective was not just to integrate various forces but also to incorporate a number of different civilian agencies to work together:

> When I was director of the Balkans in the Ministry of Defence, we created a model for Lord Ashdown, which was a much more integrated, multiagency model, to run Bosnia. Previously, we had an organization called S4, which was NATO, and we would have the officer, high representative, and a whole lot of other actors kind of working sometimes together and sometimes not together. So our idea was [that] when Lord Ashdown was going to become the EU special representative . . . was to put him in charge of the EU military, law and order pillar, development pillar. So there would be a much more coordinated [effort] reporting to him in the Balkans.[38]

As one of its strengths, the *Barcelona Report* was drawn from the experiences of members within ESCG. For example, one of the members of the group who supported the idea of a joint civilian-military multilateral task force was Klaus Reinhardt, a former commander in the German army. As an officer earlier in his career, Reinhardt was involved in combining the East and West German armies and also worked with NATO to prepare the Polish, Czech, and Hungarian land forces as they became a part of that organization. Later in his career, he was commander of the NATO-led Kosovo Force. Following Kosovo, Reinhardt was adviser and supervisor in multilateral training courses across Europe and in the United States for groups such as NATO and on exercises, such as Viking, a multinational civilian-military exercise based in Sweden. When asked why he disagreed with those such as Petraeus who said such a task force was impossible, he declared that "if you go abroad today *without* a multilateral force, you better stay home."[39]

According to Reinhardt, one of the criteria for successful intervention today is a joint-led civilian-military multilateral force, a conclusion he drew from his own experience as a commander during the NATO-led intervention in Kosovo. Reinhardt assumed the role of commander once the air strikes were completed and the multinational land forces had arrived in Serbia. Working under the leadership of his civilian counterpart, Bernard Kouchner, then UN special representative and head of the UN Interim Administration Mission in

Kosovo, he found that the objective of the operations, which were predominantly led by land forces, was to stop the violence. But, according to Reinhardt, he ensured that operations were civilian led and that he worked closely with Kouchner to lower what they described as the "crime rate" in Kosovo to the level that is experienced in Western countries:

> I basically subjugated my organization to [Kouchner], which people in NATO did not like at all, but I said, "If we ran that country, [Kouchner] was the highest political authority, and I was the highest executive authority." . . . And we met every day for the entire period of time there. . . . After a short period of time, we were called the "twin brothers." I said, "Bernard, whatever we decide here, you will be the speaker, you will engage the public, and I will support you." And we had some very tough differences and different ideas on how to proceed. But I said, "Whenever we leave this room, we will have the same opinion, or we don't leave the room . . . [because] we have to be united." . . . I remember the first visit of the NATO council in early October–November, and we could basically show them in our statistics that the murder, the arson, all these atrocities, had stopped totally, and that Kosovo was a more safe place than Washington, DC.[40]

Nevertheless, for Reinhardt, the biggest lesson in his experiences in Kosovo, which influenced his input into the *Barcelona Report*, was that, although the initial phase of the multilateral task force had curtailed the violence, it was not enough. The country had no government.

Prior to the war, a Serbian-led government had administrated Kosovo, but its politicians had all fled, as the violence ensued, leaving the country without its own parliament or bureaucracy. The Kosovars needed to rebuild their country, and the costs and skills required to run the country had not been factored in by nations that had deployed land forces. Reinhardt recalled:

> But if you are to run a country you need a budget; otherwise you cannot pay a teacher, or a doctor. . . . You lose credibility in a very short period of time. . . . This was simply not thought through by those nations that had deployed their forces into Kosovo. . . . When [Bill] Clinton came, about ten days after I had my meeting with Solana, he asked the same question. [Clinton] asked, "How much money do you need?" I said, "I need a half a billion in US dollars per year." And he told me that this is quite a lot of money. I said, "No, sir. We bombed Kosovo and Serbia for seventy-eight days, and every day cost NATO one billion in US dollars. If I get a half day out of those seventy-eight days, I can run Kosovo for an entire year." [Clinton] turned to Sandy Berger [US national security adviser] and said, "Make sure General Reinhardt gets the money."[41]

Although many components of the *Barcelona Report* were controversial, the report was important for three reasons: First, it represented the first real narrative for a human security dialogue within the European Union. At that point, there was "practically no European security discourse."[42] Second, the authors of the report "took the focus on the protection of civilians in conflicts . . . to the highest level of the [European] union . . . and . . . linked [it] explicitly with the ESDP process."[43] Lastly, the report represented "the first coherent attempt to develop a policy for intervention based on the human security concept, not only in terms of policy and legal principles . . . but also in terms of the needs of civilian-military integration."[44]

For others, the *Barcelona Report* was also a normative project that was sympathetic to the UN Human Security Commissions mandate. Moreover, the authors of the report attempted to solve the problem of how to protect ordinary people, which, some argued, required a high degree of creativity and imagination. Amartya Sen contended that Kaldor "investigated problems of human security so imaginatively and so robustly. Our report of the Human Security Commission, *Security Now,* is at a greater level of abstraction than Mary's work, but the two works are on parallel lines, and they can draw strength from each other."[45]

When members of the ESCG completed the *Barcelona Report*, their work had only just begun. Once the report was finished, members of the group began a rigorous campaign across Europe to influence policy and debate the various points in the report with European defense and foreign ministries during each of the EU presidencies, starting with the Dutch presidency in 2004 and ending with the Spanish presidency in 2010.[46] According to Salmon, in the early years, Kaldor did a lot of work with members of the ESCG to raise the profile of human security across the European Union to effect change in domestic and European policy:

> What Mary was doing during those early years was [advocating the ESCG's position]. As a nation was in charge of the EU presidency, quite often . . . they would start to hear about and understand human security through the *Barcelona Report* and through the advocacy. . . . Mary was trying to effect change in [their] policy. For [example], the Spanish Ministry of Defense, the Finnish Ministry of Foreign Affairs, the Germans were quite interested at some stage, the French up to a point, [and] Portugal was interested. So Mary would travel around Europe talking to ministries of foreign affairs and ministries of defense. And if they liked the idea, they commissioned Mary to do some work to see what they could put into the presidency agenda and presidency report as a kind of legacy, as they completed their six-month presidency.[47]

By 2010, the ESCG produced the follow-up report, *A European Way of Security: The Madrid Report of the Human Security Study Group* (*Madrid Report*).[48] They also meet with MPs, military practitioners, and policy groups, such as the Political and Security Committee, for which Mary Kaldor, Klaus Reinhardt, and Kari Möttölä, an adviser for the Finnish Ministry for Foreign Affairs, hosted a session on human security.[49]

As Serra was quick to point out, the *Barcelona Report* was not just meant to influence the European security strategy and policymakers. It was meant to influence "public opinion as well."[50] The ESCG was involved in public seminars and the publication of books, journals, and newspaper articles. Furthermore, following the *Barcelona Report*, Kaldor and Chinkin developed a human security course for the London School of Economics.[51]

A Finnish Partnership

Although the *Barcelona Report* provided details on the capability required of EU states, the next step was to operationalize the report's findings. In 2006, the Finnish EU presidency asked the newly titled Human Security Capability Group (HSCG) to further develop the earlier recommendations in the *Barcelona Report* and to review the ESDP for implementation across the European Union.[52] Erkki Tuomioja, who was, at the time, the Finnish foreign minister during the Finnish presidency of the European Union, maintained, "We were certainly very committed to the concept of human security and enhancing the EU's role in its promotion."[53]

According to Tuomioja, one of the key actors working with Kaldor "during the Finnish presidency related to human security" was Kari Möttölä, special adviser on security policy for the Policy Planning and Research Unit, then directly under the state secretary (Finland's highest civil servant).[54] By supporting the work of the ESCG, Finland's Ministry of Foreign Affairs assumed a leadership position to promote the concept of human security as a main component of the Finnish presidency. The initial "grand strategy" of the European Union, outlined in *European Security Strategy* in 2003, Möttölä maintained, precluded the term and concept "human security." However, Möttölä argued that the *Barcelona Report*, with the visible support of Solana, introduced the concept of human security into the EU agenda.

Although the concept of human security itself was not new, the question for the Finnish government was whether or not the European Union would take on the term and concept of human security in its official joint documents, and whether or not the concept of human security could be implemented as an agreed function of the European Union?[55] Tuomioja was keen to pursue a clearly defined model for human security that would be legally adopted by the European Union. According to Möttölä,

> the Finnish MFA [Ministry of Foreign Affairs] stepped in with its initiative to promote human security as part of the incoming Finnish presidency by supporting the work of the Kaldor group as a primary tool. Human security was compatible with Finnish foreign policy thinking—although the concept itself was not used in the Finnish *Security and Defence Policy Report* of 2004—and there was already a wide international "codex" on the idea. The *Barcelona Report* and the continued work of the Kaldor group, however, was by far the most developed project, and, in addition, it was tailored for the pur-

pose of the European Union. It was natural to look at possibilities for supporting and cooperating with the group.[56]

The Finnish government contributed not only financially but also intellectually to a continuation of the study. After the *Barcelona Report* was carefully scrutinized by the Finnish Policy Planning Unit, Eija Limnell, the director of that unit, met with Kaldor in London on 12 January 2006 and then participated in the rebranded HSCG meeting in London in February 2006. As a result of the engagement, the Finnish Ministry of Foreign Affairs signed a contract with the London School of Economics in March 2006 for a project entitled "A Human Security Agenda for the European Union." The objective was to determine how to operationalize the human security concept further in the European Union, with two additional experts nominated by the Finnish ministry to join the team. Kaldor's proposal was addressed to the Finnish presidency of the European Union, and, although not a binding agreement, the proposal aimed to steer strategic planning and, more importantly, operationalize human security within and across member states.

Again, Kaldor assumed the role of convenor of the study group, and she worked with a team of activists, academics, policy advisers, and politicians. Although the group still included many of the ESCG's original members, such as Ulrich Albrecht, Christine Chinkin, Sonja Licht, Klaus Reinhardt, Geneviève Schméder, and Narcís Serra, it also now included new members with new ideas, such as Marlies Glasius.

Like the ESCG before it, the HSCG undertook a broad array of studies, commissioned papers, interviews, and workshops to come up with its findings. For example, in May 2006, a workshop on human security was convened in Helsinki, in which Kaldor and the rest of the group debated the central themes and objectives of the project with around fifty participants, among them officials and NGO representatives, many of whom went by the title of civilian crisis management practitioners and tackled the notion of human security from various viewpoints. The presentation consisted of case studies on human security in the Balkans and introduced the possibility of a training module being developed for practitioners in human security operations as an ongoing objective of the project.

In a culmination of the group's work, the *Madrid Report* was unveiled in Madrid on 8 November 2007. The launch was hosted by the Spanish Ministry of Foreign Affairs and Ministry of Defense and also involved the Finnish Ministry of Foreign Affairs. Many of the experiences of those involved in the ESCG and the HSCG had influenced the content and proposals of the *Madrid Report* and the *Barcelona Report*, and the members further attempted to adopt many of the findings and to apply them in practical ways. For example, Salmon attempted to apply many of the lessons learned in his new role as commandant of the Commando Training Centre of the Royal Marines in 2007, as well as operationally in his function as the general officer commanding the Multi-National Division (South East), Iraq, headquartered in Basra:

> Another illustration, which is probably a more operationally useful one, was actually using human security in Basra, actually putting human security in the campaign language, in the campaign end-state. . . . I was the commander of Coalition Forces in southeast Iraq for about ten months from August 2008 to 2009. So with my people and my staff, before we deployed on that operation, we used to have learning sessions every week, and we introduced human security into those learning sessions. . . . What did that mean in Basra? Actually, what that meant in Basra was first of all listening to people's needs and working out how to deliver to those needs, making connections to all sorts of different types of people to do it, and using our force—not the use of force [in the traditional sense]—but using the troops, the formation, in a different way and looking through the lens of the people.[57]

Others in the Finnish presidency also attempted to apply the findings practically. The HSCG conducted a pilot human security training course with the Finnish Crisis Management Centre (CMC) in Kuopio, Finland, on 11–15 February 2008. Thirty participants (a third of them Finnish) attended the first training session on the theory and application of the *Madrid Report*, using Kosovo and the European Union Rule of Law Mission as case studies. Mary Kaldor and academic Mary Martin, along with Andrew Salmon and Klaus Reinhardt, acted as the main teachers of the course, conducted jointly by the Finnish Ministry of Foreign Affairs and the London School of Economics.

Aki Kerkkanen, the director of the CMC, had first decided that he was interested in Kaldor's work when he read her book *The Baroque Arsenal* in the 1980s, but actually getting to work with Kaldor required something of a journey:

> I came across the *Barcelona Report,* the first one of Mary's reports, about the same time that I started at CMC Finland. I remembered Mary Kaldor from the book . . . and I came across her ideas for human security and then there was a Madrid conference. . . . But, I mean, the principles of human security struck me. I've a military background, also, in the peacekeeping. I've been in several peacekeeping tours, in the Middle East, in the Balkans, both military and civilian, as UN and EU. And having this practical experience myself . . . I mean the ideas, the principles of human security resonated very well. I felt that I can connect these principles into practice, or I could have had, if I [had] known these principles when I was serving as a peacekeeper. They resonated very well, and I became more interested. I got in touch with Mary, and we started to plan or think about what to do [with] human security at CMC in Finland. . . . She was keen on experimenting with the training. . . . We started to plan the first five-day training [course] in Finland.[58]

The human security module was also incorporated into other courses for basic training at CMC, such as those for legal specialists, police officers, human rights observers, and monitors. Those who were involved in EU and UN crisis management operations also attended. According to Kerkkanen, Kaldor also attempted to export the human security ideas so they would be incorporated into the heart of EU policy. As Kerkkanen maintained, incorporating these principles "was in fact one of Mary's ideas," and she hoped "to get this human security understood by the EU crisis management group in Brussels."[59]

Effect of the Reports

In 2008, the European Union produced a follow-up to the European security strategy, outlined in the *Report on the Implementation of the European Security Strategy*. The report had included the term *human security* in reference to more traditional notions, as outlined in the UN Development Programme in 1994. According to Möttölä, the new strategy also recognized the *Barcelona Report*'s model of human security, reflecting a people-based approach to security with access to skilled civilian and military personnel readily sourced from member states.[60]

Nonetheless, the *Report on the Implementation of the European Security Strategy* was not the *Barcelona Report*. Although the notion of human security and its underlying principles were supported by the member states, doubts remained about the practicality of a multilateral task force such as that detailed in the *Barcelona Report*. As Möttölä recalled, debate ensued concerning the (additional) legal or other binding requirements that the formal adoption of a new model would involve for the European Union. The real operationalization of the human security proposition as conceptualized in the *Barcelona Report* was yet to be realized.[61]

Kaldor continued to stimulate debate on the subject of human security. Many of her thoughts and ideas on global civil society and humanitarian intervention, developed during her work as an activist in Iraq and Afghanistan and through her work in the HSCG, informed her book *Human Security: Reflections of Globalization and Intervention*. *Human Security* explored the security gap between conventional war and new wars, which, she argued, did not solve the problem of organized violence and state insecurity, nor support civil society or politics from below.[62]

Kaldor's efforts to influence the European Union only went so far in implementing the recommendations of both the *Barcelona* and *Madrid Report* and in reflecting the concepts outlined in her book *Human Security*. Although the reports led to debate within the European Union about the concept of human security, and the idea itself was now more widely accepted, human security was still not the predominant concept of European foreign and security policy. Some within the HSCG, such as Glasius, also contended that HSCG shared some weaknesses. For example, although it included researchers such as Yahia Said, one of the major weaknesses of the study group, she argued, was that it did not really include representatives from developing or non-Western countries.[63] Moreover, she argued that the group did little to transform the EU position in any material way.

However, others argued that the study group did contribute to a shift. Javier Solana insisted that the study group was "something of a ginger group," which served to move the EU on a different course.[64] Likewise, Narcís Serra observed that the *Barcelona Report* and the *Madrid Report* led to a subtle change in the European Union's security policy: while human security was not mentioned in the European security strategy of 2003, it was mentioned in the review of European security strategy in 2008. He added, "It is mentioned as if it were the direction of [the] European vision of security."[65] Yet, Natasa Kandic has argued that Kaldor's and Solana's efforts were not just to change policy wording but to shape a new debate in the European Union on what security meant. In this way, Kandic argued, Kaldor and Solana were able to "open a new space for human rights and human security" to be debated.[66] This alone, she argued, was significant.

Notes

1. Sadako Ogata, letter to Mary Kaldor, 1 October 2004, p. 1, PA-MK-HS/PolComs.
2. See Mary Kaldor, "Humanitarian Intervention: A Forum," *Nation*, 26 June 2003, online.
3. Ibid.
4. Kaldor, quoted in Julie McCarthy, "Putting People First: The Growing Influence of 'Human Security'—An Interview with Mary Kaldor," *Yale Journal of International Affairs* (Spring–Summer 2010), p. 21.
5. Carl Tham, "Humanitarian Intervention: A Forum," *Nation*, 26 June 2003, online.
6. Richard Falk, "Humanitarian Intervention: A Forum," *Nation*, 26 June 2003, online.
7. Kaldor, quoted in Alan Johnson, "New Wars and Human Security: An Interview with Mary Kaldor," *Democratiya* 11 (Winter), 3 July 2007, p. 23.
8. Kaldor, quoted in ibid., pp. 23–24.
9. Kaldor, *Global Civil Society*.
10. Solana, "The European Union and Human Security," p. 254.
11. Narcís Serra, interview with author, 25 May 2011.
12. Marlies Glasius, interview with author, 31 May 2011.
13. Christine Chinkin, interview with author, 28 June 2011.
14. Andrew Salmon, interview with author, 19 May 2011.
15. Ibid.
16. Ibid.
17. Marlies Glasius, interview with author, 31 May 2011.
18. United Nations Development Programme, *Human Development Report 1994: New Dimensions of Human Security*, New York and Oxford: Oxford University Press, 1994, http://hdr.undp.org/en/content/human-development-report-1994.
19. Glasius, interview with author, 31 May 2011.

20. Mary Kaldor, interview with author.

21. Mary Kaldor and Yahia Said, "Regime Change in Iraq: Mission Report," Discussion Paper 26, Centre for the Study of Global Governance, London School of Economic and Political Science, 2003, p. 16.

22. Ibid.

23. Ibid.

24. Ibid.

25. Lakhdar Brahimi, interview with author, 3 June 2011.

26. Albrecht et al., *A Human Security Doctrine for Europe*.

27. European Security Study Group, *A Human Security Doctrine for Europe: Report of the Barcelona Study Group on Europe's Security Capabilities*, London School of Economics, London/Barcelona, 15 September 2003, p. 5.

28. Solana, quoted in Lluis Pellicer, "La UE estudia crear una fuera de reaccion con civiles y militares" [A Study on the Development of an EU Civil and Military Reaction Force], *El Pais* [The Country], International, Barcelona, 16 September 2004, p. 5.

29. Solana, quoted in ibid.

30. Mary Kaldor, "A Human Security Doctrine for Europe, and Beyond: A Force for Intervention," *International Herald Tribune*, 30 September 2004, p. 8.

31. Pellicer, "La UE estudia," p. 5.

32. *U.S. Army Counterinsurgency Field Manual, Field Manual 3-24/ No. 3-33.5*, Department of the Army and Marine Corps Combat Development Command, 15 December 2006.

33. David Petraeus, correspondence with author, 19 April 2011.

34. Andrew Sharpe, interview with author, 6 July 2011.

35. Ibid.

36. Chris Henwood, interview with author, 8 August 2011.

37. Ibid.

38. Andrew Salmon, interview with author, 19 May 2011.

39. Klaus Reinhardt, interview with author, 13 May 2011.

40. Ibid.

41. Ibid.

42. Wilfried von Bredow, "*The Barcelona Report on a Human Security Doctrine for Europe*: Overview and Some Critical Remarks," presented at the Berlin Symposium on Human Security and EU-Canada Relations, Canadian Universities' Centre, Berlin, 3 March 2005, http://individual.utoronto.ca/humansecurity/PDF/vonBredow.pdf.

43. Jean-Yves Haine, "The European Crisis of Liberal Internationalism," *International Journal* 64 (Spring 2009), p. 463.

44. Matlary, "When Soft Power Turns Hard: Is an EU Strategic Culture Possible?" *Security Dialogue* 37, no. 1 (March 2006), p. 116.

45. Amartya Sen, correspondence with author, 14 June 2011.

46. Marlies Glasius, interview with author, 31 May 2011; Klaus Reinhardt, interview with author, 13 May 2011; Geneviève Schméder, interview with author, 1 June 2011; Mary Martin, interview with author, 25 May 2011; Mary Kaldor, interview with author; Narcís Serra, interview with author, 25 May 2011; Andrew Salmon, interview with author, 19 May 2011.

47. Andrew Salmon, interview with author, 19 May 2011.

48. Albrecht et al., *A European Way of Security.*

49. Kari Möttölä, correspondence with author, 26 January 2011.

50. Narcís Serra, interview with author, 25 May 2011.

51. Christine Chinkin, interview with author, 28 June 2011.

52. Stijn Ottens, "The European Union's Member States Commitment to Human

Security Within ESDP," master thesis, University of Groningen, Groningen, Netherlands, 2009, p. 13.

53. Erkki Tuomioja, correspondence with author, 20 December 2010.

54. Erkki Tuomioja, correspondence with author, 20 December 2010; Pilvi-Sisko Vierros-Villeneuve, correspondence with author, 12 January 2011.

55. Kari Möttölä, correspondence with author, 26 January 2011.

56. Ibid.

57. Andrew Salmon, interview with author, 19 May 2011.

58. Aki Kerkkanen, interview with author, 14 July 2011.

59. Ibid.

60. Kari Möttölä, correspondence with author, 26 January 2011.

61. Ibid.

62. See Kaldor, *Human Security*.

63. Marlies Glasius, interview with author, 31 May 2011.

64. Solana, "The European Union and Human Security," p. 254.

65. Narcís Serra, interview with author, 25 May 2011.

66. Natasa Kandic, interview with author, 22 February 2011.

14

The Future of Security?

We can only achieve those things for which we have words. . . . Why is that so important? Because really over the past eight or nine years we have really struggled with the first-order question of "What is security in the twenty-first century?" I was faced, firsthand, with that question in my position at the Pentagon. . . . So the challenge is do we have the words . . . ?

. . . We have to lay aside our traditional arguments of "Well, that's 'defence,'" and "Well, that's 'development,'" "Well, this isn't 'your area.'" So this is how Mary and I came together. We came from very, very opposite ends of the spectrum. . . . What we need is a language of understanding. . . . It's about the [different] questions. It's about how to frame those questions and how to speak that language.[1]

IN THIS BOOK, I HAVE EXPLORED KALDOR'S POLITICAL THINKING AND ACTIVISM, focusing on the shift in her understandings of security, civil society, and the role of the state. During the course of this study, three interrelated arguments were made.

First, I have argued that Kaldor's career as a public intellectual was shaped by democratic socialist and postwar notions of public advocacy that were implicitly and explicitly informed by her family milieu. Kaldor grew up in a family where public debate and intellectual engagement with social and political problems were fostered. With "evangelical" fervor, her father was intent on rescuing postwar Europe from economic disaster and the world from the ills of "monetarism."[2] Kaldor was similarly driven by a commitment to public advocacy against the political economy of organized violence. Kaldor drew on the methods of public advocacy of both her parents, which, when combined, included activism, scholarship, and policy, to develop her own style of public intellectuality. She remained attached to academic institutions in order to safeguard her own intellectual independence and to escape the limits on public debate often imposed on civil servants and professional activists. However, she firmly orientated her scholarship toward policy, activism, and public engagement.

Second, whereas Kaldor's notion of society and the role of the state were influenced by her upbringing, her professional experiences as an activist and scholar influenced her development of concepts such as politics from below, the link between peace and human rights, and civil society. Initially, Kaldor was sympathetic to the Fabian Society's emphasis on social and political reform and the enlightened role of government; however, she opposed violent revolution as an instrument for social change. Although Fabian notions of reform emphasized social engagement in the construction of policy, they nonetheless relied upon a top-down approach to political change that depended on a faith in the state's moral and creative capacities. Kaldor's engagement with Western peace activists and Eastern European dissidents during the course of the 1980s saw her shift away from Hegelian notions of the state as morally superior and toward an idea of civil society as a more effective agent of progressive social change, with the impetus and legitimacy for such change coming from below through forms of participatory democracy. Taking part in these dissident debates, Kaldor came to the conclusion that civil society should, on some level, remain completely independent of the state.

Third, Kaldor's view on the way organized violence by the state affected society during the Cold War was further developed during her direct experience on the ground during the wars in the Balkans and the Caucasus. Initially, like her family, Kaldor was skeptical about revolution, not simply because of the violence but because violent revolutions can unleash unforeseen forces with uncontrolled outcomes. By its nature, in Kaldor's opinion, violent revolution sidelines the democratic elements crucial to effective and legitimate political settlement and, for the most part, impairs civility within society. Although initially sympathetic to more Fabian reformist tendencies, during her activism in the 1980s, Kaldor adapted her understanding of revolution to actively support "soft" revolution, such as the nonviolent Velvet Revolution and other negotiated revolutions throughout Eastern Europe, and lent from Lockean notions of political legitimacy. Influenced by experiences behind the Iron Curtain, Kaldor came to see human rights as essential for peace, concluding that a peace that left Eastern Europe without human rights was not peace at all. Kaldor's efforts as an activist to confront the horrors of ethnic cleansing in the Balkans and the Caucasus during the 1990s further shaped her theorization of how violence limits the space for civil society, and she became an outspoken proponent of humanitarian intervention. However, she qualified that, although intervention should ensure peacekeeping, it should also explicitly protect the human rights of civilians. By reframing the contemporary notion of war as new wars in cosmopolitan terms, Kaldor argued that armed intervention to protect civilians by force is a duty that Western democracies ensure for their own citizens and must be applied universally. In this way, Kaldor proposed that cosmopolitan law enforcement, augmented by a temporary UN or multilateral civil administration, must therefore move to uphold the rule of law and to protect civilians from state or quasi-state organized violence. Kaldor's experience as a member of the Kosovo Commission further clarified her understanding of how intervention must be conducted through the use of force, with the emphasis being on ground troops that protect civilians, as opposed to air strikes that target the enemy. Moreover, the experience of the Kosovo War led Kaldor to conclude that, except in the civil role of policing and upholding the rule of law domestically and internationally, states have lost their legitimacy for organized violence, both in relation to traditional interstate war and in what she called "new wars."

I hope in this book to have illuminated how Kaldor's earlier ideas of militarism and the political economy of violence were adapted over time to support military intervention and how the role of military remained an important tension in her later work. Even though this book is in no way an exhaustive or definitive study of Kaldor's life, in writing an intellectual biography, I hope to have shown how Kaldor came to her conclusions concerning security and her intent to develop a cosmopolitan response to new wars and political violence.

After Madrid

After the *Madrid Report*, Kaldor's intellectual projects broadened. She continued to work with the HSCG to produce *Helsinki Plus: Towards a Human Security Architecture for Europe*, she became a consultant to Gray Hawk Systems for a report on the future of war for the Pentagon, and she continued to collaborate with various officials and experts, such as Lieutenant Colonel Shannon D. Beebe, former senior Africa analyst for the Pentagon, with whom she coauthored *The Ultimate Weapon Is No Weapon: Human Security and the New Rules of War and Peace*.[3]

By the time this book is published, she will have completed a five-year study, entitled "Security in Transition (SiT): An Interdisciplinary Investigation into the Security Gap," which was funded by the European Research Council. Along with Javier Solana, who joined the HSCG as a coconvener with Kaldor, she developed another report in 2016, entitled *From Hybrid Peace to Human Security: Rethinking EU Strategy Towards Conflict*,[4] which was presented to Federica Mogherini, high representative of the European Union for Foreign Affairs and Security Policy, in February 2016. Kaldor's work retains her activism and scholarly trademark, and she continues to debate the role of her government on the subject of war and intervention, to respond to new wars in places such as Syria, and to work with civil society activists on the ground of political violence.

Who Is Mary Kaldor?

Kaldor's story is of one who is well connected to the establishment and the political elite. As an individual, with liberal and cosmopolitan sensibilities, Kaldor could mobilize grassroots activists while, at the same time, engaging in politics at a multilateral level. What has not been explored in this book, and should be in any further studies, is how Kaldor's gender played a role in her approach to solving problems. Francesca Klug, an academic and former commissioner on the statutory Equality and Human Rights Commission observed, "There is another dimension to the sort of work that Mary does, and that is doing it as a woman."[5] Her gender may explain her style of leadership, which emphasizes inclusion and collaboration.

During the course of her activism, Kaldor rarely made decisions alone. Rather than employ a top-down approach, she ensured that decisions evolved as a series of group deliberations. Through her experience as an activist, she attempted to understand and identify the political context, which was often complex and fluid.[6] To solve problems in a complex context, Kaldor would encourage open dialogue with a broad array of activists, politicians, academics, and practitioners. She had the intellectual and personal confidence to stimulate dissent and to create spaces for experimentation, interaction, and debate with others. At the same time, Kaldor was a fiercely independent thinker.

During the course of her life, Kaldor has attempted to direct attention to how security is framed and to offer a different lens through which to view the economy surrounding the arms trade, the mutual enterprise inherent in the Cold War, the grassroots politics that played a role in disposing of it, the importance of peacekeeping forces, and international law enforcement.

As an "academic entrepreneur," Kaldor's drive to remain independent, while oscillating among the roles of academic, activist, and policy adviser, forced her to take a rather unorthodox approach to scholarship. Although well connected, she often struggled in the 1980s to access academic tenure and to continue to fund her research, compelling her to adopt a more entrepreneurial model to her work. Kaldor's approach illuminates an alternative model in an era when many universities face difficult financial cuts. Moreover, with the advent of social media, blogging, publishing, connecting, and debating in a public sphere are increasingly viable—and perhaps, one could argue, necessary. The advent of the electronic age also means that one does not have to be a policy adviser, politician, academic, journalist, or professional activist to have a view or to debate in the public sphere. Nevertheless, one could argue that opening spaces for diversity, inclusiveness, and genuine debate has become an infinitely greater challenge.

Perhaps her most notable contribution was how security is understood. In defining new wars and cosmopolitan law enforcement, Kaldor set the agenda for a new debate on contemporary war, political violence, intervention, and security. Academic Ulrich Beck pointed out:

> I agree very much with Mary on her cosmopolitanism and her perspective of trying to redefine violent issues and redefine violent conflicts from [a] cosmopolitan perspective. But I would say [although] this normative idea is important, [her] analytical and empirical diagnosis is maybe even more significant, because actually I think the contribution of the social sciences is basically what questions we ask and how those perspectives and concepts we create from those questions open up our eyes to different new realities. And actually I think this is what her idea of new wars does.[7]

Kaldor's work raises more questions than it solves. To subscribe to Kaldor's ideas, a person or entity must

- Reconsider the arms industry and the economy that surrounds it.
- Work to improve peacekeeping and law enforcement competency.
- Develop multilateral task forces equipped to intervene in an array of varying security demands, including natural disasters or organized violence, which are not constrained by notions of citizenship.
- Reconsider how the military is used to uphold the rule of law and protect civilians.
- Train and better equip diplomats to engage with civil society.
- Include a broad range of democratic elements in political arrangements.
- Refine intelligence analysis to include notions of human security.
- Draw on lessons learned for human security policy in regions other than Europe and the United States (i.e., Asia Pacific and the Middle East).
- Develop and invest in ongoing military-civilian multilateral operational competency and training.
- Address seriously the plight of refugees as a human security issue that is not constrained by state-based politics.
- Conduct further research and engage the public in finding ways to encourage and support politics from below.

These proposals present a challenge to states that appear to harbor more nationalist tendencies. A notable example is Kaldor's home country of the United Kingdom, with many of its provinces electing to leave the European Union in a recent referendum.

Nevertheless, many of the proposals named above, if not all, have been started in some capacity. Although they are all difficult, complex propositions, they are also largely antithetical to traditional notions of war and security. And traditional notions of war and security do not provide security to those who most need it, a fact many high-level former members of the military have already conceded, such as Stanley McCrystal, who led the Joint

Special Operations Command in Iraq, David Petraeus, Andrew Salmon, Klaus Reinhardt, Andrew Sharpe, and Shannon Beebe, as well as former diplomats and politicians, such as Javier Solana and Sadako Ogata.

On the surface, Kaldor's political life is one of privilege, well connected to the establishment and political elite, which enabled her to influence and effect change in matters of security. Yet her personal politics reflects just the opposite: it suggests a preoccupation with participatory democracy, civil society, and politics from below. For Kaldor, political legitimacy lies with ordinary people and their ability to debate the number of arms their government trades, the role of the military industry and development, the parameters of organized violence, and the role of civil society, all of which require a plurality of views and a high degree of disagreement and debate. All of these debates are stifled and suppressed in the context of violence and fear.

Kaldor's political life reflects the importance of where decisions concerning security should be made in society. For Kaldor, legitimate political power does not lie solely with the state or with the heads of state, and decisions concerning security should not start with established political or military elites, nor should they be decided in boardrooms of security industries, in operational intelligence organizations, think tanks, NATO, or the United Nations. Rather, the most important decisions concerning security should be born out of a liberal discussion by ordinary people. Those least capable of determining their own security should be empowered, including in the midst of war and organized violence, to be involved in these debates and to influence decisions that ultimately affect them. Similarly, those who enjoy democracy and the rule of law have a responsibility to empower the powerless in what is increasingly a global civil society. The most important question that still remains, therefore, is not *if* we are involved, but *how* all of us, each and every one of us, is involved in the social organization of violence.

Kaldor both invites and challenges those around her to open debate to greater participatory democratic involvement, where the greatest source of political legitimacy is a global civil society based on a social contract that upholds the rule of law. For Kaldor, that means all of us have the right, and a duty, to be involved in the future of security.

Notes

1. Lieutenant Colonel Shannon D. Beebe, speech presented at "The Ultimate Weapon Is No Weapon: Human Security and the New Rules of War and Peace" Panel, Old Theatre, Old Building, London School of Economics, 26 May 2010, http://www.youtube.com/watch?v=cfJpQskyxsM. Lieutenant Colonel Shannon D. Beebe is a former senior Africa analyst in the Office of the US Army Deputy Chief of Staff.

2. John King, interview with author, 21 May 2012. King described Nicholas Kaldor's commitment and drive against monetarism as "evangelical."

3. Kaldor and Beebe, *The Ultimate Weapon Is No Weapon.*

4. Human Security Study Group, *From Hybrid Peace to Human Security: Rethinking EU Strategy Towards Conflict—The Berlin Report of the Human Security Study Group*, London School of Economics, 24 February 2016, http://library.fes.de/pdf-files/bueros/london/12373.pdf.

5. Francesca Klug, interview with author, 22 June 2011.

6. See David Snowden and Mary Boone, "A Leader's Framework for Decision Making," *Harvard Business Review*, November 2007, online.

7. Ulrich Beck, interview with author, 6 July 2011.

Acronyms

BaH	Bosnia and Herzegovina
CMC	Crisis Management Centre (Finland)
CND	Campaign for Nuclear Disarmament (United Kingdom)
CSDP	Common Security and Defence Policy
END	European Nuclear Disarmament (United Kingdom)
ENEWD	European Network for East-West Dialogue
ESCG	European Security Capability Group
ESDP	European Security and Defence Policy
FIDESZ	Alliance of Young Democrats/Magyar Polgári Szövetség (Hungary)
GDR	German Democratic Republic
HCA	Helsinki Citizens' Assembly
HSCG	Human Security Capability Group
ICDP	International Confederation for Disarmament and Peace
ICTY	International Criminal Tribunal for the Former Yugoslavia
IKV	Interkerkelijk Vredesberaad/Interchurch Peace Council (Netherlands)
INF Treaty	Intermediate-Range Nuclear Forces Treaty
ISIO	Institute for the Study of International Organisations
IWC	Institute for Workers' Control (United Kingdom)
KGB	Komitet gosudarstvennoy bezopasnosti/Committee for State Security (Russia)
MGIMO	Moscow State Institute for International Relations (Russia)

MIT	Massachusetts Institute for Technology
MP	member of parliament
NATO	North Atlantic Treaty Organization
NEC	National Executive Committee (Labour Party, United Kingdom)
NGO	nongovernmental organization
NIESR	National Institute for Economic and Social Research (United Kingdom)
OECD	Organisation for Economic Co-operation and Development
OSCE	Organization for Security and Co-operation in Europe
PGD	Peace Group for Dialogue (Hungary)
PGM	precision guided munition
PhD	doctorate of philosophy
RELEX	Relations Extérieures/External Relations
R&D	research and development
SIPRI	Stockholm International Peace Research Institute
SPC	Soviet Peace Committee
SPRU	Science Policy Research Unit
START I	Strategic Arms Reduction Treaty I
UNHCR	UN High Commission for Refugees
UNPROFOR	UN Protection Force
USSR	Union of Soviet Socialist Republics
WIDER	World Institute for Development Economics Research (Finland)

References

Albrecht, Ulrich, Christine Chinkin, Gemma Collantes Celador, Stefanie Flechtner, Marlies Glasius, Mary Kaldor, Kimmo Kiljunen, Jan Klabbers, Jenny Kuper, Sonia Licht, Flavio Lotti, Klaus Reinhardt, Genevieve Schmeder, Pavel Seifter, Narcis Serra, and Gert Weisskirchen. *A European Way of Security: The Madrid Report of the Human Security Study Group*. Madrid: Human Security Study Group, 2007.

Albrecht, Ulrich, Christine Chinkin, Kemal Dervis, Renata Dwan, Anthony Giddens, Nicole Gnesotto, Mary Kaldor, Sonia Licht, Jan Pronk, Klaus Reinhardt, Genevieve Schmeder, Pavel Seifter, and Narcis Serra. *A Human Security Doctrine for Europe: The Barcelona Report of the Study Group on Europe's Security Capabilities*. Barcelona: Study Group on Europe's Security Capabilities, 2004.

Albrecht, Ulrich, Asbjørn Eide, Mary Kaldor, Milton Leitenberg, and Julian Perry Robinson. *A Short Research Guide on Arms and Armed Forces*. London: Croom Helm, 1978.

Allen, Tim, and David Styan. "A Right to Interfere? Bernard Kouchner and the New Humanitarianism." *Journal of International Development* 12, no. 6 (August 2000): 825–842.

Ali, Tariq, ed. *Masters of the Universe? NATO's Balkan Crusade*. London: Verso, 2000.

Andreas, Peter. *Blue Helmets and Black Markets: The Business of Survival in the Siege of Sarajevo*. New York: Cornwell University, 2008.

Anheier, Helmut K., Mary Kaldor, and Marlies Glasius, eds. *Civil Society Yearbook 2004/2005*. New York: Sage, 2005.

Annan, Kofi. *In Larger Freedom: Towards Development, Security and Human Rights for All*. Report of the Secretary-General, UN Doc. A/59/2005 and annex. New York: United Nations, 2005.

———. *Report of the Secretary-General Pursuant to General Assembly Resolution 53/35: The Fall of Srebrenica: An Assessment*. New York: United Nations, 1999.

Arato, Andrew, and Jean L. Cohen. *Civil Society and Political Theory*. Cambridge, MA: MIT Press, 1992.

Archibugi, Daniele. "The Reform of the UN and Cosmopolitan Democracy: A Critical Review." *Journal of Peace Research* 30, no. 3 (1993): 301–315.

Archibugi, Daniele, and David Held, eds. *Cosmopolitan Democracy: An Agenda for a New World Order*. Cambridge, UK: Polity, 1995.
Arendt, Hannah. *Origins of Totalitarianism*. Florida: Houghton Mifflin Harcourt, 1973. (First published in 1968.)
Beckett, Francis. *The Enemy Within: The Rise and Fall of the British Communist Party*. London: John Murray, 1995.
Bell, Duncan. "International Relations: The Dawn of a Historiographical Turn?" *British Journal of Politics and International Relations* 3, no. 1 (April 2001): 115–126.
Benn, Tony. *Conflicts of Interest: Diaries, 1977–80*. London: Hutchinson, 1990.
———. *The End of an Era: Diaries, 1980–90*. London: Hutchinson, 1992.
Bentley, Michael. *Modernizing England's Past: English Historiography in the Age of Modernism, 1870–1970*. Cambridge: Cambridge University Press, 2005.
Berdal, Mats. "How 'New' Are 'New Wars'? Global Economic Change and the Study of Civil War." *Global Governance* 9 (2003): 477–502.
Bess, Michael. *Realism, Utopia, and the Mushroom Cloud.* Chicago: University of Chicago Press, 1993.
Bethlehem, Daniel, and Marc Weller. *The "Yugoslav" Crisis in International Law: Part I, General Issues.* Cambridge: Cambridge University Press, 1997.
Beynon, Huw, and Hilary Wainwright. *The Worker's Report on Vickers: The Vickers Shop Stewards Combine Committee Report on Work, Wages, Rationalisation, Closure and Rank-and-File Organisation in a Multinational Company*. London: Pluto, 1979.
Birchen, Marc. *The European Parliament and the German Unification*. Wissembourg, France: Archive and Documentation Centre European Communities, 2009.
Blanton, Shannon Lindsey. "Foreign Policy in Transition? Human Rights, Democracy, and U.S. Arms Exports." *International Studies Quarterly* 49, no. 4 (December 2005): 647–667.
Bloom, Richard. "Provoking Peace in Poland." *END Journal* 28/29 (Summer 1987): 5.
Bojicic, Vesna, and Mary Kaldor. "The Political Economy of War in Bosnia-Herzegovina. In *New Wars: Restructuring the Global Military Sector,* Vol. 1, edited by Mary Kaldor and Basker Vashee, 137–176. New York: Pinter, 1997.
Booth, Arthur John. *Robert Owen: The Founder of Socialism in England.* London: Trubner, 1869.
Booth, Ken. "Book Review: The Kosovo Report." *Journal of Refuge Studies* 14, no. 3 (2001): 336.
———, ed. *The Kosovo War: The Human Rights Dimensions*. London: Frank Cass, 2001.
———. "New Wars for Old." *Civil Wars* 4, no. 2 (2000): 163–170.
Boutros-Ghali, Boutros. *An Agenda for Peace: Preventive Diplomacy, Peacemaking and Peace-keeping*. New York: UN Department of Public Information, Yearbook of the United Nations, 1992.
Bowden, Mark. *Black Hawk Down: A Story of Modern War*. New York: Signet, 1999.
Brett, Judith. "The Tasks of Political Biography." In *History on the Couch: Essays in History and Psychoanalysis*, edited by Joy Damousi and Robert Reynolds, 73–83. Melbourne: Melbourne University Press, 2003.
Breyman, Steve. *Why Movements Matter: The West German Peace Movement and US Arms Control*. Albany: State University of New York Press, 2001.
Brzoska, Michael. "'New Wars' Discourse in Germany." *Journal of Peace Research* 41 (2004): 107–177.
Burke, Patrick. *European Nuclear Disarmament: A Study of Transnational Social Movement Strategy.* PhD diss., University of Westminster, 2004.

Callaghan, John. *Cold War, Crisis, and Conflicts: The Communist Party of Great Britain 1951–86*. Vol. 5. London: Lawrence and Wishart, 1999.
Carter, April. *Peace Movements: International Protest and World Politics Since 1945*. Essex, UK: Longman, 1992.
Chandler, David. *From Kosovo to Kabul: Human Rights and International Intervention*. London: Pluto, 2002.
Charter 77. "The Indivisibility of Peace: Charter 77 Documents on Peace, Freedom and Democracy." In *Voices from Prague: Documents on Czechoslovakia and the Peace Movement*, edited by Jan Kavan and Zdena Tomin, 22–28. London: END/Palach, 1983.
Chilton, Patricia. "Mechanics of Change: Social Movements, Transnational Coalitions and the Transformation Process in Eastern Europe." In *Bringing the Transnational Relations Back*, edited by Thomas Risse-Kappen, 189–226. Cambridge: Cambridge University Press, 1995.
Chilton, Patricia, and Jiří Dienstbier. "The European Citizens Assembly." *Peace Review* (Summer 1989): 16–20.
Chomsky, Noam. *"Human Rights" and American Foreign Policy*. Nottingham, UK: Spokesman, 1979.
Clausewitz, Carl von. *On War*. Ed. and translated by Michael Howard and Peter Paret. Princeton, NJ: Princeton University Press, 1976.
"Conference on Security and Cooperation in Europe, Final Act of Helsinki, Helsinki, 1 August 1975." In *From Helsinki to Vienna: Basic Documents of the Helsinki Process*, edited by Arie Bloed, 43–98. Dordrecht, Netherlands: Martinus Nijhoff, 1990.
Cook, Robin, David Holloway, Mary Kaldor, and Dan Smith. *Defence Review: An Anti-White Paper*. London: Fabien Society, 1975.
Cooper, Alice Holmes. *Paradoxes of Peace: German Peace Movements Since 1945*. Ann Arbor: University of Michigan Press, 1996.
Cortright, David. *Peace: A History of Movement and Ideas*. Cambridge: Cambridge University Press, 2008.
Crewe, Ivor, and Anthony King. *SDP: The Birth, Life and Death of the Social Democratic Party*. Oxford: Oxford University Press, 1995.
Curnow, R., M. Kaldor, M. McLean, J. Perry Robinson, and P. Shepard. "General and Complete Disarmament: A Systems-Analysis Approach." *Futures* 5, no. 5 (October 1976): 384–396.
de Gaaf, Beatrice. "Détente from Below: The Stasi and the Dutch Peace Movement." *Journal of Intelligence History* 3, no. 2 (Winter 2003): 9–20.
de Oliveira, Miguel Darcy. *Citizens: Strengthening Global Civil Society*. Washington, DC: World Alliance for Citizen Participation, 1994.
de Tocqueville, Alexis. *Democracy in America*. Edited and translated by Harvey C. Mansfield and Delba Winthrop. Chicago: University of Chicago Press, 2000. (First published in 1835.)
Dienstbier, Jiři, Eva Kanturkova, and Petruska Sustrova. "The Prague Appeal, Document No. 5/85, March 11, 1985." In *United States Congress: Human Rights in Czechoslovakia: The Documents of Charter 77, 1982–1987*, 163–168. Washington, DC: Commission on Security and Cooperation in Europe, 1988.
Dienstbier, Jiři, Jaroslav Šabata, and Mary Kaldor. "The Helsinki Citizens' Assembly." In *Europe from Below*, edited by Mary Kaldor, 45–72. London: Verso, 1991.
Dizdarevic, Zlatko. *Sarajevo: A War Journal*. New York: Henry Holt, 1993.
Đjilas, Aleksa. *The Contested Country: Yugoslav Unity and Communist Revolution, 1919–1953*. Cambridge, MA: Harvard University Press, 1991.

Donnelly, Mark. *Sixties Britain: Culture, Society, and Politics*. New York: Pearson Longman, 2005.
Drake, Michael S. "Sociology and the New Wars in the Era of Globalisation." *Sociology Compass* 1, no. 2 (2007): 637–650.
Duffield, Mark. *Global Governance and the New Wars: The Merging of Development and Security*. London: Zed, 2001.
European Nuclear Disarmament. "Appeal for European Disarmament: Launched on 28 April 1980." In *Protest and Survive*, edited by E. P. Thompson and Dan Smith, 223–226. Harmondsworth, UK: Penguin, 1980.
Evans, Eric J. *Thatcher and Thatcherism*. London: Routledge, 1997.
Evans, Richard J. *In Defence of History*. London: Granta, 1997.
Faber, Mient Jan. "Human Security from Below: Freedom from Fear and Lifeline Operations." In *The Viability of Human Security*, edited by Monica den Boer and Jaap de Wildle, 149–178. Amsterdam: Amsterdam University Press, 2008.
Ferguson, Adam. *An Essay on the History of Civil Society*. Charleston, SC: Bioblio-Bizaar, 2007. (First published in 1767.)
Fink, Carol, and Bernd Schaefer. *Ostpolitik, 1969–1974: European and Global Responses*. Cambridge: Cambridge University Press, 2009.
Forsythe, David P. *Human Rights and U.S. Foreign Policy: Congress Reconsidered*. Gainesville: University of Florida, 1988.
———. *Human Rights and World Politics*. Lincoln: University of Nebraska Press, 1983.
———. *The Politics of British Defence, 1979–98*. Basingstoke, UK: Macmillan, 1999.
Fry, Geoffrey K. *The Politics of the Thatcher Revolution: An Interpretation of British Politics, 1979–1990*. London: Palgrave Macmillan, 2008.
Fukuyama, Francis. *The End of History and the Last Man*. New York: Free Press, 1992.
Galtung, Johan. "Violence, Peace, and Peace Research." *Journal of Peace Research* 6, no. 3 (1969): 167–191.
Garthoff, Raymond L. "The Soviet Conception of Détente." In *Classic Issues in Soviet Foreign Policy*, edited by Federic J. Fleron, Jr., Erik P. Hoffmann, and Robbin F. Larid, 108–109. New York: Aldine de Gruyter, 1991.
Gilbert, John, John Tomlinson, and James Wellbeloved. "The Ministerial Response." In *Democratic Socialism and the Cost of Defence*, edited by Mary Kaldor, Dan Smith, and Steve Vines, 532. London: Croom Helm, 1979.
Gjelten, Tom. *Sarajevo Daily: A City and Its Newspaper Under Siege*. New York: HarperCollins, 1995.
Glantz, David M. *Soviet Military Intelligence in War*. London: Frank Cass, 1990.
Goldstone, Richard. *For Humanity: Reflections of a War Crimes Investigator*. New Haven, CT: Yale University Press, 2000.
Gordon, Stuart. "A Recipe for Making Safe Areas Unsafe." In *Aspects of Peacekeeping*, edited by D. Gordon and F. Toase, 213–230. London: Frank Cass, 2001.
Gordon, Suzanne. "From the Other Shore: Peace Movements in Eastern Europe." In *Search for Sanity: The Politics of Nuclear Weapons and Disarmament*, edited by Paul Joseph and Simon Rosenblum, 408. Boston: South End, 1984.
Gow, James. *Triumph of the Lack of Will: International Diplomacy and the Yugoslav War*. London: Hurst, 1997.
Graff, James L. "Mass Bedlam in Belgrade." *Time* 137, no. 12 (25 March 1991): 34.
Gramsci, Antonio. *Selections from the Prison Notebooks*. New York: International, 1971.
Gupta, Sanjeev, Benedict Clements, Rina Bhattacharya, and Shamit Chakravarti. "The Elusive Peace Dividend." *Finance and Development IMF*, 2002. Online.

Halliday, Fred. "The Ends of the Cold War." *New Left Review* 1, no. 180 (March–April 1990). Online.
Haraszti, Miklós. "The Beginnings of Civil Society: The Independent Peace Movement and the Danube Movement in Hungary." In *In Search of Civil Society*, edited by Vladimir Tismaneanu, 71–87. London: Routledge, 1990.
Hargrove, Erwin C. *Jimmy Carter as President: Leadership and the Public Good.* Baton Rouge: Louisiana State University Press, 1988.
Havel, Václav. "Anatomy of a Reticence." In *Voices from Czechoslovakia*, edited by Charter 77, 9–10. Stockholm: Charter 77, 1985.
———. *The Power of the Powerless.* Edited by John Keane. New York: M. E. Sharpe, 1985.
Haydon, Robert M. "'Ethnic Cleansing' and 'Genocide.'" *European Journal of Public Health* 17, no. 6 (2007): 546–547.
Hegel, G. W. F. *The Philosophy of Right.* Translated by S. W. Dyde. London: Prometheus, 1996. (First published in 1820.)
Henckaerts, Jean-Marie. *Mass Expulsion in Modern International Law and Practice.* The Hague: Kluwer Law International, 1995.
Hendrickson, Ryan C. "Javier Solana and the Operation Allied Force." In *Diplomacy and War at NATO,* 89–116. Columbia: University of Missouri Press, 2006.
Higgins, Rosalyn. Memorandum to the Foreign Affairs Committee. "The Expanding Role of the United Nations and Its Implications for United Kingdom Policy." 17 February 1993. Q.390.
Hinton, James. *Protests and Visions: Peace Politics in 20th Century Britain.* London: Hutchinson Radius, 1989.
Hobsbawm, Eric. *Age of Extremes: The Short Twentieth Century.* London: Abacus, 1995.
Hodge, Carole. *Britain and the Balkans: 1991 Until the Present.* London: Routledge, 2010.
Holbrooke, Richard. *To End a War.* New York: Random House, 1998.
Hollingworth, Larry. *Merry Christmas, Mr Larry.* London: Reed International, 1996.
Howe, Stephen. "Son of the Bani Tanwir: The Work of Fred Halliday (1946–2010)." openDemocracy, 13 July 2010. Online.
"Hungarian Meeting a Success." *END Journal* 31 (December 1987–January 1988): 8.
Huntington, Samuel P. "New Contingencies, Old Roles." *Joint Force Quarterly* 2 (Autumn 1993): 42.
Hurd, Douglas. *The Search for Peace.* London: Little, Brown, 1997.
Ignatieff, Michael. "On Civil Society: Why Eastern Europe's Revolutions Could Succeed." *Foreign Affairs* (March–April 1995). Online.
Ilyumzhinov, Kirsan, Oleg Gordievsky, Eduard Kukan, Sergey Lavrov, Vladimir Potanin, Kassym-Jomart Tokayev, Yuri Ushakov, Andrey Lukanov, Zhan Videnov, and Andrey Kozyrev. *Articles on Moscow State Institute of International Relations.* Richardson, TX: Hephaestus, 2011.
Independent Commission on Disarmament and Security Issues. *Common Security: A Blueprint for Survival.* New York: Simon and Schuster, 1982.
Independent International Commission on Kosovo. *The Kosovo Report: Conflict, International Response, Lessons Learned.* Oxford: Oxford University Press, 2000.
Ismael, Tareq Y., and Jacqueline S. Ismael, eds. *The Gulf War and the New World Order: International Relations of the Middle East.* Gainesville: University Press of Florida, 1994.
Jackson, Robert Howard, and Georg Sørensen. *Introduction to International Relations: Theories and Approaches,* 4th ed. Oxford: Oxford University Press, 2010.
Kaldor, Mary. "After the Cold War." *New Left Review* 1, no. 180 (March–April 1990). Online.

———. "The Armaments Sector." *IDS Bulletin* 9, no. 2 (December 1977): 35–38.
———. "Arms and Dependence." In *Opportunities for Disarmament: UN Special Session on Disarmament*, edited by Jane M. O. Sharpe. Washington, DC: Carnegie Endowment for International Peace, 1978.
———. *The Baroque Arsenal*. New York: Hill and Wang, 1981.
———. "Beyond the Blocs: Defending Europe the Political Way." *World Policy Journal* 1, no. 1 (Fall 1983): 1–21.
———. "A Decade of Humanitarian Intervention: The Role of Global Civil Society." In *Global Civil Society 2001*, edited by Helmut Anheier, Marlies Glasius, and Mary Kaldor, 109–143. Oxford: Oxford University Press, 2002.
———. "Disarmament: The Armament Process in Reverse." In *Protest and Survive*, edited by E. P. Thompson and Dan Smith, 203–220. London: Penguin, 1980.
———. *The Disintegrating West*. London: A. Lane, 1978.
———. "Eastern Enlargement and Democracy." In *Democratizing the European Union: Issues for the Twenty-First Century*, edited by Catherine Hoskyns and Michael Newman, 139–155. Manchester, UK: Manchester University Press, 2000.
———. "Economic Aspects of Arms Supply Policies to the Middle East." In *Great Power Intervention in the Middle East*, edited by Milton Leitenberg and Gabriel Sheffer. New York: Pergamon, 1978.
———. "Editorial." *Helsinki Citizens' Assembly, News Bulletin* (Spring–Summer 1991): 1–3.
———. "Europe After Cruise and Pershing II." *Millennium Journal of International Studies* 13, no. 1 (Spring 1984): 73–81.
———. *European Defence Industry: National and International Implications*. ISIO No. 8, Institute for the Study of International Organisation, University of Sussex, 1972.
———. "European Institutions, Nation-States and Nationalism." In *Cosmopolitan Democracy,* edited by Daniele Archibugi and David Held, 68–95. Cambridge, Polity Press.
———. "European Military-Industrial Complexes." In *Rüstungs und Militär in der Bundesrepublik Deutschland, Jahrbuch für Friedens und Konfliktforschung,* Band V, 47–65. Opladen: Westdeutscher Verlag, 1976.
———. "From Gloom to Surprise." *END Journal* 36 (October 1988–January 1989): 21.
———. *Global Civil Society: An Answer to War.* Cambridge, UK: Polity, 2003.
———. "Humanitarian Intervention: A Forum—Mary Kaldor." *Nation* 8 (May 2000): 25.
———. *Human Security: Reflections of Globalization and Intervention*. Cambridge, UK: Polity, 2007.
———. "The Idea of Global Civil Society." *International Affairs* 79, no. 3 (2003): 583–593.
———. "The Ideas of 1989." In *Reframing International Law: Law, Culture, Politics*, edited by Richard Falk, Lester Edwin J. Ruiz, and R. B. J. Walker, 70–82. New York: Routledge, 2002.
———. "Inconclusive Wars: Is Clausewitz Still Relevant in These Global Times?" *Global Policy* 1, no. 3 (October 2010): 271–281.
———. "Industrial and Employment Implications of Polaris Replacement." Memorandum to the House of Commons Defence Committee, Strategic Nuclear Weapons Policy, HC 36-VI (D43), HMSO, London, 4 February 1981.
———. "Is There a Soviet Threat?" In *On Disarmament*, edited by Michael Clarke and Marjorie Mowlam, 29–44. London: Routledge and Kegan Paul, 1982.
———. "The Military and Development." *World Development* 4, no. 6 (June 1976): 459–482.

———. *Military R&D*. A report prepared for the Swedish reference group of the UN Government Expert Study on Military R&D, Sussex University, Science Policy Research Unit, 1984.
———. "Military R&D: Cause or Consequence of the Arms Race?" *International Social Science Journal* 35, no. 1 (1983): 25–45.
———. "Military Technology and Social Structure." *Bulletin of Atomic Scientists* 33, no. 6 (June 1977): 49–53.
———. "A Movement for Peace and Democracy." In *Demokratische Reformen und Europäische Sicherheit*, edited by Peter Schneider and Peter Thelen. Bonn, Germany: Friedrich-Ebert-Stiftung, 1989.
———. *New and Old Wars: Globalised Violence in a Global Era*. Stanford, CA: Stanford University Press, 1999 and 2007.
———. "Nuclear Weapons and the Atlantic Alliance." *Democracy* 2, no. 1 (January 1982): 9–23.
———. "Oil and Conflict: In the Case of Nagorno Karabakh." In *Oil Wars*, edited by Mary Kaldor, Terry Lynn Karl, and Yahia Said, 176–180. London: Pluto, 2007.
———. "Peace." In *Fabian Essays on Socialist Thought*, edited by Ben Pimlott, 253–268. London: Heinemann Educational, 1984.
———. "Remarks of Professor Mary Kaldor." Speech presented at the 30th anniversary of the Helsinki Final Act, Finlandia Hall, Helsinki, 1 August 2005.
———. "The Role of Arms in Capitalist Economies: Processes of Underdevelopment and Overdevelopment." In *Arms Control and Technical Innovation*, edited by David Carlton and Carlo Schaerf, 322–341. London: Croom Helm, 1977.
———. *The Role of Military Technology in Industrial Development*. Report submitted to the UN Expert Study Group on Disarmament and Development, 1981.
———. "Sarajevo's Reproach." *Progressive* 57, no. 9 (September 1993): 21–23.
———. "The Significance of Military Technology." *Bulletin of Peace Proposals* 8, no. 2 (1977): 121–123.
———. "Technical Change and the British Defence Industry." In *Technical Innovation and British Economic Performance*, edited by Keith Pavitt, 101–121. London: Palgrave Macmillan, 1980.
———. "VII. 4 The Revolutions of 1989." In *Peace and Security: The Next Generation*, edited by George A. Lopez and Nancy J. Myers, 243–247. Lanham, MD: Rowman and Littlefield, 1997.
———. "Warfare and Capitalism." In *Exterminism and the New Cold War*, edited by E. P. Thompson, 261–288. London: New Left, 1982.
———. "Workers' Initiatives for Conversion: Reflections on British Experiences." In *Experiences in Disarmament: On Conversion of Military Industry and Closing of Military Bases*, edited by Peter Wallersteen. Uppsala University, Department of Peace and Conflict Research, Report No. 18, June 1978.
———. "Yugoslavia and the New Nationalism." *New Left Review* 197 (January–February 1993): 96–112.
Kaldor, Mary, and Javed Ansari. "Military Technology and Conflict Dynamics: The Bangladesh Crisis of 1971." In *The World Military Order: The Impact of Military Technology on the Third World*, edited by Mary Kaldor and Asbjørn Eide, 136–156. London: Macmillan, 1979.
———. *The Political Economy of the Bangladesh Crisis*. ISIO Occasional Paper No. 1, University of Sussex, Sussex, UK, 1974.
Kaldor, Mary, and Shannon Beebe. *The Ultimate Weapon Is No Weapon: Human Security and the New Rules of War*. New York: Public Affairs, 2010.
Kaldor, Mary, and Albert Booth. "Alternative Employment for Naval Shipbuilding

Workers: A Case Study of the Resources Devoted to the Production of the ASW Cruiser." In *Democratic Socialism and the Cost of Defence*, edited by Mary Kaldor, Dan Smith, and Steve Vines, 393–425. London: Croom Helm, 1979.

Kaldor, Mary, and Alexander Cockburn. "The Defence Confidence Game." *New York Review of Books* 21, no. 10 (13 June 1974): 24–32.

Kaldor, Mary, and Asbjørn Eide, eds. *The World Military Order: The Impact of Military Technology on the Third World*. London: Macmillan, 1979.

Kaldor, Mary, and Mient Jan Faber. "What Is Humanitarian Intervention?" May 1999. http://www.greekhelsinki.gr/.

Kaldor, Mary, and Richard Falk, eds. *Dealignment: A New Foreign Policy Perspective*. New York: United Nations University and Basil Blackwell, 1987.

Kaldor, Mary, and Sonja Licht, eds. *Yugofax Breakdown: War and Reconstruction in Yugoslavia: A Project of War Report and the Helsinki Citizens' Assembly*. London: HCA and Institute for War and Peace Reporting, 1992.

Kaldor, Mary, and Ferenc Miszlivetz. "Civilisational Crisis." *International Development Studies Bulletin* 16, no. 1 (1985): 56–61.

Kaldor, Mary, and Julian Perry Robinson. "War." In *World Futures: The Great Debate*, edited by Christopher Freeman and Marie Jahoda, 343–379. London: Robertson, 1978.

Kaldor, Mary, and Yahia Said. *Regime Change in Iraq: Mission Report*, Discussion Paper 26, London School of Economics, November 2003.

Kaldor, Mary, and Dan Smith. "Introduction." In *Disarming Europe*, edited by Mary Kaldor and Dan Smith, ix–xxiv. London: Merlin, 1982.

———. *Sense About Defence: The Report of the Labour Party Defence Study Group*. London: Labour Party, 1977.

Kaldor, Mary, Dan Smith, and Steve Vines. *Democratic Socialism and the Cost of Defence: Papers of the Labour Party Defence Study Group*. London: Croom Helm, 1979.

Kaldor, Mary, and Basker Vashee, eds. *New Wars: Restructuring the Global Military Sector*. Vol. 1, New York: Pinter, 1997.

Kaltefleiter, Werner, and Robert L. Pfaltzgraff. *The Peace Movements in Europe and the United States*. London: Croom Helm, 1985.

Kalyvas, Stathis N. "'New' and 'Old' Wars: A Valid Distinction?" *World Politics* 54, no. 1 (2001): 99–118.

Kant, Immanuel. "Perpetual Peace." In *Perpetual Peace and Other Essays on Politics, History and Morals,* translated by Ted Humphrey, 107–143. Indianapolis: Hackett Publishing Company, 1983. (First published in 1795.)

Kaplan, Robert D. *Balkan Ghosts: A Journey Through History*. New York: St. Martin's, 1993.

———, ed. *Civil Society and the State*. London: Verso, 1988.

———. "The Coming Anarchy." *Atlantic*, February 1994. Online.

———. *Global Civil Society?* Cambridge: Cambridge University Press, 2003.

Kegley, Charles., Jr., and Eugene R. Wittkoff. *American Foreign Policy*. Houndmills, UK: Macmillan, 1987.

Keller, Bill. "Armenian Capital Is Roused by Calls for New Freedoms." *New York Times,* 5 September 1988, 2.

Kenney, Padraic. *A Carnival of Revolution: Central Europe 1989*. Princeton, NJ: Princeton University Press, 2003.

King, John. *Nicholas Kaldor*. Houndmills, UK: Palgrave Macmillan, 2009.

Konrád, George. *Anti-Politics*. London: Quartet, 1984.

Köszegi, Ferenc, and E. P. Thompson. *The New Hungarian Peace Movement*. London: Merlin, 1982.

Kumar, Radha. *Divide and Fall? Bosnia in the Annals of Partition.* London: Verso, 1997.
Lambelet, Doriane. "The Contradiction Between Soviet and American Human Rights Doctrine: Reconciliation Through Perestroika and Pragmatism." *Boston University International Law Journal* (1989): 61–62.
Lawler, Peter. *A Question of Values: Johan Galtung's Peace Research.* Boulder: Lynne Rienner Publishers, 1995.
Lipschutz, Ronnie D. "Reconstructing World Politics: The Emergence of Global Civil Society." *Millennium* 21, no. 3 (1992): 389–420.
Locke, John. *The Two Treatises of Civil Government.* Edited by Ian Shapiro. New Haven, CT: Yale University Press, 2003. (First published in 1689.)
Lomax, Bill. "The Dialogue Breaks Down." *Labour Focus on Eastern Europe* 7, no. 1 (Winter 1984): 4.
Makarchuk, Mac, Andrew Pakula, and Janis Alton. "HCA." *Peace Magazine* 7, no. 6 (November–December 1991): 5.
Malcolm, Noel. *Bosnia: A Short History.* New York: New York University Press, 1994.
Malcolm, Noel, Norman Cigar, David Rieff, William E. Odom, and Charles G. Boyd. "Appease with Dishonour: Faulty History." *Foreign Affairs* (November/December 1995). Online.
Malešević, Siniša. "The Sociology of New Wars? Assessing the Causes and Objectives of Contemporary Violent Conflicts." *Interventional Political Sociology* 2 (2008): 97–112.
Mares, David R. *Violent Peace: Militarised Interstate Bargaining in Latin America.* New York: Columbia University Press, 2001.
Marx, Karl. "Theses on Feuerbach." *Cambridge, Mass. ReVision* 30, nos. 3/4 (2010): 41.
Mazower, Mark. *The Balkans: A Short History.* New York: Modern Library, 2001.
McEwen, Andrew. "Home Truths for Prague? Human Rights Violations in Czechoslavakia That Need to Be Aired." *Times* (London), 21 June 1988.
Mearsheimer, John J., and Robert A. Pape. "The Answer: A Partition Plan for Bosnia." *New Republic*, 14 June 1993, 22–28.
Melander, Erik, Magnus Oberg, and Jonathan Hall. "Are 'New Wars' More Atrocious? Battle Severity, Civilians Killed and Forced Migration Before and After the End of the Cold War." *European Journal of International Relations* 15, no. 3 (2009): 505–536.
Mepham, John. "END Supporters Conference: Links with Europe." *END Bulletin* 10 (July–August 1982): 22–23.
Michnik, Adam. *Letters from Prison and Other Essays.* Berkeley: University of California Press, 1985.
Minear, Larry, Jeffery Clark, Roberta Cohen, Dennis Gallagher, Iain Guest, and Thomas G. Weiss. *Humanitarian Action in the Former Yugoslavia: The UN's Role, 1991–1993,* Occasional Paper No. 18. Thomas J. Watson Jr. Institute of International Studies. Providence, RI: Brown University, 1994.
Minkiewicz, Jan. "Solidarity: A Test-Case for the Eighties." *END Journal* 1 (1983): 14.
Minnion, John, and Philip Bolsover, eds. *The CND Story: The First 25 Years of CND in the Words of the People Involved.* London: Allison and Busby, 1983.
Miszlivetz, Ferenc. "Understanding Civil Society Before and After 1989." *Recerca: revista de pensament i anàlisi* [Understanding Civil Society Before and After 1989], 8 (2008): 102.
Monks, Pieta. "Détente or Cold War from Below?" *END Journal* 5 (August–September 1983): 8.
Muggleton, Paul. "The Doctrine of Humanitarian Intervention and the NATO Air Strikes Against the Federal Republic of Yugoslavia." In *Righteous Violence: The*

Ethics and Politics of Military Intervention, edited by Tony Coady and Michael O'Keefe, 99–136. Carlton, Australia: Melbourne University Press, 2005.
Mundy, Jacob. "Deconstructing Civil Wars: Beyond the New Wars Debate." *Security Dialogue* 42 (2011): 279–295.
Münkler, Henfried. *The New Wars*. Cambridge, UK: Polity, 2005.
Myrdal, Alva. *The Game of Disarmament: How the United States and Russia Run the Arms Race*. Manchester, UK: Manchester University Press, 1977.
Nehring, Holger. "National Internationalists: British and West German Protests Against Nuclear Weapons, the Politics of Transnational Communications and the Social History of the Cold War, 1957–1964." *Contemporary European History* 14, no. 4 (2006): 559–582.
Newman, Edward. "The 'New Wars': A Historical Perspective Is Needed." *Security Dialogue* 35, no. 2 (2004): 173–189.
Nohlen, Dieter, and Philip Stöver, eds. *Elections in Europe: A Data Handbook*. Baden-Baden, Germany: Nomos, 2010.
Oberleitner, Gerd. "Human Security: A Challenge to International Law?" *Global Governance* 11 (2005): 185–203.
Ogata, Sadako. *The Turbulent Decade: Confronting the Refugee Crisis in the 1990s*. New York: Norton, 2005.
Ortega, Andres. "El 11-S, Una ocasion desperdiciada" [11-S, a Missed Chance]. El Pais, Madrid, 20 January 2002. http://elpais.com/diario/2002/01/20/domingo/1011502355_850215.html.
Owen, David. *Balkan Odyssey*. New York: Harcourt Brace, 1995.
Packenham, Robert A. *Liberal America and the Third World*. Princeton, NJ: Princeton University Press, 1973.
———. "Nicholas Kaldor: A Few Personal Notes." *Journal of Post Keynesian Economics* 5, no. 3 (Spring 1983): 333–340.
Pejanović, Mirko. *Through Bosnian Eyes: The Political Memoir of a Bosnian Serb*. West Lafayette, IN: Purdue University Press, 2004.
Pianta, Mario. *UN World Summits and Civil Society: The State of the Art*. Civil Society and Social Movements Programme, UN Research Institute for Social Development. Paper No. 18, August 2005.
Pinker, Steven. *The Better Angels of Our Nature: The Decline of Violence in History and Its Causes*. London: Penguin, 2011.
Politkovskaya, Anna. *A Russian Diary*. London: Vintage, 2008.
Pugh, Michael, and S. Alex Cunliffe. "The Lead Agency Concept in Humanitarian Assistance: The Case of the UNHCR." *Security Dialogue* 28, no. 1 (1997): 17–30.
———. "The Politicisation of the UNHCR in the Former Yugoslavia." *Journal of Refugee Studies* 10, no. 2 (1997): 157–161.
Reagan, Ronald. *An American Life*. London: Hutchinson, 1990.
Regehr, Ernie. "Defence and Human Security." *Ploughshares Monitor*, December 1999. Online.
Reyna, Stephen. "Taking Place: 'New Wars' Versus Global Wars." *Social Anthropology* 17, no. 3 (2009): 291–317.
Rieff, David. *Slaughterhouse: Bosnia and the Failure of the West*. New York: Simon and Schuster, 1995.
Rogel, Carole. *The Breakup of Yugoslavia and Its Aftermath*. Westport, CT: Greenwood, 2004.
Rousseau, Jean-Jacques. *The Collected Writings of Rousseau*. Edited by Christopher Kelly and Roger D. Masters. Hanover, NH: University Press of New England, 1994.

———. *Oeuvres completes* [Complete Works]. Edited by Bernard Gagnebin and Marcel Raymond. Paris: Éditions Gallimard, 1964.
Rozin, Mordechai. *The Rich and the Poor: Jewish Philanthropy and Social Control in Nineteenth-Century London*. Brighton, UK: Sussex Academic, 1999.
Rudd, Gordon W. *Humanitarian Intervention: Assisting the Iraqi Kurds in Operation Provide Comfort*. Washington, DC: US Army Center of Military History, 1991.
Ruggie, John G. "What Makes the World Hang Together? Neo-Utilitarianism and the Social Constructivist Challenge." *International Organization* 52, no. 4 (1998).
Schlesinger, James R. *Report to Congress on the Fiscal Year 1975 Defense Budget and Fiscal Years 1975–1979 Defense Program*. Washington, DC: GPO, 1974.
Schouten, P. "Theory Talk #30: Mary Kaldor on Framing War, the Military-Industrial Complex, and Human Security." *Theory Talks*, 16 May 2009. Online.
Shaw, G. Bernard, ed. *Socialism: The Fabian Essays*. London: Walter Scott, 1889.
Shaw, Martin. "The Contemporary Mode of Warfare? Kaldor's Theory of New Wars." *Review of International Political Economy* 7, no. 1 (2000). http://www.sussex.ac.uk/Users/hafa3/kaldor.htm.
Shiman, David. *Economic and Social Justice: A Human Rights Perspective*. Amnesty International, 1999.
Silber, Laura, and Allan Little. *Yugoslavia: Death of a Nation*. New York: TV Books, 1996.
Skidelsky, Robert. *John Maynard Keynes: Fighting for Britain*. London: Macmillan, 2000.
Slaughter, Anne-Marie. "Security, Solidarity, and Sovereignty: The Grand Themes of UN Reform." *American Journal of International Law* 99, no. 3 (2005): 626.
Solana, Javier. "The European Union and Human Security." In *Routledge Handbook of Human Security*, edited by Mary Marty and Owen Taylor, 251–259. Oxford: Routledge, 2014.
Soper, Kate. "E. P. Thompson: 1924–1993." *Radical Philosophy* 66 (Spring 1994): 63.
Spencer, Metta. "Helsinki Citizens' Assembly: Soul-Searching in Bratislava." *Peace Magazine* 8, no. 3 (May–June 1992): 24.
———. "Two Talks in Pugwash, Hungary." *Peace Magazine* 2, no. 6 (1987): 12.
Stewart, Christopher S. *Hunting the Tiger: The Fast Life and Violent Death of the Balkans' Most Dangerous Man*. New York: St Martin's, 2008.
Stockholm International Peace Research Institute (SIPRI). *The Arms Trade with the Third World 1971*. Stockholm: Almqvist and Wiksell, 1971.
———. *SIPRI at Forty: 1966 – 2006*. Solna: SIPRI, 2006.
———. *SIPRI Yearbook of World Armaments and Disarmaments 1969/70*. Stockholm: Almqvist and Wiksell, 1970.
———. *Yearbook of World Armament and Disarmament 1968–69*. London: Gerald Duckworth, 1969.
Strachan, Hew, and Andreas Herberg-Rothe. "Introduction." In *Clausewitz in the Twentieth Century*, edited by Hew Strachan and Andreas Herberg-Rothe, 1–13. Oxford: Oxford University Press, 2007.
Thatcher, Margaret. *The Downing Street Years*. London: HarperCollins, 1993.
Thirlwall, Anthony. "Biography." In *Nicholas Kaldor's Raffaelle Mattioli Lectures: Causes of Growth and Stagnation in the World Economy*, edited by Ferdinando Targetti and Anthony Thirlwall, 143–190. Cambridge: Cambridge University Press, 1996.
Thomas, Daniel C. "The Helsinki Accords and the Political Change in Eastern Europe." In *The Power of Human Rights: International Norms and Domestic Change*, edited by Thomas Risse and Kathryn Sikkink, 205–233. Cambridge: Cambridge University Press, 2002.

Thompson, E. P. "Beyond the Blocs." *END Journal* 12 (October–November 1984): 12–15.
———. *The Making of the English Working Class*. London: Gollancz, 1963.
———. "Notes on Exterminism." *New Left Review* 121 (1980): 21–31.
———. *The Poverty of Theory and Other Essays*. London: Merlin, 1978.
Tickner, Arlene, and Ole Wæver, eds. *International Relations Scholarship Around the World: Worlding Beyond the West*. Abingdon, UK: Routledge, 2009.
United Nations. *A More Secure World: Our Shared Responsibility, Report of the High-Level Panel on Threats, Challenges and Change*. UN Doc. A/59/565, 2004. Online.
———. *Report of the Secretary-General: The Relationship Between Disarmament and Development in the Current International Context*. Department of Disarmament Affairs, Document No. A/59/119, 2004. Online.
US Helsinki Watch Committee. *Violations of the Helsinki Accords: East Germany, a Report Prepared for the Helsinki Review Conference, Vienna, November 1986*. New York: US Helsinki Watch Committee, 1986.
Voon, Tania. "Closing the Gap Between Legitimacy and Legality of Humanitarian Intervention: Lessons from East Timor and Kosovo." *UCLA Journal of International Law and Foreign Affairs* (Spring/Summer 2002–2003): 31–97.
Wainwright, Hilary, and Mary Kaldor. "Tuesday Women (Between Friends): Out to Change the Real World." *Guardian* [London], 27 September 1988.
Walzer, Michael, ed. *Toward a Global Civil Society*. Providence, RI: Berghahn, 1995.
Wapner, Paul. "Environmental Activism and Global Civil Society." *Dissent* 2 (1994): 389.
Ward, James A. *Ferrytale: The Career of W. H. "Ping" Ferry*. Stanford, CA: Stanford University Press, 2001.
Weber, Tom. "The Hungarian Peace Movement Today." *Pacifica Review: Peace, Security and Global Change* 7, no. 1 (1995): 77–83.
Weiss, Thomas G., and Don Hubert. *The Responsibility to Protect: Research, Bibliography, Background: Supplementary Volume to the Report of the International Commission on Intervention and State Sovereignty 2*. Ottawa, Canada: International Development Research Centre, 2001.
Weller, Marc. *The Crisis in Kosovo 1989–1999*. Cambridge, UK: Documents and Analysis, 1999.
———. "The Rambouillet Conference on Kosovo." *International Affairs* 75, no. 2 (April 1999): 211–251.
Wendt, Alexander. "Anarchy Is What States Make of It: The Social Construction of Power Politics." *International Organization* 46, no. 2 (Spring 1992): 391–425.
West, Rebecca. *Black Lamb and Grey Falcon: A Journey Through Yugoslavia*. New York: Viking, 1943.
Western, Jon. "Sources of Humanitarian Intervention: Beliefs, Information, and Advocacy in the U.S. Decisions on Somalia and Bosnia." *International Security* 26, no. 4 (Spring 2002): 112–142.
Wheeler, Nicholas J. *Saving Strangers: Humanitarian Intervention in International Society*. Oxford: Oxford University Press, 2001.
White, Andrew. "Open Dialogue in Hungary." *END Journal* 1 (December–January 1982–1983): 15.
Wimmer Andreas, Richard Goldstone, Donald Horowitz, Ulrike Joras, and Conrad Schetter, eds. *Facing Ethnic Conflict: Towards a New Realism*. Oxford: Rowman and Littlefield, 2004.
Wittner, Lawrence. *Confronting the Bomb: A Short History of the World Nuclear Disarmament Movement*. Stanford, CA: Stanford University Press, 2009.

———. *Toward Nuclear Abolition III: The Struggle Against the Bomb*. Stanford, CA: Stanford University Press, 2003.

Woodward, Susan L. *Balkan Tragedy: Chaos and Dissolution After the Cold War*. Washington, DC: Brookings Institution, 1995.

Wylie, Gillian. "Social Movements and International Change: The Case of 'Détente from Below.'" *Journal of International Peace Studies* 4 (1999). http://www.gmu.edu/programs/icar/ijps/vol4_2/wylie.htm.

York, Herbart. *Race to Oblivion*. New York: Simon and Schuster, 1970.

Zakaria, Fareed. "The Reagan Strategy of Containment." *Political Science Quarterly* 105, no. 3 (Autumn 1990): 373–395.

Interviews

Abdullayeva, Arzu (Helsinki Citizens' Assembly activist), Baku, Azerbaijan, 29 March 2011.

Albrow, Martin (scholar), London, 8 June 2011.

Anderson, Paul (European Nuclear Disarmament activist, journalist, and scholar), London, 14 June 2011.

Archibugi, Daniele (scholar), London, 22 June 2011.

Ashdown, Paddy (former UN special representative for Bosnia-Herzegovina), via correspondence, 30 June and 4 July 2011.

Bayandour, Anahit (Helsinki Citizens' Assembly activist), via correspondence, 27 November 2010.

Beck, Ulrich (scholar), via telephone, 6 July 2011.

Brahimi, Lakhdar (ambassador and UN special representative), Paris, 3 June 2011.

Burke, Patrick (European Nuclear Disarmament activist), London, 10 May 2011.

Chinkin, Christine (scholar), London, 28 June 2011.

Coates, Ken (member, European Nuclear Disarmament, director, Bertrand Russell Peace Foundation), via correspondence, 20 April 2010.

Cortright, David (activist and scholar), via correspondence, 29 April 2010 and 31 May 2011.

Esche, Dieter (European Network for East-West Dialogue and Helsinki Citizens' Assembly activist), Berlin, 31 March 2011.

Faber, Mient Jan (Interchurch Peace Council [IKV] and Helsinki Citizens' Assembly activist), Amsterdam, 30 May 2011.

Falk, Richard (scholar), via Skype, 13 May 2015.

Gannushkina, Svetlana (memorial activist), via correspondence, 30 April, 15 May, 5 June, and 11 June 2011.

Giddens, Anthony (scholar and former director of the London School of Economics), via correspondence, 7 June 2011.

Glasius, Marlies (scholar), Amsterdam, 31 May 2011.

Goldstone, Richard (international jurist), via correspondence, 2 May 2010.

Grebo, Zdravko (Bosnia-Herzegovina lawyer and Helsinki Citizens' Assembly activist), Sarajevo, 7 March 2011.

Held, David (scholar), London, 18 May 2011.

Henwood, Chris (former group captain based at NATO Allied Joint Force Command in Naples), via telephone, 8 August 2011.

Holland, Stuart (scholar and former Labour Party member of parliament), Coimbra, Portugal, 23 May 2011; via correspondence, 1 June 2012.

Hoskyns, Katharine (Mary Kaldor's eldest sister), via telephone, 10 July 2012.

Howard, Michael, via correspondence, 27 May 2014.

Kaldor, Mary, London, 11 May, 20 June, and 24 June 2011; Brighton, UK, 10 July 2011; via correspondence, 31 October 2010 and 20 September and 25 October 2012.
Kandic, Natasa (activist), Belgrade, 22 February 2011.
Kavan, Zdenek (scholar and brother of Jan Kavan), Sussex, UK, 1 July 2011.
Kerkkänen, Ari (former director of Crisis Management Centre), London, 14 July 2011.
King, John (scholar), 21 May 2012.
Klug, Francesca (scholar), London, 22 June 2011.
Kostovicova, Denisa (former journalist and scholar), London, 9 June 2011.
Licht, Sonya (Helsinki Citizens' Assembly activist), Belgrade, 22 February 2011; via correspondence, 4 May 2011.
Martin, Mary (scholar), London, 25 May 2011.
Martirosyan, Natalya (Helsinki Citizens' Assembly activist), Yerevan, Armenia, 17 March 2011.
Miszlivetz, Ferenc (independent Hungarian activist), Budapest, 18 February 2011.
Möttölä, Kari (adviser, Finnish Ministry for Foreign Affairs), via correspondence, 26 January 2011.
Neild, Robert (former director of the Stockholm International Peace Research Institute), via correspondence, 16 April, 16 May, and 9 August 2010.
Ohanjanyan, Karen (Helsinki Citizens' Assembly activist), Stepanakert, Azerbaijan, 21 March 2011.
Owen, David (British politician), via correspondence, 19 September 2012.
Pankin, Alexei (former analyst with the Soviet Academy of Sciences), 5 October, 7 October, and 12 October 2010.
Petraeus, David (former commander and director of the US Central Intelligence Agency), via correspondence, 19 April, 20 April, and 21 April 2011.
Reinhardt, Klaus (former commander of Kosovo Force), Starnberg, Germany, 13 May 2011.
Rusetsky, Alexander (Helsinki Citizens' Assembly activist), Tbilisi, Georgia, 24 March 2011.
Salmon, Andrew (former commandant general of the UK Royal Marines), Mons, Belgium, 19 May 2011.
Sampath, Niels (archivist, Oxford Union Library), via correspondence, 24 February 2012.
Schméder, Geneviève (scholar), Paris, 1 June 2011.
Sen, Amartya (scholar), via correspondence, 14 June 2011.
Serra, Narcís (former Spanish minister of defense), Barcelona, 25 May 2011.
Sharpe, Andrew (brigadier, head of land strategy at Defence Concepts and Doctrine Centre in the British Ministry of Defence), Shrivenham, UK, 6 July 2011.
Simai, Mihály (former director of the World Institute for Development Economics Research at the United Nations University), via correspondence, 28 January and 30 January 2011.
Skidelsky, Robert (scholar and Keynesian biographer), London, 23 June 2011.
Smith, Dan (scholar and activist for the Campaign for Nuclear Disarmament and European Nuclear Disarmament), London, 4 May 2011; via correspondence, 14 April 2010.
Steel, Jonathan (journalist), London, 13 July 2011.
Stewart, Frances (Mary Kaldor's sister and scholar), Oxford, 10 June 2011; via correspondence, 30 May 2012.
Strachan, Hew (scholar), via telephone, 8 July 2011.
Tham, Carl (former Swedish member of parliament and a member of the Independent International Commission on Kosovo), via correspondence, 6 June and 7 July 2010.
Tuomioja, Erkki (Finnish politician), via correspondence, 20 December 2010.
Van Creveld, Martin (scholar), via correspondence, 13 April 2010.
Vierros-Villeneuv, Pilvi-Sisko (Finnish politician), via correspondence, 12 January 2011.

Index

About the Book

ALTHOUGH MORE THAN A LITTLE CONTROVERSIAL, MARY KALDOR'S ACademic work and ideas have both stimulated and influenced debate in the Pentagon, the United Nations, the European Union, NATO, and beyond. How did this come about? And how did Kaldor reach the conclusions outlined in her seminal books?

Melinda Rankin traces the evolution of Kaldor's work, revealing how her thinking developed from her years as an anti–Cold War activist and scholar in the 1970s–1980s, through her direct experiences of war in the Balkans and Caucasus, to her present support for rights-based international law enforcement to defend civilians from state and quasi-state violence.

Melinda Rankin is lecturer in international security and an associate of the Centre for International Security Studies at the University of Sydney.